KARMA, THE GREAT TEACHER

DR. HELEN ROBERTS

GNOSTICOEURS PUBLISHERS
Box 208 Grand Island
Florida 32735 U.S.A.

i

Karma, The Great Teacher
by
Dr. Helen Roberts   2-86

ISBN #0-915151-12z
Library of Congress card #83-81111

Excerpts from the Loehr-Daniels Life Readings used by permission of the Religious Research Foundation of America, Inc. All personal names, dates, etc. changed to protect anonymity, but otherwise excerpts are verbatim.

Typing help by Elizabeth Murray. Computer processing by Helen Roberts, Leah Linzer, Hazel Ray, Marie Sanders. Editing by Franklin Loehr. Typesetting by Dianne Stultz, Jayne Fisher, Marlene Hassell, Mary Hays. Special acknowledgment to Sandra Sherrod for her extensive assistance in the early research and writing of this book. Book manufacture by McNaughton & Gunn
Printed in the United States of America.

2 3 4 5 6 7 8 9

GNOSTICOEURS PUBLISHERS
Box 208   Grand Island
Florida 32735   U.S.A.

KARMA, THE GREAT TEACHER

BY
DR. HELEN ROBERTS

Helen Nethery Roberts, daughter of Birmingham, Alabama, bankers, took her college degree in Education *magna cum laude* from the Western Connecticut State Teachers College, and did graduate work in Psychology and Counselling at Georgia State University. Mother of three, she has worked full time in Religious Research since 1978, and currently is Dean of Research Studies of the Religious Research School of Spiritual Studies. She holds the cultural doctorate *honoris causae* Doctor of the Philosophy of Education.

Dr. Robert's first book, *The Soul That Sinneth—It Shall Die*, was published in 1981 and republished in 1986 entitled *Destiny of the Soul*. She is co-author of the 1983 book *Dr. John: He Can Read Your Past Lives*, and is preparing *Growth Is The First Spirtual Law* for 1986-87 publication. She is also the author of a series of Reincarnation Quickbooks, including *Karmic Roots*, *Karmic Justice for Women*, etc.

Dr. Roberts writes, teaches, lectures, leads seminars. She is an experienced counsellor, holding the certificate of Master Psychographist from the American Psychographical Association, Inc. Currently she is the major conductor of the Loehr-Daniels Life Readings.

iii

AUTHOR'S DEDICATION

To

The Rev. Franklin Loehr, D.D., S.Ph.D.

Director of Research (since 1952)
The Religious Research Foundation of America, Inc.

Author: *We Don't Cry for Heroes* (1946)
The Power of Prayer on Plants (1959)
Diary After Death (1975, 1986)
*Science and Religion, and the
Development of Religion
As a Science* (1983)

Deep-trance channel (medium) for the Loehr-Daniels Life Readings (since 1951)

————and my personal mentor and friend.

SPECIAL ACKNOWLEDGMENT

For his steadfast confidence in this book throughout the four years of its preparation, his conviction that this is knowledge which will greatly benefit the human race, and for his personal sponsorship of this first printing, to

MR. C.J. WILLIAMS
of Newnan, Georgia

Twelth Degree Rosicrucian and many years member of the Religious Research Foundation of America, Inc.

KARMA, THE GREAT TEACHER

GLOSSARY OF TERMS OFTEN USED IN THE LOEHR-DANIELS LIFE READINGS

Akashic records - Each soul has a record of its past lives. This includes major factors of each life such as the approximate place and time, the person's gender, occupation, age at death, accomplishments, failures. These are spiritual records and not easily read; only a few high beings are trained to decipher them. The Christian Bible calls them God's Book of Judgment. They are sometimes called soul records. The modern computer helps us understand how this vast storehouse of information is both possible and very logical. (More detail in *Dr. John; He Can Read Your Past Lives.*)

Astral plane - Refers to spiritual plane of existence which person goes to at death. Lower astral (also called "Post Mortemia." See *Diary After Death*) is entered immediately after death. Although it is spiritual (non-physical), the lower astral is very similar to physical earth. (More detail in *Death with Understanding.*) Higher astral refers to more spiritual planes, not similar to earth, entered as the person progresses after death. Still higher levels often called etheric.

Aura - Personal spiritual sphere or force field surrounding each living being. Affected by emotions, health, etc.

Beingness - Essential nature.

Cohesion Stage - Stage immediately above the soul stage, after incarnations on earth. Also called "Sons of God." Beingness is the main development emphasis in this stage, as doingness is in the incarnations-of-the-soul stage. (More detail in *Destiny of the Soul.*)

Conductor - Person who is conducting the life reading. Experimentation with many ways of giving the life readings in their early days led to the conclusion that the most efficient way is for a carefully prepared conductor to act as personal representative of the person getting the reading, asking his or her person-inquiries and questions of the akashic record reader, Dr. John Christopher Daniels.

Co-Creator - Refers to an Individuated-God-Being who has progressed far above the soul stage. (More detail in *Destiny of the Soul.*)

Cosmic cousin - See cosmic family.

Cosmic family - During the soulhood stage, the time of earth incarnations, souls are put into cosmic families. Members of cosmic families have a close spiritual bond and will incarnate with each other more often than with other souls. New members enter as new souls are individuated from the reservoir of God-Beingness, and old members graduate. Cosmic cousins are similar but one step removed from cosmic family members — just as on earth cousins are one step removed from sisters and brothers.

Cosmic school - God has many cosmic schools in which His children can learn and grow. Most of these schools are spiritual and not in the physical universe, earth being the exception. Earth is a true cosmic school and is often referred to as the laboratory where the soul puts into practice what it has learned. As such, earth is a highly important cosmic school for souls.

Council - Usually refers to the council of guides and teachers. See guides.

Crystallization - Refers to a soul becoming stuck in a certain pattern. E.g., a soul having a series of lives in China may become crystallized in Chinese thought and refuse to incarnate in another area of Earth. Crystallizations which hold back a soul must be broken through. (More detail in *Dr. John: He Can Read Your Past Lives.*)

Daniels, Dr. John Christopher - Chief spirit guide for Religious Research, leader of "upstairs team," and akashic record reader for the Loehr-Daniels Life Readings. Affectionately called simply "Dr. John." Has a quiet sense of humor.

"Downstairs team" - Used to designate the members of the Religious Research project who are in earthliving at the present time.

Elder Brothers from Space - UFO beings who have visited or will visit earth.

Elohim - Refers to the next stage beyond the Cohesion stage. Individuated-God-Beings in the Elohim stage are often called "lords," meaning they must take responsibility for something beyond themselves. Only about one-half of one percent are associated with earth. In the Elohim stage one must learn not only to discriminate but to discern ever more directly the nature and the way of God. (See *Destiny of the Soul* for detail.)

Excarnate - Personality after the death of the body.

Feminine Soul - For the purpose of earthliving each soul polarizes into a masculine and feminine half. These are the two "soulmates." They rarely incarnate together, but join into their wholesoul in other realms. On earth the masculine half has its on series of incarnations and so does the feminine half. The feminine half is called a feminine soul; the masculine half, a masculine soul. Each half-soul has its own development, including incarnations in its non-native gender. (See *Dr. John: He Can Read Your Past Lives, Destiny of the Soul*, and the Study Courses of the Religious Research School of Spiritual Studies.)

Given life - See "Grace-of-God life." Given life may also refer to a certain test life for an older soul. Detail on this type of given life is found in *Growth is the First Spiritual Law*.

Grace-of God life - Refers to a lifetime in which a soul is allowed to incarnate in a personality with qualities above the level that soul has yet attained. This helps the soul learn and can be likened to teaching an infant to walk by letting the baby walk while holding an adult's hands before it can walk alone. Also called "given life" and "walk-through life"

Guides and Teachers - Each person has "blessed invisibles" who help him/her through life and its decisions and problems. Some are called guides and teachers, or the council of guides and teachers. Guides and teachers come and go as the person goes through different steps of life, but there is a small core group which may stay throughout the life. Not with us constantly; a soul, or an excarnate personality, undertaking the guide/teacher function (as all must do for their own growth) may be member of 50 such councils. Our immediate, constant upholdment, always with us unless we deliberately and willfully step out of it, is the flow of God's beneficence, His loving care and provision for us.

Incarnate (Incarnation) - Living on earth - in the body.

Individuated-God-Being (Individuation) - A begotten child of God, with individuation and free will. This includes souls, but also refers to other spiritual beings.

Jesus Christ - The most highly developed Individuated-God-Being now in touch with planet earth, Co-Creator of souls, leader of the current cosmic redemption project.

Karma - In the spiritual law of cause-and-effect, the result of a cause. As the Bible says, "What ye sow that also shall ye reap." Usually refers to carried-over experience from a past life, but can also refer to receiving just reward (positive or negative) in same life.

Loehr, Dr. Franklin - Medium (channel) through whom Dr. John speaks; Dr. John's soulmate; Director of Religious Research and leader of the "downstairs team."

Loehr-Daniels Life Reading - Each person has a soul record of its past lives (*see* akashic records). In a Loehr-Daniels Life Reading, Dr. John reads the person's soul records and transmits the information to earth through Dr. Loehr (in deep trance) with the help of a conductor. Past lives with particular significance for the present life are included, as well as the purpose and other helpful information for the present life. Write Religious Research for free life reading information.

"Lords" - *See* Elohim.

Masculine soul - *See* feminine soul.

"Masters" - An ill-defined term used differently by various psychic, occult and spiritual groups to mean anything from a deceased relative who establishes some sort of communication to a very highly developed Individuated-God-Being far beyond the person or soul stage. The ultimate Master recognized by Religious Research is Jesus Christ.

Mini-Creator - Refers to Individuated-God-Being who has progressed far past the soul stage. Above the Cohesion and the Elohim stages, but below the Co-Creator Stage. (See *Destiny of the Soul*.)

Moses - The leader of the Hebrews in their famous Exodus from Egypt to the promised land in the 1200s B.C. The Moses soul is, we understand, the chief adjutant to the Jesus Soul, has had many incarnations, including the Old Testament Joseph and Joab and Elisha, and the New Testament Lazarus.

Native gender - When a masculine soul incarnates as a man or a feminine soul incarnates as a woman, each is considered to be incarnate in its native gender.

Non-native gender - When a masculine soul incarnates as a woman or a feminine soul incarnates as a man, each one is considered to be incarnate in its non-native gender.

"Other side" - In general this refers to the excarnate planes of personal life, but can refer to any spirit plane, any realm of being or plane of expression other than physical.

Post Mortemia - *See* astral.

Reincarnation - the soul incarntes meaningfully 60 to 100 times with different personalities (always in human form) with a primary purpose for its own growth and a secondary purpose for the redemption of evil. Because of high birth and infant mortality in most human generations, there may be another 100 or so incarnations of no real significance to the soul in addition.

"Second death" - After the death of the body the person will continue as an individual entity as long as it is potentialed and energized; then it becomes one with its soul. The "second death" refers to that joining of the personality to its soul. Eastern religions may call this "nirvana". (See *Death with Understanding.*)

Solity - A level of beingness and expression less than the whole soul but more than any one personality of the soul. It incorporates traits, experiences and abilities from several of the soul's personhood (incarnations).

Sons of God - *See* Cohesion stage. (More information in *Destiny of the Soul.*)

Soul records - *See* akashic records.

Sponsor soul - A new soul is sponsored into earthliving by an older, close soul friend called the sponsor soul. Nearly always a cosmic family member. (Detail in *Dr. John: He Can Read Your Past Lives.*)

Supervisory council - Refers to council above the council of guides and teachers. Just as the council watches over and assists the person and soul, the supervisory council observes the work of various councils and helps when needed.

"Upstairs team" - Refers to members of Religious Research project who are not in earthliving at the present time - the spirit part of the team, led by Dr. John Christopher Daniels.

"Walk-through-life" - *See* Grace-of-God life.

Wholesoul - In earthliving each person comes from either the masculine or the feminine half of his/her soul. "Soul" usually refers only to that half. Dr. John uses the term "wholesoul" when he wants to refer to both halves together.

CHAPTER ONE

RESEARCH OF REINCARNATION

How does one research reincarnation?

Actually it turns out there are five ways to scientifically research reincarnation: the psychological (or psychographical), historical, psychical, spontaneous, and philosophical.* These five ways to objectively research reincarnation evolved one by one, as through the years researchers discovered and developed them. It was not all that tidy in the beginning. Actually reincarnational research dropped into the Religious Research program by accident. It was not even considered as a research project when Religious Research organized in 1948. What those early seekers were trying to find was good evidence of life after death. They were an independent group of young university-trained ministers in the Connecticut River valley of New England, who came together under the leadership of the Rev. Paul McClurkin, Ph.D. They called themselves "the Hadley Workshop" because they met in the parsonage of the Old Hadley Massachusetts Congregational Church where Dr. McClurkin was pastor.

For two years (1948-1950) they met a half-day or more each week, studying various ideas and movements for bettering their profession, seeking better ways to serve their parishioners. Life after death was recognized as a major area of interest, because proof, or strong scientific evidence, for life after death could bring hope to parents who had lost a child, greater solace to a husband mourning the loss of a beloved wife, firmer courage to old people facing the increasing limitations of their waning days. To show, in acceptable modern terms, life after death as a reality would be a professional

---

* These are summarized in SCIENCE, RELIGION, AND THE DEVELOPMENT OF RELIGION AS A SCIENCE, Loehr, Gnosticoeurs 1983, and developed in detail in the lesson series THE SCIENTIFIC EVIDENCE FOR REINCARNATION of the Religious Research School of Spiritual Studies.

breakthrough of the first magnitude.

The group felt their time well spent, but disbanded after two years without a major breakthrough in this area. Dr. Franklin Loehr, later to become Director of Religious Research, accepted a call to be Collegiate Minister of the First Congregational Church of Los Angeles, California, then the largest Congregational Church in the world. Dr. McClurkin continued his ministry, research, and large counseling practice in Old Hadley and Northampton, Massachusetts. The several other ministers went their ways.

Then came the "lucky accident." While experimenting with some counseling techniques presented in the 1948 book *Dianetics*, Dr. McClurkin found that he could put a client into a deep relaxation and take him back into childhood, then infancy, then the birth experience, then pre-birth happenings in the womb, and then into a pastlife—another incarnation, the same soul but a different person, in a different time and place. Things that happened back then, perhaps many centuries ago, were still very much alive and influential in the personality, relationships, and other vital factors of the client's present life. Here were new answers, supplied not by the therapist but by the client himself, which bore uniquely and immediately upon the present life problems.

With his Ph.D. training and long experience as minister and psychotherapist, Dr. McClurkin realized this was a new validation of Sigmund Freud's history-making discovery of the dynamic subconscious—that things in our deep memories of which we are unaware are still very much alive and are strongly influencing us.

Hence, Freud's great dictum, "look farther back." To find answers to present questions and problems, look back to what happened before, farther back than yesterday or last week, farther back even than we remember, farther back into the forgotten yesterdays and yesteryears. Here lay the hidden reasons. Dr. McClurkin's discovery was that our "dynamic subconscious" conditioning goes back not only to childhood and infancy, not only to pre-natal conditioning, but that there is pre-conceptual conditioning also. Things that happened before our present body was conceived influence us. Dr. McClurkin was not the first to make this discovery, but he was one of the first to use it in counseling, and to understand the larger significance of it.

Early in 1951 Dr. McClurkin followed Dr. Loehr to Los Angeles and shared his findings. Now the question of life after death had not only a new answer but a whole new perspective. The reason most people do not believe in life after death is that they do not know of life before birth. But if you lived before your body was even conceived, of course you will continue to live after it—the body—dies.

Beyond that idea a new horizon loomed: Here was the opening door to the study of the soul itself. That which was *you* before your father ever smiled upon your mother, that *you* which carries over from one body to another, with periods in between with no body, that is in reality your *soul*. So reincarnation is the evidence for the basic religious claim of incarnation, that there is a soul incarnate, embodied, in each of us. And here in careful, long-term reincarnational research was a way to study the soul and its progression, learn the laws governing it, discover the spiritual principles and values of God at work.

Dr. Loehr immediately signed up for an intensive six-months personal course in self-discovery with Dr. McClurkin. He recovered a score of his own pastlives and truly discovered himself. Now he knew who he was in the chain of incarnations of his soul, and his present life's roots and purposes, abilities and limitations. The missing link, the link to his soul, had been found. The old question of life after death was answered, and the research of the soul's nature and experiences began.

After personally experiencing the insights and integration this brought, Dr. Loehr started using pastlife recall in his counseling work. This had to be done discreetly, for reincarnation was still a "naughty word" in the early 1950s in America, especially among church people, and Dr. Loehr was a prominent minister. As he reported years later in the Religious Research Monthly Journal, the pastlife recall counseling crept into his work in an unusual way:

> One day in late August or early September of 1951, I was at my desk as usual as collegiate minister of the First Congregational Church of Los Angeles, and the phone rang. Nothing unusual about that. A woman was calling, asking for an

appointment—nothing unusual about that, either. But when this woman came, her particular request was unusual enough for me to remember her opening words: 'You are the minister I want to have help me offer up unto God as a spiritual sacrifice my yearning to have a child.' I thought this was spiritual sublimation of an unusually high order, but asked the woman, 'Why can't you have a child?' And her story came forth: She and her husband had been married two or three years. They both wanted children. No children came. So they went to their doctor, who after tests and consultations reported that with her the fallopian tubes were firmly closed.

'That could be psychosomatic, you know—something in your subconscious mind closing down on the tubes,' I said. 'Oh yes,' she replied, 'they told me that. So after the physical tests and treatment they sent me to a psychologist, and even a psychiatrist. They went all through my life, but couldn't come up with any reason. We've tried everything. Finally my doctor has told me that I've just simply got to accept the fact that I never will have a child, and that lots of women cannot bear children, and I must learn to live with it. I'll never have a baby. And I heard you speak several weeks ago at a CFO (Camp Farthest Out) meeting, and you are the minister I would like to have help me to offer up as a spiritual sacrifice to God, my yearning to have a child.'

At this point that overworked but sometimes unpredictable guardian angel which God has assigned to me, opened my mouth and put his big foot in it. I'm sure it wasn't I! Oh, he used my lips and breath, and the sound came from me—but the words were utterly ridiculous. The words I heard my voice saying to that poor woman were, 'It still could be psychosomatic, but with the cause in a previous life'—!!

I thought to myself, 'Oh, my goodness! Here she's not even a member of our church! I'm busy, I've got lots to do. What have I said? Reincarnation!! She doesn't know anything about it—I don't know very much about it—.' I knew only that I had found the missing links of myself, the missing parts of me and the answers to my own life, the truth, the key, and the sustainment that had brought me through my own Gethsemane and which had made me more of a person than I had ever been before, in the recall of some twenty of my own pastlives. I had found the missing parts of me, and the missing answers I so desperately needed, in this way. But really, I knew so little about it! Reincarnation! Why, only a few short years before I had taken up offerings to send missionaries to the poor benighted heathen who believed in reincarnation! And this woman before me—I knew nothing about her, except that her heart cried out to have a baby, and she was trying to accept in the best way she knew the brutal 'fact' the doctor had given her, of being doomed never to have her own child. Yes, the doctors—the doctors who had examined her, the doctors whose business it was to help women, the doctors who were the experts—they had told her that her sterility was beyond help. Why should I raise, even momentarily, foolhardy expectations that almost certainly would be doomed to even further disappointment?...So I tried to dissuade her.

'I don't suppose there's one chance in a hundred—one in a thousand—' but she answered, 'That's all right, if there is any chance at all.' 'It will be a long process, very likely,' I continued, 'and you'll have to work hard in it.' 'That's all right,' she said, 'let's try.'

So I was in for it. With some choice but unspoken thoughts for my guardian angel for having gotten me into this, I made an appointment for the woman to return, and we set up a tentative schedule for a psychographical session once a week.

Well, we found it. We started work in September, and I think it was in early October that she recalled a former life that I could see probably held the key to her present life sterility. I was not too sure in those early days about reincarnation, despite my own self-discovery and integration through it—but at the very least, this picture that came forth in her third or fourth session, even if it were only symbolism as I told myself then it might be, could hold the key to the powerful psychological forces in her subconscious mind shutting off the tubes in her body. After finding the cause, as it did turn out to be, we still had to work with it for several months of really intensive, hard, psychotherapy. But the diagnosis proved true, the work was accomplished, and her healing came. In December of 1952 their first child was born. And the second summer after that, as if to underscore the fact of her healing, their second child was born. (Journal XIV:2h-i)

In hindsight this experience and others were part of a predestined plan, which led Dr. Loehr toward the scientific research of religion and away from his successful professional career as a parish minister. On September 15, 1952, Religious Research opened an office in Los Angeles, with two major projects on the agenda. The first was the prayer-plant work, the second was reincarnational research. The prayer-plant project culminated in the publication of the 1959 Doubleday bestseller, *The Power of Prayer on Plants*.

Even though reincarnation research was among the early projects, it was also a necessary outgrowth. Religious Research had little financial support and Dr. Loehr fell back upon his extensive counseling experience (professional training in Seminary, in the Army Chaplains School at Harvard, then the Air Force Chaplains School, and years of private counseling) for the necessary monetary means to keep the organization going. Only this time it was different. The word quickly got around the Los Angeles "spiritual underground" that there was a minister from the prestigious First Congregational Church who could help you recall your own pastlives and discover how they affect your present life. Therefore his work touched a new group of people, not just people who needed personal therapy, but also people who were interested in why they had the sense of having lived before, or why they had a certain deja vu experience, or simply wondered: Is there really life after death?

During these first seven years, before the success of the prayer-plant work took Dr. Loehr on a four-year speaking tour, a solid basis for reincarnation research was built. He carefully charted each client's pastlives in a chronological order, which provided the first objective insights into the soul and its progress. For the client, here was the connection between life and death, between the soul and the person, between the problems of his pastlives and the solutions in this and future lives. For Religious Research here was a tool to study the soul.

It was quickly discovered that usually several, but not all, pastlives will impinge majorly upon any present life. No one pastlife is tapped exclusively in pastlife therapy, as a number of previous incarnations may feed into the present. Other things also made themselves known to the careful observer, such as the independent way in which reincarnation proceeds. There is no set time period between incarnations, although five to seven incarnations in a thousand years is a fairly prevalent pattern. Another point that became evident was that the client has an "inner knower," or an inner director, who decides which lives would surface from the subconscious to the conscious mind, and in what sequence.

The introductory method used to bring out the pastlife of the "inner knower's" choice is for the client to be gently led to imagine a quiet, personal theatre-like setting. The present consciousness takes a seat and allows the subconscious mind to take the stage, presenting whatever it has ready for the person. Usually he finds that a personality from a previous incarnation is on the imaginary stage re-living key experiences, feeling again the emotions, which can reveal the hidden springs of present-life relationships, problems, and abilities, and help explain who a person is now and why. The life presented may be the life immediately preceding his present incarnation, or it may be one from long ago.

Here we discover the workings of karma. For the unfinished business of the past is in the individual's subconscious mind waiting for the right time, the right incarnation, to come to the surface and get worked out. Unfinished business must be finished. Incomplete mastery of life situations must be completed. These recalls, and the counseling following the recalls, act as a clearing house for fear, anger, and other negative emotions which have become pockets of irritation in the soul, draining into the present life personality.

Unfinished business is what karma usually is. Yes, there are times when some dirty deed of a past personality of the soul comes back to haunt the present person. But usually the problems are unresolved fears, frustrations, hurts from the past. Karma is a great teacher more than a great judge. Karma is helping us to grow, to progress, rather than sitting with a giant club waiting to clobber us for some former misdeed.

For instance, Wanda recalled a pastlife when her father drunkenly watched her mature into a young woman and then ravaged her. It was approximately 1900 in the slums of New York City. The then incarnation of the Wanda soul was from a poor Irish family—her mother worked as a housekeeper, her father spent his time working odd jobs and drinking. As the young Irish girl matured, her father began making sexual advances toward her. She avoided him for four years, but finally he cornered and raped her. She ran away from home and started a new life, earning her living as a telephone operator. Several years after the rape she met and married her Prince Charming and did live happily ever after.

But the fear, hatred and frustrations of the early childhood were not resolved. These continuing emotions were like a prickly pear in the beingness of her soul, a buried cancerous sore which needed healing. Wanda, the present incarnation from that soul, became the one to reap the harvest and clear this pocket of negativity from the soul.

As a child Wanda remembers shaking with fear whenever loud people made advances toward her, and crying for hours for no reason, or hiding in closets or bathrooms shaking with uncontrollable fear. As she grew older the fears subsided, but she had a low self-image. After the pastlife recall uncovered the cause and continued counseling worked it out, her fears and self-doubt fell away.

Was this karma? The young Irish girl was a victim, not a villain. Yet it was Wanda who had to overcome the hatred and fear. The Irish girl had pushed the experience into her subconscious mind, aided by a happy marriage and kind husband. But it was this unresolved situation that haunted Wanda. The young Irish girl never told anyone about her father raping her. She simply ran away, found a job and started a new life. Yet the four or five years of apprehension and fear as her father made sexual advances, and finally the rape, was not something that could be forgotten. It was simply absorbed into the soul to be released at a later date.

Wrongful or frightening death is another strong source of unresolved emotions. Pamela had a skin sensitivity which was traced to a pastlife in the late 1700s. She recalled being a young mother who tried to save some children, several of them her own, from a burning church. Even though her long dress was in flames, the young woman went back into the church several times to bring out more children until she was finally engulfed in flames and died in the fire.

It was not possible for the 1700s personality to resolve the traumatic death, therefore it surfaced in Pamela. The pastlife recall and subsequent psychotherapy helped heal those old wounds and the skin sensitivity diminished. Again what might appear to be karmic, the sensitive skin, proved to be a pocket of pent-up emotion that had to be drained from the soul beingness.

Sometimes a soul will harbor unresolved emotions for centuries, until it has strengthened its own soul beingness and has a strong enough personality to handle the situation. The days of the Roman Empire produced much cruelty as well as human advancement. Henry recalled a pastlife as a Roman gladiator. Being the slave to a powerful Roman senator, he was first trained as a soldier then later as a gladiator. Considering the circumstances, he lived a relatively long life. Henry discovered from his recall that the games were usually rigged—the survival or death of the gladiators depended on the power and prestige of their owners. Of course they had to give the Roman citizens a good performance.

This gladiator was well taken care of, provided with women, excellent food and wine; but the killing began to seep into his daily life until he imagined blood streaming from his hands. Finally, nearly mad, the gladiator arranged his own death. Defying the commands of his owner, he arranged to be killed by a friend and fellow gladiator in the arena.

From this life Henry could pinpoint some of his childhood fears, particularly a fear and revulsion at the sight of blood. He had an early aversion to anything related to violence, whether in real life or in the movies. What Henry was re-experiencing was some of the emotions and fears of that strong, proud gladiator, who could not acknowledge his fears or permit them in his consciousness. But these emotions were stored in the beingness of the soul, until they had cooled sufficiently to be passed down to Henry for release 1800 years later.

Pastlife recalls also supply a great treasure of afterdeath experiences. There is really no reason anymore for ignorance or fear of the death experience. So much positive research has been done in this area by so many competent people and organizations that death should be understood more as a part of life rather than an ending of life. Our forthcoming book, *Death With Understanding*, for example, combines the Religious Research study of the death experience with knowledge gained by many other researchers. The pastlife recall work opened an obvious opportunity to study this phenomena, by simply taking the client through the pastlife, then gently stepping over the line between that life and the afterlife, into the astral realm. Of course anyone with a closed mind or fearful or ignorant of death might be apprehensive about making that crossover. Yet in pastlife recall the death has already occurred and the client is only remembering, with new insight and the assistance of a supportive counselor, the past experience of death.

It emerges that the important thing in dying, as in living, is not so much what happens to you as how you cope with the situation, what you do about it. Deaths caused by war, for instance, may be traumatic, but many are relatively uneventful. Often a client whose pastlife person had been killed in battle will simply say, "Well, I'm dead now," in almost a ho-hum comment. The first question may be quite natural, such as: "Where is my horse?" Or, "Where was I hit?" This is quite common. The newly dead person may search his body looking for the wound. One client who had been a bagpiper in a Scottish and English war was concerned about his bagpipes, since they were on the ground and someone had stepped on them. Another past personality, who had been killed in fierce Arabian hand-to-hand combat, kept fighting even though dead, swinging his long curved sword, swearing and yelling that they couldn't kill him!

After the personality has accounted for his immediate concerns, his thoughts usually turn to the people left at home and he wonders how they will fare without him. As a general rule the newly dead will go home to see the family, before continuing on to the astral planes. It is the principles the person fought for, the trauma of the battles, feeling for people left behind, and of course, the experience of a life cut short, that usually are impressed upon the soul forces and need be resolved in another lifetime.

If a client is open to exploring the personalities as they evolve in the astral realm and beyond, the counselor often can follow these personalities into the death experience and beyond it. Again we use the example of war deaths because they are particularly interesting. Since the Civil War is a fairly recent historical event in this country, a number of people incarnate today lived in America during that period, often in the opposite lifestyle: Southern people now living in the North, former Northerners now living in the South; black slaves as whites now and the whites as blacks. One such client, who now lives in the North, fought and died fighting for the South. The personality was taken through the death experience: he was shot in the chest by a volley of bullets which killed him and his horse. His immediate afterdeath emotional needs were met; he went home to visit his family and tried to repress the anger he felt at being killed by a "damned Yankee." Then the personality continued into the astral planes, where he accepted further teaching. Later he bivouacked with ten or twelve soldiers in the astral, some from the North, some from the South. As they sat around the fire and told their war stories, the young Southern gentleman realized that the Northerners were not just stupid factory boys as he had thought. They were just as smart as he and could ride a horse equally as well. Thus the young Southerner was able to watch the rest of the war from a more elevated level of understanding.

The client who experienced this pastlife/pastdeath recall had only a minor carryover of this war death. The intensity apparently was lessened because the young Southern gentleman had accepted additional teaching after his death. Even a traumatic death can be eased if the astral personality can be reached with more knowledge than it had at the point of death.

What became evident from the pastlife/pastdeath recall work was that not all situations which appear to be karmic in their nature are caused by some nasty villain of yesteryear. The roots of these difficult present-life situations are often the pent-up fears and sorrows of a victim, the emotions trapped in the soul beingness and stored in the subconscious of the present personality. When these pockets of fears and frustrations are tapped, it is the responsibility of the person living now to handle them, clear them, work through the negativities, gain the spiritual growth, resolve the problems, and reintegrate these forces constructively into the present person.

Karma, it was discovered, has more than one blade in its sword and can cut in more than one fashion. Just what are the factors working to make karma the great illuminator, the great teacher, that it is? After much review, of both his own clinical experience and the work of other people in the field (some of whom he had trained), Dr. Loehr began gathering up and sorting out reincarnational facts, mentally mulling them over, looking for their spiritual as well as practical significance. He approached the subject of karma in an article in a 1964 Religious Research Monthly Journal:

> There is a basic justice in this world. The scientist recognizes
> it in a fine form, as the law of cause-and-effect. The moralist
> recognizes it as basic in human nature and relationships. The
> deist (believer in God) recognizes justice as a fundamental
> decree from God, a foundation stone of our world as created
> by Him. Reincarnation shows this basic principle of justice as
> bringing unto us the kind of action we give to others.
>   This is known as 'karma.' 'Karma' actually is only a word
> meaning effect, or reaction-to-action. In my high school days
> in Stillwater, Minnesota, I did some duck hunting. For this
> I had a trusty old 12-gauge single-barrel shotgun. In the science
> classroom I had learned that one basic scientific law is, 'For
> every action there is an equal and opposite reaction.' From my
> shotgun I learned that law in actual practice. For when I pulled
> the trigger and exploded a shell, the powder in the shell not
> only pushed the charge of shot through the barrel in the direc-
> tion of the flying ducks—it also pushed the gun backward
> against my shoulder. That gun shot to kill—at both ends!...This
> essentially is what karma means. It is a very scientific word,
> indicating that in human actions, as well as in shotguns and
> scientific discoveries, there is action and *reaction*. It is part of
> the orderliness, the overall pattern of justice, of God's crea-
> tion. What we send out to others has an equal and opposite
> reaction—it comes back upon ourselves. St. Paul expressed it
> in this way: 'Be not deceived—God is not mocked—for **what-
> soever a man soweth that shall he also reap**' (Galatians 6:7).
> Karma does not mean that we've got to make up for everything
> we do ounce by ounce, act by act—it is NOT an 'eye for an
> eye, tooth for a tooth' sort of thing. Reincarnation turns out
> to be basically above that level. It simply means the reaction
> of our own actions.
>   This is akin, of course, to our actions toward people, but
> it extends our growth into another area. We are to take mastery
> of every major type of human life situation—that is why we
> are incarnated at least once in every major race, continent, col-
> or, religion, culture, economic and social class, type and con-
> dition of human life.
>   In the book of Genesis—first book in the Jewish Scriptures
> as well as the Christian Bible—the first two chapters tell and

retell the story of creation, as understood by the ancient spiritual seers and teachers who cast it in these terms. A key part of this story is the injunction given by God to man to 'take dominion'—to extend human mastery 'over the beast of the field, the fish of the sea, the birds of the air' (see Genesis 1:26). Man collectively, and in a sense individually, is to take dominion over the earth. As the reincarnation research points up, this includes mastery of every basic type of earth situation. So the more we take mastery of the situations in which we find ourselves at the various times of this life, the more we are progressing, and the less there will be that we must achieve in our future incarnations. This is a basic form of growth.

In actual practice, as we observe the progress of a soul from one lifetime to another, we find that this mastery of earth situations is often achieved in two stages. We must take sheer earth mastery of earth situations if we are to survive upon earth, and much of man's early mastery is on this primitive, animal level—through powerful and trained muscles, shrewdness of mind, driving purpose to succeed. But that is not enough. We must learn to take mastery of earth and its many situations in *terms of what we are*—which means, in *terms consistent with our spiritual nature* as children of God. So we find that a soul which in its early incarnations develops shrewdness, must later learn to stand by principle instead of expediency. Although this principle holds true, we find in the reincarnation research that often it is only after a number of earth incarnations that a soul comes to standing by principle and refusing expediency. But before we are through we must take mastery of earth situations as a child of God of whom neither we nor God need be ashamed—'a workman...handling aright the word of truth.' (II Timothy 2:15)

More than once as a quantitative analysis student I would spend an afternoon in the chemistry laboratory working through some analysis, only to discover at the end that I had done it wrong somehow. Sure, I had an answer, an analysis. The only trouble was that my answer was not the right one. Then I had to do it over. Just so there are incarnations in which we take mastery of some earth situation or other—perhaps, say, the earning of a livelihood—and think we have done well, only to learn when the period is over that we have gone at it in a wrong way and have essentially a very wrong answer. Then we have to come back and do it over again, and perhaps again, until we do it the right way. (Journal XIV:6c-e)

The idea of taking spiritual mastery over earth and all its experiences offers a new approach to understanding karma. Let us apply this idea to some of the pastlife recall cases—for instance Wanda, whose father raped her. There was something to learn here. One of the questions the counselor asked during the pastlife recall session was, "Why didn't you talk to your mother about the situation?" Her answer, "She has too many problems already. How could I give her any more problems?" This was most likely how the young Irish girl felt. It is a reasonable answer. But, we ask, should not she have done something earlier about the situation? Left home earlier? Talked to her mother? Talked to her priest? Could she and should she have turned to other people and could they have helped? We don't know. But the soul must have felt it could have done a better job, since it chose a quick comeback (only about five years between the death of the Irish girl and Wanda's birth) to face this unresolved problem.

In the case of lives cut short, such as Pamela in the fiery death and the war deaths mentioned, all souls must learn that not all incarnations can be lived to a ripe old age. Life situations in the cosmic school of earth do not always go according to plan. As someone has said, "Life is what happens when we are expecting something else!" This concept the soul must grasp. Sometimes the shock of a sudden death will leave a blotch on the soul and this has to be worked out. Accepting and facing the unexpected is an important skill to develop.

Also it is evidenced over and over in pastlife recall work that the Creator does not set us adrift. Although life circumstances may devastate us, there is a great loving hand that guides us. For instance Henry, after he recalled the life of the gladiator, experienced the distinct feelings of hatred, aloneness, loneliness, disgust with the human race, and above all the smell and taste of blood. In the next session Henry recalled the soul's next incarnation. The unhappy gladiator would not have recognized the sweet, happy shepherd girl who sang as she herded her sheep over the hilly country of Greece, at peace with the world and bringing peace and love to a wounded soul.

Sometimes the afterlife of the personality will have a healing effect, as presented earlier by the example of war deaths, when special healing and love was brought to the young Southern soldier. In Pamela's case the woman that died in the fire watched her children grow up from the astral realm. After her husband finally remarried, providing a good home for her children, the astral Pamela felt free to drop her concern for her family and to go on her way.

Karmic growth seen from the standpoint of taking mastery over earth situations is a different concept than some dastardly character who victimizes others. However there are dastardly characters in the world. The Irish father who raped his daughter was one. The Roman senator and others who decreed life or death for their gladiators are other instances. Although the lives and soul experiences of these particular pastlife personalities are not available for our perusal, reincarnation research has provided substantial evidence that indicates they somehow met the unbreakable reality of the spiritual law of cause-and-effect, called karma. Since karma makes the punishment fit the crime better than any human could devise, it is impossible to conjecture how the warp and woof of God's justice worked in their cases, but their passions and greed turned upon them somehow. The retributive karma is just as real and exacting as the karma of growth or taking mastery over earth experiences.

Karma was not the only spiritual idea studied through the pastlife recall work. Other reincarnational patterns emerged in those early days. The most important was the difference between the soul and the person. As Dr. Loehr witnessed a client gradually recall lifetime after lifetime, often two successive incarnations being very different in nature, he realized it was not the previous person who came back, but another portion of the soul which incarnated as a different person, and was born to experience a new set of life circumstances:

> I gradually realized that only a portion of the soul is incarnate at any one time. Later, talking this over with Aldous and Maria Huxley, who were two of my advisors in this early research, we came to see that the soul is a large complex of energies, like the nucleus of an atom, and only a few energies are detached at any time to form a new personality. This way the soul would experience from different portions of its beingness in different races, countries, religions, and of course,

both sexes.

I suppose I really saw this when Lilla, a delightful retired school teacher now, went back to a lifetime as a lovely, consecrated, Spanish nun in the 1500s. Then in the 1600s had an incarnation as a roistering Brittany fisherman off the coast of northern France, never darkening a church door, but delighting in his strengths and courage, daring the sea and eventually dying, gloriously, in a storm that engulfed his boat. What happened to the demure nun? She was not lost. That was one part of the soul and the strong fisherman was another part, each adding experience and balance to the whole soul.

As we studied these facts, it became apparent that 'reincarnation' is not an accurate term. What it seems to say, does not take place. It is not that a person incarnates, then dies, then incarnates again, or re-incarnates. Rather it is that the soul has a series of different incarnations, each with its own purpose and concentrating on its own beingness, each its own person. Reincarnation is the wrong word, and 'sequential incarnation'—that when the soul comes to take its earthschooling it does so in a number of different persons, each uniquely made for that life ('tailor-made'), each from the same soul but each person different from all the others—is more correct. We shall continue to use the word 'reincarnation' for that is the word entrenched in current usage, but let us understand what it really means.

Another important aspect of this discovery of sequential incarnations is that each person has an afterdeath life which is not cut short nor affected in any way (with a few exceptions) by the birth of its soul's next child. This means that death frees us to go on in the astral and etheric realms just as far as we as persons are potentialed and energized to go. This gives respect to each individual person of the soul. We are each our own person, in a very real way. Just as each person is individually responsible for his own growth, so each person is individually loved and encouraged by God. How could God's infinite love be expressed if we as persons could not develop to our fullest, both in the material realm of earth and then after death in the ascending spiritual realms? Each person is a continuing separate entity of the larger complex of the soul, until it accomplishes its fullest nature. (Journal XIV:9c-e, 1964)

It was during this early discovery period—the prayer-plant project and the pastlife recall work—that Dr. John, the chief Spirit Guide of Religious Research, introduced himself. He is not an ordinary spirit guide, but one who has studied the akashic records, also known as God's Book of Judgment, with the purpose of introducing another aspect of spiritual knowledge, the values of God, during the early part of this early scientific era on earth, thereby balancing the scientific material facts with the spiritual values of God. (The particulars of Dr. John, the spirit guide, and the steps taken to create the bridge between the non-material—or upstairs team as we refer to them—and the material Religious Research, headed by Dr. Franklin Loehr, often called the downstairs team, is discussed in detail in the first chapter of the first book of this series, *Dr. John: He Can Read Your Pastlives.*)

The approach of understanding God through the method known as science is also embraced by the upstairs team as brought out by Dr. John in a 1979 teaching session in Atlanta, Georgia:

> Dr. John: The first part of establishing the Kingdom of God on earth is to find out what is God's particular way for earth. This involves at least two things. It involves what are the facts, the truth of what God has done. The best way of discovering this is not through pronouncement, is not through psychical means. The best way is to find out *objectively* what God has done. This is why our team emphasizes finding the objective truth of what God has done in this physical universe, particularly planet earth.
>
> Now this is a new development. The 'spirit of truth which shall lead you into all truth' as the Master said, we believe to be the *method of science*, which is the search for truth, not for inspiration, first. Certainly not for personal gain and personal opinion.
>
> The Religious Research approach is essentially the understanding that the method called 'science' is a tool, a very superior and valuable tool, for finding out what God has done and is still doing. Remember, science does not make a thing true. Science never made a thing true. It only finds out what God, the Creator, made true, and then what God's children can do with that truth.
>
> Along with the facts, the objective facts, of what God has

done, and that is the essential truth, lies also what God values. In other words, God has certain purposes to be attained. And so I have said from the beginning, use the test the Master gave, 'By their fruits ye shall know them.' This is what we bring; this is our emphasis upon science, meaning the objective understanding of what God has done; this is our emphasis then upon values, which involves, of course, feeling and commitment as well as cold understanding of objective truth.

The scientific method has proved the best way mankind yet has for discovering what the Creator has done (and is doing) in creation. The scientific researcher says in effect, to the object or process he is studying, "Let me understand you objectively, in terms of what you are, regardless of what has been said or taught or presupposed about you in the past. Let me examine and re-examine you, find your components, see how they fit together in the logic of your own being. I want to know what you really are.'

This was the approach used by the Hadley Workshop group in 1948 as the ministers gathered there were asking: What are the *spiritual* facts of God? Although they did not use that terminology, and may not have even understood they were asking that particular question, this was their approach. They were saying to the spiritual facts of God, "What are you?" as they went about discovering them objectively.

Finding the non-material portion of ourselves, the soul, was started in the pastlife recall work and proceeded very naturally and with special guidance to the life readings. This was to become Dr. John's major role in transmitting the knowledge he had gained in his extensive study in the etheric realms, bringing that knowledge to earth through his specially prepared channel, Dr. Loehr, his soulmate as well as his partner in this work. Since the pastlife recalls laid the basic foundation of soul information, the life readings were checked against the facts gathered by the downstairs team of Religious Research. This process was carried out intensively for four years before any public announcement was made of the life readings, and the continuing cross-check credentialing has held solidly for more than 30 years now (1985).*

---

* *CROSS-CORRESPONDENCE AMONG THE LOEHR-DANIELS LIFE READINGS, Professor Horton W. Amidon, 1985.*

As with the pastlife recall work, the life readings are done on an individual basis; therefore, the various spiritual principles can be applied to each soul in the problems as well as the growth potential. Hence the life readings supplement the pastlife recalls and expand them both in number and depth. A program of pastlife recalls has its limitations, in that it does not identify whether your soul is from the masculine or feminine half of its whole soul, nor does it give the placement and purposes of present life, etc. A life reading supplies more information from an objective source.

Karma has the same force and emphasis in the life reading material as in the pastlife recall work. What is the past mistake or partial mistake that now reappears as an opportunity to grow in the present life? What was gained by holding onto this or that principle, what was lost in overlooking or misusing an opportunity? Applying the spiritual principles to these areas is the insight Dr. John brings through the life readings. Therefore the study of karma continued and expanded with the life reading material.

The pastlife recall therapy has developed its own identity and is now being called psychography, meaning the graphing, the mapping, of the forces that make up the personality. It is still an important part of Religious Research, as therapy and self-discovery. Psychography has its own integrity, providing personal growth and enrichment possibilities, as well as a means to tap and evict unwanted negative emotions from the subconscious.

The life reading program also is an ongoing portion of Religious Research, with life readings being given on a basis of three to four a week. There have been approximately 4800 life readings given to date, each reading averaging seventeen pages. Dr. John has indicated that this portion of his work will be accomplished after six to seven thousand life readings have been given, which should build a substantial library of spiritual teachings. From this vast source of material the spiritual aspects of man and his universe, his relationship with God and God's all-important value-system, can be studied on a "discovery" basis, of who we are and what we are attempting to accomplish on planet earth. Although these life readings are not all-encompassing, all-knowing, they do bring new understanding of our role in the continuing process of soul growth.

Early in the life readings, Dr. John brought out that souls are of different ages. He uses a five-fold division: (1) "Just-starting" (about five to eight lives), (2) "well-started" (perhaps seven to twelve lives). These two first stages are sometimes called "young souls," and their early incarnations are designed to get them oriented to earth and off to a good start in their 60-100 significant incarnations.

(3) "Around-the-midpoint." These are what we call "middle souls." This is when about sixty percent of our incarnations take place, as the soul takes on the more serious and important experiences of earth learning. Dr. John sometimes refers to these as "the karmic lives," using karma to mean learning or growth.

(4) "Well-along" and (5) "nearing-the-end" are what we call "old souls," and the emphasis here shifts from our own learning more to service of others, in a way returning to earth what was received by the soul in its early incarnations. Thus karma is of a lesser nature for the old soul, though it must clear up any tag ends of unresolved business or emotions, and get whatever lessons may have been missed, polishing up its mastery of earth experiences before going on to the next stage.

The first book of this series dealt primarily with young souls and the lessons learned in the first two stages. This second book and the next (*Growth Is The First Spiritual Law*, presently set for 1986 publication by Gnosticoeurs) present an in-depth investigation of the middle soul. A fourth book will deal with the old soul.

There is so much, and so many interesting facts, to learn about the soul—your true immortal self—and its progression of incarnations.

Karma, the great teacher.

CHAPTER TWO

CYCLES

A person rarely understands himself in terms of the present life only, for pastlives do influence us.

When we think of the effect of our pastlives upon us, we usually think of how they affect our present life now. This is natural, for this is where we live, this is who we are, this—our immediate life—is óur primary responsibility. But also the study of reincarnation shows that certain growths are accomplished in a series or cycle of lives, and our present life may be—often is—one of a cycle. So to better understand ourselves we need to understand these cycles.

Dr. John often refers to the long cycles as "cycles-of-seven," and the shorter cycles as "cycles-of-three." These are terms of convenience and do not indicate a hard-and-fast number of lives. There is nothing magical about the number. A cycle-of-seven may have only six lives or stretch to eight or nine. A cycle-of-three may actually take four incarnations, or in rare cases may be accomplished in two. Moreover, in a long cycle usually there are non-cyclic lives interspersed. For example, in a long series of masculine lives there will usually be a feminine incarnation or two, and vice versa, to keep the soul from becoming crystallized in the emphasis of that cycle.

The long cycles are to help the soul attain and become comfortable in some major accomplishment, such as development in the non-native gender, or the melding of the spiritual with the material in earthliving. The short cycles can be used to concentrate in one area and also to experience different viewpoints of a social or religious issue. One frequent reason for a cycle-of-three series is to achieve a balance in some quality. Following somewhat the thesis-antithesis-synthesis pattern, the first life may swing too far in emphasizing a particular trait. In the second life corrective factors are introduced. An older, more adept soul can gain the balance in that second life, but a younger soul may experience a "swing of the pendulum" too far in the other direction. Then a third lifetime is needed to bring the soul to a balance in this quality.

Pendulum swings often seem characteristic of large-scale human behavior as well as individual learning. Early industrialization saw the owner and manager in the driver's seat. Then the rising labor movement of the 1900s reversed the flow of power. Now, hopefully, a cooperative equilibrium is being established. Late nineteenth century Victorianism repressed sexual expression and the twentieth century has swung far the other way into promiscuity. Now a more moderate view of sexual freedom, with respect for one's self, hopefully will emerge. Growth requires change, but sometimes early change becomes so violent that the previous good seems nearly lost. Thankfully God gives souls the time to learn from their excesses and gradually achieve a balanced growth.

This chapter includes four illustrations of how short cycles are used: to teach by thesis-antithesis-synthesis; to demonstrate different sides of a situation; to thoroughly instill a quality; to watch a civilization rise and fall.

FRANCES

The life readings bring many examples where various forces— grinding poverty, a ruthless state rule (as with the Incas in Peru), a driving personal work ethic, etc.—produced a life of ceaseless work. This is not balanced. Such repression may plant corrective seeds of desire for a lifetime with more play, producing perhaps a quite frivolous life next in that series. Then, having experienced both, the soul can see that a life of only hard labor, or only fun, does not bring satisfaction, and the pendulum swings to the middle as the soul learns to achieve a good personhood and incarnation without either imbalance.

Frances is a woman in her sixties, in the second of a cycle-of-three lives:

> Dr. John: Frances Simpson. Yes.
> In a very particular way, this life and the immediately prior one, which was back in India, and it was really quite a life of

privation but with a certain tantalizing touch with people who did not know privation. It was in a trading city, a seacoast trading city, where the extremes of wealth and poverty were, well, extremes. There was a great gap between, and she was on the poverty side of the picture. The necessity of just plain hard work, the lack of money, and the lack of nice things for much fun in life, were dominant emotional factors in that life.

In that life she was married. She had a certain vivaciousness despite the poverty, and she was attractive despite the fact that she was pretty much in rags all her life. She won the attention of a young man in her same general economic status. Both of them had a bit more intelligence than was needed for a life of privation, so both had a certain outreach.

They married rather young, as marriage went in those days. They had several children, and the responsibility of the children increased their privation. They knew of some people who rose out of the deprived status by means that were not legal—by smuggling, by theft, by crime. So they talked it over. Their upbringing, their parentage, had been mildly moral, but when they married they moved more into the downtown ghetto, so to speak.

They tried a bit of minor crime, a bit of theft from the merchants in the bazaars, who were pretty sharp. They got away with a few things. But before long they were caught red-handed. There was no such thing really as a trial, and they were executed on the spot. Their children were small, less than five years old, and starved to death after the parents were executed.

This lifetime was one of the tragedies of which earthlife holds so many while evil is as rampant as it is. Evil is less rampant now, and more curtailed by the very processes of law and of social concern. But it did set up in the desires of each of them the strong wish for a different kind of life, a better material basis of life and one with more fun in it.

The girl had had a certain vivaciousness. She wanted a life in which she could be somewhat coquettish and an attractive young female. The young man wanted a life in which he could be more materially successful and have a quite different type of family life.

Since in a way the answer depended upon the man, he was given such a life in the 1800s in Ireland and England. He was an Irishman but he would live occasionally in England and he would live occasionally in France. He had a better mind and a more capable nature than before. He was born into a family that owned land and managed it well, and there were enough of them so that they could individually escape from watching the land, while one of the brothers did it, and travel abroad.

They usually managed to turn the travel abroad to some business significance. If they had had to justify it on some tax record, they could have. But they also enjoyed learning what life was like in other places. So he had that better life, partly better than he as a soul had yet earned. The grace of God put him into a family in which he was brought along, as it were.

Both Frances and her husband come from very young souls who have not yet attained a great deal. God wants His children to succeed, and His grace is operative in many ways. Usually souls must earn a better life but sometimes they are given one to help them learn. Dr. John says this is similar to the way in which parents will hold a toddler's hands as he walks, until the child is able to walk alone.

Another example of a grace-of-God life is one in which a feminine (or masculine) soul is given a very masculine (or feminine) personality before she/he is able to build such a person. This type "walk-through" life can help that soul learn how to develop in future non-native gender lives.

Dr. John: Now they come back together in this life, again as husband and wife, their second time, and the general thought is that they are just going to have fun. Well, they did, but they learned that that also is not the key to a good life. In the 1700s life they could have really made a better life for themselves in a way, if they had returned to their parental region and worked on the farms. Even though it was poverty and hard work, they would have lived and their children would have lived and they would have had the happiness that can come even in a poverty family, a family of hard work and not much luxuries but still enough to eat.

So in a sense they made the wrong choice in the 1700s, and in another sense they made a good choice because they were not content with the status quo but struck out for something better. But in striking out for something better they were really not equipped with the extreme cunning and ingenuity and such to be successful thieves. They did not have the contacts to get in with organized crime. Both of which were probably fortunate for the souls. So in striking out for something better they rather quickly struck out. But at least it was an attempt. In the present life they have more the frivolity, they have more of the fun of life. They can buy the things which they had seen others eat and imbibe and do, to a small extent anyway. But again they find this is not really the answer. The persons are more capable. They endure more and achieve more. The souls are learning, but are still young.

Here is where what we sometimes call the 'pattern of three' holds. The first life in such a 'pattern of three' sees the pendulum swing pretty far to one side. The second life will see it swing rather to an opposite. The third life in the pattern hopefully will see it come to a better middle course without the extremes of either.

So it is hoped that these two individually, if not together, possibly together but not necessarily, will come to a more balanced view of life in the final one of this 'pattern of three' lives. These three in the pattern need not be sequential. The first two have been for Frances and have not been for her husband.

The third one may be the next life. We rather believe it will be for Frances anyway. I am not reading the husband's records, so I do not know for him.

The Frances person has a mind which is certainly not stupid. The restrictions upon her have been more karmic. The desires set in motion, with quite some force from the past, of what she wanted in this life, did not particularly coincide with education. They coincided much more with flirtatiousness, with coquettishness, with enjoying herself, with escaping restrictions, with 'being free,' things such as that.

So she has had that experience—one might say 'fling,' but that may not be quite the right term. She had that experience and she found it was not really what she was seeking as a person or as a soul. She is seeking something else.

She has a spiritual thirst, we would say. She is seeking to advance that portion of herself which is more than earthly, the portion that we call the soul but which is represented within the personality by spiritual interests and by activities that feed another portion of the being, that bring a different kind of satisfaction.

It is somewhat late in life for this, she might feel, and yet not too late. There is ample time for new interests. The early stages of coquettishness have been had and were good, an answer to those desires. The middle stages of raising children who did not starve, who did not die because the parents were executed, who presented some difficulties, challenged her, but she stayed with the children. She stayed with the assignment of motherhood. She achieved. She in a sense completed that task, although in one sense the role of motherhood is never completed by most women who are mothers. At least until after the incarnate days are over and the excarnate stages bring a larger understanding and a new relationship.

So Frances is enabled now to give time to the new chapter which, her council tells me, has begun. A chapter of seeking something more, to bring more in the way of satisfaction, of fulfillment, to the real nature and the whole nature of her being. It is really an interesting life that she has had. Its difficulties have not been too unusual. Her mistakes have not been damning.

She has learned from the difficulties and the mistakes as well as from the pleasures, and she has enjoyed the pleasures, and this is good. The having of the pleasures has in one sense fulfilled a pre-requirement for going on. Because to accomplish these, to satisfy these desires, which were very strong and carried over, was a pre-requirement for going on to something more.

She can start her third life in the pattern of three in the remainder of this life, and perhaps begin the attainment of it. As she attains this more balanced view about life, she will have a new basis for living in most or all of the subsequent incarnations. Some may have certain emphases which vary from this pathway, but on the whole now she's had a pretty good pointing of the way that really leads to life, to progression for the soul. Is there a question so far?

Conductor: I believe this introduction to Frances has already answered one of her questions: 'Why did I in my youth prefer men who had bootlegged, and why did I have a hatred of policemen and a fear of the noise of a police car or an ambulance, a fear that was almost panic?'

Dr. John: It was the authorities of law that trapped her and her husband red-handed, then hauled them before the person whose establishment they had raided and there was shouting, there was anger by the merchant whose goods they had taken and which were upon their persons, and there was execution. This could very well carry over in a fear of policemen.

They had come to admire in that 1700s life the people who got away with this sort of thing. So possibly this could be the reason for her admiration of the bootleggers. I say possibly. Maybe it was that some of the bootleggers plied her with liquor during the prohibition days. I do not know. There was the admiration of those who 'got away with it,' and this might have been interpreted in her present life as being attracted to men a decade or so older than she. These are possiblities.

Late in the reading the conductor presents a question which has bearing on the life in India:

> Conductor: Her next question is a rather unusual one. She says that she has had a habit of holding her hand on her chest just below the collar bone. She drew a picture of this. People will even ask her if she's in pain. She does it unconsciously and she wonders if there is any reason for it, that you can see.
> Dr. John: The execution of the 1700s India young woman was by beheading, and it may have been that when the head was severed from the body that instinctively she reached for it. I am not sure, but this would be a possibility. Otherwise, it may be just sort of a habit beginning in some now forgotten episode. She might recover this in some type of recall program of past experiences. (A2105:1-5,15)

The pendulum swing is being used to help Frances balance work and play in earthliving. The 1700s India girl longed for a different kind of life, one with material success and fun. This second incarnation in the cycle of three has been releasing those pent-up desires as the pendulum swings to the opposite extreme. Now in her sixties, Frances is realizing there is more and is thirsting for the spiritual. Her next life, the third in the cycle, should introduce a woman eager to live a well-balanced life.

PHILLIP

In the previous example, the pendulum swing was used to release forces of desire. For Phillip, the second in a cycle-of-three lives helped release forces but also increased his understanding by showing him the opposite side of the picture. As an American Indian in the early 1700s, he watched with anger and resentment while the white man gradually took control of his homeland. Along with the negative emotions, he was filled with the desire to know why this was happening. So the pendulum swung him in the 1800s to an incarnation in England, a source of the white man. In the following excerpt, this third life in the cycle-of-three finds Phillip in the same general area as in the 1700s. He is integrating his learning from the past two lives as he releases the remaining forces set up by the Indian incarnation:

Dr. John: The soul now expressing as Phillip is in the third stage, and just slightly over the midpoint of the third stage. This particular life is somewhat in two chapters, in that it is the end of a cycle of three lives, and that is its major function, but also it is a beginning on a new phase of the soul's growth and service. This new phase, really beginning just pretty much in the present, that is, within the past several years, will extend through the balance of the years of this incarnation.

This is quite an interesting picture, conductor, and I would share it with you, and of course with Phillip, at this time. The first of this particular cycle of three lives, which really is quite an unusual cycle, but it makes a lot of sense and the soul had quite a hand in choosing the second and third lives of this cycle of three—the first was as an Indian, an American Indian, pretty much in the area in which he now resides, that of New England. Although, of course, the Indian did not know of it as New England. He knew of it more as his ancestral lands.

Lands of hunting, lands of fishing, lands of being out with nature on the hills, the high hills, the mountains there, the trees, the game. Game was plentiful, and he studied it and made friends with it to some extent, as well as hunting and killing it when need be, always with a certain reverence.

He had the fortune—let us not say either good or bad fortune, because it was both—to be born in the late 1600s, with most of that life extending into the 1700s. It was in the masculine expression, which is his native gender, in that he is an incarnation of the masculine half of his whole soul. Each whole soul is polarized into the masculine and feminine soulmates before coming into earth, as I have brought out many times, but expresses as a whole soul in most of the other realms.

Of course, each 'half-soul' operates with the soul quality of bringing life, hence functions really as a soul as it comes into incarnation. I can expand on that at some future time, but let us proceed now with Phillip.

This Indian man was a good provider for his family. He had a wife to whom he was quite faithful, as was the custom there. She was quiet and made no demands upon him, which was good in a way, because it allowed his mystical nature to develop. This mystical nature, of course, had roots in past feminine incarnations as well as in the nature of the soul itself.

In another way, it might have been better had the wife made more demands upon him, because he developed qualities in the mystical hours which were tending to draw him, as it were, away from earth. However, these qualities have been corrected, these tendencies have been corrected, while the goodness of the qualities is still there.

As I said, he had the fortune of being born at this particular time, and this was the time when the white man was pushing farther out from his early settlements and staking more land. The white man, with his better weapons and his greater sophistication and his own sense of self-righteousness, was in effect pushing the Indian off the land.

This man belonged to a relatively small group of Indians. The hunt-and-forage tribes needed larger areas than the more settled agricultural tribes, hence were smaller as a general rule. This tribe was being pushed rather inexorably out of their ancestral lands bit by bit. Sometimes the white man would trade with them or reason with them, and usually got the better of the bargain. They didn't quite know how they were persuaded when they were persuaded.

When they rebelled, they met up with the white man's guns. Although they killed some white men, they lost enough of their own people to make quite an impression upon them, and to see that really they could not that way hold onto their ancestral lands. They were pushed further north and into some of the

Canadian areas, I believe. It could be interesting to follow this little streamlet of life which that tribe was. However, we have other things to do.

The then incarnation of the Phillip soul was a good man. He was a respected man, a strong man, but he had no interest in politics. He was not on the governing council, although many times the little governing council called all the men together as they faced this or that decision. I repeat again, it was a number of 'this and that' decisions that were pushing them out.

There was not a frontal attack, as it were. There was no great battle which they lost. They were just faced with many decisions which their forefathers had not had to face and for which they had no guidance in the history of their tribe or in the religion of their tribe. They were politically and economically somewhat naive, of course, compared to the white man.

They put up resistance as best they could. They turned to their religious leaders, who gave what guidance they could and what help they could. But this was an inexorable, historical development. They were pushed out, and I believe that little tribe was in time reduced quite a bit in numbers and then possibly attached to or absorbed into another tribe, but that was after this man's death.

He had three children who lived and grew to at least young adulthood. This quiet, comfortable wife, who made no demands—he provided all the game and fish they needed—provided the vegetable side of the diet. It was not a difficult life. They knew how to survive by the traditional survival wisdom of their people.

He was greatly disturbed at being pushed out. Not just for his own sake and his family and his friends, his peer group, his contemporaries, but also because this he feared was, and it was, the end of their history and their ancestral lands. This really bothered him a great deal. But as he pondered it, he also—let me begin again:

As he faced this situation, he did not merely develop anger— he did that, anger and resentment and such—but also he pondered why this was allowed to happen. Were the gods of the white man stronger than the gods of his people? What were the white men like? Why was this happening? They were superior in shrewdness, in being able to talk and bargain and make things in their favor seem logical. They had superior weaponry and even a superior social organization. They could communicate with each other more fully. They had more to talk about and they had more resources upon which to draw. Also, they had seeds, and they planted crops and they settled down. So his pondering on this really included a great development of curiosity as to who these white men were, where they came from, how they got that way. This led to the next incarnation, the second of this cycle-of-three.

This was in England in the 1800s. Again, he was born on the cusp of the century. He was born in the late 1700s but lived most of his life in England in the 1800s, again in the masculine expression.

In a way, the soul was acting out a play in these three lifetimes. In a way, the soul understood. But what the soul understands in the spiritual dimensions needs to be translated into the consciousness of its own earthbeings, its personhoods, for their sake and because the great requirement made upon the soul in its incarnational experiences is to be able to construct somewhat, along with its guides and teachers, and then to guide, along with its council, earthbeings, earth human persons, through certain experiences successfully and into certain learnings, a growth of consciousness in this level of beingness, the personal level, on planet earth.

Is this clear, conductor?

Conductor: Yes, Dr. John, it is, and I thank you. I'm sure this will help him. He was very interested to know about the earlier American Indian life.

Dr. John: He sensed one, did he?

Conductor: Yes. Perhaps more than one, he's not sure.

Dr. John: There may be more than one. We will look for others later on. It is interesting that he did not come back as a white man in New England or in America somewhere, but he chose to go to the source of the white men who came to New England, he went to England.

There, again drawing on past experience of the soul, but cast within the framework of an answer to the quest of the Indian, as I have explained, he was a businessman, a merchant. He did quite a bit of business with the ships that imported things from the new world, from New England. He was acquainted with some of the traders who went back and forth. He did not go himself. He stayed in England, because the true source of the white man was the white man's way of thinking, which had its origins there in England, you see. He not only studied it, he experienced it.

He was a merchant, he was an importer, although he did not own his own ships. He bought from those who did bring the things over. In his life, he knew the value of buying things from the new world to sell in old England: food and such. He knew that he had to send to the new world then, or someone had to, things that the new world wanted and for which they would exchange what they had in the way of trade. This man in the import business came across an import that was not from New England. It was from the new world. Of course, by the time he was in business in the early 1800s, the new country was fairly well established. There was the skirmish in the early 1800s between the two countries, and there were frictions, but there was a growing amount of commerce between them.

Products from the southern and central portions came over as well, including this strange oblong leaf, a large leaf, which when rolled upon itself or shredded and encased within itself and smoked, produced some interesting effects upon the body. This person became quite addicted really to tobacco. He liked the strong tobacco. He became somewhat of a connoisseur of tobacco.

There was a dark tobacco, wrapped into smaller cylinders. As this man's use grew and his addiction grew, he turned to the stronger tobacco which was his favorite, and he became quite addicted to it.

The Indian's curiosity was being answered, you see, by letting him live a life as a white man at the source of the white men who had come into his area.

There is a principle of balance which is a spiritual principle, and it makes often for a 'pattern of three,' which in turn can make for the small cycles-of-three life patterns. In the first there is usually a swing of the pendulum to one side, and in the second a swing to the other side, and in the third, hopefully a balance is found.

Although that British merchant, who was married, and who was born into a merchant family—there were several siblings, brothers and sisters—then he married in his class. He wouldn't have dreamed of marrying outside of his class! It was not the top class. He was not one of the 'gentle folk.' But he was not one of the peasant group either. He was in this merchant group, which was a group that was gaining respect in England as being a very necessary and productive group. The Crown and the whole establishment of the Crown was taking note of the merchant class and working with it, while still retaining their own superiority. Sometimes the superiority of the 'gentle folk' was anything but gentle. Although some of them were truly gentlemen and ladies.

The soul, with a little bit of bemusement, observed the personhood of that English merchant, who became a bit plump and would really fuss around. He was pretty good. He was active. He would bustle around, 'bustle' is the word. He would bustle around, and he insisted that those who worked for him do their share of bustling, at least when he was present.

He threw his weight around a bit, for he was a merchant and a successful one. Not a grandly successful one, but his family lived well and he had money with which to operate. This was really the totality of his personality. He did not get interested in politics. It was not too wise. He was somewhat fawning upon those who were over him, which was wise.

In a way, he did not have the strength of character of the Indian. But likewise, the Indian did not have the strengths and qualities that the Englishman developed and added to its soul.

As the soul was considering its next life, it pondered how to somewhat bring the two together in a synthesis which in itself would be a step forward for the soul and for humanity, as represented by the incarnations of that soul. This has led to the present life.

The present life has returned him to the same general New England area. I could not say if it is the precise area. It probably is not. For the Indians in their hunting occupied a rather large area, and a small hunting party might be away from the tribal village for several days journey and then back. They did certain explorations. In general, the Indians that they met were few and peaceful and rather civilized and not on a warpath. So they roamed an area there, certainly larger than what this man roams in his usual week, let us say.

In each life, that is, in each incarnation of a soul, there is a pickup of some events and relationships and developments of qualities of beingness from some of the past lives. Once in a while there is a lifetime which has almost no connection with the past lives of that soul upon earth, but these are usually test cases and special cases.

The present life as Phillip Farrington picks up from both of those two immediately prior lifetimes in various ways. The council is suggesting that his questions will help to bring out some of these ways, and I defer to them.

As Phillip's life reading developed it was shown that a number of the people who shared a part of this life had been in either the 1700s Indian or the 1800s English life. For instance, his paternal grandfather was the father in the English life and the present father was his brother. His older brother was the former undemanding wife of the Indian man, while his sister was also a sister in the 1700s. Two of his present-life friends played a relatively important part in the life of the Indian—one was the medicine man of the little tribe; the other a fellow tribesmember who watched from the other side as his friend lived the English life.

As the guides and teachers had indicated, some of Phillip's questions brought out more ways in which these two pastlives feed into the present. There is an interesting possible carryover brought out in the answer to this question:

> Conductor: Dr. John, he as a young person had a very unusual craving for drink and smoking and cursing. This has disturbed him through the years. It has entered into the marriage.
> Dr. John: The addiction to tobacco in the Englishman's life would be the explanation of that. The Englishman drank, but I do not see that the drink was really such a problem. You say cursing also?
> Conductor: Cursing, yes.
> Dr. John: I will hazard a guess on that: I see the Englishman merchant down on the docks making sure his goods are delivered and perfectly in good order and everything, and listening to the sailors curse and thinking, ah, that is an even greater, stronger expression of manhood. But he himself did not curse. He wasn't allowed to by his social standing and his business. So there may have been a wish to curse which came out in the present life.
> Knowing that should be sufficient to release him from it,

because the present is when things are changed. Consciousness is where forces like this are taken up and we make our decisions on every level of spiritual beingness.

When the conductor asks the following question Dr. John further explains how the present life is balancing the experiences of the last two:

> Conductor: He says, 'I am interested in my present-life purpose and how I am to fulfill it.'
> Dr. John: He has done a very fine piece of work in reclaiming the land that was taken from him before, and in fulfilling that portion of the unfulfilled desire and force of the Indian lifetime. This has been an accomplishment far beyond simply meeting that pastlife force, of course.
> What he has done is in some ways a much greater achievement than what the English trader did, because the Phillip person in this life began, as it were, with no advantages from society and asking no favors. What he accomplished is to his credit, and it is a very fine credit.
> So in one sense he has accomplished the first purpose of this lifetime, which was to live a good strong life as a New Englander, within that framework, within its difficulties, and with the difficulties of his birth and environment, but also with the strengths of his birth and environment. And to make those strengths his own, and they are his now, and they belong now to the soul. He's been a helpful person all through this, helping others hopefully to build and gain strength of achievement, various kinds of masculine strengths.
> This he has achieved. Were he to die tomorrow, this life would rate a very fine grade, for it has contributed good qualities to the soul and it has been a life well lived within a certain experience-framework. But he will not die tomorrow, at least as far as I can see. (A3125)

MELODY

Cycles-of-three are not necessarily pendulum swings. Sometimes a small cycle is used to thoroughly learn a difficult lesson. Our third example is taken from a life reading for a two-year-old girl. Her parents were interested in discovering the life purpose for Melody and found that she had just finished a series of three lives in the Orient. Because the soul is eager for the freedom of the Occidental world, the girl should "bust loose" in this incarnation. Unlike the Phillip soul, the Melody soul was held to the series of three lives rather than choosing to satisfy its curiosity:

> Dr. John: She has just come out of a cycle-of-three lives in the feminine valance, with at least two of them in the Orient. I see her in the mid-1800s. It began earlier, of course, but the major portion of the life came into the mid-1800s, and I believe she died in 1859. She was born probably about 1815. I do not usually get these dates quite as precisely, as you know, and I do not know why I am now.
>
> She was in the feminine expression and in Japan. She was the third daughter and had two older brothers as well. Then there were two siblings younger than she. Her father was a minor functionary of the temple, although he earned his livelihood by his own hands. He farmed, and the whole family worked. They had a small farm but they made it very productive.
>
> He also was, I believe, a general handy-man. He could do many things with his hands. He could help a neighbor sow or harvest. He could help butcher an animal and cut it up. He also could make things of wood, and he could fix things.
>
> He was a very trusted man because of his very fine, although somewhat rigid, character. He took his religion seriously and, one might say, the whole family took their father's religion seriously. As far as it affected his third daughter, it meant that there was a very structured environment in which she lived.
>
> There was kindness, there was compassion. There was also discipline and a certain amount of rigidity in that the cultural pattern as reinforced by the father who saw to it strenuously that he and his family 'lived up to' the temple religion, which prescribed quite carefully what a girl and a young woman and a woman and a wife and mother, and grandmother, all of which she was in due turn, should do and how to behave.
>
> This proved a bit irksome, particularly because it was the third such life. Going back into the 1700s and rather late into the 1700s, the mid and late 1700s, there was a life that was just about the same and in China. Here the father was a merchant and there were not as many children.

The father provided a little better for this family, in that they had meat more often and their clothing was a little richer, especially the 'dress up' clothing. But the pattern was about the same, though here the pattern was set and reinforced by the culture and by the mores of his class, rather than by any particular religious motivation. Although the religious motivation was there and was taken seriously.

Here, this one was the third child and the second daughter. The life just preceding that one, the first in this triad, was likewise in China. It was in the late 1600s and quite early 1700s, and feminine again. In this one the soul carried in quite a bit of freedom and did not take too well to the discipline and regimentation, and really did not like the life.

She was born into a peasant-farmer family in the vast interior of China. They had enough to eat nearly all the time, but life was rather dull and boring to this soul, which had known more excitment in the other realms and the other planes of the spiritual, and had known more excitement in earth as well.

This life saw quite a bit of rebellion to it. It took the form in the early years of being somewhat of a tomboy. Not because of a masculine urge within the person or soul, but as a means of rebelling against the role of woman in that culture. She saw that her brothers had more freedom and she was going to have more freedom, too: to speak her mind, to do what she wished, go where she wished, and such.

Discipline descended rather heavily at first, but the parents discovered that the discipline did not really accomplish its purposes, and eased up on the girl. Which turned out to be a good thing, because then the girl found that the parents were not the source of the regimentation and repression, but something bigger than the parents. The whole system was the source of it.

So in this triad of prior lives the soul experienced what it was to be a woman where a woman was a restricted being, and the role model of woman was very much structured; and the individual, unless she was fortunate in marriage or in wealth or some other way, really was forced to conform.

That is a good learning. That is an earth experience, hopefully more of the past than of the future, and the soul did manage by the third time to really settle in. Well, the second time pretty much too, but the third time for sure, and accepted that type of a life and guided its personhood successfully through it in the Japanese and in the second of the Chinese lifetimes, but particularly the Japanese one.

Against this background the soul was really very delighted, almost overjoyed, at being given the opportunity of a life now in the twentieth and early twenty-first centuries as a woman in an enlightened culture where woman is almost as free as man to discover and develop all that she is and all her qualities and abilities, and both man and woman are much more free to do so than they have been in nearly all the cultures of nearly all the centuries.

This will make for quite a quality of joy in this little one. This that I have given the parents can be a major guideline in understanding her. She should be allowed to express a great deal of joy.

However, there also is a slight difficulty here, in that the soul, understanding the freedom and the opportunity to live life to the fullest and to discover and develop her own beingness to the full—well, that quality in the soul will translate at times into a certain strong-minded willfulness on the part of the person of this little one.

She will know what she wants and want it, and set out to get it. She is an able little person with a good mind and a good body and a good personality, and mostly she should get what she wants. However, one should get what one wants when one wants the right things, and she will have to learn what these are. So a rather firm parental restraint in these early years, built on this guideline of letting her get what she wants when she wants the right thing, but compassionately, gently, firmly guiding her away from wanting the wrong things, and not letting her get them.

This will make an interesting lifetime for the three of them, particularly as the girl is coming along. But it is important that she learn this lesson in her very early years, in infancy and early childhood. Because as life opens up more and more to her, as she comes into the ripening of her body and then the openings that education will bring her and the career choices and all the other choices, if she can build on a wise and solid foundation, which in a sense she has had herself in her early years but guided by the parents, this will see her through well. Otherwise, there will be some rather tempestuous times of more difficulty than we hope she will have to meet. (A4176)

As Dr. John pointed out, Melody would need special supervision in her life to keep her from running away with her new-found freedom. The person who assumed the task of keeping a parental eye on her was none other than her former grandmother in the first Chinese life. This grandmother had watched the little girl rebel against the yoke of the Oriental society and was now back as her father in this life. It was the father who requested the life reading. Several years later, he wrote to the Religious Research headquarters office to let us know that Melody was eager to be a part of life and a special delight to him, and was responding favorably to the early discipline.

CARRON

Cycles-of-three lives can also be used to study historical cultures. When Carron asked about her grandmother, three interesting lives appeared:

Dr. John: Yes. They were friends, Roman matrons, with a concern for the welfare of at least their portion of society. This would be in the early, well, in the latter part of the first century and the early 100s, the early part of the second century, A.D., with the major part being in the early 100s A.D. They were in Rome. They were not senators' wives nor of that level. But they were of the type who today could help sponsor a benefit concert for some worthy cause, the type which will take a direct personal concern not only in the welfare of the young people but also in the cultural policies affecting that welfare.

In other words, they were capable, competent members of society, both of them women, in a civilized culture. This was leadership. This was certainly contributive to the betterment of society. They do have a cosmic relationship, and that cosmic relationship was well expressed in their earth partnership.

Now we follow them down to the breakup of the Roman Empire. Well, I find them three times here in that culture: (1) In the early 100s; (2) in the 300s. This is Rome, this is feminine again. And this is a time when ideals have been relaxed. And to begin with they, mainly from their subconscious remembrances of their earlier time in Rome, were against the relaxing of the ideals. But then they went along with it. And this was a part of the deterioration of Rome, as they were to find later.

(3) In the 600s, again feminine and again in Rome, but this time in a suburb outside of Rome. And they learned the terrible cost of a civilization that goes down. They learned the horrible setbacks that come in human living when civilization is lost. This has helped to place within the soul of each of them a very real and continuing concern for social welfare, for social ideals, for standards of human living. And this can fit into the present life, this does fit into the present life, as a source of some of the dynamics in it. She wants in her way to see that civilization is maintained and furthered, and that standards of human living are kept high rather than lowered. (A3700:3)

Experiencing the "rise and fall of the Roman Empire" through a cycle of three incarnations is certainly a good way to prepare a soul to work for the betterment of civilization. Participation in that civilization at its height, then as it made the transition downward, then at its depth, could have been accomplished only through reincarnation.

Thus through the use of a small cycle the soul can observe different cultures as they rise and fall, getting first-hand information on the factors involved. Cycles-of-three lives similarly enable a soul to follow economic conditions in a certain country, experiencing such fluctuations as inflation, recession, stability. Likewise, experiencing changes in social situations can be another way to use the cycle-of-three. To illustrate, a soul could choose to incarnate in France as a member of the aristocracy, then again as a peasant during the Revolution, the third time as a French soldier in World War I. Another possible cycle-of-three lives during slavery in America is: slave, master, abolitionist. When one adds to these economic and social lessons the correction of biased attitudes or characteristics, the development of finer and stronger soul qualities, and similar growths, the choices are further extended.

As a person observes the limited parameters of any one-life framework compared with the expansion offered by even a small cycle-of-three lives, let alone the total of many lives, the significance of reincarnation again stands out. It is the schoolroom for karma, the great teacher. How thankful man should be that God does not limit his soul to only one lifetime!

CHAPTER THREE

CYCLEMATES

Cyclemates are two souls who pair up for a series or cycle of lives. This is one of the loving, wise provisions of our Creator. God has established various supportive and companionship roles for us as we go through our incarnational experiences—good karmic relationships from pastlives, cosmic families, cosmic cousins, sponsor souls, twin souls, soulmates. And cyclemates.

Cyclemates are not as close as soulmates, who are the two halves (masculine and feminine) of the same soul. Cyclemates are different souls who agree, and who are selected, to incarnate with each other more often than with any other soul during a specific cycle. These cycles may be for a short span, small cycles (cycle-of-three) or large cycles (cycle-of-seven), but more often the cyclemates work together for a longer period of time, perhaps several thousands of years.

Usually cyclemates are from the same cosmic family, and frequently of opposite gender, but neither of these is an absolute requirement. We find souls of no cosmic relationship but of an innate soul congeniality making excellent cyclemates. And souls of the same gender can provide the supportive partnership of a cyclemate team. The pairing depends more on soul individuality and congeniality than on any set rules.

The two souls involved in the cyclemate team often come together several times before entering into the relationship, perhaps testing the bond in a difficult incarnation to be sure they have a genuine love and regard for each other in the earth realm, as well as a good cosmic rapport. And most cyclemate relationships do not continue as such beyond the specific purpose of the cycle, but the two souls may continue to incarnate with each other occasionally.

Young soul cyclemates support and reassure each other in their early lives, when the two souls are getting acquainted with earth. Middle soul cyclemate teams will prod, push, challenge and compete with each other in their sinew-building incarnations. Older soul cyclemates make good teams for cosmic projects such as leadership in needed earth developments, scientific breakthroughs, or various religious or artistic projects, etc. They may leapfrog with each other, one spearheading the team first, the other taking the lead the next time around. Or one (usually feminine) may find its God-given and fulfilling role in a quiet, loving, personal support of the other through several important incarnations. The cyclemate relationship has various purposes and is as flexible as life itself. But basically it is a loving, mutually helpful, sustaining soul element which carries over into our earth episodes called incarnations.

PIERRE AND DAPHNE

Pierre and Daphne are from the same cosmic family, and married in this life. Both are young souls and in a change-of-gender life — Pierre, a feminine soul, in a masculine incarnation, and the opposite for his wife Daphne. In this life they have a loving relationship—with a few "bumps" in it, which is almost inevitable for relatively young souls and especially in their early non-native gender expressions, but close and supportive.

The Pierre and Daphne souls have incarnated together a number of times since the 300s B.C. in different roles, but usually within an earth family situation, being supportive of one another, as Dr. John brings out. Daphne is the first person Pierre asks about in his reading, and we begin this excerpt after her name is given:

> Dr. John: These two are cosmic family members and really quite close cosmic family members, and are cyclemates for the present cycle.
> The term 'cyclemates' can refer to various cycles, of course. The present Daphne is not the cyclemate for the entire cycle of earthlives with Pierre. Neither has she been the cyclemate for the entire cycle to date. Rather, she has moved into the cyclemate position really as both of them started into the 'around-the-midpoint' stage, which is the third of the five stages into which we, for ease of reference, divide the soul's progression through incarnations and through its own soulhood—its

early stage of Individuated-God-Beingness.

The two souls, who are quite close within the cosmic family as brother and sister souls, the Daphne soul being a masculine soul, were brought together as cyclemates. It was suggested to them and they very happily agreed to be cyclemates for a span of twenty or twenty-five lifetimes. This does not mean that they will take all of those lifetimes together. But they may very well take ten or a dozen of them together.

It means that they will incarnate each with the other more often than they incarnate with any other one soul during this particular period as they come into the 'around-the-midpoint' stage and proceed over the middle point of this third stage. As they come into the latter part of this third stage they probably will not incarnate together as much, and may each have a different cyclemate for that further position.

The present incarnation sees these two, Pierre and Daphne, really with pretty much the same purpose for each—which is, to gain competence. First, by gaining experience, more experience, within the non-native gender expression type of personhood.

These two were together in the immediately past incarnation, which was in the 1800s. They did not take much time in between, as you see. In that life they were each in the same expression as now. In other words, Pierre was in masculine and Daphne in feminine expression. This was in the same country as the present, France.

They were born after the Napoleonic era, and they were in the southern part of France. So they were not too much caught up in great national world events. They were brother and sister in a sunny part of southern France. It may have been a bit to the east of the midline, as it were, of that country. They were in a small village which was majorly agricultural. They were close enough to the sea to know of the sea and to have fresh fish brought in occasionally by traveling vendors. They also had that enlargement of life which comes from some contact with the men who sail the seas.

Aside from that, it was more just a little simple experience of each in the non-native valence. The sister was married but died in the first childbirth. This was partly one of the vicissitudes of earthlife, and partly that the soul was not too adept at coping on its own with that experience, and partly—

there is a third element here, a minor causative factor—partly because the personality itself was really not too feminine and was rather happy when the opportunity came to exit. This third factor really is an outgrowth of the second factor, but has a certain significance and causative force of its own. The brother married and became a father, which is rather easier than becoming a mother, of course, and he was a success as a father. The demands upon him were rather simple. He had two sons who lived. They were rather stolid, in that they did not have a great curiosity or an inquisitive intelligence about them. They fit quite well into the village pattern. They both grew up to become successful farmers and had their own homes and so forth.

So the father, who was brought up in that pattern by his parents and by the village, raised his sons in the same pattern that he had known. Thus fatherhood was not too difficult. The father did a very commendable job within rather narrow parameters.

It was from this life and the experiences of it and at least the partial success that each one had in it, that they were encouraged then to come in together now to be husband and wife. With the greater encouragement that the cosmic family and cyclemate relationship gave to each, the masculine soul, the present wife, was able to go further in womanhood, successfully bearing not just one but several children.

The feminine soul, the present husband, went further in fatherhood by bringing up three girls. This is a little more of a test of a man than bringing up two boys. Likewise, the incarnations of these daughters presented more problems than did the incarnations of the two sons before. The problems were more for the souls and the persons having those incarnations, the daughters themselves. But an incarnation of a child who has more problems does present more of a challenge, let us say, and more problems, to the parents.

Let me say at this point that the council of Pierre's guides and teachers, of whom three are present, say that he is doing a good job with his children, with his marriage, and with himself. Likewise, that the present wife is doing a good job of it.

Now let us go back further. We would go back to the late 1500s. We find the Pierre soul in its native gender expression, the feminine, and the cyclemate, the present Daphne, in its native gender expression, the masculine. This is in that area—I am not sure if it is in the area that is now northern France or southern Germany. At that time, of course, it was not so defined, but defined in terms of its own time.

This was more in a coal-mining area. But neither of these two nor their fathers or brothers participated in that type of work. It was more of a small animal husbandry situation. This meant contact with buyers of their products. They were pretty much villagers, but it was a larger village than that late 1800s. They were brother and sister. In this life in the native gender expressions they found no difficulty in marriage and parenthood. Each soul was well versed by this time in carrying through a full incarnation.

The brother and sister were close because of the soul closeness. When they married they stayed within the same village. The brother stayed within the family home, and his wife was congenial. His mother died, but the father lived on. The father was not a difficult sort to have around; that is, not very difficult. So he stayed in the son's home.

However, the daughter lived nearby and, as it were, the son and the daughter took care of their parents together—although the mother was not a care. She was quite active up until within about ten days of her death. She was stricken with something and went rather quickly. The father likewise remained pretty well active and productive up to very shortly before his death. He went even more quickly. He went within one day, possibly within a matter of just several hours. I do not see precisely what took him, but he went very quickly.

There was a third sibling whom I do not see. The relationship of all three of the children who lived was good. But it was these two that we are following through now, and these two had quite a special bond between them. Although they were close to the third sibling also, simply because they were siblings.

Let us go back farther. These two, Pierre and Daphne, really have quite an interesting number of incarnations together. I see one in Indonesia in the 1100s, each in its native gender expression. Here Daphne was the husband. Life on the whole was rather simple and rather easy. It was well structured by society. A man knew who he was and what a man did, and a woman knew who she was and what she did, within that culture.

The training in it, the social training, was rather precise. The physical living was not too much. They were not on the poverty level. They had enough to eat usually. There were several times in that lifetime when food was scarce, but they managed. They had a certain native wisdom whereby they had secreted away food which helped to carry them through, as most of the people then did.

They had children. I think possibly one of their present daughters was present in that life. We will find out later.

I'm looking for another type of life, to see if they had a 'given' lifetime when they hopefully worked together. Yes, in the non-native valence. I would preface this by saying that before a soul comes into a full life in its non-native expression on its own, so to speak, it usually is given a 'given' life, in which the person is formed not so much by the soul itself but by its council, and is then led through that life, not so much on the basis of its own soul's direction and expertise, which it doesn't have much of as yet, but more as one would take the hand of a child who is learning to walk and hold the child up and lead him forward as he progresses from the crawling to the walking stage.

This is a way of helping a child to learn to walk on his own two feet, and it is a way of helping a soul to learn how to handle a non-native expression on its own.

I find this life way back in the 700s, and I find the two of them together, but not as husband and wife. It is an expression for the Pierre soul of a good masculine life. This is in what is now known as the Near East, or the Mid-East. I believe in what is now known as Turkey, probably.

The man was not one of the leaders of the community and he was not one of the strongest and he was not one of the smartest, but he was a good citizen and he was a good man. The then incarnation of the Daphne soul was his brother, an older brother, who of course was then in his own native gender expression and could be a wayshower to the younger brother.

The younger brother had a good life there with a wife who was quite suitable to him, and the winning of her was an achievement. They loved each other and each felt comfortable with the other, and each felt respect for the other. They had five children, of whom three lived into the teen stage. One died at the age of about thirteen, into the fourteenth year. So two came into full maturity. That is the essence of that experience. Let me probe a little further. I'd like to find when these two started being cyclemates. I see a life when they were sisters in the 900s A.D. in which, as it were, the Pierre soul returned the compliment to the Daphne soul of being a wayshower. This time as an older sister. I am not given much in the way of details, except this was in China.

In the 300s B.C. I find them, both in their native gender, the Pierre soul in the feminine expression and the Daphne soul in the masculine expression. This was in early Rome. It was north of Rome. It was in Italy. But it was enough on the outskirts of Rome to be considered Rome, I suppose. The city was their orientation of thought. They were caught up in some of the exciting things happening there.

They were again in the agricultural area, but they also processed some of the things which they produced for transportation to and sale within the large city. I am not shown much further on that.

Conductor: Were they sister and brother?

Dr. John: Yes, although they had different mothers. The then incarnation of the Pierre soul was born first. Her mother did not die in childbirth, not in that childbirth anyway, but died about a year later. The father then remarried, and the half-brother was born between three and a half and four years after the sister. This meant they would not have been particularly close just by sibling placement, but the soul closeness brought them together.

In fact, this was one reason for this half-brother/ half-sister relationship, although the major reason was the concern with the two mothers and the father. But if they were going to root their cosmic family relationship on earth now in a cyclemate relationship, the fact that they overcame some factors that could have led them to be not very close and did develop a personal closeness, was a certain achievement, you see.

The councils of each soul then saw that these two really did reach out to each other in earth expression as well. So all this is good.

We have spent a good deal of time on this relationship, but this is really the most important single relationship within this life of Pierre. Is there a question?

Conductor: Not a specific question. He does say, 'My companion,' meaning his wife, 'through the good and the bad times' she has been his companion. 'We are very close, even though we don't always agree. She is a very devoted mother to her entire family and gives of herself and of her time to the sick.' His last sentence regarding her is, 'She is rather suspicious.'Dr. John: This sounds as though they are doing a good job, and it sounds like a pretty normal pattern for a relationship. Secondly, that she is doing a good job also. That soul, as it has more experience in handling and living as a person in its non-native expression, will become a little smoother about it. The same can be said for Pierre. But both appear to be doing quite well. His council nods approvingly as I say that, and they have a better view of the wife than have I. (A123:3-7)

So these two souls have each acted as guide for the other during a change-of-gender incarnation. In both cases, the soul in the native gender expression was an older brother or sister when the other soul was in its first major non-native gender life, each serving as a wayshower for the other. The test life came in the 300s B.C., when the two personalities, directed by their souls, bridged the age gap and the half-brother/half-sister relationship to become close in that life. This set up the forces for the cyclemate team to be formed.

Since the 300 B.C. life was the "test life," the souls probably had a previous incarnation or two together, even though it was not brought out in the life reading. These two souls will have other lives together, in different situations and settings. The team has built a good comradeship for the duration of this cycle—the building of the soul strengths in the around-the-midpoint period referred to as the karmic major-learning lives.

This excerpt is an example of how the cyclemate partnership is formed, how it works and the purpose it serves. The council of guides and teachers, who have a somewhat greater understanding of the overall plan and goal of the two souls as well as knowledge of the individuality of each, assists in bringing the two souls together. The two souls need to prove they have a cosmic and an earth companionship; secondly, both souls have to give their approval to the cyclemate union. This balance of love and understanding is the basic framework of the cosmic twosome.

FERN AND BLANCHE

The cyclemate relationship is a loving force that carries with it certain responsibilities. These cosmic friends are expected to be supportive whether the incarnation is easy or difficult and even when the earth relationship may be strained. If one member of the cosmic team makes a mistake, the other must have the patience and fortitude to sustain the partner. This does not mean either soul must always condone the actions of the other, for each must maintain its own individuality and integrity as well as grow at relatively the same pace. The responsibility of the cyclemate partner lies more in the area of "helpmate." Fern and Blanche demonstrate this "helpmate" aspect.

Although both are now in feminine expression, and sisters, Fern is the masculine half of the cyclemate team and Blanche the feminine. The Fern soul had a difficult feminine incarnation in a 1700s French life. Her masculine soul felt it did not handle well that incarnation as wife to a demanding husband and as a mother. Since this soul has a desire to do well in all its incarnations, it carefully went about making amends. After the 1700s life was over, her soul needed to regain its confidence and chose to swing back into a masculine incarnation, its native gender, in the 1800s.

In the present incarnation the soul returned to the feminine, but elected to live a less demanding feminine role. Her cosmic sister, and earth sister in this life, has stood by her cosmic brother in this series of lives, serving now as a wayshower. Both Fern and Blanche remained single and had successful careers, since this was the type of life the Fern soul elected to live in this incarnation. The tag "spinster" was usually attached to unmarried women of their generation, as they were born in 1910-1911. But Blanche, the cosmic sister, stayed close, being a helpmate.

Both women received life readings, therefore portions of both readings are presented. First, Fern, the soul having the problem:

> Dr. John: This is a feminine incarnation from the masculine half of her whole soul and, in a sense, that is the most definitive feature. The soul has had some feminine incarnations before

but felt it did not do a very good job with them. The soul is quite conscientious and wants to do a very good job. The soul has a knowledge of itself as being a child of God and wants to accomplish all the growth expected of it in the total picture of its beingness and in the growth of each particular earthlife. Actually the soul could have undertaken in this life a little more than it did, but it chose to, as it were, limit its reach to make sure it got well what it did get within its grasp.

She is doing very well, which, of course, is one reason I say the soul might have tried for a little more. When we find a soul doing very well in the accomplishment of a particular lifetime, it is sort of a sign the soul might have tried a little more. But really there is no other reason why she should have. She, as a soul, wants to do well that which she does. She has learned this not only from conscientiousness but also from the realization that progress is built upon each step as it is taken, and hence that step should be solid, because if it is shaky, then a future incarnation might be shaken by the poor foundation underneath it and be one of undue hardship and possibly even then the learning of the previous life would have to be revisited and firmed up.

She has a good concept of growth as a child of God and is not imposing her will upon the council of her guides and teachers and upon the general structure of progression which has been established, really by God Himself, but rather is content to accept this direction and, as I said, build firmly that which is built in any one lifetime.

Of course, this realization, really, of the many-stepped nature of progression of the God-child, brings an ease to the mind of the soul, the realization that it does not have to do everything and be everything in any one incarnation, and the soul, which is in close touch with this person, has firmed this and has extended this assurance, as it were, to the person, yes.

As we get into relationships we probably will get some nature of a past feminine life or two, which will help Fern to understand the nature of the present feminine life.

When Fern asked about a special friend, Dr. John presented the 1700s life in detail. This friend had been her sister in that life.

Dr. John: Yes. I find them in the 1700s when the then incarnation of the Fern soul was in feminine expression. She was born rather early in the century and lived to pretty close the midpoint of it. This was in the eastern part of France, toward the Italian border but not on the border, oh, 50 or 100 miles from the border. And this was the feminine life which the soul felt it did not handle very well.

The girl was born into a family which, for its particular village, had a little more affluence and influence than most. I believe the father—well, the father and his two brothers had inherited from their father some land which they tilled well, but they also had a bakery. The bread was quite different from the bread today but it was good. It was good bread. Also, to operate a bakery at that time in human knowledge and history had a few more problems than in the present day, although perhaps missed some of the present day problems.

The flour, the wheat, was ground from whole grain, and this included the oil, the germ of life within it, which did not keep well after being ground. The flour could become rancid and 'spoil.' And quite often bread baked in a bakery could have that little tell-tale taste.

These brothers had been taught well by their father to utilize the flour while it was fresh and to avoid that rancidity, also to take care of the flour, keeping it out of sunlight and keeping it somewhat cool, which, of course, helped to slow the oxidation of the fat element, the oil, and delay it becoming rancid.

But even with proper care the flour had to be used quite promptly, and so the brothers had in their bakery establishment a mill. And here again there was a problem of getting the right amount ground to make the bread that would sell that day. They wanted to have enough because they certainly did not want to miss a sale of even one loaf. The bread would hold over to another day but not much beyond that. The flour was likewise perishable, as I have explained. Thus the 'shelf life' of each was limited by the state of the art of baking of that day.

So there was a constant vigilance in this way, which actually was a matter of keeping the quality high.

Now, I apologize for being somewhat drawn into this of my own interest. It did not really have too much to do with the then incarnation of the Fern soul, who was the wife of one of the brothers, the brother who had the particular responsibility for the baking end of the family enterprise. Now, he was not the easiest man to get along with. The standards of excellence which his father had instilled within him and which his brothers likewise expected him to maintain, became a trait of expectation in his personality, in his character, and he required his wife and children to measure up likewise. He didn't realize that he was carrying from one realm certain traits and expectations into an entirely different realm. It was not all bad, of course. But the then incarnation of the Fern soul, being the wife of this one and mother of his children, found it really was not quite prepared, it felt, to undertake such an exacting feminine incarnation.

The result is that she felt 'run ragged,' not so much by the work involved, because they had ample money for food and livelihood and even for a servant if needed, and the husband was not stingy. He was not exactly generous, but he was not stingy, and he did love his wife.

But she felt 'run ragged' in trying to live up to his expectations. The children were to be dressed well and just so, and they were not to have runny noses, and if they did, they were certainly to be wiped clean before the father came home, and he came home for lunch. The business was very close to the home. So there was a constant need to be a good mother, a good housekeeper, a capable wife, and the soul felt really hard-pressed to do this.

Actually it did a pretty good job. But as the result of this, the soul said when it was able to terminate that life—it did not terminate it until the end did come, the destined end—but it said a great big 'Whew!'

Because of that sense that this was pretty strenuous, as it was, although a more experienced soul in feminine living or a more feminine soul probably wouldn't have found it so, the next incarnation the soul went back into the masculine, into an area where it was very competent, you see, and its sense of competence was restored by that.

The next result was the present life in which the soul came into femininity, but without the inborn drives that would have taken it into wifehood and motherhood. As I say, the soul could have attempted a little more. It would have made a very fine wife and mother to the right husband within the right setting and all. But instead of that it chose not to undertake those responsibilities, and instead what has happened, and this is partly by the planning of the guides and teachers, who are good and whom the soul trusts, came into a different phase of expression as a woman and has done very well.

The soul now has built a more sure foundation under itself for feminine incarnation. For the masculine it already had that and has it. But now it knows it can live a very good feminine lifetime and all the way through.

In the very next incarnation it very well may come back in the feminine and become wife and mother in a rather capable situation. In other words, not married to just a 'common laborer' type of man but one who has a little more to him in ability, in responsibility, in that which he has undertaken. Oh, she won't be the wife of a great political leader or such, but she could be a very fine wife now to, say, a teacher or a merchant who is also a 'pillar of his community' and such. She can keep his home. She can mother his children. She can walk beside him with confidence.

And so this may be the next lifetime. It is not set for sure. The soul wants to finish this lifetime and get in the full picture of what it has accomplished before it really gives its assent to the pattern for the next one. And there is no hurry upon it. It will probably be fifty years or more before it comes back. That is a rather quick comeback, of course, but it's not too quick. The soul will prepare well in the cosmic schools of preparation for the next incarnation, and in the assimilation and fuller understanding of this life and its place in the progression of its competence in feminine earthliving.

After the difficult feminine life in the 1700s, the soul decided to regain its confidence with a masculine life in the 1800s. This life was brought out when Fern asked about her cousin, Carolyn. The conductor gave Dr. John Carolyn's name and birth information. He replies:

Dr. John: They were together in the early and mid-1800s. This was a masculine incarnation for the Fern soul. It was in this country. He went as a child, a pre-teen child but not a young child, with his parents as they went west. They were not among the real pioneers, they did not 'fight Indians.' But they did push west. They were, well, somewhat below—somewhat south of Pennsylvania as they went west, and went into the area which now would be known perhaps as Indiana or perhaps western Ohio. The parents had farmed and had acquired some money, and knowledge, which was even more important. They took with them not simply a covered wagon in which to live and food for the trip. They took some livestock. They had, well, at least five cows and one bull. They took seed. They knew pretty much where they were going and what the nature of it was. Some friend of theirs or maybe a relative had been there and either written back or come back, so it was quite an intelligent trip. They found land which they liked. It was not on water but there was a small river not too far from it, mainly which provided trade, as the rain provided water.

So the parents settled there. They had to not so much clear the land of trees—although there were some trees but these were largely kept as a wood lot for fuel—but they had to 'break the sod.' It had not been farmed before. And so they were in that respect pioneers. They were very constructive pioneers. They were really building the growing edge of the country.

They were definitely not caught up in the Civil War. They were too far away from it and really not interested, so none of their children became soldiers and they were not in any area of fighting nor of the passage of armies. The general purpose was simply, as I have indicated, to build a good life for themselves. This was typified by the fact they had three houses. The first one they put up was a small one but adequate shelter, and then a better one, and finally even a better one. The third one incorporated the second one. They rebuilt rather extensively, enlarging the second.

And the other purpose accomplished was the extension of this growing country.

The then incarnation of the Fern soul was a son who came into his teens very quickly. He was perhaps 11, maybe 10, when they took the trip. He helped his father and his older brothers in getting established, and he was within a few years really quite a young man himself. The soul is natively masculine and was quite at ease in the masculine. In fact, this was a return to the masculine from the feminine life which had been a bit of a trial to the person, and the soul had felt it did not do a very good job with that previous feminine life. (A1913:1-2,4-5,12-15)

These two previous incarnations are the problem and corrective lives the Fern soul experienced. Even though the soul's performance in the 1700s feminine life was not exceptional, there was no failure, simply a feeling of losing control. Coming back into the masculine permitted the soul to become comfortable in earthliving. And now this present incarnation completed that earth lesson. Therefore the soul is ready for a more conventional feminine life in the future.

The life reading for Blanche was given the same day. Dr. John began her reading in the following manner:

> Dr. John: Yes, her records are here. I have been expecting her. We gave a reading for her sister this morning. The two of them are cyclemates, and in one way that is the nicest thing of the reading, for them to discover that.

When Blanche asked about her sister, Fern, we find she was present in the two previous incarnations mentioned.

> Dr. John: I must probe for this a bit. She had been born as a sister to Fern in the early 1800s, in the present country of the United States, to a farm family with very fine parents who, after due preparation, went to the growing frontier, the outer edge, the outer established edge of the country. Not way out to carve a new edge, as it were.
> Conductor: That was what you saw this morning with Fern?
> Dr. John: Yes. The Fern soul at that time was in masculine incarnation, the Blanche soul was in feminine incarnation and passed her second birthday and did not reach her third. This was before the family went west.
> Now, they did not go west because of the loss, but the going to a new location not too long after the loss did help them to overcome their sense of loss of their baby daughter, by going to a new location and by doing something new and different, yes. The family was a rather close-knit family where all the members cooperated. They were not in competition with each other. They were not working at cross-purposes.
> So there was that relationship with the present sister and, even though it was a brief one and in that time, there was established really a desire to see each other again. It was not greatly important that this be established, because as cyclemates they would come back together again anyway, but it was there.

Now they were together in the life just before then, and I will come back to this 1800 period in a moment. This was in France. The then incarnation of the Blanche soul was an aunt, a sister of the mother of the then incarnation of the Fern soul. The two sisters were close, the Blanche incarnation being a bit younger, and she took quite an interest in the children of her sister, including of course, this cosmic family member, this cyclemate, who at that time was in a very interesting feminine experience which I delineated this morning and which held certain difficulties.

The aunt, being natively feminine and, of course, being of the generation just ahead within that same family, understood and helped the younger woman to make a success of that life, as did several others. The success belonged to the younger woman and yet the help of several was important in assisting her to achieve the success.

Then concerning the present life, Dr. John congratulates Blanche for her willingness to help her cosmic brother:

Dr. John: The relationship with Fern has been of more helpfulness and love and service than Blanche has realized. Fern has subconsciously felt it with a deep appreciation, and Blanche knows there has been this force in her life.

But neither has known (1) that they are cyclemates, and (2) that Miss Fern is in an important early feminine incarnation of the masculine half of her soul. So, to have the feminine incarnation of her sister with her and being so much like her, really, has been an additional service.

The sister could well have gone into a more typical feminine life with a good husband, children, even grandchildren, but instead she chose the pattern of femininity that the Miss Fern soul was taking in this life. I outlined this morning why the Miss Fern soul is in that type of femininity and she may care to share her reading with Miss Blanche, and that would be good, and vice versa.

Now this did not mean a deprivation of the Blanche soul from experiences which could have been better. This type of feminine life is good, is a good experience and builds many good qualities, and it certainly lays a basis for the new type of woman-expression upon earth in which even those women who have homes, who are mothers and wives, will have a greater outreach into the world of what's going on around them, will have careers as well, or at least some recognition and expression of that fashion outside of the home.

So it has been a good life for Blanche, but there is this added element of kindness and of love in taking that pattern of life now, when it was so purposeful for the Fern soul to have that pattern now.

So this is much appreciated by the Fern soul, and by the Fern person as well, and it is the kind of thing that a close friend, a close soul friend, would do—particularly a cosmic family member and especially a cyclemate.

So it has built even more largely, more substantially, and more deep—well, I mixed my adjectives and adverbs there; I apologize—it has added to the very real substance of the relationship and love of those two souls. This means that the processes of God and the councils assigned to these souls will have all the more to work with as they plan and work out the future incarnations particularly of these two together, of which there will be quite a few. The ones I have mentioned are only a portion of the ones they have had in the past and there is more ahead of them than there is behind.

So the present life together has helped to provide bonds that can make for a good teamwork of these two in the very interesting and historically very important New Age ahead when the true human era upon earth can be inaugurated.

In addition, they enjoy each other now. Each is a separate individual and maintains the integrity of her own being, but neither of them threatens the integrity of the other's being. This, in itself, is really quite an accomplishment for any two people. It is more easily done, of course, when the two have a deep soul closeness, and it does require a congeniality of personality temperament which they have.

Actually, their life, if viewed from this level, turned out to be quite unusual and their accomplishments quite unusual. I congratulate them, and their council of guides and teachers congratulates them, and the achievement is noted by those higher up who direct us all. Yes. And so the Master's words are earned, 'Well done, good and faithful servant. Thou hast been faithful in these things. We'll have more for you ahead.' That's a rather free quotation. (A1943:1,6-7,15)

These two souls have had other incarnations together, but the essence of the supportive cyclemate element is demonstrated in these three lives.

Presently Blanche and Fern are retired and live together in Florida in a retirement community. They both speak highly, appreciatively, and fondly of each other. This, of course, is right in line with the purpose of this life and cyclemate relationship, and the goodness of each of these fine, interesting women.

This chapter illustrates cyclemates who are paired through the early karmic, or major-learning, series of middle lives. For these particular four souls the cycle will probably extend into the 3000s A.D., perhaps further. Of course these cyclemates will not be together in every lifetime ahead, but each will be a supportive friend to the other when the proper incarnational pattern is set in motion for them to come together. After these major-learning middle lives are over, each of these souls may pair with another soul for a different type later cycle.

Older soul cyclemates and cycles have a different nature, for the incarnational patterns and life experiences of older souls are different, as will be brought out particularly in later books of this "Dr. John" series. Older soul cyclemate teams in general have more freedom of choice. The length and nature of cycles and of the cyclemate relationship depends upon the purpose of the cycle, the particular nature of the support needed by each team member, and the individuality and purpose of each soul.

CHAPTER FOUR

KARMA INCURRED
FROM CRUEL LIFETIMES

Karma, the great law of spiritual cause and effect, is one of God's big leveling agents. Through this law the villain of one life becomes the victim in another. What we sow, we truly will reap. Jesus' great commandment to do unto others as we would have them do unto us, is a most practical application of the law of karma. For research into the Loehr-Daniels Life Readings shows that the way we treat others does determine how we will be treated, either in this life or in another. This applies whether a person is kind or cruel.

Justice is one of the reasons for karma. A cruel despot may not be punished in his lifetime. Many fiction and non-fiction stories tell of powerful people taking cruel advantage of others. These stories usually dwell on how unhappy the tyrant is and try to stress that such behavior is not rewarded, but the facts often show otherwise. If we depended only on man's justice, crime *would* pay. But God, not man, rules the world. Justice becomes understandable when one realizes that the despot will have to return to earth to experience being oppressed. Indeed, it may take several lifetimes for him to make amends.

Although God is just, retributive karma does not exist solely for punishment. In fact, the prime purpose of karma is growth. Our progress, as souls and as persons, is mirrored in how we behave toward others. What better way to grow than to experience the results of our own actions? If those actions include abusing others, then receiving similar treatment can help a soul to master the essential lesson of consideration for his fellowman.

But percentage-wise how many really cruel people are there? Perhaps there are more now than in former times. But over the centuries merely a small percentage of the population has victimized others. In our research we find that only about five percent of those getting life readings have negative karma as the major force of their present incarnation. This certainly makes sense if earth is a cosmic school for the soul's growth, for the soul could not progress if most of the lives were spent primarily making up for past mistakes.

Nevertheless, there are times when incarnations produce such major negative karma that at least one entire lifetime is required in recompense. If atrocities are committed, it is usually necessary to devote more than one life to paying the debt and mastering the lesson of brotherhood. This chapter presents four such studies.

DOLORES

Dolores is a woman in her early forties with a strong desire to help others. Although she has a good mind, her ability to serve is hampered by her poor physical health. She had an unhappy childhood and was particularly mistreated by her mentally-ill mother. For Dolores marriage was a great blessing, but her husband has been impotent during the entire twenty years of their wedlock.

At the beginning of her life reading, Dr. John explains the forces from a pastlife that are now causing Dolores so much misery:

> Dr. John: Once in a while, there is a lifetime which is very much the result of the immediately preceding lifetime. So much so, that that one prior life outweighs in many matters all other pastlives in the aspect of its effect upon the present life.
> That is the case with Dolores. The immediately prior life of this soul produced certain results for which the present life is the very direct karma.
> Before getting into it, I should say that Dolores is a feminine incarnation, a very good feminine incarnation, from the masculine half of her whole soul. The soul is in the third stage, around-the-midpoint, and is close to the centerline of its progression through significant incarnations. So it is not a young soul at all. It is a good, solid, middle soul.
> In the life preceding this one, the person was subjected to temptations to which the person gave in, and the soul lost control. It is not that the soul itself went all the way along with the temptations. It lost control of the person of its incarnation, because the person was too caught up in the temptations.
> So the present life is a karmic life for Dolores, and it is doing a great deal to absolve the past one, to resolve the results of the temptations which were given in to in the prior life.

That life was in the early 1800s and was in India and was in the masculine expression. The person was the second son of a raj, a ruler of an Indian area, a province or two. This was before the English rule brought some basic reforms into much of India. This was a fairly small rajdom and a bit out of the way. The raj was an absolute monarch, an oriental despot.

This boy was the second son and did not expect to succeed his father, was not trained for it. The older boy was brighter, was strong, healthy, and was expected to succeed his father. But the older boy unexpectedly died, and the father died within not more than two weeks afterward. So the line of succession had gone back to the father, and from the father then came to the eldest living son. If the father had died before the elder son did, then the line of succession would have gone to that son's son.

The second boy was thus catapulted into the position of power and wealth. He was not prepared for it. He had not been expected to take it, by his council of guides and teachers. He was expected to have a different kind of life under the rather benevolent rule of his elder brother. The two of them had gotten along well and it was expected the younger brother would work under the elder brother and learn some of the aspects of rule.

When he was catapulted to the throne, he was frightened. He was a victim of palace intrigue. Some of the more crafty advisors saw their chance and took advantage of it, undermining the more stable advisors, and the result was extremely bad.

Taxes were increased. The poor were not considered in their own right. It got so bad and the young king's fears were so played upon by some of the crafty advisors that he actually had his own brother's sons murdered. There were two of them—no, there were three. One was just an infant when his father had died. Within a year and a half, this really foul deed took place. It was covered up in some way so it could not openly be laid to the younger brother, the king. But it was widely known that he was back of it.

This guilt lay heavily upon him. He had enjoyed his young nephews before he had been persuaded that there might be a rebellion to put them on the throne and he should get rid of them. He responded to the guilt by blocking off his finer sensitivities, by blocking his spiritual nature, by blocking the sense of guilt even, and going even more into debased acts. In his own life, he discovered the pleasures of sex and that he could demand any type of sex. So his own life lacked nobility. That was the general picture and it was a sad picture. He was killed in a rebellion. There was a palace coup arranged by some of the older, wiser advisors who at first had been willing to accept him. But when he caused the murder of his own brother's sons, they rightfully were outraged within their own beings, although they did not dare say anything, and were convinced that this man had to be removed for the good of the country, for the good of everything.

He was on the throne about five years and in that time he caused a great deal of suffering. His personal behavior became erratic. If he saw a woman he liked, even though perhaps she were newly married, he would take her away. The husband might be killed or might be exiled or might be simply thrust aside. When he was through with a woman, he did not keep her in his entourage but thrust her back into the streets.

He had some children, but he felt so guilty over the murder of his three nephews that he could not take happiness in his own children.

The soul was aghast at what happened. The personhood, that oriental despot, even after he died could not be reached. Evil was reaching out toward him on the lower astral side—but he had been first reached by some who were good, his own mother was one who had reached him in consciousness when he was murdered and went over—he was rather quickly put permanently to sleep and did not have much of an afterlife.

But the evil that he did lived after him and was 'karma on the doorstep' for the Dolores incarnation.

The soul, as I have said, was quite aghast. It recognized its part. It had been titillated by some of the prerogatives of wealth and power and had gone along with it at first, although it had not gone along with any of the more debased acts, such as murder of the nephews. But the soul, in addition to that, knew that it was responsible for its incarnations. This incarnation had gotten away from it, but that did not relieve the soul of its responsibility.

The present life was chosen as the first of two karmic lives to start making up for what went wrong. In this life, there is suffering. Not as much as the oriental little raj caused to others, but there is deep suffering in the life of Dolores. But this is redemptive suffering.

In the next incarnation, there will not be the suffering but there will be a rebuilding. The person will have to start from 'behind scratch,' so to speak. It will have to really work for its education, for its success, for its spiritual rebuilding. But every indication is that it will achieve this, so that by the end of these two corrective karmic incarnations the soul will once again be a good solid child-of-God middle soul on the right path. The whole episode of these three lives will be a very constructive episode, actually, in the soul's total progression.

Is there a question so far?

Conductor: You have answered one question. She wanted to know, 'What is the purpose of my life in this incarnation?'

Dr. John: This is a purpose which could not have been gotten from psychology or religion or any way we know. You see, conductor, when the truth is known of the relation of the soul to its many incarnations, then there is more knowledge to be had. Knowledge which can set one free from ignorance and on the right path of understanding and achievement.

It is a quite fine bit of progression that psychology has developed to where it has. But psychology is essentially the study of the person in terms of one lifetime only, and a person never can be understood in such limited confinement. So I am glad to bring to Dolores this larger understanding of who she is and what she is doing and why, and the fact that she is doing a good job of it.

Remember, it is not Dolores that was the oriental despot. That was a different person. 'Reincarnation' technically is an inaccurate term. It is not that that oriental despot of a hundred and fifty years ago has reincarnated as Dolores. Rather, it is that Dolores is the next incarnation of that soul. The soul takes a succession of incarnations to accomplish its earthliving, its earth learning. Dolores is the next incarnation. She is a redemptive incarnation. In a certain way, she is sharing in the redemptive suffering that Jesus the Christ underwent. He took upon Himself the sins of the world. She has taken upon herself, the soul did, some of the sins of her soul's immediately prior incarnation, and her sufferings are redemptive.

This is very important to realize. The same person does not incarnate again; it is another personality of the same soul that comes. The guilt of the despot does not fall on Dolores. However, it does fall on her soul, the larger beingness of Dolores. Through the personality of this lifetime that soul is expiating past wrongs committed by the raj.

We now go to some of the persons of whom Dolores inquired. First the father:

Dr. John: He was one of the citizens of that Indian province. He was a husband and father, a small businessman. He and his family raised much of their own food but they were not essentially farmers. He was a small businessman. He found the levies imposed upon them greatly increased, the standard of living of his family going down, and the standard of the economy went down so it was harder for the businessmen.

The men who were responsible for the exchange of goods and services, upon which the livelihood and the welfare of the whole nation depended, found their work much harder because of this silly, crazy king. The king had the means of power in his hands, the army, and he paid them well so they would be loyal to him, and he was not above allowing a certain amount of looting by his royal forces.

This man suffered from it. He thoroughly despised the king. He was very happy when the change came, but he had suffered while this young man was on the throne.

There is no cosmic relationship of the two and there is no other pastlife acquaintance of them. It is not expected that they will be together in the future. They would have been probably, except that Dolores has taken this life really in pretty good spirit. She has not allowed great vengeance, vindictiveness, to grow within her. She has not let the difficulties of this life break her spirit nor break her personality.

She will be through the karmic relationship and the continuing incarnational acquaintance with this one who now is her father. Actually he could have been much harder than he was, but he has a certain dignity of his own within the personality, coming from the soul. She is fortunate that he and not some other was her father.

Conductor: She has a question. She says, 'My father is a totally self-centered man who is incapable of a meaningful human relationship. Why was I given such a disturbed man for a father?'

Dr. John: She knows why she got him, but her judgment of him may not be completely right. In other relationships and in other aspects of his being, he may be a finer person than she thinks. I do not see him. I am working with her records and staying quite closely with them for her reading.

But supposing she withdraw judgment on him, withdraw not only emotional judgment but also intellectual judgment. Let him be himself. He may be doing a better job than she realizes, so just let him be, and take her entire judgmental apparatus and weight off from him.

Conductor: We next go to her mother (name, birth information given).

Dr. John: Instead of trying to figure out just what she was to the young man, I will say she was the sister to the wife of the elder brother. This may have made her a sister-in-law or something like that to the young man in that early 1800s life.

It was never proved that this young man arranged the murders of her sister's three sons, but she was pretty sure of it. When she discovered that that one was back as her daughter, there was really quite a mix of forces. There was the natural force of love of a mother for her child, of concern for this fruit of her body. But then there was the mix of the forces of hurt and anger, of hate, of uncertainty.

The result was precisely what was wanted. It produced the difficulties that the Dolores person was supposed to face from the very earliest part of this life. It likewise gave that other soul the opportunity to vent some of the forces, and really quite legitimately, upon this one who had so hurt her sister, the mother of the three boys.

They have not had other pastlife acquaintance. It is not expected that they will come back together again. It is possible that the forces of anger and hate and revenge and the shock of it all within the mother could bring her back again, and in somewhat of a similar relationship to Dolores. But it is hoped that Dolores, through prayer, through magnanimity, through forgiveness, will cut all those ties, so that that other one will find its redemption in some other way.

The Dolores person really is in a very wonderful position of redemptive possibilities, you see, and part of them is that she must forgive. To understand will help her forgive. Yes, she is the 'innocent bystander that got shot,' to use a term I have used before, in that she is the corrective incarnation of her own soul. But let her forgive her mother. Be kind in such ways as she can be, because the mother-daughter relationship has a certain nature of its own. Let her reinforce the good of that when it can be done in a rather quiet way.

Then let her feel a redemptive sorrow for the mother, for the mother is experiencing pain and suffering from the immediate pastlife as well, you see.

Conductor: She has a question but I believe you have answered it, Dr. John. She says, 'My mother is mentally ill and capable of great cruelty. Why was I given such a cruel and disturbed mother?'

Dr. John: Because she was a very cruel person in her own pastlife, and disturbed, but even more cruel than this mother ever was.

Both parents were victims of the raj! It is easy to see how the unhappy childhood came about. Dolores is to be commended for her positive reaction to her father's mistreatment. But to escape further negative karma Dolores must also forgive the mother. Later Dolores asks about her husband and Dr. John replies:

Dr. John: This is an incarnation from the other half of her soul. This is the soulmate. She is from the masculine half and he is from the feminine half of the whole soul. He is in a life of some difficulty, of some corrections, I see. I do not see just what they are, but it was a wise and merciful provision that brought them together this time.

They can help hold each other up, so to speak. They can be supportive, they can be nourishing to each other — 'nurturing' is the word, excuse me.

Soulmates very seldom incarnate together. This is their first time. Being the two halves of the same soul, they are together in other realms but usually not in personhood. Each one develops in personhood that which will bring a greater fullness to the combined soul, the whole soul of them. Is there a question?

Conductor: Yes, Dr. John, she has two questions. First she says, 'My husband and I have a marriage in which we love each other very much but cannot physically consummate the marriage due to hopeless sexual impotence which my husband suffers from. No treatment has been effective for twenty years in helping him. Why are we not permitted to consummate this marriage?'

Dr. John: So that is the problem he is facing in this life. I do not see the background of that problem. That would be in his records. But if he is going to face a lifetime with that problem, then it is really quite appropriate that the soulmate come to be of assistance, and at a time when the soulmate also has a very severe problem or a set of problems, as I have pointed out to Dolores. So the two face together this problem life of each.

This is very interesting, conductor, and certainly a marvelous service each to the other.

Conductor: She wants to know if they are destined to remarry in a future life?

Dr. John: They are the married halves of their whole soul, but they are not destined to come together as persons again that I see. Maybe some time far up ahead.

I can feel Dolores becoming a bit discouraged at this. But no, because the soulmate in her next life will not be incarnate but will be close to her on spiritual levels and helping her in that way. In this life, he incarnated. In the next life, he will be on spirit levels helping her, inspiring her, sustaining her, picking her up when she is down, and things like that. So they will be together very meaningfully and with a great amount of love the next time, but he will not be in the body with her.

A wise and merciful God provides the soulmate to help Dolores get through this difficult life. But it is fitting that the husband took an incarnation which prevented their complete fulfillment together.

Not all of the reading is pertinent to the subject of this chapter, but several more of her questions are. They reflect what Dolores is going through as a direct result of the cruel actions of the raj personality.

Conductor: Her next question is, 'Why did God give me such a brilliant mind, such a strong desire to serve other people, in such a sick body with severe asthma and severe emotional handicaps, so that my ability to help others is so limited by my poor health?'

Dr. John: That is answered by the fact that this is a karmic life. If there were no costs put upon her now, she would not be expiating the wrong done one hundred fifty years ago. It has to cost her. There is no other way. The soul has to be working with an incarnation that is paying the karmic debt, and the soul is held rather close to experience the frustrations and the disappointments of the Dolores person.

Conductor: She next says, 'I want to serve God by doing everything I can to help relieve human suffering, both by helping individual clients in counseling and by helping millions of people through my articles in national magazines. In which of the following does God want me to put most of my energy: (A) psychotherapy and pastoral counseling and psychonutrition, or (B) writing articles on nutrition and medicine to try to help thousands throughout the country?'

Dr. John: Let her do what she can, wherever there is an opening. But she'll be blocked, she will be frustrated many times in many different ways. The great service of the Dolores life is to her own soul. It is not going to be some outstanding service to mankind.

The soul had the position of leadership as the oriental despot and misused it. It does not have a position of leadership, of world acclaim, or even of large acclaim right now. This is one way in which a missed opportunity is handled, you see. I do not see that Dolores will be of major help really in either or any of these ways. Let her do what she can. But there are too many limitations for her to have grandiose ideas, and to cast those grandiose ideas in the form of serving God is a camouflage for ego and for a wish for greater self-achievement and recognition.

Let her do what she can, but let her be realistic. Don't let her get over-blown in her ideas of her abilities or of what she is going to do, because simply calling it service to God is not going to change the facts. Her service to God is going to be much better achieved if she will very realistically face the facts of her life and understand them now in the light of the akashic records, and see that her life is accomplishing a very important service to her soul.

Then, be like a seamstress who must choose the pattern for

any new dress she were going to make, to fit the amount of cloth she has. If she has just four square yards of cloth, she could not take a pattern that would call for seven or eight. She'd have to find a pattern for her dress that she could make with what she had.

Just so, Dolores must find a pattern for her life to fit the resources of health, of personality, of education, of ability, of mentality, that she has. Yes, she can work to increase the resources which she has. But there would be only greater frustration and rather foolish expenditure of prayers and dreams if she were to be completely unrealistic, you see.

Conductor: She last asks, 'I am a very pro-life person, but if I were to have the misfortune to outlive my husband, I would have no way to survive on my own because my health is so poor and he takes care of me. If he were to die and I were left alone, I would have to choose between suicide or a life worse than death in some institution for the chronically ill. In such a place, I could not use any of my creative talents and would just die spiritually. Would I be punished for choosing suicide in that circumstance?'

Dr. John: Her soul in a pastlife brought great restrictions onto some thousands and tens of thousands of people in the tyrannical practices of that young raj. If she experiences now some such restrictions and frustrations, it is only appropriate and, likewise, it is enlightening.

I would point out likewise that if she does have to be institutionalized, she will experience the good of society which is doing its best to provide for the limited and the restricted people, you see. So in a sense she would be receiving good in place of the evil that she dispensed in the last several years of the young raj incarnation.

Now as to whether to choose suicide in preference to institutionalization, I will not advise her. There are times when the intellectual decision to end a life has much to be said for it. On the other hand, the knowledge of the spiritual factors involved is still so small within human knowledge that such a decision could be made on the basis of inadequate information.

I trust that the total picture I have given her of herself will be of some helpfulness. Remember, the guilt for the young raj is not Dolores' guilt. It would seem as though she is being punished for his mistakes, and that is true. But to serve constructively one's own soul for its redemption, is a high calling in God indeed, and this is her calling. (A864:1-9,11-13)

Through Dolores, her soul is reaping the harvest of the inhuman seeds which were sown by the raj. This lifetime is also hammering in the lesson that power is not a license for heartless actions. The next incarnation will find the soul rebuilding, on a more solid foundation, what was torn down in the 1800s. Cruel lifetimes are often expiated only after two full lives, or more.

EVELYN

Alcohol has been and is one of the demons bedeviling humanity. Although she did not drink, Evelyn was surrounded by the problems that overindulgence in alcohol can bring. Her father drank too much and her sister was an alcoholic. But the real tragedy came for Evelyn when her husband was killed while driving and drinking. With no one to turn to, Evelyn had been forced to put her four sons into an orphanage for seven years. She married again, but it has been a stormy marriage.

In her life reading, one finds that this is indeed as might be expected, a karmic lifetime for Evelyn. We will begin right after Dr. John is given her name:

> Dr. John: Evelyn....Yes, her akashic records have been brought here in preparation for this reading. Four members of her council, her band of guides and teachers, are here. They look not grave, not sober, but serious. This is an event of importance, they feel, in the life of their protege, to help her to understand this life.
> The present life is karmic in an interesting and not unusual way. It flows from the immediately prior life when the Evelyn soul was in masculine expression and was in Germany and as a brewmaster who also—well, let me look at this: he had an inn; he supplied brew, alcoholic brew, to three inns, one of which he and his brother owned. It was not an inn but a drinking place. This man was a manufacturer of brew, which was a kind of beer, and was rather potent.
> The village was fairly small and a little bit off the mainstream. The religious leadership in the village was rather

impotent and had been for a while. There was a Catholic church with a priest who got pretty old. Then there was a small Protestant group with a minister who was quite strict but not very smart. He was rather young and did not understand life, and was not effective in coping with it to make this little church group an effective force in that society. He gathered a few people to him who were as committed as he, as strict as he, and in general the whole group was ineffectual. They provided a good support and fellowship for themselves, but they did not provide a strong force in the community. Also this village served as a center of an agricultural, rural area. So many more people came to it than actually lived within its boundaries.

So in effect, there was really no strong counterforce to the tavern, the saloon, that this man and his brother owned and ran, and the two subsidiary drinking places which I believe were also inns. One was an inn and one was an eating and drinking place.

These two men were gruff, the then incarnation of the Evelyn soul being the stronger of the two and somewhat the leader. He was a gruff, big-bellied man, rather gross, although the whole life there was rather gross. The influence of the saloon and the inns and the drinking-eating place all contributed to quite an earthiness, which was rather gross, as I have said.

Hence this man and his brother, who quite agreed with him, brooked no interference from those who would diminish the amount of drinking done in that whole area. The young Lutheran minister would preach against it, but he was in general laughed at. The brewmaster laughed, and led the rather simpleminded peasants who were characteristic of the area, to laugh at the minister and what he stood for.

The Catholic priest did not pay too much attention, even in his prime, to that sort of thing. He was caught up more in a simple mystical observance of the rites and rituals of the church. As he grew into a rather early old age, he became rather doddering. So in a way he was aware of the sinfulness of the parish, and he did protect some of the people who were his parishioners from the evils of this sinfulness. But it was not a very active or weighty counterweight. It was not a very effective counterweight to the influence of those who would hoist a container of brew.

The containers were sometimes rather fancy. In short, drinking was one of the more accepted elements of life and events of society there. It was mainly the men who gathered in the tavern, the drinking place, the saloon, but they were encouraged to bring women as long as they had the money or the chickens to exchange. A chicken would get three medium-sized tankards if it were a big chicken.

In short, this man increased and encouraged drinking because he profited from it. This was his way of life. That person got out of control of its own soul. The soul had not particularly assessed the way in which alcohol had been truly an instrument of evil, a bedevilment of some members of the human race and some communities through many cultures, centuries, and generations.

The soul did not quite realize that this personality was going to become so taken over really by the forces of darkness, as it was. It was not a directly evil person. It was just a low-ceiling type of person who made potent brew and sold a lot of it and encouraged people to drink it. He was shrewd enough himself not to drink very much, because he kept his eye on business.

He would extend credit a bit. But then if he extended credit, you got not even two tankards for one chicken but you got three tankards for two chickens. He was really 'shrewd' and pretty grasping.

He ate well and his family ate well. They did not dress too well, because he did not have enough sense of that which was artistic or nice. They were well fed. He had a good sense of food. He had resources. He had actual cash coins hidden away. He bought up some small holdings and was beginning to become a bit of a landholder, a grasping type.

The soul, in despair, said to its council, 'What can I do? I am not able to handle this person.' The council agreed likewise and appealed to a higher council, who, after due deliberation, and after looking the whole situation over, asked the others who had charge of it to terminate that life, which mercifully was done.

The man was in his forty-second year when he died. I believe they stopped his heart, which probably was not too difficult, since he had laid on quite a little fat with his hearty eating.

The evil that was done continued. It takes a while for momentum such as that to be slowed down. Events took place which helped to bring the community into a little better balance with decency and spirituality. I do not see just what they were. But the soul was really quite aghast. After the transition, the excarnate person proved intractable. An attempt was made to show him some of the damage that had been done within families, wives and children who had had to do without food and clothing and a few simple pleasures because the husbands had become alcoholic and would go down of an evening to the tavern and hoist the tankards with the fellows and find their enjoyment of life, their 'high,' in that manner rather than in family life and love.

An attempt was made to show him how he had contributed to the non-progression or even the regression of some souls whose personal expressions had come into this type of personality. But the excarnate person refused to look. More importantly, he refused to feel. He simply closed his eyes to what was being shown.

He had not developed in the incarnate stage a sensitivity to others, nor a spiritual interest. Nothing but the rather gross and materialistic interests. So in the excarnate stage they had very little to work with. So they caused him to close his eyes and sleep, and the life force was withdrawn. In short, he was killed off in the second death.

As in the case of the raj, the brewmaster after death was no help to the soul. If either villain had seen his wrong, he could have made partial recompense on the excarnate plane, thus making it easier for both the souls and the persons of Evelyn and Dolores.

Dr. John: The entire making up for this fell upon the soul. The soul consulted its guides and teachers, and they talked over various possibilities of what to do next to partly make up for the evil that had been done, and to strengthen the soul so it would not let any future incarnations given unto it get away from it in this way.

The task was to raise the consciousness and stability of the soul. Since consciousness is affected by experience, it was rather quickly seen that experience in the next incarnation, probably in the next several incarnations, should be used to raise the consciousness of the soul, particularly in this area of the evil done by alcohol.

So the present incarnation was designed to produce a person, or to give to that soul a person, more sensitive and who was capable of better things, but in whose life repeatedly would come some of the suffering and some of the disasters which were associated with the promotion of the sale and consumption of alcoholic beverages. Also, the costs of finding one's happiness in such activities.

The next incarnation—and I go to it now—will likewise be karmic, but in a different sense, and I think Evelyn will be very happy to hear this. The next incarnation will be with a personality actively engaged in social uplift, in improving the lot of others within the communities in which that one lives.

It probably will be masculine, because this one does have masculine strength and masculine leadership. In fact, the brewmaster certainly showed masculine strength and masculine leadership, but without that sense of spiritual values, without that regard for other people, which this present incarnation is truly adding to the soul.

Or the next incarnation may be in the feminine, because the feminine has the touch with other realms, and thus can bring into the earth realm the values of the spirit realms. These values include a concern for others. These values include a certain sense of identification with others in which the good of the person himself or herself is linked with the good of others.

This experience happens in motherhood, but this experience is not limited to the children of a woman. It extends to the siblings, it extends to the parents in a fashion, it extends to friends, and it extends to the community. The feminine, with this touch with other realms, is more open to the spiritual elements of society, represented by churches and spiritual movements. So the next incarnation may be in the feminine.

Or these qualities may be sufficiently established in the consciousness of the soul in this life by its—well, horror is not too bad a word or too strong a word to use to describe the soul's response when it was shown the degree of hurt and harm which it had helped cause in other lives in that past incarnation.

So the next incarnation may be in the feminine.

For when the excarnate personality simply closed its eyes, the soul had to take over quite directly and see the details of individual children and of women and of families who were hurt by this. And of women who got caught in the drink habit and camaraderie themselves and became quite besotted and lessened in the finer aspects of their womanhood. And of men who were lessened in their outreach to other things by the contentment they found in the lesser spirits of alcohol rather than the greater spirits of their own nature and spiritual challenges and in family life and love and community advancement and worship in the churches.

So this is the setting of this life. If Evelyn spends much time on regret for that former incarnation, she will mistake both the content of this reading and what it can bring to her and the nature of the present life. She is not that brewmaster. Every incarnation is a different person. Her soul took a much greater hand in the formation of this Evelyn personality right from the very start, from long before the body was conceived. The soul has invested quite a lot of itself in this personality.

The whole soul never incarnates in any one personality, but only a portion. But her soul has invested a great deal of itself in this personality of Evelyn.

Along with this—and here I jump ahead a bit—there is a factor of how will a soul face disappointment, which is a major factor for her children rather than for herself. As she observes her children experiencing this, she will experience what many mothers experienced in another sense, of being deprived of the wherewithal to adequately care for their children and to bring to their children the advantages that they would have liked to have brought, because the father had wasted the resources or at least a portion of them and partly wasted himself, there in the life-style encouraged by the tavern and the two other drinking places.

The tavern had become the chief community center, and it robbed many a home and many a mother and many a child of their patrimony, their birthright from the husband and father. This is being observed, but also for the soul's correction, for the personhoods of various souls who experience disappointment, a change of plans from what they had expected as they came into incarnation.

It is quite an experience, an inescapable experience, because all souls must bring some of their personal expressions, some of their incarnations, through lifetimes in which that which had been planned and which the soul had been allowed to expect or even led to expect in that incarnation, underwent a very drastic change.

So I bring that as a bit of a foreward, for we shall get into that type of experience as we come into the consideration of her own children.

This is a very determined soul now, determined to help make things aright. It incarnated into a community and a society and a setting in which she experienced this degradation of too much alcohol and of making alcohol and alcohol-camaraderie too much the center of happiness or of the 'high' experiences of life. But the soul is determined to help bring some of the corrective factors into the picture.

The soul saw how the two little churches in that community, had they been more active in developing a strong spiritual life within the community, could have been more constructive. The soul saw how the understanding of spiritual things would help lift persons above grossness of the flesh and help them to better withstand temptations such as presented by much drinking, and would help these souls to progress in their real nature which is of the spirit and not of the flesh, the flesh being a time of testing and of opportunities for developing the spiritual strengths.

So this is the very interesting matrix of this lifetime for Evelyn McFee, and she has much of this life yet to live. Her council has had a hand, of course, in bringing her to this reading, and of delaying the reading until she as a person was sure she wanted a spiritual understanding of life itself and of her life in particular and of how she can live it better.

Let me say, she is doing quite well. This life already is certainly on the plus side. But there are ways to improve. There are ways to raise the grade from passing, and from a C grade to a B grade, in this life. She can and she should add more to the accomplishments of this life. The soul intends to, and that intent of the soul has been imparted also to the person— and it is as a person that Evelyn lives her life—and the person has the intent to find the better ways and the better things, even though the way to them may involve effort and suffering that require persistence and dedication.

There is more to the soul than this, of course. The soul is a strong, relatively young soul, although well started. But this is the point of emphasis within the soul right now. This is the point of progression. This is the grade of school in which she is now making the mark. This is the grade of school in which she is making the grade which will be the mark of her excellence in accomplishing this grade of school.

Is there a question?

Conductor: There is only one. You said her immediately prior life—I take it this was in the 1800s?

Dr. John: Yes. I think it ended in 1869. It was in somewhat south-central Germany. Of course, Germany wasn't Germany yet then, but it was in that area; possibly Bavaria. Incidently, the community was largely untroubled by world events. It was a rather small community off by itself and away from beaten paths, which is one reason why the brewmaster made his own brew and had his own market right there.

There was not much trade with the outside. Possibly it was back in some kind of mountainous area, although the land was flat and tillable. But the community during this twenty years or so, in which this particular man became an adult and developed and expressed the forces within his own beingness, as I have outlined, was largely untroubled by outside events.

Conductor: Shall we go now to the persons she has inquired about?

Dr. John: Yes.

Conductor: The first person she asks about is her father (name, birth).

Dr. John: He was one of the village men back there. In this life he was somewhat repeating that pattern, although with some improvement. He was a customer, a rather undistinguished member of the community but one who did not buy his brew on credit. He had more integrity than that. But he spent many a chicken on brew, so to speak.

He is a younger soul, and sort of repeating that pattern of what was considered the good life then. Is he still alive?

Conductor: No, Dr. John. He died in 1952, twenty-five years ago.

Dr. John: Then there is really no way Evelyn can reach that one. However, as Evelyn progresses, he has been shown her from the other side. He is not close to her now. I am not sure if he continues to exist on the astral side. I think his excarnate personhood has run its course and expired.

She might pray for his soul, very literally for the soul. I would suggest to her that she find a Catholic church and light at least three large candles for him. Not all at once and not necessarily consecutively, but the kind of candle that will burn for a week or ten days. Light it for the enlightenment of his soul to the finer things of life, particularly as made available through and expressed and brought by religion. Because this is the way the finer things of life often are brought into the peasant type of life, as it were.

I would strongly suggest this, and also that Evelyn give to a priest of a Catholic church money for at least one mass, for the—how shall we put it?—not exactly for the intentions of the soul but the intentions of God for that soul of the father. This contribution, I believe, can be a minor one of five dollars or so, and then there will be a mass said. Make this gesture, which will be more than a gesture, and it can be helpful to the father soul.

The father was Catholic. Therefore, the soul of the father can better be reached through using Catholic rituals.

Next Evelyn asks about her alcoholic sister:

Dr. John: No, there is no pastlife between them. But the guides and teachers are telling me that this is an example to the Evelyn person of the difficulties that drink can introduce into an individual's life. Not so much into some other individual's life as victim, but the individual himself or, in this case, herself as victim.

The lesson is really being driven home. Although Evelyn has not yet quite seen it, this reading partly is to open her eyes to what is one of the great lessons of this sequence of several lives, that alcohol is not just a social lubricant and not just a pleasantry, although it can be either or both of those on occasion. But it also is possessed of horns and a tail if it gets out of hand. That which can be a mild servant if kept mild, can become a very cruel taskmaster if it is allowed to become strong in a life.

So the Evelyn person, through experience, is certainly bringing additional knowledge to the consciousness of the Evelyn soul, and this sister is one instance of that. I have said they have not had past life acquaintance. This sister is not a reincarnation of one of her former customers.

Future? Probably not. There is really not that between them to make much to work with for the future. It could be, but certainly is not patterned. The other one's life will go its way insofar as it goes, and Evelyn's life will go her way.

Observing her sister as she wastes her life away through the use of alcohol is not pleasant for Evelyn, but certainly a good learning experience for her soul.

The next relationship which stems from the brewmaster life is that of the first husband, victim of his own drunk driving:

Dr. John: This was perhaps the most telling experience in her life, of the wrong of that in which she was engaged in the prior lifetime. I do not see that in that prior lifetime any of her customers got drunk in the tavern or either of the other two places and went out and mounted a horse and broke his neck. It may have happened but I do not see it.

However, a number of men with families were more gradually taken from those families, either completely or in part. So in this life the Evelyn person experienced in one quick experience the death of her husband, caused really through alcohol. So the death of the husband definitely was karmic for her.

I am not looking into his records. However, he did not come into this incarnation only for this purpose of serving her. The event also was meaningful in his life.

Here is where is introduced one of the other elements which I brought out earlier, the element of disappointment in a change from the life pattern that was expected. This is true for her in her marriage and all the years of her life remaining after the death of her husband. It is true also of their children, of course. This we will go into as the children are presented.

Evelyn and her first husband are cosmic family members with several pastlives together and the souls are quite close. Even though the husband's untimely death was used to teach Evelyn, it was of course not only for Evelyn's benefit. God does not sacrifice one person for the good of another. But He does, with the help of guides and teachers weave one purpose in with another. As Dr. John puts it, "God plays both ends against the middle."

This same principle holds true in the case of the four boys who were placed in an orphanage. We'll see what Dr. John has to say about two of them:

> Conductor: Let's go to the sons now. The first son (name, birth).
> Dr. John: He had fully expected that the father would remain in his life as father. The soul has not yet really assimilated the change, the difference in his life from what he expected. The home broke up, didn't it? And then re-formed?
> Conductor: She had to put the four boys in a home for seven years. She had no other choice.
> Dr. John: A foster home? An orphanage?
> Conductor: Yes, an orphanage.
> Dr. John: This would qualify then, as I saw the home breaking up, but then was re-formed. The soul of this son has not quite yet accommodated itself not only to the actual experience but to the philosophy, as it were, that there are times when definite plans are made for a lifetime and then something happens to change the plans, something that is not an accident but is very purposeful. This soul still feels that 'it had the rug pulled out from under it,' which is, of course, exactly what happened.
>
> Now what will the soul do with a person who is undergoing that type of experience? This the soul has not yet quite decided. The soul may take some time to decide. The personality is a quiet one, not pushy, and the soul just may take a while to decide what to do in a situation like this.
>
> I believe there is a girl, a woman, who is going to be brought into the picture, but maybe not for a while. This should make quite a difference. She will be brought in purposefully, as I see it, unless the soul decides that it does not want marriage.

Now the youngest son:

> Dr. John: Here is a younger soul and a younger cosmic family member. He is from the masculine half of his whole soul. But he is acting like a baby over the death of his father. He is rebelling at life. He is in danger of having a negative result to this lifetime, this incarnation. However, he is still young and he may grow out of it.
>
> Evelyn will ask for suggestions as to what to do about him. Possibly she can enlist his older brothers in helping her to make

a man out of him or to challenge him to 'make a man out of himself,' or to 'grow up,' etc. There are weaknesses to which this one has given in, weaknesses of disappointment, weaknesses of not wanting to try hard. This is not good. The outcome is not decided. Let her 'hang in there,' let her get all the help she can to help him take a good firm hold in a positive way of his own life. Because this is that upon which will hinge the success or failure of this incarnation for her young son's soul. Is there a question?

Conductor: The only question is how she can help him, but you have covered that.

Dr. John: He is young yet and he partly is in the process of working out some of the difficulties of being young in a culture where it is a little more difficult than usual to be young. But it is time for him to come out of the young stage and become an adult, a young adult.

The last relationship which stems from the brewmaster lifetime is that of her second husband:

Dr. John: He was one of her former customers in the 1800s. He was one who was encouraged to find his happy times in the tavern rather than in his home. They have not had other pastlives. They may or may not have future together. Is there a question?

Conductor: Yes. She goes into the many difficulties she has with him, and this pretty much explains why. She wonders if there is something she can do to help the relationship?

Dr. John: Let's put it this way: Their relationship is in their own hands. Their guides and teachers work with them, but each of them is a person. They are living personal lives. They are not souls, they are persons. They have souls and they are incarnations of souls. The souls are influencing them. But Evelyn is a person and her husband is a person. How will they as persons conduct their relationship? It is pretty much a long life, and one goes on or one goes backward. One does not stand still. So will their relationship progress or will it regress?

The relation of the soul and of its personhoods, its incarnations, is a two-way street. Forces in the soul affect the person, but what the person does and feels reaches the soul, too.

Remember, it is the former incarnation of the Evelyn soul, not Evelyn, but the man back there a hundred and ten years ago or more who encouraged the then incarnation of the present husband, and not the person of the present husband, to find its happy times in the saloon. He encouraged the lessening of the companionship with the wife and family, he encouraged the spending of resources for the brew, and so forth. She might wonder should this marriage continue? That is entirely in their hands. If they agree it is not really productive, if they balance all factors involved and come up with a negative answer, then why continue?

Of course, if either one of them balances all factors and says, 'Hey, I've had enough of this,' then they either work out a new basis for a relationship, or just continue the relationship for what comfort and conveniences it holds, or terminate it. It is quite in their hands. Really in the hands of each of them as well as in the hands of both of them. The decision can be made at any one of three points, each as an individual or the both together.

Conductor: I take it they are not cosmic family members?

Dr. John: Correct.

Conductor: Will they have future together?

Dr. John: Not necessarily. The Evelyn soul is paying for the past sins now. If they do develop a closeness now, if the husband-wife relationship really develops a bond, a force, a usefulness, a niceness, that is something that can be used again. But it's not settled.

Several of Evelyn's questions reflect her problems and also bring a better understanding of how retributive karma can operate in a life:

Conductor: She has had a kidney condition that she has not been able to cure. She gets a lot of pain from the infection and it has given her quite a bit of trouble. She wants to know if this is karmic.

Dr. John: Let me first extend my sympathy. Where there is pain, I would extend first my sympathy. The major reason that my next incarnation, which will be my first in some four thousand years, will be as a medical doctor in the 2000s, is to join forces with others upon earth in the elimination of as much pain, ailments, disease, incapacitation and such as possible, and to bring more healing into the more advanced human race at that time.

Secondly, I must say, yes, this is karmic. It is part of the general karma of this life. Those whom the brewmaster and tavern owner encouraged to drink of his brew and to make that the high point of their simple lives each week suffered, many of them, deterioration of internal organs.

Now the Evelyn person is having that experience herself, experiencing the other side of the coin. This experience is affecting the consciousness of her soul.

Thirdly, do keep in touch with medical science, which may find something to do. Do take care of any infection as best you can. Do not fear it unduly, as I believe she does not. She has continued to make a good life despite this. Know that if it should bring about her death, she will have accomplished much, by the direction that she is going and by the intent and persistence and commitment that she has to that direction.

Finally, she might find in some of the more ancient approaches something that would be helpful. Modern medicine is finding much of helpfulness in some of the ancient approaches. Mankind is an animal geared to the physical conditions of this planet—to the sun and its rays, to the herbs of the field and the flesh of the animals, etc. God has given Mother Earth all that His children need on earth.

It is possible that she might find some nature remedy of old, something that would be truly helpful. I do not know what such would be, I do not know if such exists, but I make this suggestion. I believe there is something in the herbal line which could be helpful.

You say this is a condition of the kidneys?

Conductor: Yes. She says she has quite a few kidney stones as a result of it.

Dr. John: Small ones?

Conductor: Small and large. Let me quote: 'I had a calcium buildup, but they did not know what caused it. Extensive tests were taken.' First they thought she had a metabolic bone disease. What she was born with was 'sponge kidneys.' That is the common name, and these kidneys almost always develop stones.

Dr. John: This is karmic and was designed. The soul knew it ahead. The soul winced in accepting it and knowing what

Evelyn would go through with it. The soul experiences the pain with her. The pain makes a real impact upon the consciousness of the soul. Evelyn is, in her suffering, being redemptive unto her soul.

I trust that will truly help her, and then I trust that prayers and possibly some discovery and some of the nature wisdom of some culture or other might bring further helpfulness. I shall add a prayer of my own for the alleviation or the cure of this ailment, if such be rightful in the accomplishment of her purposes to the glory of God and the service of her soul. And I salute her. She is a brave person.

Conductor: Yes, she is. Thank you, Dr. John.

Her next question—she is a very high-strung person. Her mind never wants to rest even when the body is over-tired. She has to take pills to sleep. Would this be because the soul is determined to do so well in this lifetime?

Dr. John: The soul is upset, which makes for a restless and hyperactive person. If there are material means for assisting her in sleep, I see no reason why she should not follow the medical advice in accepting such helpfulness.

Conductor: She is also very sensitive and gets hurt easily. Even just in conversation she's afraid to let her feelings show.

Dr. John: Quite likely her soul's attitude, which is healthy, has given to the subconscious mind of the person an uneasiness that something detrimental will be found out. Of course, in this reading it has been found out. She may share the reading if she wishes, she may hold it to herself if she wishes. We suggest that she first listen to the tape alone and then decide.

However, I feel that 'now that the cat is out of the bag' and has come to her consciousness and she sees it for what it truly is, she will see herself not as the brewseller but as the redemptive swing of the pendulum upwards into light, and can come to a greater confidence in herself, a greater liking of herself. She is one of the saviors of her soul. This is a rather high calling by God.

Jesus was called to be the savior of the world, and she is called to be one of the saviors of her own soul, her Individuated-God-Being child of God. It is a high calling. So while it might take a while to get over the habit of being sensitive, it also is possible that this enlightenment will simply drop that away as an old dead skin which has been outgrown. A snake has to wriggle a bit to get out of its old skin, and something coming out of a discarded cocoon has to wriggle a bit to do so. She may have to wriggle a bit, but she can leave it behind. (A2524)

A father who was a drunk, an alcoholic sister, a beloved husband killed while drunk-driving, four sons in an orphanage for seven years, marriage again with a difficult spouse, and kidney problems. What a price Evelyn is paying for her soul's past callousness! Evelyn's debt will not be fully paid when this lifetime is over, but the next lifetime, of service, will be much more pleasant.

Both the soul of the brewmaster and that of the raj were appalled at what they had allowed to happen, but this did not negate the karma. In fact, a good soul who gets into trouble will want to make amends. The righting of the wrong that has been done is a very good way to strengthen that soul. Then it is less likely to fall into temptation again, for the lesson is well learned.

ELWOOD

Women have been the most exploited group of human history. Within the other minorities—race, caste, slaves, or whatever—man, the physically stronger human sex, could take out his own frustrations upon physically weaker woman. And he often did.

Yet the justice of God is not denied. Reincarnation, a far greater equalizer than civil rights legislation, brings the unjust and unfeeling into the position of their victims. Many persons have experienced karmic lifetimes of learning what it is like to be an exploited woman.

The soul of Elwood produced several incarnations who had little concern for the feelings of women. But in his immediately prior lifetime he paid a large chunk of his karmic debt through experiencing extreme cruelty as a woman in an American Indian tribe. Elwood, the person, is still affected by the last life and is also completing his lessons on proper treatment of women. Dr. John begins the life reading for Elwood:

> Dr. John: The lifetime immediately prior to this one is affecting the present life more than is usually the case, and this

is the first key to the understanding of the present life and the person of Elwood.

The immediately prior lifetime was a century ago; a good hundred years separates the two. It was in the feminine expression in an American Indian tribe, and the Indian girl was in her late teens when there came the disastrous contact with the white people. The white people who came into her area, which was in the American West, but not as far north as his present birthplace of Montana, were a very rough lot. It was a group of men, and not of families. These men were adventurers, they were roisterous, they were not of a very high intellectual standard; they were shrewd and gimlet-eyed.

Naturally, they had little regard for the people already in the land to which they came or through which they passed; and likewise naturally, they had their eyes out for the native women. Unfortunately, the then incarnation of the Elwood soul was one of the native women whom they took with them. Not that they kept her with them for very long. They used her cruelly, although not with deliberate cruelty. The cruelty of it was in taking her away from her own people.

Of course they made her a group sex object. Several of them could very well have intercourse with her in one night. This was such a change from her way of life that the poor young woman was really in a state of shock nearly all of the several months that she was with them. Fortunately—and this was a wise provision of the loving God—she was not of a very high intellectual nature nor really very sensitive. This does not mean that she did not have feelings, but it does mean that those feelings were not of a high enough pitch of intensity for her to either have had a very fine life if left alone, or to suffer as much as she otherwise might have in her abduction.

The low mental level, probably an I.Q. of about 80 if you'd measure it today, means that in her mind she did not suffer as much either. She missed her people and her homeland, but not as much as if she'd had normal intelligence. She wondered about the future when she was taken off by this band of really despicable marauders (although they did not think of themselves in that way), but she did not have enough of a mind to fear the future as much as a normal person would have.

As I have said, this was a wise provision of a gracious and loving God, to cut the suffering quotient of that life. That life was known and intended, it was a karmic lifetime to help to right the balance for some of the things which this soul had allowed its previous incarnations to do which were wrong, particularly wrong towards women, and it did right that balance. It also had the carry-over into the present life of some of the shyness, some of the withdrawing, some of the unwillingness now to make a full commitment of the self. The mental and emotional faculties, however, are not under the cloud they were then.

This is the essential placement of the present life in the sequence of incarnations of this soul. The soul handled the immediately prior lifetime and is handling the present lifetime, really quite commendably. The soul is at the midpoint, or perhaps just a tiny bit shy of the actual midpoint, in its earth incarnations, and a little bit less than that in its experience and training in the other cosmic schools which souls attend while they are in contact with earth and in the sequence of their incarnate and personal experiences. It is a masculine soul, as we use the term, meaning that it comes from the masculine half of the soul. Is there a question so far, or does one of his questions fit in at this point?

Conductor: When was this lifetime?

Dr. John: It was in the 1800s. I am getting two ages; I am getting the age of nineteen and the age of twenty-three. I think the girl did not know quite how old she was. She had a nice body, she was attractive physically. She would not have had a good marriage, simply because the mental tool primarily was retarded, and the emotional tool also, so that she could not really have entered into a continuing and flowering personal relationship with a mate. I believe she died at nineteen. As I said, she was taken by this rowdy group of hard-living men, and their lot was not easy really, although they had chosen and made it that way. After several months she did die, which was a good thing.

The only two relationships included in this chapter are those of the wife and a former girlfriend. These two should paint a good picture of how the karma was induced, and bring more of what Elwood is learning this lifetime.

First, Dr. John researches the wife:

Dr. John: They were together in a life in the 1600s and early 1700s. Again, the Elwood soul was in the masculine expression. He had come from Spain to the new world, and for some reason or other he and some others were established for several years upon one of the islands in the Carribbean. Let me look at this more closely...they were placed there as sort of an outpost garrison.

This island was used as a re-provisioning and somewhat refitting port for Spanish ships. The garrison would gather food. That is, in essence they knew where the food was, so that when the ships came it could be gathered. They made sure that the natives did what had to be done so that food would be available, food from the sea and from the land. The ships that came by knew what could be gotten from that island, including, of course, fresh water and some fresh vegetables and fruit, which they would take aboard and which would stay fresh for several weeks on the way of the return trip home.

The members of the outpost garrison made somewhat of a practice of finding a native woman and living with her during their tour of duty. This tour of duty lasted usually two or three, sometimes more, years. The present wife was a native woman taken as wife, or rather live-in companion woman, by this one during his tour of duty there. The native woman was really quite impressed at being so chosen, for she did not think too highly of herself, although she was a comely and a capable young woman for that time and place.

But to have this white man, who had come almost from heaven on those great ships with those great sails, the ships that would appear from over the horizon and disappear over the horizon—for her to be chosen to be the live-in companion for one of these god-like creatures (to her simple mind) was very impressive to her and gave her life great meaning.

Of course, when he left, he left her, and pretty much abruptly. He really made no provision for her. He was not going to return, and if he had he probably would have picked a different woman. The rather free and easy society at that time allowed her to reintegrate herself again within that society, and she was welcomed back. But she did feel chagrined and demeaned by his sudden abandonment, even though she put up a good front.

Does this mean that this present-life marriage is karmic? Yes, it does. It also means that—well, two things are in effect here: First, here is the opportunity for this soul to right what was really a wrongful treatment of the other one. Second, here is the opportunity for this soul, the soul incarnating now in the personhood of Elwood, to correct its own concept of love and life with this other one. This is not a 'hit and run' or 'love her and leave her' occasion now. This is a relationship which has held meaningfulness and joy, which is to expunge from the river of his experience the 'leave her' factor, and which has real promise of good qualities for him.

I feel that I am not saying this too well, but his guides and teachers say they think he will understand. Is there a question?

Conductor: Well, he explains in a way what you have said: 'I feel that she loves me, but I am not sure I have ever loved her. However, I feel very close to her and very protective of her, and she is really a very nice person.' But he does say that in his mind their relationship is a question mark.

Dr. John: May I suggest, and this suggestion comes first from his guides and teachers but I concur with it, that he dwell upon the 'niceness' of the relationship and of his wife. There may be stirring in him impulses and desires for more, and that is quite correct. For in this life there is to be more to the relationship with her, more fulfillment, more depth, more content, than in the immediately prior lifetime, of course.

Of course, that immediately prior lifetime was necessitated partly because of the way he treated the native woman in this earlier Carribbean life I have just detailed.

But this is a very positive and constructive approach to a relationship. As he explores the positive features and the constructive aspects of a 'nice' relationship with his wife, he can find more content and depth and satisfaction developing within it for himself. This is strongly recommended to him.

It is expected that they come back together again, possibly in the very next lifetime, as husband and wife with a greater depth and degree of fulfillment. You see, this will be a three-life pattern then of their relationship as husband and wife. The Carribbean relationship did not have much depth or fairness to it. The present life certainly has more. And it could, if the present life is properly approached and lived, not only have a greater fulfillment but also lead to truly a very happy life-long relationship and marriage in the next one.

It is expected that his next life will be in the masculine, and within another hundred years or so after the end of this one. However, what he does in this life will help to determine the timing and the nature and the pattern of the succeeding incarnations. How he handles his whole life now is one of the major factors determining the next life. We have confidence that he will not slip backwards.

Now the former girlfriend:

Dr. John: She was his wife in a 1300s lifetime. They were quite happy in the manner and after the fashion of being happy in that place and at that time. It was a good life in South America in the mountains, with a rapport with nature.

They will be together in a future life, and she was brought into this life for a very interesting purpose. She is, as it were, a 'tantalizing' point of experience, which has come and has been withdrawn and is to be left withdrawn as part of the making-up for times in the past when the Elwood soul in masculine expression has mistreated women. Now this has been more in the farther past, and in more primitive tribes and methods.

For instance, the Elwood soul was one of a Viking band which did great feats of derring-do on their voyages and in their various exploits, but who also wrought a great deal of grief and harm and brought a great deal of sorrow and disaster to many others, including the women. There have been several lifetimes in this general type of environment and activity. As part of making up for that, this particular woman has been brought into his life now and then taken out, and he is not in position to command her nor the situation. Rather, he is suffering after a fashion because of the experience with her. Is this rather subtle point clear?

Conductor: Yes, and does explain his anxiety about their relationship. This bothered him.

Dr. John: I trust it will give him the guidelines for that relationship as well. And properly handled now, this can result in their coming back together in some future earthlife in a very happy way. But not now, not in this incarnation. If she still is in his life, she probably will be taken out of it, and this I hope will forewarn him. If that does happen, let her go with as much grace as he can muster. He will suffer from it, but this suffering itself should be handled in a redemptive way. Let her go, let the experience be a redemptive experience for him. I have indicated why and how. (A3077)

Much of the karma from cruelty to women was expiated in his last lifetime, but Elwood is still learning. The carryover of disturbances in his mental and emotional processes inhibits him and reminds the soul to keep a closer watch over its incarnations. The relationship with his wife is expunging from his soul's consciousness the urge to toss aside women after using them. At the same time the inaccessibility of the girlfriend teaches the soul what it means to lose a loved one—a lesson he has given others.

COREY

The effects of karma from a cruel life are not easily removed. Just as Elwood has a carryover of effects from his lifetime as an abused Indian woman, another soul may find its consciousness muddied from a former karmic life. Corey is suffering from a residue of pessimism which comes directly from a past lifetime of karma.

Through Corey's material for his life reading, it was obvious that his major problem was several business reverses. He was most pessimistic about his future in business. Dr. John brought out an incarnation in which the Corey soul, through its then personality, had used its shrewd business sense to take great advantage of others. To right the scales of God's justice, a process went into motion. The next life found the soul incarnate as a woman whose family was thrown out into the streets. This life taught him that "you don't get away with it." The next incarnation was designed to turn against him the forces he had previously wrongly used. With a below-average mind, this personality was continually conned and "plucked as a pigeon."

Corey's soul has met its karma and paid its price, but within the soul is still that consciousness of, "Whatever I do, I can't succeed." Our excerpt begins with Dr. John's first words to Corey:

Dr. John: Well, this is a rather capable soul and a rather capable person. He is an incarnation from the masculine half of his whole soul. He is in the third of the five stages into which for convenience sake I have divided the soul's progression, the God-child's progression through soulhood. He actually is a bit over the midpoint.

The purpose of the present life is two-fold. One is for the soul to get the experience of this incarnation and to successfully guide a personality, its own personhood, through this particular lifetime. The second purpose of this lifetime, or the second major coloring of it, is to let a certain momentum in the soul run down. And this is rather interesting. It's a momentum of consciousness rather than a momentum of actual outside forces.

This one has had some pastlives which would not be judged by present standards as being completely fine, let us say. In the 600s there was a life as a nomad Arab. This was in the masculine expression. They rode camels. They prided themselves on being fierce. They weren't very nice. He was a strong man, and whereas they had sort of a home oasis with dates and water and goats and wives and children, they really gained quite a bit of their livelihood from rather daring raids. They knew their part of the desert quite well. They could spy on a caravan without being known and carefully calculate just whether or not they would hit it and if so, when and how, usually at night. And on several occasions they killed all in the caravan, although if they could capture a woman or children, they did, but then they were very apt to sell them as slaves. And this is interesting. They made raids on some other settlements but they were shrewd enough not to raid the most nearby settlements. None of them were too nearby, but they would go two hundred or three hundred miles and raid a settlement and make off with plunder and loot. They also did some legitimate trading. They would trade some of their loot for some foodstuffs in the more nearby towns. That was not a very nice life but it did make qualities of masculine strength and courage and fearlessness.

I see him again in the 900s. An incarnation in somewhat the same area but a little north in, well, sort of the outskirts of Persia; this time as a trader, a merchant trader, not as much outside the law but a very sharp trader and one who had discovered certain uses of credit. He would extend credit but only when he really thought the customer could not pay him back, and then he would exact the pledge, which could be a child or anything else the person had of value. And he was pretty shrewd. He had a good mind and he devoted his mind to his own welfare. His own family lived rather well, quite well. He was affluential and because he was affluential, he was influential. His acquaintances did not know too much of his business. He had two sons and as they came along into their teens and later teens he trained them in the same kind of business tactics he used. He had capital and he had things that—well, he had quite a wide stock in trade, including foodstuffs, and so if a family were really hungry, he might advance them foodstuffs. First, of course, selling it and then when they really could not buy it, he would use blandishments. He was an oily one, yes. He would descend upon them and take their pledge. It was in writing and it was witnessed and his two sons would be with him and if need be, another strong henchman or two. It was not good.

And then in the 1000s—well, after that 900s life the council of guides and teachers knew that they had to do something or that soul was really on the wrong track. So they called in a member of their supervisory council, who called in another, and they used blandishments to get the soul to accept a lifetime in the feminine valence in a Persian town as the daughter of a man who was affluential and influential, a trader probably or a politician or both. The Corey soul, knowing how he had made his family comfortable and his daughters were spoiled and married well, etc., was quite happy. But he did not know that it was scheduled that his new father was to fall out of favor with the ruler and be stripped of all possessions and thrown into prison and as a political prisoner stayed there, I think, until he died, and his family was thrown out on the street. This had a good effect. As I said, this is not a young soul, and the soul by experiencing the results of what it had been doing in the masculine previously, 'saw the light.'

So then it came back in the 1100s in China, coming back into the masculine again, and the soul knew that this would be a life in which some of the karma from the 600s and 900s, especially the 900s, would be met. It was a little less from the 600s because that was their code and 'If ye did not know it was evil, it is not held as much against you,' as the Master said. Some karma, of course, had been met in the 1000s feminine life. Now in the 1100s, there was the karma of financial reverses. In the 1000s there was the learning of that which had been done, 'You don't get by with it.' In the 1100s some of the forces which he had used wrongfully for his own gain were turned against him. There were individuals in that life who took advantage of him, were shrewder. In that life he did not have the most shrewd of minds. It was pretty good, but there were others who conned him, took advantage of him, took him in, plucked him as a pigeon, yes. I find that term in the concept bank here.

So whatever he did seemed to go all right for a little while and then, then he'd be toppled. He'd work hard, he'd get a little way and then something would happen, the rug was pulled out from under him, and that was the nature of that life. There were those who supported him, but the experiences still happened to him, you see.

After that, he swung into a different kind of life. Well, several, of course. Different kinds of experiences. And now in the present life actually a thread from the 600, 900, 1000 and 1100 sequence of lives is picked up and this is quite interesting, conductor. The actual karma is over, the soul has learned and has 'turned from its evil ways' or from the ways of evil and misuse of powers, meaning of its mind and energies, and those others who had a burning desire for revenge have had their day, although they have not been allowed to take burning revenge. But there was in the soul a residuum in consciousness, a feeling that bad luck still dogged him, that he could work hard and things would still go wrong.

So in this life the soul rather expects bad luck and this opens the door for it to come about, for there are always in the world as yet forces of evil that will take advantage of the doers of good whenever they can. As the Master said, 'Be ye wise as serpents as well as harmless as pigeons.'

So he will be asking now what can he do about it.

Conductor: Yes, Dr. John.

Dr. John: Well, born 1925—he is now fifty-five. Bind with his transcript our sheet on 'Talking to the Subconscious.' This can help.

Majorly, though, the answer is going to be in the assertion of good judgment and ability and business effort to very logically and objectively conduct his affairs with good decisions, good judgment, and carry through into success in that way.

Now this success may not be a huge financial success, but it can be a financial success. He has knowledge in the present life and from pastlives, upon which to draw. The trader, the merchant in the 900s in Persia, and also the legitimate activities which were a part, anyway, of the 600s Arab, provide a certain background. And there has been success in other kinds of earthliving, feminine and masculine, so the soul has background and the person has foreground for producing a modest financial success in this life.

Here let the person take the lead, let the person say to the soul, 'Move over. You've had a wrong idea too long. There's been this residuum. You almost don't know it's the 1900s instead of the 1100s, that it's in the United States now instead of China, and that I am now Corey Smith and not—' that other name, that Chinese name which had a sound like 'chan' in it. I do not get the rest of it and I will not probe for there are more important things to do in this reading.

So the person can take the lead here. Really, of course, the answer is going to lie in the correct application of business principles, which means to do that which he knows about. Don't feel that he may get lucky, because that is a gambling feeling which has led to more losses than wins.

So it's rather mundane, conductor. The answer is to be found right in the walks of life, that which he chooses, and his ability to walk them with success and not expect or invite failure.

Well, that is the introduction to Corey. (A1433)

In this material-centered world, business success is so often top priority. But whether or not Corey is able to take the lead from his soul and attain prosperity is really of only small consequence. For his ongoing beingness, the Corey soul, is gaining "prosperity" in this lifetime as difficult lessons are being learned.

One may note that each of these four examples of karma incurred from lifetimes of cruelty involve masculine souls, and the question could arise, "Are tyrants usually from the masculine?" This is often—though certainly not always—true, because the male half of the soul contains the survival values of competitive drive, strength, and wisdom. These are the qualities which can more easily be warped through power.

The urge to succeed at all costs, which is inherent in the masculine soul, could cause that one to get so involved in success that it falls into the trap of thinking that the end justifies the means. The characteristics of strength and wisdom would make the power so much more easy to come by. Until the masculine soul has developed the feminine qualities of God's values, there can be temptations to commit cruelties. However, this in no way lessens male attributes. The original gender split was made for good purpose. For the human animal to succeed on planet earth, physical survival values were essential.

It also must be understood that the feminine half has its own characteristic temptations. Although the feminine qualities of cooperation and reach to the spiritual realms make it less susceptible to the temptations of greed and cruelty, it is more likely to allow its lack of strength and wisdom to get it into trouble. Examples of ways in which feminine souls commonly incur negative karma are shown in succeeding chapters. The characteristics of each half of the soul are purposeful, necessary. This is why it is so essential to have successful incarnations in both gender expressions to develop the good qualities of each.

It is true that until the masculine soul adds feminine values to its beingness and comes to know the value-system of God, it can produce cruel personalities. But the justice of God is genuine. "The mills of the gods grind slowly, but they grind exceedingly fine." Each of the four villains in this chapter will, in the long run, suffer as his victims suffered, and learn from his mistakes.

Yet God's sentencing of the soul to pay for its wrongdoings is so much more than just a balancing of the scales. It is a learning, growing process designed to teach the God-child the necessity of adhering to the values of the Creator who establishes the soul's realities.

The great function of karma is not to punish. It is to teach.

CHAPTER FIVE

KARMA, THE GREAT TEACHER

In the cosmic school laboratory of planet earth, the soul puts into practice lessons taught in other cosmic schools. Karma often acts as the laboratory professor, for karma is the law of spiritual cause-and-effect. The God-child who causes action that is against the Creator's values will get negative results, if not in the same lifetime, definitely in another.

Although only about five percent of the readings show retributive karma as the major purpose of a life, it is rare to find someone in the first, second, third or fourth stage who is not experiencing at least some negative results from pastlife causes. In the growth lives this is certainly logical, because correcting our mistakes is an essential part of progress. Dr. John states, "If you cannot look back and see errors that you have made, then you are not growing." Karma, the great teacher, takes the soul into the laboratory of incarnate life on planet earth, to master the spiritual principles which have been taught in other cosmic schools.

As the soul grows, part of the divine imperative upon it is to do its best in every endeavor. No earthlife can be lived perfectly, but each person must try to do well. If a soul allows its person to live a slovenly lifetime, or to terminate prematurely an incarnation, it is wasting an opportunity. This is a backward step. That which is taken for granted in one life, the unappreciated portion, may then be removed in another, thus teaching the soul to appreciate opportunities.

Another way in which a soul may inherit karma is through becoming overbalanced. Something which is essentially good can become not-good if carried to excess. For example, souls should like and respect their cosmic teachers. But to confuse a teacher with God is definitely wrong, and the soul that does so must be shown the teacher's "feet of clay." Or a very fine soul may enjoy spirit realms so much that it hurries through its incarnations without concern for loved ones left behind. This is both unfeeling and unthinking. The God-child must balance its priorities.

Probably it is in the area of relationships that we find the most examples of karma incurred. A victim of one life may become a relative in another. But it is interesting to note that the one victimized does not necessarily come back himself to punish the villain. If the victim is forgiving, then the karma may be worked out with another. As the readings indicate, "Make friends with your enemies. Then you won't have to meet them in another life."

This chapter displays seven illustrations of the teaching methods of karma.

CLARA

Clara was born in the twentieth century in the slums of New York to parents of low capabilities and status. She felt, correctly, that they were dumb, stupid, and she was ashamed of her family and environment. But her home situation actually began two lifetimes back, in Italy in the 1700s. At that time the Clara soul had incarnated in a rather upper-middle-class family, but chose to lead a lowly life. Caught in the excitement of a rowdy gang that pillaged the neighborhood, she eventually married the leader of this gang and her life continued downhill. To make up for that slovenly life, she came in the 1900s into humble circumstances and is purposed to climb out and become more:

> Dr. John: Clara is an incarnation from the feminine half of her whole soul, so she is in her native gender expression. This makes the incarnation a bit easier (which is in general true of native gender incarnations until the soul has had enough experiences in both gender expressions to feel completely at ease and adequate in each).
>
> That also is the framework for the confluence of experience streams within this lifetime. They could not have flowed together in a masculine lifetime, and this will become more evident as the reading goes on.
>
> So a part of this lifetime is karmic in the usual sense, that of paying a debt or meeting some unfinished business or business not well handled, not satisfactorily completed, in a

former life. It also is karmic in the larger sense in which I usually use the word, of meaning this is a life in which the soul itself is adding to its quantity of earth experience and building within itself the qualities it must have if it is to go forward as a child of God into the greater and ever greater realizations and expressions and developments of its Individuated-God-Beingness. Is there a question so far?

Conductor: No, Dr. John. It's very clear.

Dr. John: Then let us have relationships.

Conductor: First her father (name, birth date and place given).

Dr. John: Yes, they have had a pastlife relationship as mother and son, Clara being the mother. This was in Italy in the mid-1700s and into the latter part of that century. This life was one of net regression for the Clara-soul, and is the particular life for which the present life is making amends.

In that life she was born into a good middle-class family, but was a rather high-spirited girl, not really in the good sense of that term. She was pretty, she was sexy, she was quite willful. She quite early developed a certain disdain for her parents—in the early teens, let us say, and the immediate preteens.

She started going with 'fast company,' people of her peer group in age but not her peers in culture and social status and the economic class of her family and what she could have become. She became compromised sexually a number of times, and with her quite willing approval.

She became really the dominant female with a certain group of young people around her own age who were—oh, I shake my head as I look at them. They too had broken loose from their families, several of them coming from families where one parent had died, and at least one being an orphan, I see, orphaned when he was about eleven or twelve.

They did not ride motorcycles only because there were no motorcycles at that time. They knew the back alleys and the interweaving of streets, so that if they were apprehended by police or good citizens in some small crime as petty thievery or such, they could scatter and flee like fleas. They would be gone so quickly that no one could really put a hand on them.

They became somewhat known, but their leader was smart enough to operate in different portions of Rome, the city. Since the then incarnation of this one was the outstanding female in their group, the leader claimed her for his own.

Then an event happened which really sobered them up partially. She would be away at night at times without her family knowing it. She was quite adept at slipping in and out. But the family knew enough of her character so as to be very apprehensive. Some stolen things were found in her possession within the home, some things she liked. For she had a certain appreciation of the finer things. I think this was a ring, and possibly a few other bits of jewelry or clothing, for which she gave the best explanation she could give, and she had a glib tongue.

Although her father tended to accept her explanation whether he believed it or not, the mother knew it was not correct and that these things had come either by theft or as a gift of some man they did not know. So the girl decided that the better explanation to keep peace at home was that these were the gift of a young man, and she introduced the leader of their gang as the young man.

The family did not like him, the mother particularly. But the father thought, well, if this is her young man it's her choice. He then suggested they get married and rather soon. The young man was not too averse to this, and besides, another event happened about this time.

Two of the gang were caught in some episode, and very shortly after apprehension were executed. It may have been that the shopkeeper or whoever it was they were stealing from caught them himself or had some rather burly assistance to put them to death. Or it may have been the law. At any rate, the law, if it did not execute them itself, was quite approving of their execution.

This event cast a cloud on all of them, and it seemed to the leader that it probably would be good if he and the girl were married, and married in church, which they were, and really settle into a fairly acceptable lifestyle. To do this, the girl, now cast full time with the boy, had to accept his dominance. She was strong but he was much stronger. His dominance included a certain way of life. It was a gruffy way of life, a scrubby way of life.

She gradually became rather slatternly. He got a job. The gang broke up. He got a job as a laborer, and that suited him. He managed to become somewhat of a foreman and unionized his shop, so to speak, under his dominance and collected tribute from all those who worked under him, a half-dozen or more men. So in a sense he provided fairly well for his family.

He did like children. He would be gruff with them, but he enjoyed them and was a strong father. The home was dirty and cluttered, and the mother would scream at them all. This was the level of life to which she descended, when really the level of life she was supposed to have had was much higher than that. So it was a life of regression for the soul.

The present father was a son, either the third son or the third child. I believe he was the third son and the fourth child who lived. He grew up within that environment and copied his behavior from that of his father, reflected the home environment and, of course, the mother within it. For the then son, a younger soul, it was not a life of regression. It was a life in a certain type of earth environment which was successfully lived, and he survived.

He met a girl—of course they were not in the gang stage—he met a fairly decent girl and married, and she established a better home for them.

At times the mother, the then incarnation of the present Clara, would think of the life she had had as a younger girl. She knew when her sisters and brothers married and the homes they had, although she was never invited because she was too dirty and her language would deliberately shock them, so they pretty much just dropped her. Although her parents continued to have a certain parental regard for her, her siblings, with that rather brutal honesty that siblings may have, decided they wanted nothing more to do with her, and they had nothing more to do with her.

So at times, particularly in the early stages, she thought of what might have been, but very quickly she pushed those thoughts into a far recess of her mind and went on with the life she did have. It was too bad. But this sort of thing can happen and does happen, and represents how a giving in to temptations can lead to evil within a life. For it was evil for her. That was a life of regression rather than progression for the soul.

The soul was not quite smart enough and strong enough then to guide its high-spirited, willful girl with the quick mind and the glib tongue into a better life. The soul made what proved to be the fatal mistake of letting the early temptations enter and not realizing their seriousness. Temptation is like the camel's head under the tent, and pretty soon the camel comes in and takes over the tent, in that earthy fable of the East. So there was that life. Really, the both of them, the mother and the son, have progressed beyond that life, the son's wife getting more credit for his progression than the mother. They may or may not be together in the future. They were together this time, and in a sense the tables were balanced and things were made better than they had been the last time. So they may not be together again, or they may. It is not patterned. Is there a question?

Conductor: No, Dr. John. I assume they are not cosmically related?

Dr. John: Correct.

Conductor: We go now to the mother (name, birth).

Dr. John: Her ties are with her husband. There is no pastlife and no cosmic tie with her daughter. The 1700s daughter, having been so disregardful of her own mother, in a sense did not deserve to have in this life a mother with whom there were past ties or with whom there was cosmic relationship.

This is part of the justice of God, which is a great principle but more than only a philosophical principle. The justice of God is a force expressing itself to right wrongs, and this is one way in which it operates. Do you see this?

Conductor: Yes. That's very interesting, Dr. John, and it certainly explains why she was the mother this time.

Dr. John: It is not expected that they be together in the future. It might happen.

The council suggests to me here, and I pass the suggestion along with my general concurrence—I do not know the situation as well as they do—that Clara may be able to make her relationship as daughter with her parents a little better for her and for them than it is.

This is not to become a major project. There simply is not too much to work with there with her parents. However, within that framework of what they are and of what she is, and the framework of the fact that she really has more quality to her, being an older soul and having gotten that bad bubble of the 1700s life out of her being—if she, operating from the superior position of intelligence and soul knowledge, can find a way without encouraging closeness of the type that interferes, to express the good aspects of parent-and-child, this would be a real accomplishment for her. It would also be an accomplishment requiring enough thought and ingenuity to make it rather special in a small way. However, it should not loom as a major thing in her experience. She broke away from parents who could have done more in the 1700s. Now in the 1900s, essentially she must break away from parents who would hold her to less, if she were to remain really close to them. But within that framework there might occasionally be a call, a Mother's Day call, a Father's Day card, something which did not lessen her own independence, which needs to be made more instead of less, but still could recognize and get some of the good out of the inherent parent-child relationship.

She can think of this, and a way may open. She may figure out how to do it, as a small thing timewise in her life, not a major element.

So this feminine Clara soul abused the opportunity to be a part of an upper-middle-class family and is now seeing what it is to be born into lowly circumstances with a desire to rise above one's environment and heredity. This marrying beneath herself is a not uncommon way for a feminine soul to make mistakes. Had Clara been from the masculine half she would have had an inherent drive to succeed and climb upward, and therefore been less tempted to settle for a scruffy life.

In her present life, Dr. John identified several others karmically connected by that Italian incarnation: a sister, mother-in-law, and husband. But the essence of the soul mistake and manner of correction has been brought out by the relationship with the father and mother.

However, there is a lifetime sandwiched in between the 1700s life and the current one which is worth noting. The conductor asked if the "scruffy Italian life" is the last prior life:

> Dr. John: There was one in between. It was a short one. It brought her into quite a different setting, in about 1845 or 1846. She was born a female in the American South, the southern part of Virginia, into a lovely family where the chivalry of the

gentlemen and the gracious living of the ladies was very real. She grew up to the age of thirteen and then died. The purpose of this was, of course, to erase a lot of the scruffiness of the previous life. The soul repented of itself and was really quite dejected at what it had allowed its personhood in the 1700s to do and to become. Although that 1700s personhood was a pretty capable person. Given that life pattern, that person demonstrated a lot of capabilities and strengths. It just did not hold onto some of the things it should have held onto, and it did embrace some of the things it should not have embraced.

So really by the grace of God and somewhat in answer to the sorrow—not the prayers, but let us say the sorrow, the penitence—of the soul which had failed and knew it had failed, even though it stood by and did the best it could with that willful person, there was this mid-1800s lifetime in a setting of graciousness and human beauty.

She was taken out before the Civil War began, so did not experience that. That's pretty much all there was to that life. It was an act of the grace of God, and it, too, enters into the present life. (A3189)

Karma is not necessarily met in the immediately following incarnation. Karma, the great teacher, has many classrooms and its teaching-reach spans many centuries. In Clara's case, God's grace gave her an opportunity to have a short but gracious lifetime to set the soul again on its true course before the ignoble birth in the twentieth century. Clara has now been able to erase the scruffiness of the 1700s Italian life. Hopefully her soul will never again be tempted to become less than was intended!

POLLY

Even as karma does not have to be met in the next lifetime, so also it is not necessarily handled between the same two souls. The one who incurs the karma has to meet and pay his debt, but the victim might not have to be present with the villain again. This is true usually when the one who is hurt does not hold bitterness and resentment toward the transgressor.

Polly met her negative karma in this lifetime by caring for an invalid husband. But the husband's soul was not one of Polly's past victims. In her life reading, Dr. John told her that she was filling in a missed piece of the jigsaw puzzle of her soul. He referred to this missing portion as a "dropped stitch" of karma. Meeting it is only a part, but an important part, of the purpose of the present life. When the second husband was asked about, this interesting insight emerged:

Dr. John: In this life the soul went back to pick up some 'missed stitches' of karma. There is an element of karma here and it represents a dropped stitch.
Yes, and I believe there are two stages. I go back quite a ways into a primitive tribe in Africa. They are blacks. This would be about the sixth century B.C., the 500s B.C. The then incarnation of the Polly soul is expressing in the masculine, and concentrating on learning and exercising the strengths of survival in a quite primitive society and not too friendly an environment. They are in the southern portion of Africa, below the great desert.

The particular tribe is not too big, so they must live in a rather fearful respect for other tribes which are bigger. There is really no sense of brotherhood, excepting within their own tribe. The brotherhood within their own tribe is not too strongly developed. There is not much of a moral sense.

Within that setting, this one fathered a son who had a birth injury to one leg, to the right leg. Something in the hip. It could be a dislocated hip rather than a crippled leg. A disadvantage of that nature was a very serious disadvantage in that tribe. The father, as the nature of the disadvantage became clear, made a somewhat intelligent but also rather quite callous decision that that youngster be simply left behind once when they picked up and moved. The father decided that the boy's chances of survival were not very good, and that his own chances of survival were less if he had to carry a limited child with him. So once when they moved the father simply waved with his hand. The mother knew that the boy whom she was calling was not to be called and brought with them.

The little one had heard and was coming as best he could. He was walking in his own limping way, in a slow way. He saw them go out without him and he did not quite understand. He survived through the first night. On the second or third night some wild animal made a meal of him. It was a rough experience for that one. But life had many rough experiences, and it was constructively used for that soul, in that that soul in that lifetime met several requirements of earth experience. It had the basic earth experience of being rejected by its family. It had the basic earth experience of a tragic death. Several basic experiences were worked together, you see, so in a way that soul got its money's worth out of that life, even though there was fright and there was fear and there was some pain, although wild animals who live by their prey have learned to kill the prey quickly, so that the prey does not get away. So the death took place, the actual physical death, took place rather quickly.

But back to the then father. Here was an experience where he could have had the experience of caring for someone who was physically crippled, and he did not. We cannot fault that father too much, but it was a mistake in soul growth. And it left an empty place in the picture.

Now we come up to a second time. Let me say that the present husband was not the son then. This is a karma of experience, not of people.

We come up to the second century A.D., the 100s A.D. This one again in the masculine, a Roman soldier. This had even less fault attached to it, but nonetheless did entail a karmic carry-over that was very active and real.

The soldier, in one skirmish with his sword, hurt a young man who was fighting him. It cut some muscles. The young man lived, was pulled back by his side. The skirmish didn't last very long. There were a few bold people in an area where the Romans came who dared to resist for a few minutes. They lost several dead, and this one was wounded.

This young man lived but he was incapacitated in some way. Again, this was not the present husband, and I do not see the particulars of the incapacitation. But having incapacitated someone there, this was joined to the sin of omission, as it were, from the lifetime some seven hundred or so years before. This made a gap in the picture which is being fulfilled now as she takes care, of her own volition, of a person who is incapacitated but not by her.

As she reaches out to this other one with love and with care, a continuing care, she is filling in this portion of the total picture of the life experiences of her soul. Is this clear?

Conductor: Yes. Her main reason for getting this life reading was to find out why she married him. And this answers that question.

Dr. John: She and her present husband are cosmic cousins. They were not very close in the cosmic cousinhood, but they knew each other. The purpose of the other one's life—that one is from the masculine half of his whole soul—in this life fitted in with Polly's soul, putting in this missing piece in her life, in her soul life, her soul experience of human life. This was known on the other side before they incarnated. They discussed it with their councils, and their councils discussed it with them, and it was agreed by the two of them as souls. Actually, the husband soul is more alert, more adept, more adventuresome, and in a sense more attractive than the husband person. And this is good to know. Really she has, to a certain extent, plumbed her way through the person to the soul touch. Although it is a rather clouded plumbing through or tunnelling through or seeing through, but she has to some extent. He has, too, to some extent, but with less clarity than she has, but perhaps even more appreciation that she would do this for him in this temporary stage of their soul development, in these latter years of the present incarnation.

I do not find them together in a pastlife relationship, although—well, this is interesting. Each one, as part of the preparation for their present life chapter together, was shown several pastlives of the other. As it were, each took the other in hand and showed the other some of these pastlives, as souls that is. So they have sort of an acquaintance, even though they were not incarnate in the acquaintances.

'There are more things wrought in earth and heaven than you have yet dreamed of, Horatio.' If Mr. Shakespeare is around and if I have misquoted him, I trust he will forgive me. But what he said there is certainly true!

These two will be together in the future, in quite possibly the second lifetime after this, because the husband will be freed of this experience. Incidentally, what is his incapacitation in this life?

Conductor: It is cerebral palsy.

Dr. John: He will be free from it. And it will not carry into the excarnate stage of this personality, although on the excarnate stage he will have quite a lot of growing to do, to make up for the growing which was inhibited somewhat by the incapacitation of the incarnate stage. But it will come. In the second life ahead they will be together. Not as husband and wife, probably not even as immediate family members, but as good friends, and possibly working together in some way or other.

I trust that what I have said will help Polly in various ways to accept or to continue to accept and to make the most of and in a sense to make more of, spiritually, the present framework of her present incarnation. (A145)

Although the Polly soul's 'crimes' were certainly not heinous, she did stray from God's values. In one incarnation she missed an opportunity to learn by caring for someone who was crippled; in the other the soldier inflicted a disabling blow. Her second husband was not in either life, but his purposes this time did include having cerebral palsy. So karma, the great teacher, could teach Polly her lessons while also helping her husband through his lessons. Combining purposes in this manner, karma is most efficient. God does not waste!

LOIS

Often the question arises, "What happens when a person commits suicide?" Just as each soul is unique, each suicide is for different reasons and produces various consequences. In general, God is more lenient with suicides than is man. On rare occasions taking one's own life is the correct solution to a problem, but most suicides represent a wasted opportunity, an easy way out of a difficult situation which should have been faced.

Lois is a lovely girl in her early twenties whose father killed himself when she was seven. Her lifesketch refers to how as a young girl she had always felt that if life became too rough she would end her existence. Because of her insecurity and over-sensitivity, Lois experienced time as a "great vat of molasses that I was wading through." At age eighteen (as the reading reveals, that age is significant) she underwent surgery and discovered that she did want to live. Since then Lois has coped better with her world, although she does have problems.

In the beginning of her life reading, Dr. John describes the immediately prior lifetime, which ended in her suicide:

> Dr. John: Since the nature and the purpose of this present life is closely tied up with the immediately prior life, I shall go directly to that life, rather than waiting for it to emerge in the relationships, as it probably will. I do not see that yet.
> In the immediately prior lifetime this soul had a feminine incarnation in the American South, the northern part of the American South, in Tennessee. A number of traumatic events took place, leading the girl there to take her own life at the age of about eighteen. Although the traumas which led to that began closer to when she was in her sixteenth year, shortly after her fifteenth birthday.
> She lived in a close-knit and loving family. The father and the mother loved each other very much. They came from two families who were close. I see three siblings, two brothers and one sister, in the children there. They were modestly well-to-do. The father was a gentleman farmer, but yet active in the farming. Although in a border state, they sided with the South in the Civil War. They were from the South and of the South.
> The girl was the youngest of the three children but not by much. The next older brother was only about eleven and a half months older. The other brother was almost three years older than the sister. There was about two years between the two boys.
> When the Civil War came, the older brother was caught up in it. He was rather thoughtful, and he was caught up not so much emotionally as for philosophical reasons, for ideals which he felt to be at stake. I do not see precisely what those ideals were. Possibly 'freedom' as exemplified in the conflict particularly by 'state's rights' versus the right of the national government to impose a nationality over the states, as it were.
> So he joined the Confederate forces. Life in the forces was more difficult. He developed a certain skill at survival, and he saw quite a bit of action. He was with a Southern force that had a leader, a general, who, as it were, was acquainted with jungle fighting. Not that there were actual jungles in which to fight, in which the war could be fought. But there were lands somewhat like jungles—tangled wild wood growth, some swampy—into which this band of soldiers could melt away,

and with their superior woodsmanship be lost to pursuers. They then could make their way, often traveling at night, to strike unexpectedly someplace else. They were not a great decisive force in the war, but they were a sting-and-retreat, hit-and-run force, which not only took its toll of the Northerners but also kept them off balance and kept a number of them on guard against depredations of this group, and hence out of the other active conflict.

So this group, although relatively small for an army or a portion of an army, tied down more than its size, two or three times as many of the enemy as would have been required to meet it in conventional, active battle, open battle.

This one, the brother, as I said, developed skills of survival. But after two years of this he 'caught a bullet.' He was not killed immediately, and was taken with his group back into the swamps. But there was not proper medical care even for then, and the 'proper medical care' then did not know how to combat the infection and the fever which came upon him. He lived between eight and nine days and then died.

Word got back to his family, who took it very hard. Her next brother wanted to go, but he was crippled. He could get around, but he certainly could not take the rigors of army life or of marching and such. He suggested going into the cavalry, but he was not a horseman either. So there wasn't much he could do except stay home and work there.

But the father, after a long talk with the mother over a period of twelve days, felt it really was his duty to take his son's place. So he joined. He was not assigned to the swamp group, the jungle fighters, but was made an officer in a larger combative force. He was rather quiet. He was careful but he also was courageous.

In this period, the mother's younger brother was sort of a favorite uncle of the girl, and he also was killed. He was in the cavalry, and in some charge he was killed instantly. A bullet caught him in the head or the heart, and he was killed quite instantly. This was another blow to the family, including the girl.

Then in the fourth year of the war, after about two years of being in it, the father was killed. He was killed in one of the major battles. At this point the mother, who had wept a great deal from the time of her son's death—well, actually had worried much. She was of a rather delicate nature, as it would be called. Her son going to war had been bad enough, and the death of her son was a great blow.

Then her husband going to war, although she supported him and agreed with him in the idealistic stand and had confidence in him, yet she worried. Then the loss of her younger brother hit her again. The loss of her husband then was more than she could take, and she went into a mental decline from which she hardly emerged. It led to her withdrawal from life even before her death.

The daughter had an older girlfriend and confidant who was quite a source of strength, and who carried the daughter through when the family sort of fell apart. That is, with her older brother off to war and then her father off to war, and her mother doing her best to carry on but really withdrawn into her own sorrow and worry. And her younger brother doing his valiant best to carry on, which took all his time and effort and strength; carry on the home and the agricultural work there. They raised crops and such. The girl, in her teens, was left without anybody really, but found a great comfort in this friend of hers who was several years older.

Now let's see, just where are we? The older brother is gone. The mother's younger brother, a favorite uncle, is gone. The father is gone. The mother in a sense is gone. Then the final blow—this close girlfriend died accidentally in a fall from a horse. She was in very good health, and she was a good horsewoman in an amateur way, and was strong. But in this fall from the horse she went into a coma for several days from which she never recovered consciousness.

When the older girlfriend, older by several years, died, this other girl now about seventeen or eighteen had no one to turn to, and took her own life. Her mother didn't even know it. The mother was so far withdrawn from reality that she didn't even know it. The brother was the only one left and I do not see what happened with him. But this girl took her own life, which is understandable but was still an act of weakness. She could and should have stayed and sustained her next older brother for they had been close in that which he was undertaking, and there was a pattern of life for her.

It would have meant going through a reconstruction period. But a difficult period within the environment, within a culture such as that, can really build strength. There was a husband waiting and there were several children waiting. There was a pattern of life and there could have been happiness found in it. Happiness that grows out of a bed of sorrow can have a sweeter fragrance, a deeper truth to it, than happiness without its roots in sorrow. Without its roots deep in. Sorrow makes for deep soil for roots.

Out of that background—well, let me first pursue what happened with the girl after death. She was met by her father. Her father was the one who was brought to receive her when she came over. He comforted her greatly. She then met her older brother. The father really was the better philosopher of the two men, and he by that time could see the truth of both sides of the war, and withdraw his allegiance from only the one side.

The brother still was very strongly supportive of the Confederate side, but was beginning to get the larger viewpoint. The daughter had not really engaged in the philosophy of it too much. She accepted her philosophy, her sense of cultural values, from her parents and her brothers. She was a woman who was much impressed by her menfolk, which is a way of saying it.

Now these women were not oppressed, but as a general thing they accepted as their position what the menfolk determined the family stand to be on any issue, also the family course in any major action. Within that framework, these women if they were capable could make a very fine life for themselves and know an independent existence and growth and much happiness.

She also met her uncle and other friends, and before long resumed friendship with her girlfriend, the older young woman who had died in the fall from a horse. So the excarnate being there—the name I get is Belle, but I'm not sure on this, that may have been a middle name. It may have been a name, or a name that meant the same then. We shall call her Belle, for she truly was beautiful, and the beautiful part came out, as it were, on the excarnate side after having been under a cloud for three or four or five years on the incarnate side, especially for the three years since her brother had died.

Belle went on into a good life on that side, but there was a pattern of living which had been set up for her on the incarnate side which, of course, now was not fulfilled.

On the other side she watched her mother on the incarnate side. The mother's husband from the excarnate side ministered unto her, and gradually the mother's life was drawn again to be with her husband. Those around her thought the lady had lost her mind and was hallucinating as she would speak her husband's name and smile and would converse with him and reach out her hand as she spoke with him. The mother did not remember these things if anyone would speak to her about them, but the mother really was mostly in that other world before her body ended its existence in the physical plane, you see.

So the step-over was a short one for her when she did come, and easy, although it took a little while to bring her consciousness then fully into the other estate. This girl watched that on the excarnate side, and having watched it there knows about it now on the soul level. That excarnate Belle entity or person, through its experience, brought this into the soul's consciousness on the level in which that consciousness experiences personhood, personal existence, this watching of the mother in this period when the mother was gradually crossing the line, as you see.

So that knowledge is in the subconscious mind, that portion of the soul mind which is carried in the person's subconscious mind, and the knowledge is fairly near to the surface. Perhaps it can be consciously recalled, or perhaps only the learnings of it utilized. I do not see, but it is there.

The excarnate Belle also saw the brother who was left, who struggled through and who made it. He lost a great deal of what they owned. Not that they owned a lot, but he lost more than fifty percent of it. But he was able to hold onto enough, including a building, that he could reestablish himself as a productive, self-sustaining member of the post-war economy. The building he made into a home. It was a little home, not the larger home in which they had lived.

He eventually married, had children, and became a solid citizen. He went through the reconstruction period, and the soul really gained a great deal, more than in two or three normal lifetimes without such large incidents.

So the soul of his sister, seeing what could have been for itself and how it could have helped the brother, gained a new insight. When given the chance to try again, she accepted it.

Now this life, the twentieth century incarnation for the Lois soul, is different, of course. It is not possible to reconstruct exactly the framework of the former experience. However, there are certain portions of it with her now. The favorite uncle is present in this life. The older young woman friend is present in this life. I do not believe the then father, mother, and older brother are present. However, when we come to relationships it may turn out that they are.

But the karma of it, the righting of the mistake, is being accomplished in a very unusual way. It is not that she picks up the pattern of that other life at the age she laid it down or abandoned it, at eighteen or so, and carries it on now. It is rather that at the age of eighteen or so she no longer has a set pattern for this life, but must devise one of her own with the help of her guides and teachers.

This is a rather unusual way of meeting karma, you see. But it is a very effective one, and the karmic balancing of the picture here is that a pattern was abandoned, and now the entity comes into a time without a pattern, when she must go on without there being a set pattern. She must proceed. As she proceeds then, she must choose—with the help of the guides and teachers, but essentially the choice is her own, and the soul working with her must experience the choosing through the person doing the choosing—and then with the choosing, she must build the pattern of this life.

That is the basic picture from the akashic records of her present life, growing out of the immediately prior one primarily. Is there a question to this point?

Conductor: No. It is extremely interesting and very clear. I would like to make one comment of interest: in her lifesketch, up until about the age of eighteen, interestingly enough, she always felt that if life got too bad for her she would just end it. Around the age of eighteen she decided that she would never end her life and that she wanted to live.

Dr. John: The soul, you see, decided that. This was the soul's decision reflected into the person's own decision, and that was very good. The soul is working with her, you see. She has so much going for her. And the soul's enlightenment and determination following the prior lifetime is very strong and wise and good.

It almost seems unfair that the Lois soul should suffer negative karma from a suicide under such tragic circumstances! But karma, the great teacher, knows best. The Lois soul is in the third stage and old enough and wise enough to recognize the chance for growth she could have had. And the chosen way to make up for the mishandled opportunity—no set pattern this lifetime after the age of eighteen—should strengthen the soul's future hold on life.

If Lois had been from the masculine the innate soul strength might have prevented her from taking her own life. This is not to say that a masculine soul will never commit suicide or settle for a scruffy life when a better opportunity is there. Nor is it true that a feminine soul will never become a tyrant. But the divergent native qualities give each soul-half different strengths and different weaknesses.

To further assure her resoluteness, the Lois soul was brought into a family with karmic ties from the 1800s.

First, the present-life father who committed suicide when Lois was seven years old:

> Dr. John: This was the 'favorite uncle.' He was close to his older sister and he loved her children. He was married. He was, I think, ten or a dozen years younger than his older sister, who was the mother of the then incarnation of the Lois soul. This younger brother was married and he had children, but he did not marry and have children until the sister's three children were rather well grown. I think the girl was six and the boys were seven and nine.
>
> This uncle had been very close to them before he married and before his own children came along, and that closeness was maintained. It was just a natural and a loving thing. They have that past-life acquaintance.
>
> Have they other pastlife acquaintance? Not on earth. They were well acquainted in other cosmic schools associated with the soulhood stage. They have taken various learnings and lessons together in some of them. But this is only their second time of incarnation together.
>
> He is what we call a cosmic cousin, but a rather distant one. Not, as it were, a first cousin, but a second or a third cousin, as it were. However, when the pattern of this life was drawn

up for that one with its known difficulties but its unknown outcome, the Lois soul was approached about coming in as a daughter, and the Lois soul gave quite glad acceptance. The excarnate Belle had been so glad at finding her uncle again. His name I think was Harvey, but I don't think they pronounced it Harvey. I think it was 'Uncle Harve.' I believe that was his name, but maybe it was nickname and it may have been an attenuation of his real name, but 'Harve' is what I hear.

So the Lois soul, not realizing completely what it was getting in for, but making the decision no matter what it was getting in for, said, 'Yes, I shall be glad to come in as daughter to Uncle Harve, and somehow I'll be there to help in whatever way I can as he faces and goes through the rather difficult assignment of this lifetime.' This lifetime for him did not grow primarily out of the immediately prior one. That one was more wrapped up complete while incarnate and polished off in its excarnate phases. This lifetime for him goes back to his general pattern someway.

Now for Lois, there was this commitment out of love and out of a rather quick generosity and out of emotion to accept the position of daughter, and she would do it again. But there was also (since her soul is not a greatly wise, greatly old soul) less detachment, and the impersonal aspect of life was not very well developed, or the impersonal aspect of personal relationships, so that this experience of her father's suicide affected her psychologically and within the pattern of this life very deeply.

However, this was used in her case as providing, as you can see and as she can see, a certain framework of difficulties to test her determination as a person, implanted by the soul and by the normal processes of personal living, that wants to live rather than to die, to test that determination and see if it would hold up and if her soul could guide this person adequately— not quite skillfully but adequately—through the experience into the next chapter which lay ahead.

The soul did, and the Lois person and soul are evolving a pattern for this life. As they do, the great supportive nature of life itself, of God's spiritual universe, works with them, as well as many other factors.

Conductor: That pretty much answers her first question about her father. She wanted to know what the purpose was in choosing him for a father and what was the purpose interrupted by his death. You have answered this, unless you have any more comment.

Dr. John: A question would be, will they be together in the future? I would think yes. It is not patterned as yet, but these two had many positive forces and there are certain unfinished measures and expressions of love between them, uncompleted forces of love, which in all likelihood will draw them together again in some future incarnation when the father is cleared of the darkness which he experienced in this incarnation. Lois will be ready after this incarnation to meet him again. He may be ready the next time, and the two could come together as, say, good 'friends. I believe it would not be a family nor a lover relationship, but as good friends. Possibly both of the same gender but possibly of opposite genders.

Conductor: She will be pleased at that. There was a close love bond and a warmth. However, she speaks of when she was around the age of thirteen, and this was after her father's death, of a 'struggle between my darkness and light, and an experiencing of dark presences.' Some of these dark presences she thought were her father. She felt both terror and fascination with these unknown forces, which hit a peak point when she overdosed on alcohol at age fifteen and almost died.

The question is, was her father from the excarnate side influencing her toward this, or is he using any influence on her now, particularly of a negative nature?

Dr. John: He is not allowed to get that close. However, one might say the memory-thoughtform of him was a focusing point through which came to her negative forces growing out of her own pastlife experience. Is this clear? In other words, the darkness that came really was composed of two things: (1) There is darkness around all earthlings all the time, just as there are germs in the air. But this is the normal environment. Now if the skin is broken, the germs may get into the inner system and bring a certain poisoning, even a rather crisis condition. In which case the forces of healing must certainly be rallied and applied at the point of danger. Psychically and reincarnationally and spiritually and simply because of incarnation, every earthling walks in an atmosphere of good and evil external forces during all of the incarnate life. As long as the defenses are up, the germs of darkness, as it were, are kept outside. If for some reason or other they get within the astral being, they can set up quite a lot of difficulties, many different kinds of difficulties of varying degrees.

(2) In Lois' case, the difficulties she had experienced in that former life, in the last five years of the life, had never been resolved. They had never been fully met and digested in her experience—the good, the strength, of them being assimilated, and the rest of the experience, that which was simply the carrier, the roughage as it were, eliminated.

So in this life there was quite a job of digestion of experience to be done, even though the experience was primarily from the past and precipitated or triggered by the suicide of her father. Even though it was triggered in this life by the suicide of her father, the major portion of it came from her past and entered at that point, and simply the life forces had to rally and overcome the death forces. The light had to overcome the darkness. The unmet difficulties of the past had to be met and conquered. The growth which conquered them had to be achieved. The experience had to be digested as good, assimilated as strength in the beingness, and the rest eliminated as simply being the carrier of the experience, the carrier of the nutrients of the experience.

This is pretty good expression in earth terms of that which took place spiritually and which takes place not only with Lois but with many, many others.

The fear of dark forces from excarnates is prevalent among many. Actually, if the person's "spiritual skin" is healthy, "germs of darkness" need not be feared. But if one is filled with spiritual pride, need for proof of significance, or negative psychological forces such as deep insecurity, then the spiritual skin may be broken and there is reason for caution.

In the case of Lois the forces from the immediately prior lifetime were triggered by her father's suicide. It was painful for her, but necessary. The negative energies were cleansed in somewhat the same way as alcohol burns an open sore while purifying it.

Lois' brother was also in the 1800s lifetime. Even though she is close to him, Lois has always felt antagonism from the brother. The reason became known as his name was given:

Dr. John: This was the intended husband of the immediately prior lifetime. They had met, and then the young man had gone off to war. But he carried the picture of this one, and it was sort of his romantic picture during the war. When he got back he found that she had taken her own life, and it just didn't seem fair to him when he had survived what he had endured, which to him seemed much more than she had faced because he had seen much more of death than she had experienced, and he resented it.

He carried over that resentment to be expended in the present life. Of course, the framework of brother-and-sister has its own closeness. It has its forces. So these pastlife and present life forces help to neutralize each other; unfortunately, the resentment could help neutralize the good of the brother-sister relationship even as the good of the brother-sister relationship helps neutralize the past resentment force, you see.

We would suggest that she in wisdom gradually see what she can do to constructively build that relationship with her brother into a greater meaningfulness.

Conductor: The only question she had about him was about the tension between them and what to do about it.

Dr. John: This was a very real thing with that young man. As he came back into the reconstruction period he rather blamed her for not being there waiting for him and helping him to establish his own home. It took him quite a while before he got over it. So there was a rather strong force of resentment, which he needs to understand. If the time does come when he's open to this, she might mention it, but certainly not now. But let her recognize there is a certain legitimacy to his resentment. In its own framework it is legitimate. Counteract it by providing so much of the positive that any residual negative is overwhelmed, washed away, balanced out, totaled out. One moment...a member of her council is saying 'totaled out with a positive remainder.'

Bringing the boyfriend in as a brother is a clever way for karma, the great teacher, to lighten the dark picture of their former relationship.

Near the end of the reading, the conductor asked for Lois the question, "Why is there an ever present sense of pain and fear in me about pursuing my life, and how can I best overcome it?''

> Dr. John: This grew out of the past, plus the fact that the immediate future of the present is up to her. But she need not meet it with fear and pain any more. The fear and pain have been amply gone into, both in her experience and now in her understanding, and can be let go. They have been experienced, now let the events be open, let them be ventilated out, as it were. Really it's a rather exciting adventure to determine her own future! (A4151)

The study of Belle's tragic suicide and its aftermath, in both the excarnate and her next life, is only one example of what can happen when a person takes her own life. Every self-murder is an individual case. Man sees the act, but ''God sees the heart.'' However, in most instances suicide is taking the wrong way out of a rightfully difficult lesson. And karma, the great teacher, wisely does not let the soul get away with such evasion of learning.

MONICA

Suicide is a *person* taking his own life. Usually, the *soul* makes the decision to end the person's life, based on when the purpose is accomplished and convenient means are available. This is supposed to be in alignment with God's will and in conjunction with the advice of the guides and teachers. But a soul can build up karma if this decision is callously made.

A woman in her late sixties, Monica, requested a life reading. It seemed there was no reason for her to continue living. Her beloved husband and daughter were deceased; life held very little for her now. She was told that her soul had several times pulled out of incarnation without consideration for loved ones left behind. And now she was reaping that karmic harvest. The Monica soul is dear and fine, but had come to love spiritual realms so much that she rushed through earth incarnations. We pick up the reading immediately after the conductor has given Monica's name and birth information:

> Dr. John: God delights in the Monica soul and the Monica person, and her council, of whom four are present plus one from the...well, three of her council and one from their super-

visory council and one other person, who may or may not identify himself to me as the reading goes along, or herself. I believe it is an excarnate entity who was in the feminine expression while incarnate and, of course, is still feminine in the excarnate personality experience, too.

Well, Monica is an incarnation from the feminine half of her whole soul, so she is in her native gender, but she has had good experience in masculine incarnations as well as feminine, so there is a good balance there.

But there is a certain imbalance in the soul in that it has been a bit—well, I won't say tardy in taking its earth incarnations, but it has been so interested in the spiritual realms, in the cosmic schools for souls other than the cosmic school of earth, that it has gotten ahead there. It is—well, the soul is in the third stage, and well along in the third stage, over the center line; whereas in earth incarnations, it is just entering the third stage of around-the-midpoint.

There is a very interesting purposefulness right now. She is— well, she is almost sixty years old, and in some ways major purposes of her life have been accomplished, but there is one more major purpose which she is accomplishing now, and that is simply to enjoy earthliving.

This soul in the past, because of its spiritual slight imbalance—imbalance is too strong a word here, but because it has taken spiritual experiences with a certain accentuation of importance and has let its incarnate earth experiences lag— the soul has rather treated earthlives as simply ways of accomplishing certain experiences and gaining certain qualities.

Now this is purposeful. This is direct. This is straightforward. This is good in a way. But it misses one thing. For instance, when the major purpose of an earthlife is accomplished, this soul would usually terminate that earthlife. It did not stick around to see what earth itself was like in its own right.

Now the two major personal purposes of this life, to be with her daughter and with her husband, have been accomplished and ended. But the soul now has a third purpose, which has been a major purpose of this life all along, and that is simply to live earthliving.

Earth is a cosmic school of learning for the soul. Earth has its good things, and if she would awake in the morning, just lie there quietly in bed, enjoy the feel of the warm bed, think of God, think of herself as a soul having now the blessed experience of incarnation, being in a warm house or apartment or wherever, having some friends and having all the richness of human life upon earth open to her—and then get up to enjoy that during the day—this would really bring to her certain joys and certain choice goodnesses which really are attained in no other way.

There are such interesting books to read. There are churches to attend. There are plays and concerts and lectures and demonstrations and museums. There is the visiting of persons or groups of persons or displays. There is the vast richness brought into the home by television from which to choose the good things. (By 'richness' I perhaps mean more richness of material offered, a rich variety, many programs—not all of them are 'rich' in themselves! But there is such a profusion from which to choose.)

Yes, she might get interested in following one or several television series of programs. The public television sometimes will have things of a little more worthwhile nature than the commercial kind, more worthwhile for her.

But the point is, earth offers a rich profusion of interesting, rewarding things, and so the balance of this life, and I do not know how long this will be, can be well spent—well spent, I repeat—in simply enjoying earthliving.

Now, as I have said, there is no place else other than earth one can get this. She must do it now. Likewise, her major responsibilities are over. She has the leisure to do it. Likewise she has had the education, has the intelligence, the background, and the good mind to enjoy these things.

And thusly, she will be learning that the cosmic school of earth is one of God's wise, good provisions for souls, along with the other cosmic schools in which the soul has learning and experience.

She has lots of time. This soul has been in too much of a hurry when it came to earth. It wanted to get back to the more spiritual realms. But earth is a spiritual realm. It is the spiritual realm in which the soul has living contact with and experience in the material realm. It is the only such realm, the only such plane, the only such cosmic school. Don't hurry away from it. Don't get bored with it. Don't feel that time spent here is time wasted or half wasted. She can spend the rest of this life, and how long that will be I do not see, enjoying earth. Now this is not a counsel I give to very many. All too many are enjoying earth too much, are too wrapped up in the material aspect of living, and to them the message comes from prophets of old and from ministers and teachers and life readers of the present day to remember that the spiritual realm is the true home of the soul and the area of the more important values. But she already knows this. She has gotten a bit imbalanced in denigrating earth. As a soul she has not appreciated what earth has to offer.

Now in these golden years she has the freedom, she has the leisure, she has the opportunities to simply enjoy earth. If she were to do this for ten, twenty years, it would be good for the soul. It is not time wasted.

Yes, her spiritual interest comes first, and that is good. But that is already established. In her reading, let her branch out. Let her read some history. Let her read some novels, if she will, as well as spiritual books. In her activities such as they are—television, going out with some friends, or whatever— let her have the social, the artistic, the historical, the current news interest and such. Let her have some good earth interest as well as non-earth, spiritual interests!

This is the particular purpose for her at present. I can see it from her akashic records; and her council, all five of them— well, all four of them—are nodding, whereas the one from the supervisory council is watching quietly the council members and their guest. Yes.

This is the general placement of Monica and the purpose of the life at present. The other major purposes have been accomplished. This one stretches on and it can be good. It can be rewarding. It can be enjoyable. It can be relaxing. It can be done in a leisurely way, simply enjoying each day, each week, each month, each year as it comes along for what the earth brings to her. The earth is a very, very, very interesting place in which to be, especially in these days!

So many philosophies paint the picture of earth as evil. Yes, the soul meets and is to redeem evil on earth. But God has provided earth as a cosmic school for souls, with lessons which can be learned nowhere else. As a high school student one may not like mathematics, but it is definitely a required and valuable subject. Planet earth is a required and valuable subject for souls and should not be down-graded.

To illustrate the Monica soul's tendency to pull out of earthlives without considering others, we will bring in two pastlives which surfaced during the course of her life reading. The first one:

> Dr. John: Well, I find them back in the Roman Empire in the late 100s and early 200s A.D. This was a masculine incarnation for the Monica soul and it is rather interesting. The Monica soul chose to come and be a soldier in this vigorous world empire of Rome, this vigorous nation with its expanded reach which meant culture, which meant education, which meant wealth, which meant a certain laying of tribute upon the conquered areas.
>
> So the soul came in a good masculine body. It chose a family that had good heredity and where the, not the father but an uncle, was in the military service and secured for the nephew a rather good appointment. The nephew came in, did his basic training, did it well, developed skills with the weapons of war, and also a certain skill of understanding and administration.
>
> So he could have gone more into a staff position as it were, but he enjoyed the marching, the physical strength and exercise and exertion. So he, oh, he might be considered a sergeant today, a corporal, a sergeant, but he was definitely with the troops.
>
> And he was with the troops in their foreign expeditions. He saw much combat, relatively. He liked that and he was very skillful at it. He did not take undue risks. He protected himself, because he enjoyed his life.
>
> So having had that experience, then somewhere in his thirties—when he was about thirty-six, he was not yet thirty-seven—the soul decided it had had that experience in full, as it really had, and rather promptly died. It did not even have the graciousness to return home to die. It just decided it had all it wanted from that and it simply pulled out. It allowed some kind of a fever to come upon the body and it died within two days, I believe somewhere in the Egyptian area.
>
> This was really ungracious because the mother and others in the family had quite an outreach of affection and pride. At the very least, the soul should have waited in compassion and

in consideration for them until its next furlough home, which was due in a year or two, and had regaled them with his adventures and so forth, then after being home for six weeks or so, then die.

Of course, it would have been better in a way if the soul had lived out the full potential of that life, but the soul has had a habit of accomplishing what it wanted to accomplish and then pulling out. That is another reason why in this life if it will realize the full potential of the life energies within the Monica person by simply enjoying earthliving as I have pointed out for the remaining years, it will be a good accomplishment.

So the mother was still alive when her soldier son died, and when she got the word of it, it was quite a shock to her really. She, of course, was in her fifties or so and did not have the resilience of early youth—she may have been in the early sixties—the shock meant more to her in a physical strain than it would have had she been younger. Her hair visibly whitened and her spirits were dampened. It was not a nice thing to do to the mother, although the mother did not hold it against the son. The mother had no idea that this son's soul had had a part in this. She simply knew that the son had been a casualty. That strong man who had done so much and been so many places was stricken down, and so she mourned his loss.

The soul of the son rather dismissed this, saying, 'Well, men must die and women must weep,' and did not realize that he could have mitigated this blow, this grief, to his mother had he accommodated his own quick wishes or strong purposes to the larger picture. Yes.

They have had other lifetimes in which they have been supportive. They will certainly be together in the future. It is a good relationship. They really are growing together as souls. Yes.

The second illustration concerns a nephew:

Dr. John: Yes. He was in the 1400s A.D. with her. Well, this was as an Amerind, in a vigorous tribe. it's sort of on the United States and Canada border in the Great Lakes area, the eastern Great Lakes area.

They were in an advanced tribe. It was really quite a confederation of tribes, one with an advancing political development. They were beyond the hunt-and-forage stage of existence. They still hunted and it was a prolific place for game. It supported a larger population than many areas would have. They could range a bit south in the winter and a bit north in the summer. They knew their area quite well. The neighboring tribes were part of the same confederation. They did not fight one another. They were strong and they did not get marauded by those on their border. They did a bit of marauding themselves but mostly they knew where they lived and the others stayed many miles away. They knew where certain vegetable foods were. They had fish and fishing. They had some deliberate agriculture, raising of some crops, the maize and such.

It was an experience in this type of earth experience.

The then incarnation of the Monica soul was in masculine expression. The then incarnation of their nephew soul was the father, was a capable man; he was not one of the chiefs, one of the chief men, but he was one of the strong men who took part in the political decisions and the social decisions. He was physically quite strong, and rather large for the place and time.

The Monica soul saw that this would be a marvelous opportunity to have that kind of a life, so it came and had that kind of life. The son was not quite as strong or as large as the father but it learned from the father. The boy was more wiry and became more athletic. He had a good hard body which he trained by discipline and exercises. He was a good hunter. He was a very good swimmer. Swimming was not a usual undertaking of the Indians, but he had sort of a natural knack for it and he very much enjoyed it. Now, swimming was not a way of catching fish. It was more for his own pleasure. He loved to display his skill at this swimming, which was a real skill. He had almost a dancer's coordination of the body, coming probably from some pastlives of the soul in developing in the dance expression, and this enhanced his swimming.

So he was well known as a swimmer. When there was some other swimmer, he delighted to challenge him in speed and grace and such and he nearly always won. But he was not a braggart in that way. He was confident in himself, and not too many of them were really swimmers.

So that was a good life. He fathered two sons and a daughter who lived, had a wife who adored him. But again as he reached about the age of 40 the soul decided well, it had made a suc-

cess of that life, and so it pulled out leaving the others behind, the wife, the sons, the daughter, and grandchildren. This soul has been not meaningfully cruel but certainly thoughtless in accomplishing what it came to accomplish and then calling that incarnation done. Yes.
Conductor: Thank you. Very enlightening.
Dr. John: And that's one reason that she is alone now. Others have been purposeful in her life and their purposes were accomplished and they are gone, the husband and the daughter, and now she is alone. Yes. And she should experience it. But she can make the experiencing of it good, as I have pointed out. Yes. (A1299)

So karma, the great teacher, now has Monica experiencing "the other side of the coin." Before, she thoughtlessly, callously, pulled out of life leaving others alone. Now the others are gone and she is alone. But karma mitigates this lesson by opening to her an accomplishment for her soul, if Monica learns the value and the enjoyment of the cosmic school of earth.

PETER

Earth is not the only cosmic school for souls. There are many other cosmic schools in the spiritual (non-material) realms where older souls can be teachers to their younger brothers and sisters. Then, if they come together into incarnation the teacher can provide further training, by example, for the younger student-soul. the pupil can watch the older soul put into practice what he taught.

Admiration of the cosmic teacher is quite common and most useful, but must not be overplayed. if regard for the teacher approaches worship, the younger soul is out of balance and must be taught to keep his priorities straight. This is the lesson that the Peter soul is learning. The karmic result of becoming attached to a teacher in cosmic schools was to bring Peter into a lifetime in which the incarnation of the teacher had "feet of clay."

The life reading for Peter was given at the request of his mother, who wanted to better understand him. Peter had been badly disillusioned by his father—so much so that when the father died Peter had to have psychiatric help:

Dr. John: Peter is in his native gender expression. That is, he is an incarnation from the masculine half of his whole soul. The soul is into the third stage, the around-the-midpoint stage, and is perhaps about a third of the way through the total soulhood experiences. This includes incarnations and the other cosmic schools associated with the cosmic school of earth.

The soul ran into a certain deviation, possibly it might be called a detour of spiritual growth but actually it was more dangerous than that. It was a deviation of aim, as it were, even though the situation and the actual deviation had many good things among its causes.

It attended one of the cosmic schools, a cosmic school dealing with the understanding of incarnational experience and why souls have such experience and the general nature of them. But here, in essence, it became enamored of a certain teacher. The teacher was from the masculine half of its own soul, so the enamorment did not have the outlet of a 'crush,' an amorous love outreach. Rather, it was a very strong intellectual outreach.

It thought this teacher was a most wonderful teacher. And truly he was very fine. The concepts which the teacher taught and which the student understood opened new doors to the student, and the light that came in carried really an emotional content. So that there was a deep gratitude to the teacher, which had a great feeling-tone along with it.

This would seem as though it were a fine thing. But it tended to 'edge God out,' and the injunction included by Moses in the first of the commandments, the first four, which dealt with the total commitment to God, wisely includes the words 'for I thy God am a jealous God and will have no god before Me.'

In a small way this teacher began to, as it were, 'take the place of God' in the student's eyes. The teacher succumbed to the temptation to enjoy, to somewhat revel in, the student's worshipful adoration. This was not good for either of them, of course, but the teacher is farther along as a soul and the necessary corrections were more easily made. Partly because the deviations and meaningfulness to the teacher of the student's high approbation, was not as much as the meaningfulness to the student of this appreciation and emotional commitment to that teacher.

He put the teacher on a pedestal, and it was seen by the council for the Peter soul that he would have to be shown that his idol had feet of clay. This was done by bringing him into an incarnation with the teacher also incarnate, where the personhood of the teacher would have certain cracks in his story, so to speak; certain deficiencies in his own behavior which would reveal deficiencies in the soul's knowledge and ability to guide incarnations. This would result in a healthy disillusionment for the student.

The mother was brought into the picture, because this is the lifetime in which that disillusionment took place, to be a stabilizing factor for the son, the son-person and the son-soul, as it went through this painful but very necessary disillusionment and readjustment of sights and understandings and values.

The teacher to whom I refer was a cosmic family member, and the incarnation of the teacher to which I refer was the father in the present life to Peter as the son.

In the present life the Peter soul saw that his worship as it might be called, for it had in it at least some of the beginning stages of some of the elements of worship, which he felt for the teacher, had gone overboard and had gotten him out on thin ice—I really am mixing up my figures of speech here. But I trust that which I am saying is clear: That the son discovered that the father was not the all-wise person, the all-knowing one of how the soul could successfully guide its personhoods through the experiences of earthliving. And that the teacher soul was not all-good, and was therefore not really completely aligned with God and the processes and structuring of God. It has been a difficult experience for the person and for the soul.

If it were only a disillusionment for the person, he probably would have recovered more easily. But the disillusionment was for the soul also. So when the person was rocked by the experiences of disillusionment, finding his father was after all quite human and did not handle all the experiences with all wisdom and did not withstand temptations with all strength and commitment to goodness-the fact the soul was rocked meant that when the person reached inwardly within his own being he found even greater disturbance than there was on the outer level of his personality consciousness.

So it has been a rough go, but a very needed one. The soul already is recovering a bit as it begins to accept that which it has been forced to see by the events which have occurred. Is this clear?

Conductor: Yes, Dr. John, I believe it is.

Dr. John: This is the essence of this particular incarnation then as Peter. The person of Peter also has the experiences of being born, of growing up, of being a son, of becoming a young man, of becoming a man, of choosing a craft or trade or profession, of making livelihood, ordering his life. As you present the persons of whom inquiry is made I will know more about him. What I am saying here is that the person of Peter is a person and within the stream of life of a certain environment and a certain flow of events.

This regular business of living exists right alongside this problem with his father. In fact, the life might be called the river that carries him along, and the disillusionment with the father and then his own inner adjustments are, as it were, the boat upon the river within which he is travelling.

This disillusionment with the father is greater than it should have been. The father is only human, or only a soul, and soulhood itself is the very young stage of the Individuated-God-Being, the God-child. The father is not unusually bad. The father-soul assumed he was better, stronger and wiser than he really was. So the father-person reflected this aspect of the soul, in a personal assumption of goodness and moral ability and innate wisdom which really he doesn't quite have.

The toppling of the father from the pedestal occurred in the son's consciousness. But there is a certain corrective aspect in the present life and its, let us say foibles perhaps more than failings, which are a corrective for the soul consciousness of the father as well. That is being really brought to the father soul. The father has passed over, hasn't he, made his transition?

Conductor: Yes.

Dr. John: At such a time there very often is a review of the events of the life. Why? Because a new stage of life is beginning. This is why we ask that when a person comes for a life reading that he review the events and the personnel and the meaningfulness of his life to that time, because we hope the life reading will start a new chapter for him.

The person and the soul of the father have reviewed the incarnate life of the father. Both of them see the deficiencies. This is a soul that is advanced considerably beyond that of his son. He is well at or slightly over the centerline of soulhood and incarnations, perhaps a little bit more than slightly over the centerline, but not an old soul really. He will learn. He has enough stability in himself and enough graciousness to admit the mistakes, to see the mistakes. And yet he has enough character that he is not 'thrown into a tizzy,' as the saying is, by seeing his mistakes.

The son, on the other hand, does not have this greater substance to the soul and to the person, which comes from experience and deeper insights, that the father soul and person have. So the son is much more rocked on the surface level and on deep levels in the subconscious, on the soul level as well as on the outer personality conscious level.

Does his mother ask for him of the relationship with the father?

Conductor: Yes. That is her first person asked about.

Dr. John: Let us go ahead and take him now.

Conductor: The father is (name, birth).

Dr. John: A very fine man. But, on second look, not quite as fine as at first appearance, but I have gone into that. As the saying is, 'There is nothing wrong with him that reincarnation won't cure.' Also, the person and the soul have taken the revelations of his own need for further growth with graciousness, with acceptance. But I have spoken of that already.

These two were together earthwise in the 1700s in a German university. The father was a teacher, a teacher of philosophy and theology, but with a good general knowledge of that which was known in other fields. He was somewhat of a 'Renaissance Man,' in that learning interested him and he mastered it easily. In his classes he spoke from a broad background of contemporary knowledge and of historic knowledge, which very much impressed the students. He was a very good teacher.

The son was a student. The earth experience there reinforced the cosmic school experience which had already been established, and of which I have spoken at some length in the forepart of this reading.

The student admired the teacher and kept in touch with him, and was not disillusioned in that life. The teacher was a scholar and did not enter into the social or political life of that time. The teacher was not married. He had been married and there were two children, but the wife had died. The professor, for such he was and head of his department, had given the children to the wife's sister who brought them up.

The professor missed his wife. He had honestly loved her. Her loss threw him all the more into complete commitment to his learning and his teaching. He did not marry again. He did not take an interest in another woman. He used his loss to plunge him ever more deeply into his profession. This impressed many of his students, and certainly the student who was the then incarnation of the present son.

They have been together once before in a different circumstance. This is very interesting. This goes back into the 1100s, and it began in England. Again they are both in the masculine expression. The present father then was a duke or count or something, one of the peers of the realm, and a very able man socially, financially, and politically.

He was a real master of the practical aspects of living at that time in that place. Yes, he inherited his position and his lands, but he was very able in administering them. Also, in the general politics which swirled around the king. But the duke knew that the king was sustained actually by the support of his nobles. With this knowledge judiciously applied, without confrontation with the monarch, the duke 'walked tall' and strode with confidence, albeit quietly, in the national affairs of the country's politics and welfare.

When the crusades came along, the duke also showed his organizational ability and his military ability. He organized a unit which joined the crusade. His company was well equipped, was trained before it started out, and logistical preparations were made.

The then incarnation of the present son was one of the retainers of the nobleman, one of the younger ones. His father was one of the nobleman's retainers. The son went along on the crusade, admired the nobleman, found he could trust his judgment. He took care of his contingent of soldiers. He had a much stricter discipline than existed in some of the groups.

He also had a practical wisdom which did not accept completely the guidance of the clergy involved. He would say, 'Yes, Father, that is certainly right and this is the cause that we serve. Now as we serve God in this cause in this particular situation, we face certain factors and I would suggest we take this particular course of action.' The clergy involved may not have seen as deeply and might not have been ready to advise that course of action, but it was much wiser when they did, because the nobleman was wiser in practical matters.

Likewise, even if the clergy with the crusade would suggest something else, the nobleman went ahead and did things as he thought. He fortified their encampments when they were in places of possible danger. He planned certain strategies as they reached their goal and as they entered into battles. He knew that his strength depended upon the strength of his soldiers, his unit, and he saw to it that they were well fed, well led, well disciplined, well protected.

So in that life the then incarnation of the present son came to have a very honest and rightful admiration for the nobleman. The soul's openness to the nobleman was then used to bring the soul of the son as student to the soul of the nobleman, the present father and a teacher in a cosmic school. That was sort of the beginning of it.

The rest of the story I have outlined. That fine cosmic school start, the teachings, the reinforcement of it all in the German university life, the getting too far involved by the soul of the son and the father soul giving way to the temptation of accepting the adulation and assuming a superiority beyond what he actually possessed, and the corrective factors of the present life—this is the large picture within which I hope there are some elements of greater understanding for the mother of her son, Peter. (A2409)

Karma, the great teacher, knows that it is better for one to be disillusioned than illusioned. Peter's illusions about his cosmic teacher were certainly shattered and corrected by his father's present-life shortcomings. The problems that Peter has had in accepting that his god had feet of clay should teach that soul to refrain from again worshipping a false god.

MARY

Probably the most common examples of minor karma in the Loehr-Daniels Life Readings are found in relationships. A soul may make a passing grade in a lifetime, yet fail with one or two of the persons with whom he relates, thus building up negative karma.

One of the ways in which persons build up negative karma is through possessiveness. Each soul and each person is an individual and entitled to make his own decisions. Free will is not only one of our prize possessions but is one of God's firm values. If a parent, or any authority, imposes his own ways on a child without regard for that one's integrity, karma steps in to teach that free will belongs to all.

Mary's children do not listen to her, but turn aside much that she has to give them. Their attitude stems from a lifetime in Greece with Mary as a very possessive mother.

Dr. John: In the latter years of the 1700s and the early 1800s, in a lifetime in Greece, she was in feminine expression. She was of peasant stock, and she married above her. That is, in the sight of the personalities of that time, she married above herself socially. But the man she married was a weakling. With her strong roots and the characteristics of the peasant stock, she was the matriarch, and her home and the individuals in the home were her domain. She ruled with a great deal of firmness, although not always with wisdom. That life established some of the problems and relationships of the present life.

Her two children of the present life were among her children in the Greek life, and she did not do wisely with them. Both of them came from the realm of creativity. They expressed in very creative personalities. They did so in the Greek life and they do in the present life. In the Greek life, the peasant mother was not wise enough to recognize their creative temperaments. She was a practical 'let's make money'—'don't rock the boat'—'let's have no nonsense' person. She forced the children into modes of conduct and activity that were not their modes, that thwarted the creativity within them and therefore caused a good many problems and heartaches.

The children are with her again, and now she is much wiser. She learned by her failures in that Greek personality life, and she further learned when she got to the other side and could look back and assess. She is a wiser mother. But in spite of her wisdom, her influence upon her children is somewhat removed. She does not have the influence and control the Greek mother did. She has done well with them in this life, but she has more to give them than they will accept. The fact that they have not accepted and will not accept all that she has to give is karmic, and is because of subconscious resistance on their part, stemming from the Greek life. They subconsciously shy away. They want to accept, yet something within them keeps them from reaching out and taking more than they do take. This is right; it is right for them and it is right for this soul. This soul must learn she cannot direct and command and shape other human beings, even her children. The process of physical birth does not make them hers. This she knows; we do not have to expand upon it. (AB731)

A dominating mother may get by with controlling her children in one life, but sooner or later the cause she put into effect will return (this is what karma is) to teach her that she cannot shape another's life.

HENRIETTA

Petty jealousies between two persons can build up over more than one lifetime to hatred. And that hatred can cause a person to do unspeakable deeds. This is exactly what happened to the Henrietta soul. This masculine soul developed a rivalry with another man in the 1300s which mushroomed into hatred and murder in the 1500s. After that lifetime the Henrietta soul was appalled at what it had done and was filled with self-reproach. the other soul was resentful and angry. Although some help was given to both in that afterlife, the present incarnation brings them together to handle the negative forces—as father and daughter! (Henrietta is the daughter.) It is no surprise that there has been much conflict between Henrietta and her father. She describes their connection as a love-hate relationship. There are pastlife reasons:

> Dr. John: They were together in a lifetime in the 1300s in India when India was divided into many small states, each with a ruler. Perhaps we should say provinces or districts rather than states. These two were in masculine expression, and were rulers of two rather prominent provinces, prominent in the sense that they had wealth, prominent in the sense that they were strong and had a way of reaching out to attach more land to themselves and increase their borders, and such.
> It was inevitable that conflict over who should have some

of the smaller fiefdoms would arise between these two strong rulers. And although the early conflicts were resolved it was also inevitable that in time the desire for growth and increased strength for each province on the part of both leaders would bring them into serious conflict with each other.

They were both very strong men. Each became very jealous over the 'haves' of the other. But they were constantly besting one another in different ways. The personality expression of the Henrietta soul was the superior one and did outdo the other, which created a jealousy on the part of the other. These forces were never resolved. Actually, had they come into open combat it might have been a good thing. An open combat leading to a winner could have been an expression-point to drain away the competition and the jealousy that existed between them. But it did not come to that. The situation was not resolved, so that lifetime ended with these competitive forces and their backlog of jealousy very much alive as personality forces which flowed into the soul entity of each.

They came together again in a life in the 1500s rather briefly. This was a life in Arabia in which each was a member of rival desert tribes. They were not the leaders of the tribes, but each had a devotion, a commitment, to his leader.

Now very interestingly there was a certain sense of honor and, as it were, rules to play by, among these desert tribes. These two met as solitary figures. They met unexpectedly at a water hole during a period of cessation of hostilities. It was the perils of the desert recognized by the tribes which gave them rules of honor and conduct.

The personality expression of the Henrietta soul was at a watering hole when this personality, member of the rival tribe, came to it literally on his hands and knees. He was very much in need of water. But the personality expression of the Henrietta soul disregarded the rules of the desert, the rules of fair play. He saw an advantage over an enemy. He approached the other one and literally stood with one foot planted on each hand of the other. The other was weak and could not move, could not struggle, could not get to the water. The personality expression of the Henrietta soul taunted the other, teased him, tormented him, and then drove a sword into the back of his enemy, and hurried away, carefully covering his tracks so that he was never discovered.

Now this incident of course released the soul presently the father into the excarnate stage, in a state of much suffering and even more anger and hostility. They have not met since that time. They could not meet in the excarnate plane because first the hostility and resentment on the part of the soul now incarnate as the father had to be diluted as much as possible by cosmic teaching and healing.

When the Henrietta soul was released from the personality expression, and as it surveyed that personality life from the other side, it entered into a state of quite extreme self-reproach and recrimination. And that had to be, as it were, cut down to size. It was more than the soul could handle had the two of them met. So they did not meet in the excarnate personality plane.

These forces, created in that lifetime, and of course to some extent stemming from the earlier life in India, were handled to some extent in a cosmic school of learning. And the two souls were readied to handle the continuing forces which could be handled within the framework of an incarnate life. That has been the present life.

With the Henrietta soul carrying in a great sense of inferiority and a sense of reproach and self-blame, and with the other soul coming in with some of the jealousy and resentment and anger still present, it was rather inevitable that they come into conflict.

The other soul, the father, was prepared to—that is, prepared by his own assumption—to meet this soul in masculine expression. Finding it in feminine expression somewhat threw him. It was a counter, it counteracted at least some of the continuing hostility. It put a rein on some of the expression of the hostility. This situation would probably have been worse had the Henrietta soul been in masculine expression. But also the Henrietta soul in its self-reproach in a sense 'asked for it.' It said in a sense, 'I'm no good! I've done a terrible thing. Do unto me as you will,' which is not too wise an approach on the part of any soul toward another soul.

So this lifetime has been a releasing of negative forces from both souls in regard to each other. We would say that the negativities have been cleared away so that in forthcoming lives these two can begin a rebuilding not accomplished in this life. But they have cleared the way and reached the place where they can build together positively in future lives.

The major thing of importance we would say to Henrietta in regard to this relationship is to use her spiritual insights and understandings to forgive and to love. A little exercise we might give here to help in the process of forgiving is to use the Lord's Prayer. Use the phrase, 'Forgive us our trespasses as we forgive those who trespass against us.' Now on one hand, as it were, she might place herself with the wrongs she has committed in this life and in other lives—she does not need to know them or itemize them, simply knowing there are mistakes is enough—put them in one hand. As it were, put her father in the other hand. And in the prayer-framework reaching out to God, ask to be forgiven for her own mistakes even as she forgives the other soul and the personality for his mistakes. Allow the one to balance out the other.

This is a prayer exercise which would be of much spiritual benefit for both of them. That is, we do not expect the father to do it. We suggest Henrietta do it. But in the doing of it there could accrue spiritual benefits for both. (B3193)

The Henrietta soul allowed its jealousy in the 1300s to grow into murder in the 1500s. But through this life as Henrietta, the soul is not only paying its karmic debt but also is beginning to learn how to get along with the one it wronged.

When one hears of the law of spiritual cause-and-effect, the first tendency is to think of karma as God's great justice. But also it is His great teacher.

A soul which misses an opportunity can learn by coming into a lifetime without that chance. Through her humble birth, Clara has come to appreciate the advantage of being born into a high-middle-class family. The present life is teaching Lois to value every incarnation, whatever the difficulties. And Polly is increasing her respect for disabilities.

Karma can also help a soul to balance its priorities. Even a good thing can be carried too far. Because he has been so drastically disillusioned with his present-life father, Peter will hesitate to worship another soul. Monica is experiencing the pain that can result from too quickly leaving earth to return to her beloved spirit realms, and hopefully her personal hurt now will keep her soul from forgetting that courtesy to others in the future.

Many, many souls learn consideration of others by experiencing the effects of thoughtlessness. Through her children's attitude, Mary should increasingly respect the free will of individuals. Henrietta and her father, both strong masculine souls, in their karma together are mitigating and expiating past strong-men mistakes.

Karma, the great teacher, insists that the God-lessons, the God-values, be learned. Karma sets up the schooling and provides the laboratory for that learning.

CHAPTER SIX

THE SPIRITUAL COMPONENT
OF HUMAN BEINGNESS

In the preceding chapters, Dr. John several times used the term "the values of God." A soul must learn the values of God before it can progress, before it can even comprehend the importance of a failure in an incarnation. Therefore in order to understand this important learning progression of the soul, the values of God—spiritual components—should be explained.

Usually when the soul first enters into incarnate life it comes with spiritual doors open, but soon it must close these doors so it can concentrate on the materiality of earth. At some later point, frequently in the forepart of the third stage, the soul gradually opens again to the spiritual.

The materiality of earth is expressed in the physical facts of God's creation, while the spiritual (or non-material) is expressed more as the values of God, the good which God has His heart set upon for incarnate life on planet earth. Discovering the material facts of God is the earnest pursuit of the soul in its early incarnations—learning how incarnate life operates, how to take mastery of the earth body, how to operate successfully as a human being in the material realm of earth. The spiritual, or the values of God, is more of a secondary quest until the soul has firmly established itself in the material.

But the very reason for attaining success as a human being on earth is to bring in the values of God. Establishing the facts, mastering material survival and knowledge, is essential before the soul can build the values of God upon a firm foundation. These values have been aptly expressed by the ancient Greek philosophers as truth, beauty, and goodness.

The masculine-feminine division of the soul for purposes of incarnation has a place in this material-spiritual progression. The masculine half has major responsibility for the physical success, the very survival of the race, and therefore it has a greater gender affinity for material factors. The feminine half has major responsibility for the development of those qualities which make the human being more than just an animal—the values of God, the discernment and achievement of the Creator's purposes in bringing His children into incarnate life. Hence the feminine has more of a gender affinity for the spiritual components of life and the universe.

After our considerable study of the soul, certain incarnational patterns have emerged. For instance, a masculine soul will customarily open to the spiritual during a feminine incarnation and after a number of them. But likewise we have observed that the feminine soul needs a solid grounding in the strengths and realities gained primarily through masculine incarnations before it can successfully and productively open to the nonmaterial, or spiritual, components of incarnate life. The soul really is not ready to undertake the adventure of discovering and developing the spiritual values of God on earth until it has sufficient incarnational strengths and soul individuality to handle the nebulous, nonmaterial aspects of God's multi-faceted values.

Awareness of life after death is for many of us the primary orientation in the spiritual component of our beingness. This is a growing edge for both the person and the soul. Recognition of life after death and the experience of some of the psychic phenomena associated with it, prepares the consciousness of the personality for more than only its own incarnate existence. This awareness is one of the keys to expanding the consciousness, both while incarnate and after the death of the body.

A very material personality is doubly handicapped. Such a person simply misses a great deal of the richness and diversity of human life, which spiritual awareness opens to us. Then when the person dies, the consciousness is not prepared for a continuation of life. Therefore a very material personality may be absorbed into the greater beingness of the soul after a relatively short time, losing all personal consciousness.

But when a personality is conscious that there is more to life than the material body, it has the necessary incarnate preparation for a start on life after death. As it grows further spiritually on the excarnate plane of personhood, it can explore the astral and etheric realms for hundreds or perhaps several thousands of years before the personality co-mingles its forces with the greater beingness of the soul. A personality open to the spiritual can continue to be a growing edge for the soul long after the death of the body.

With the introduction of the personal spiritual forces, a new dimension is added to the soul's beingness. Future incarnational experiences will carry a growing knowledge of the values of God. Although there must still be a number of lifetimes directed primarily toward the material, the soul will have in its beingness a deeper understanding of the Creator's value-system. It may find spiritual satisfaction in simply observing God's work in nature, or it may express its spiritual awareness in an appreciation of the arts. Or the soul may develop a material personality but with sufficient compassion to help others. Once introduced to the values of God, the soul can manifest these qualities in a number of ways.

Melding the spiritual with the material in earthliving is an important new beginning for the soul's education and this learning is taken step by step, just as carefully as the soul has learned to walk in the materiality of earth.

JORDAN

The values of God are something that have to be sought. They are not presented within a formula, although certain life settings provide a better framework than others. The life can be very humble. In Jordan's previous life his father was a poor Jewish man in New York City, happy with his lot in life since he was able to come to America where freedom provided opportunity. The Jewish father instilled his philosophy in his son, now incarnated as Jordan. This simple life paved the way for continued spiritual growth in his present life.

Since Jordan is a seeker after truth, Dr. John began his life reading by giving some basic explanations of the soul's advancement in searching out the facts and values established by God. We begin this excerpt with the indentification of Jordan's soul progress to date:

Dr. John: Yes, his records are here. This is an incarnation from the masculine half of his whole soul. He has had a rather busy session of earthlives bringing him to his present soul position, and this is an interesting point. He is in the third stage, the around-the-midpoint, in which the largest number of incarnations of any of the five stages of just-beginning, well-started, around-the-midpoint, well-along, and nearing-the-end, are had.

He is not yet at the centerline but is approaching the centerline of the third stage.

When the soul comes into incarnation, at times it has, in its very first lives, doors rather wide open to the spiritual realms which are more native to the soul. Life is native to spirit, not to matter, and the soul, being an Individuated-God-Being, a God-child, is particularly native to non-physical or spiritual realms rather than to the realm of matter.

So in the earliest incarnations, at times, not always but at times, the soul carries into incarnation open doors and quite an awareness of spiritual realms. But the time comes when this must be closed off so that the soul can, while incarnate, specialize, concentrate, focus on the necessary work of incarnation.

What is the necessary work of incarnation? Well, from the soul's standpoint it is to have and successfully pass through all the major experiences which can be had in incarnation. But what is incarnation? It is actually the soul being in a living, vital association with an earth animal being.

The human being really begins as an earth animal being. It partakes of all the evolutionary processes which have evolved life from its simplest beginnings, that is, evolved life in matter, from its simplest beginnings up through the vegetable and the animal realms or kingdoms. Then, when under the direction of those who were working with this development eons ago, it came time for the soul, for certain reasons, to make a personal vital living association with an animal form, the animal form that was chosen was rather carefully selected as having qualities which were deemed to be most conducive to the purpose of the soul in coming into incarnation. And then this animal form was given a little extra boost, as it were.

Then the soul 'squeezed down' to make living contact with it. You might say it aligned its current or its vibration or whatever with that form so that it could take a very direct part in the life of that form, even to the extent of the mind of the soul operating in and through the brain of the animal, the human animal, the person. In fact, the person is the interaction phenomenon, actually, of the soul, the Individuated-Godchild, with the, as we would say, highest form of animal life upon earth.

After the human species has been established as one which lives in conformity with the truths of God—which are both facts and values; in other words, to know what the facts are of God's structuring of this phase of His universe, and then what God values, what God is purposefully endeavoring to obtain in the human walk of life—then the person, the human being, guided primarily by the soul, is to not merely know and accept but to enthusiastically accept, to desire, that which God has structured, as being God's way, God's truth, for incarnate life upon Geos, planet earth. This is what truly is 'Thy will be done, Thy kingdom come upon earth as it is in heaven'—the Greek word of heaven there being the word indicating the spiritual rather than the material realms.

Now how does this apply to our friend, Jordan? The soul, as I have said, must learn how to focus upon earthliving because this which I have outlined is quite a job. Life in matter is alien to the soul but it must learn how, because as a child of God it is 'learning the business from the ground up' and must learn what God has structured, what God has willed and brought about, in every realm of being and every plane of expression within each realm into which it comes, and these patterns are different, of course. Even as God is the same, He has certain patterns which differ for the different planes of expression within the different realms of being.

So the soul is learning that which is God's will, God's way, in each realm and plane into which it comes for expression and for development. It must do so to grow in God-nature and in God-powers, and to increase in compatibility with God and in companionship with God.

Now this earth learning is, as I have said several times in this reading, of sufficient complexity and importance that it requires the focused attention of the soul even to the extent of not paying too much attention to its own spiritual nature for a period of time from the early lives up into the time when it is doing a pretty good job with earthliving. Then the time comes to reintroduce into the soul's earth consciousness the awareness of other realms.

The Jordan soul has reached that stage in this Jordan personality lifetime, this incarnation.

Now this is, of course, one of the initiations of the soul. An initiation is simply a further beginning, a coming onto a new level, the breaking into a new life in consciousness. It is a graduation and a commencement, a graduation from one level and a commencement of another, and the graduation and the commencement usually overlap.

But it is not something which is only an insight. It begins with, as it were, an insight, a light in consciousness. But to bring the spiritual awareness into more and more consciousness during earth beingness is quite a process, really. It makes a great difference. The great dividing line of humanhood really is the dividing line which separates those humans who know there is a spiritual component to their being, and that the spiritual component is the eternal component and certainly the most important component in the long run of immortality—from those who do not know in consciousness that they are more than only a physical material being.

This is the great dividing line. Jordan has reached it. He has crossed it. And this is the initiation, the beginning of the process of bringing spiritual knowledge and values into earthliving and as a human being, and this process will continue for many, many, more lives.

Well, Jordan as a soul has reached the stage in this incarnation, of the reintroduction of the spiritual component into consciousness, into the consciousness of the earthbeing of his incarnation. This is not something that is completed in any one lifetime. It is a new beginning. It will mean a difference in the lives to come. It means a difference in this life.

It also means that in pastlives this soul has really successfully completed a number of requirements, of taking mastery of earthliving in various manners and experiences.

That is the introduction to Jordan as a person.

"The person, the human being, guided primarily by the soul, is to not merely know and accept but to *enthusiastically* accept, to *desire*, that which God has structured as being God's way, God's truth for incarnate life upon Geos, planet earth.'' This important discovering of God's way and God's truth is many-faceted. The enthusiastic acceptance was expressed by Jordan's previous-life father, the Jewish man, and passed on to his son. That was the first spiritual life for the Jordan soul and served as a good springboard into the present incarnation.

When Jordan asked about his wife in this life, it was brought out that she had been his older sister in the Jewish life:

Dr. John: In the immediate pastlife she was an older sister. Now this life began in the Balkan area and then came to the present country. Well, the then father and mother came. They were from a persecuted Jewish group. They came to this country, they came into New York, and the father became a 'sheenie'—I suppose that is spelled s-h-e-e-n-i-e—a term I use with certain endearment.

Yes. With the ingenuity which marked them, he found work to earn a livelihood, driving a horse and a wagon—first a pushcart but then through a bit of sacrifice in living, acquired a horse and a wagon and hence enlarged his livelihood, and had his regular route. He would buy rags and paper and bottles and metals and he would pay the people enough so that they would sell them to him, and then he would have his own outlet for selling what he had collected, and he made enough to support his family.

The present wife was a sister then. Both of them were children to the sheenie. The father and the mother instilled in their children a great appreciation for this land. They did not ask for welfare. All they asked was a chance to make a livelihood and to express themselves as best they could. They were rather devout in their Jewish community, which was of a particular kind. I do not see quite what. But it had its own rituals and such and they were very appreciative of this land giving them the freedom to be themselves and do their own religion. They instilled this appreciation very deeply in their children.

The then incarnation of the present wife was at that time his sister, about two years older. She and the brother were close, the cosmic family bond manifesting in that way. The brother, when World War I came—or rather when this country got into that war—enlisted with a great enthusiasm, with a great happiness at being able to serve this great country which had given them the opportunity, because the parents had told them of the life which had existed for generations before in the ghetto where they had been, and then the cruelties and the persecution which had forced them out even of that rather unhappy life, and the freedom here was so appreciated by the parents and they passed that on. They instilled that appreciation within their children.

So this one was quite happy to enlist. He was a foot soldier. He was killed in action. He was—he saw his seventeenth birthday about the time he enlisted but he was killed shortly before his eighteenth birthday.

The parents missed him and mourned him but they also honored him and the gold star which they displayed in their window was a badge of honor, a mark of their love of this country and the fact that they, too, served and had given something for this country.

Now, the young man's life was cut off at that point. He did not regret it. He knew when he went in there was a possibility he would die. He served well. He was just a private in the ranks. He was a foot soldier, served in the mud and in the trenches and all, endured the hardships well, and when he was killed there was no great bitterness at all on his part. This was part of what he had done. He was met on the other side by those who were then working with the soldiers, and taken on. He was congratulated for his loyalty to duty. He was a good soldier, not one of the world's brightest but certainly bright enough, and he obeyed orders. He had trained well and he was a good soldier.

But the consciousness was limited. That being went on, I do not see just how far, but I would doubt if it went very far beyond the lower astral plane, and whether it is still in expression I do not see.

There was not then the spiritual outreach that there is now, but the ground for it was laid because of the Jewish faith and devotion of the parents. They simply knew that there were certain things that were more valuable than any comforts or any social acceptance or even life itself. They held to them irrationally because they did not try to defend them rationally. They knew that these were values, the values of their culture;

and that, in a way, was a certain spiritual outreach. It was centered in their religion, of course, their religious teachings which he would not really accept very much now, but it laid a good grounding for this bringing into earth consciousness of spiritual awareness, yes. And this will mark the consciousness probably of all the succeeding incarnations of the Jordan soul.

In this life Jordan is seeking the spiritual, trying to find the values of God through various religious teachings. He is not a church member in this life, and in the question portion of his life reading he asked why organized religion was not part of his religious seeking now:

> Dr. John: The sheenie's religion is not enough for this incarnation of the Jordan soul. It had its value. We hope he sees that it had its values. But really the past and present major formulations of religion have only a small portion of total spiritual truth, and he is seeking the larger. Even as death seems to be the negation of the spiritual nature of man but is not, because life continues on after this experience of the bodily death, so the present presentation of religion leaves too much to be desired to be satisfying to the earnest seeker today. He is seeking more, and that is quite good.
>
> As the Master said, 'He that seeks shall find.' Not all in one quick moment, but in the much more productive and satisfying way of continuing to find through all the days of his life, yes.

Even though the religion of the 18-1900s Jewish sheenie is not enough for Jordan in this life, it was a good introduction to the values of God, and certainly has its beneficial effect on the present life.

At the end of the reading, Dr. John noted that his present-life father, who had died, was quietly sitting in the council area listening to Jordan's life reading. This father is an older cosmic family member serving as a wayshower to his son in this life and other lives. He sent a message back to his son, telling him he is doing a good job. Then Dr. John pays his respects to the former father, the Jewish man:

> Dr. John: The present-life father has been quietly sitting in

on this reading, at the invitation of Jordan's council of guides and teachers.

The father is a little older soul than Jordan and on the soul level was pleased to learn of some of the pastlives of his son. The father is somewhat of a wayshower although is not the sponsor soul. I do not see the sponsor soul. But the father has been a wayshower, an older brother soul, let us say, and he sends his love and his greeting. He says, 'I knew you could do it.' And he says something else—something like, 'Now you know what you've done and I hope you are more satisfied with yourself.' I do not quite understand this but I presume it is some kind of a message. Maybe the father used to joke with his son a bit saying, 'You are doing better than you know,' or something like that.

Did we identify the sheenie son's father?

Conductor: I don't believe so.

Dr. John: Well, he is one to be respected and Jordan might, as it were, send a postcard to his own father to be put up on some celestial bulletin board for the father in that immediately preceding life, to say, 'Thanks, father, for the good things you did for me then as father and instilled in me, which have carried on.'

That about concludes it, I believe, and we wish him a happy bon voyage on the way ahead. May each day be one with at least an extra sunbeam of light and some days with quite a large additional ray of light, for this, the walk ahead, is into greater light. But sunlight and spiritual illumination are so large it will take a number of lifetimes, a great number, and then going beyond the soul stage and into the other stages of growth as a God-child. So do not believe that you can encompass the full sun in any one lifetime. It would be quite blinding and it would kill him if he did. But as he grows in capacity there will be ever more light to be grasped and made his own in which to live. (A3604: 1-4,8-10,18,19)

The immediately prior Jewish life was a simple life, but one dedicated to the values of God within the structure of the parents' understanding. And it withstood the pressures of their difficulties. Also it was important as a guiding light for Jordan's soul in opening to the spiritual. Jordan is building additional spiritual understanding in this life and certainly the lives ahead, as the nebulous non-material aspect of the values of God encompasses a wide variety of experiences.

CHRISTOPHER

The arts manifest one of the values of God—beauty—and are spiritual in their nature, since they are generated through the mind of the artist and are non-material until expressed in a form such as painting, sculpture, dance, music. This type of expression of God's values also can serve as a spiritual opening for a soul, as in the case of Christopher. In a 1400s life as an artist, he captured on canvas the life around him. Although he did not go down in history as one of the great artists, his soul experienced the values of God in that life, and that feeds directly into the present life:

Dr. John: The Christopher incarnation is a breakthrough point of the soul in the regaining of knowledge of the spiritual dimensions of reality and of his own beingness, and the incorporation of that knowledge with the physical knowledge of earthlife and with the physical events of earthliving.

This has certain advantages, because certainly the person who is cognizant and intelligent about the spiritual as well as the physical components of himself and the universe knows more, has more knowledge, has more wisdom, has more of 'the truth that sets us free.' So it is very handy in that way.

Likewise, it is particularly satisfying to a soul that has never lost its touch with God. The soul that has always known it is basically spiritual and did not let a too intense physical consciousness during some incarnation or other 'hook' it onto the material plane—that soul will find a particular joy as it is allowed and encouraged to open the spirit doors into its personality while incarnate—open those doors again, I should say.

This is that particular lifetime for Christopher, but he had a past lifetime of preparation for it. Going back about five hundred years into the country of Italy, he was born into the masculine expression with a somewhat frail body. The frailty was a part of his real nature then, and not from any accident or illness.

He had an artistic ability. He lived in a fishing village, lived there all his life. He, of course, had a father, but the father died. I do not see any other siblings. He took care of his mother, who was very congenial and close to him, a cosmic family member. He provided her livelihood by his artistry expressed in painting.

His painting was recognized as good. He painted the sea, he painted the life of the fishing village. The people who lived in that village knew the sea and knew their own life and recognized that in his paintings he had caught not only the appearance of it but some of the essence, the spiritual essence, of the sea and of their life in that fishing village. The word of his artistry spread, and people came from a distance and bought his pictures well. So he provided a good livelihood.

Now there is a close association of true artistry with the spiritual dimension of life. Both of them go beyond the mere physical dimension and mere material considerations, you see. So that life, which was a fairly full life—he lived most of forty years or so—was a preparation of a sort for the present life. Let me say, it was a first step in this reintroduction of the spiritual component into the earth consciousness of an incarnate existence.

So what is the purpose of this life? It would seem as though the purpose is to reintroduce the spiritual consciousness, but that is not really the purpose. The purpose is to reintroduce that spiritual consciousness in a particular way—which is, to keep it in a good balance with the physical. He is quite right not to have become a hermit or a monk, not to have secluded himself in some way.

When the spiritual is reintroduced into incarnate consciousness by a progressing soul, it must not be as an alternative to the material interests and undertakings, but as a part of a well-balanced life. This is a larger achievement, it is a larger spiritual achievement. It is carrying the knowledge of God—in the sense of the knowledge of the spiritual components, the nonmaterial components of man and the universe—onto a higher level. Now it is not simply knowing that these components exist, but it is knowing that they are a part of the total being, which by now has incorporated physical living and certain physical mastery as well.

Many lives in the spiritual are everyday-life centered, not completely devoted to a religious order such as found within a monastary or convent. The life-oriented spiritual incarnations promote a more balanced understanding of God's values, since they blend the spiritual components with the material. The arts are definitely one way of dealing in both the spiritual and the material.

When Christopher asks about his father in this life, Dr. John brings out that he was the father in the 1400s life, but died when the boy was between two and three years old. Therefore these two souls are picking up a relationship interrupted five hundred years ago:

> Dr. John: This is interesting. It turns out he was the father in that 1400s Italian life, but he did not live very long there. He sired his son, he enjoyed the baby and loved him, and loved his wife. But he died when the son was about two-and-a-half to two-and-three-quarters years old. So he was quite glad to have him back as a son this time.
> Now that death was not done voluntarily by the father at all. The father missed his wife; the father missed his son. The father had his own plans to continue in that life, and it was a good life and he was a success within it. Actually, the father in heredity contributed more to the artistry of the son. The father, by heredity, had a fine voice and loved singing, and people liked to hear him sing and would sing along with him. He had artistry, which with him came out in a musical way and with the boy came out in the way of painting, of drawing and essentially painting.
> The father and son are not cosmic family members. They may be third cousins, so to speak, but they are not close within the expanse of cosmic family. He was chosen to be the father in the 1400s because his hereditary makeup included some genes of artistry which were seized upon for the personality of the boy. This was why; and of course they are back together now to finish the relationship begun then. They may not come together again or they may. It is not patterned. There are forces there.

The "artistic genes" can manifest through any one of the art forms. Also the artistic nature is carried in the soul forces. A soul interested in the arts may express through music in one life, dance in another life, then have an incarnation as a poet, and perhaps have a culminating life as a great painter. And these lives usually are not consecutive. There may be a life in the 100s B.C. in dance, for instance, then the soul will continue its development in another area.

By the 400s A.D. the soul may be ready for another artistic life and choose to be a poet in India. After further soul development, there may be another artistic life in the 1100s as a proficient musician, followed by a life as a talented painter in the 1600s.

When Dr. John speaks of "genes" in the life reading, he is speaking of physical heredity, not soul development. The 1400s incarnation of the Christopher soul did not have the soul forces behind him to be a great artist, but he had the hereditary forces of the father to help bring in the artistic qualities in that life, which provided the necessary impetus for the soul to have its first major expression of the values of God.

In the present life Christopher is again a seeker. He works in a government job, but has a part-time avocation in the spiritual. One of his questions dealt with meditation and he asked Dr. John to give him some advice in achieving more through his meditation:

> Dr. John: My general answer is that Christopher, although quite correct in his over-all search, is making a bit of a mistake in this detail. He will make more progress in activity than in meditation. He is not geared for the contemplative life. I think I have mentioned that he would not have made a good hermit or monk. He is in a life of activity.
>
> He may feel that this blocks him from achieving what some people achieve in meditation. That is true. But (1) very few achieve greatly through meditation, and (2) he is not geared for that. He is geared for active study. He is geared for exploring, for knocking on many doors, sampling, getting what is good in each.
>
> He is a hummingbird, drawing from a thousand flowers rather than concentrating on one. He simply is not geared to becoming a great meditative mystic or entering into psychic progression in that way. But on the whole, hardly one in a hundred who try it find that which the masters in the field proclaim for it. Meditation is not necessarily the best way.
>
> Here he might consider corporate worship in a group; the scripture reading and prayers in a church on Sunday morning may bring him more in spiritual insight than his own forced meditation might. He may find that singing with a group, singing hymns, Sunday School songs and such, may bring him

more spiritual experience than a forced meditation would.
There are many doors. If meditation does not yield to him,
do not waste himself trying to kick in that door. This would
be my counsel.

Conductor: Very good, Dr. John. This does complete the
material I have for Christopher. Do you have a final word for
him?

Dr. John: Yes. My final word for him is a rather interesting
one: Let him view his spiritual achievement not as being a
mountaintop guru, not as becoming a great teacher, but as
himself joining the onward march of those people who are
growing in spirit. This is a minority in the human race, but
there is a very fine companionship with them if he can see that
it is his growth in potential, rather than his achievement of
leadership, that is success for him in this life—all the time keeping it well-balanced with a sensible, successful physical earthlife.
Here is where he will find his greatest joy and satisfaction,
because this is that for which he is geared and that which is
purposed for this lifetime. (A1192:2-5,16,17)

This does not mean that incarnations completely given over to
religion—a monk, nun, guru, meditative mystic, etc.—are not right
for certain lifetimes. But the spiritual seeker working in the everyday world has more opportunity to explore in many directions. And
with the explosion of opportunities opening in the twentieth century,
this often has proved more fruitful than meditation, not only for
Christopher, but for many of us. The spiritual components, the
values of God, are more readily available now to the true seeker than
in the past.

The present life of Christopher is only the second incarnation of that
soul with the good earth achievement behind it to re-open now to
the spiritual. The first earth "genes of the spirit" came in the 1400s
life. Now his search has broadened. But as yet there is not the solid
achievement in incarnation to successfully participate in extensive
meditative practices. If the soul wishes, then in some future incarnation it may be able to follow a fulltime religious profession. Now
is the time to blend spiritual practice with day-to-day living.

ESTHER

One of the values of God is the nurturing of others. There are many
ways in which this can express in life. A loving mother may come
first to mind, but there are innumerable avenues for this flow of
helpfulness one to another. In this life Esther is finding her way
through psychology. This particular way of experiencing the values
of God directly relates to her immediate pastlife, when her soul first
opened to the spiritual while in earthliving.

In the 1800s the Esther soul experienced an incarnation as a nun.
The personality had a choice of marrying a young man from her
village or entering a convent. Since her masculine soul was not too
adept at feminine living, it felt some uneasiness at accepting a full
feminine life as a wife and mother. The life as a nun offered another
way. Dr. John points out that either choice would have been correct. Since her friend, the present life sister, joined the convent, the
1800s personality of the Esther soul finally decided to become a nun,
too.

But this choice had its problems. This masculine soul found itself
wondering why certain practices were accepted, why certain people
acted one way and other people another. She wanted to ask questions, but the convent was not the place to do that. She was expected
to conform to the traditions of the past centuries. In this life, circumstances have provided her soul with a personality and life
mechanism for finding answers to the questions the former nun asked
within herself.

The life as a nun was brought out when Esther inquired about her
sister, who is an older cosmic family member:

> Dr. John: Now in that immediately prior lifetime, the nun
> life, the sister nun, the cosmic family brother, the present life
> sister, was able to really enter into the mystical part of it, the
> contemplative part of it, to accept the framework, perform the
> rituals and do the service, really without question, entering in-
> to that experience-framework for the experience which it held.
> But the Esther soul rather fretted within her own self. She
> wanted to understand more. She had not yet progressed far
> enough in the feminine to be as fully acceptive of a nun-life

framework as was her sister. The masculine forces were a little closer to the surface in that feminine personality. She wanted to understand more. She wanted to be able to discuss the doctrine, to question some of the teachings, to find the why and such, and she found this was not really encouraged among the sisters.

And she wanted to understand more about people. Why were some people nuns and others mothers, and some quite nonreligious and non-maternal even though feminine? Why was there this great diversity of human reaction to the same sort of experience? Why could some accept a teaching quite easily, and some could not? Why did some get a great deal out of the prescribed prayers and others, including herself, really didn't get what she saw her friend getting? And she wanted to understand people more, the personness of a person. That little nun sometimes came fairly close to getting into hot water, but was wise enough to shy away before getting burned; but within herself there was an incomplete acceptance of that which she was taught and of that framework of life.

This of course sowed good seeds for the present life and for several future lives as well, and God does welcome a soul with an inquiring mind. Yes, God could also enjoy, let us say, the sweet worship of the other nun. That did rise as a perfume to Him, in a manner of speaking. But He chuckled a bit, let us say, at the then incarnation of the Esther soul, who in her prayers had one corner of her mind asking questions. And so He has given her now an incarnation to ask her questions, to find some more answers. And she will be asking questions for several more incarnations as well. And finding answers as well. Yes.

In centuries past there must have been many people who asked questions that could not be answered by the traditional means—the whys of how people thought as well as the whys of our universe. In this century many questions have been answered through the objective, factual knowledge of science. What really was an impossible dream a scant hundred years ago has opened some answers to the little nun's many questions through the present day field of psychology.

Actually the whole area of science has built roadways to new thoughts and illuminated the facts—we now have medicine out of witchdoctoring, jet travel instead of horse-and-buggy, etc. But the essential ingredient left out of the scientific exploration to date has been the spiritual, the values of God. As Dr. John brings out in the next excerpt from Esther's life reading, scientists are discovering the parameters of God's universe through the factual but without including the purposes of God. Facts and values combined are needed if we are to have the whole truth. He also names the field of psychology as one of the important advances of mankind:

Dr. John: There have been stages in human history, and these are usually particular to some environment, some culture, rather than general for all humanity, when certain developments took place. Now I am speaking primarily of major developments, because the change taking place now is destined to be truly as major as was the introduction of the scientific method, or the coming of the Industrial Revolution, or the change from the hunt-and-forage type of early tribal life to the settled type with agriculture, or the change brought about by the domestication of animals. These all are important historic changes, as you know.

The historic change of importance now is in human understanding of itself—people's understanding of what humanity is. The major change which will be brought into this is the recognition within a scientific framework of a spiritual element.

The spiritual element has been prominent in some past cultures, of course, but it was in the old framework wherein what the people know—or thought they knew—was by the prescientific methods of getting information such as I have outlined before, tradition and authority and special revelation and such. Well, I might as well add intuition and speculation and personal experience, and there we have the six major ones. And so the spiritual component was kept in the thinking and the philosophy of the people through the nature of the religion of their culture. This has been a very important factor of religion, overlooked by many of those who rather shallowly think that they have outgrown religion in the new knowledge of their day—whatever that new knowledge of their day might be. Yes.

But there has been introduced into essentially the western culture, from which it has spread quite widely, a new way of

knowing what God has done, what truth is, and that is the way
called science. It is the way of objective, factual knowledge.
I have gone into this upon a number of occasions, and I believe
that Esther is acquainted with our teaching on this matter.

Now the important thing is to introduce the spiritual components of man and the universe in which he lives, into the
'scientific' world view. Yes. This must be done in the full integrity of the scientific approach. There may be up ahead a
way of knowing that supersedes the scientific, but it will be
reached only through the scientific, and there is no shortcut
to it. Likewise, it is the scientific way which is the way for now
and for the next century largely. Yes.

So into this must come not only a knowledge of what God
has done—the actual material facts of this physical creation
(and I might add parenthetically that the scientists *must* come
to a realization that whatever is true has been made true by
the Creator of it all)—but also a concept of the *purpose* of the
Creator in whatever He has done. This involves, as I have said
before, the aspect of values. I would place values alongside
facts in this categorization, although the values themselves are
facts and extremely important facts of God's creation. To
understand what God has done, and perhaps how some of it
can be replicated, without a concept of the values, is to miss
the purposes of God; and a man then 'thinking the thoughts
of God after Him' to the extent of taking mastery of some of
the aspects of the material creation, but without the purposefulness of God, without a knowledge—I don't mean only
a glimpse, but a knowledge—of the values which God has His
heart set upon, would be to use the developing God-powers
of man in a most un-Godlike way.

This is the big purpose in which Esther can have a part.
Esther can find her place in this enlargement of human
knowledge, or build her place, in several different ways. It is
not by accident that she has been in the field of psychology,
meaning the understanding of human behavior, the cause-and-
effect framework of it and just what the causes are that lead
to effects and how bad effects can be ameliorated, and how
wrong causes can be found and set astraight. Now this is important, and in the whole field of psychology the aspect of value
is rather large. It is not simply the communist approach to

psychology, finding out how people work and then pulling the proper strings and ringing the proper bells to get them to do what the masters want them to do, to control behavior in that way.

Rather, in the western approach the whole approach of psychology is really value-oriented: How can human behavior be understood, ameliorated, changed, built, to achieve certain values, to the individual first and to society next, values of peace, values of tranquility, values of creativity, values of joy, values of problem-solving—sometimes values of problem-evasion, of course. And so psychology as she knows it and has studied it is right in this line.

Now also, there is the matter of the spiritual component of mankind which psychology, desperately seeking substance and acceptance by being 'scientific,' has largely avoided as yet. But man never will be understood or understand himself, nor know how to live the good life, nor be taught how to live the good life, with an evasion or the downplaying of the spiritual element, the nonphysical component of his being and his life.

This would be like trying to explain the rainbow without the color red. It simply could not be done, no matter how you emphasize the blues and the yellows. And so to understand man simply in terms of material values and animal nature does not explain man and does not understand man. That vital color of the spirit must be added.

Esther was born into the present family because there are ties with the family members as I have brought out, but also because this family has sort of a family purpose as I have said, and it gave to Esther a framework for having a part in the pioneering of the adding of the spiritual element to the understanding of human behavior. Yes. (A4406:7,20,21)

Fortunately for Esther, she was provided with the family setting that emphasized the spiritual but encouraged her to get a good education, thereby combining the facts and the values of God. As a psychologist the little nun who "made God chuckle" has this lifetime and several lifetimes ahead to find the answers to her many whys.

Science itself is asking questions, placing them within the factual parameters of discovering DNA, space travel, the "Big Bang," etc. These are important factual discoveries. But as Dr. John emphasizes, leaving out the purposes of God—the spiritual element—is the same as denying one-half of God's reality.

Facts and values are both part of God's structuring, though the facts are easier to find first, since the values—the non-material element—are more nebulous. The soul coming to earth discovers the facts first, and the values are brought in when the soul is more firmly established. The new field of science is discovering the facts first, but is nearing the time for purposes to be introduced—to add the color red to its rainbow.

ARIETTA

Not all spiritual learning for the soul is accomplished in the earth realm. Other cosmic schools the soul attends also provide spiritual knowledge for the young God-child, the soul. What the soul learns in other cosmic schools about spirituality is interpolated into the earth realm as the values of God, and this covers a number of facets.

Arietta's soul has attended classes taught by the Master, Jesus the Christ, in other cosmic schools. This is not unusual. It is part of the divine order that more spiritually advanced souls and personalities teach in other cosmic schools. This, of course, includes the Master.

In this life Arietta is a mother, therefore her soul is expressing the values of God in a nurturing role. But there has been much suffering in her life. Two of her sons have died. One son was killed in a car accident. Since she does not ask about the other child, we do not know how he died or learn from Dr. John the reasons behind the death. But her spiritual nature, which has been definitely tested in this life, has held firm:

> Dr. John: This is an interesting soul. The Arietta person comes from the feminine half of the soul, and thus this lifetime is in the native expression, the native gender of that soul. The soul exhibits in its beingness many of the qualities and characteristics called feminine in earth persons. It is a trusting soul, and yet it has learned not to trust too openly. Even as a girl on earth, growing into womanhood, must learn to guard herself, and to guard her heart, and to give her trust only where it is deserved. This is simple prudence.

So although this soul has much of the quality of trust, it has likewise learned to guard itself and to place its trust only in that and those who win that trust. It has learned that it can trust God. It has known this with a deep knowledge as a soul, and that knowledge has never been shaken. It has learned also that it can trust Jesus the Christ. This is more of a learned trust, an acquired trust. She has acquired this trust in Jesus the Christ because of teachings she has received, both on earth in various incarnations, and in cosmic schools other than on earth.

She has met the Christ in some of the other planes. She knows Him as a wondrous Being, and this is enough for her so far, as she has been in the group listening to Him. She has personally accepted Him as her Leader, her Master, as the One who understands life and can lead her safely through it.

Yes, she has both seen and known suffering in this life. More than most in some areas, although it is difficult for anyone to truly know the amount of suffering another has experienced, or to know how to judge that suffering. An experience which would be a little suffering for one person, can be a lot of suffering for somebody else. So when we think we are experiencing a great deal of suffering, and more relatively than others, we really cannot tell. From that we can learn several things: Of course, not to judge another. But also we can learn that since there are others who may experience that which we call great suffering, but somehow not be shaken by it as we, we can learn from them how to undergo our own suffering without quite so high a cost to ourselves.

In this realm the soul, through its many incarnations, experiences pain and suffering. It is part of earth, since this is the dwelling place of evil. Yet the pain and suffering could be diminished if people understood more about death. Death is not the ending of life, but a new beginning. The first stage after death is the astral realm, which is similar in structure to earth. When Arietta asks about her son, who was killed in a car accident, Dr. John indicates that he is enjoying life more in the astral realm than he would have on earth had his life here continued:

> Dr. John: I shall now say something which is impossible and yet is a guideline for her: Do not grieve at Jerry's death. This was a part of his probable life pattern from the beginning.

Every soul must have several incarnations in which the life is not lived out fully to a 'ripe old age.' There was no particular purpose in taking him over at this time, other than to give the soul the experience of experiencing and of managing a person, one of its own personal expressions, its own incarnations, who had expected to go on, had plans to go on, and then quite unexpectedly and suddenly was taken out of earthlife. The soul is handling it pretty well.

We speak of this now as being an experience for the soul, you see. Just like an infant death is an experience for the soul and for the parents, rather than for the person of the infant who dies. The Jerry person has likewise taken the experience really quite well. It was more of an eye-opener to what he is now into, than a grieving experience for what he left behind. He did not have, really, any great commitment to the Jerry incarnate life. Sure he had ideas, he had friends, he had things he'd like to do, places to go and see, and such as that. But really, when he came over to the other side, he was quickly caught in the greater opportunities that are there, and he has more interest in these larger life dimensions.

He had a certain artistic nature, and he can do more with beauty on that side. He can do more with pleasing lines and form, and there are more colors with which to work. So instead of being caught in a consciousness of being deprived of the further years of this incarnate experience which he had expected, he is caught in a consciousness of what he is into now as a greater experience, a greater dimension, a greater world in which to live. He tries at times to get this word through to his mother, also to his father and to the others in the family, and he is thankful that we are getting this word to his mother now.

Jerry will be there to greet his mother when she does step over at the end of the incarnate stage of this life, and he will have much to show her and to share with her. Although she will not be bound to him, nor he to her. But they will be together for the full extent of their love and their companionship, and it will be quite a healing time for Arietta.

Incidentally, she can enter into this healing time now. She will understand more of this. She understands enough of it now to make a start of the healing relationship with Jerry. He will not be present very much of her time. He has things to do also.

But she can know his company. She may feel his approach at times, or she can call out to him at times; and he will come to her at least occasionally when she calls. And she will not be holding him back if she calls to him and he comes. Something like calling by long distance a grown child in this life. You don't call every day, but when you feel like it you do, and on birthdays and holidays and Christmas and special occasions, why yes, put in a call. (A1349:2-5)

So one of the soul's various incarnational experiences is an early unexpected death. It is part of the learning process. Of course, those left behind can be overwhelmed by their grief. Even understanding death does not take away the pain, but healing can be accomplished sooner if there is the realization that life does exist beyond the earthly body. In the book *Death With Understanding*, the death experience and the life after death are explored in depth.

Arietta's son has caught the larger expansion of the astral realm and is working with the designs and colors there. One of the purposes of the astral is to complete life. Many people die wishing they had done more. A personality who catches the larger potential of the astral can live out life's dreams.

MATTHEW

The "second death" is spoken of in the Holy Bible. (Rev. 2:11—"He that overcometh shall not be hurt of the second death.") What does it mean? Dr. John uses the terms "first death" for the demise of the physical body and "second death" for the termination of the personality. When Matthew, a true spiritual seeker, had his life reading, Dr. John brought through some extensive teachings about the first and second deaths. The following excerpt begins with his introductory words to Matthew:

> Dr. John: Yes. Well, the introductory statement for this one really would be in the words of the Master, 'Blessed are they that seek, for they shall find.' Now seeking is more than just a matter of ten minutes. Seeking is a quality of life. It is a knocking upon many doors, discovering the doors that open, entering in, sampling what is there, and deciding to stay in that open door or to seek another.

Matthew is a seeker and that is the major element of this incarnation and its purpose, its placement in the ascending ladder of his many lifetimes.

But a second element is that those who find must use what they find, and so along with the Master's words, 'Blessed are they that seek, for they shall find' must be placed the parable of the talents which the Master told. The servants who find are among the servants to whom things are given by the very giver of life and giver of all knowledge, and that which they are given is to be used. It is not to be buried. It is not simply to be savored by themselves, although it is to be enjoyed of themselves. But it is to be used as opportunities come.

Now for the identification of the soul: Matthew is an incarnation from the feminine half of his whole soul, but I want him to understand this. This does not indicate any effeminacy in his character or personality, but it does mean he carries from the very nature of the soul many of the finer qualities which are needed to mix with and improve the masculine qualities.

Without the feminine contribution, man would be only another earth animal and the most dangerous predator of them all and a predator upon himself. But with the feminine qualities man realizes that he is essentially a spirit—being begotten of God; not simply a collection of matter which has been structured and given a pattern of beingness by the Creator and impressed with some particular consciousness, but a child of the Creator, begotten of God, possessed of potentials of God-nature and God-powers.

Now these potentials need to be discovered, and then a decision made as to what are the values that the individual places upon them, and then to develop these qualities if the individual does value them.

Matthew values the things of the spirit. Matthew knows that these are really primary to immortal life. The values of the spirit are not necessarily primary in mortal life. The human animal can survive, at least for several decades, without the values of the spirit, but upon the death of the animal body what then would be left? It is the knowledge of the spirit component, it is the development of the spiritual nature, it is the valuing of the spirit above the flesh, which gives 'treasures in heaven.' Actually this is what gives life after death any significance and continuance. It was a bit of a primitivism, but not entirely a mistake, when some of the early mystery religions said that in their teachings of the spiritual nature of man they were *bestowing* immortality upon that individual person. If an incarnate human being on earth has utterly no concept of himself as a spiritual being which will survive the death of the body, he may in consciousness fully die when the body dies. You see that this is so?

Before the personality can survive beyond the initial entry into the astral realm, it must be aware of life after death. This is one of the "treasures of heaven." It is the bestowing of immortality upon the individual.

Dr. John: He has identified himself as being the body and/or he has identified life as being the life of the body. If then this is a hard-set consciousness with no chinks in it through which a greater light can come, then death can be death for him.

Now, somewhat as a diversion of thought and yet a line of thought which Matthew will appreciate, let us turn from this first death, which is the death only of the physical body, to the second death. This is, in a sense, the termination of the personality.

Now there are some whose spiritual sights are so low, whose spiritual ceiling is so low, there is no concept of beingness beyond the body. And so for them, although there may be a carryover of life from the incarnate to the excarnate phase of the personality, they do not progress beyond what we call the lower astral realm. And here, conductor, please send to Matthew, with our compliments, a copy of our book *Diary After Death*. This explains what we mean by 'Post-Mortemia, a suburb of heaven,' and the lower astral realm and the chance to progress far beyond that into higher spiritual levels for those who are potentialed and energized so to do.

Now, what do we mean by potentialed? Well, some persons have a beingness which simply does not have the potentials of going beyond the physical or the lower astral planes. But those who, particularly in the incarnate phase, develop a consciousness of other dimensions of reality and other dimensions of their own inherent innate beingness greater than are expressed in the physical expressions or greater than can be fully realized upon earth, those folk have a potential in consciousness as well as in beingness to become more, you see. So when they drop the body, which is a limitation, they are potentialed to go farther.

Now, as they are interested in it and as they have poured some of the life energies of their being into the study of the spiritual, they are energized to make the start and then as they do make the start on the upward ladder to where the ladder is left behind and the wings are used, in a manner of speaking, there is further energization. The great energization available to persons and to souls and to God's children is to love God, because in loving God a love is returned. We open ourselves to the greater love of God and this is the highest energy. God is love. Man does not understand that fully. We do not understand that fully in our higher plane, either, because this is a tremendous aspect of the Creator. We understand the Creator more as we grow in our own God-nature, but there is always more. The God-child is to develop his God-nature and his God-powers.

The love of God! Who can understand it? But even on Earth, as we His children come to know and appreciate Him, we can begin to experience His love for us.

Dr. John: So the person leaving the incarnate plane of expression behind at the death of the body comes into the excarnate plane. Many earthly spiritual exercises give him glimpses of this plane or perhaps a very brief little insight into it or experience of it, but this is not too important. If he knows that it is there, it is not too important that he visit it in an out-of-body experience or astral projection with consciousness before he goes over. If he knows it's there, it is there waiting for him, and he knows the way. If he has a spiritual nature which can express itself in mysticism and in worship and in spiritual studies and in certain philosophic outreaches, or in any of these, he has made contact with that plane. He knows in his consciousness that it is there and he can await God's timing for him to enter into it more fully and experience it, even as while incarnate he is experiencing the physical plane and life as God's child in this plane most fully.

However, the person, the personality, the personhood, is not eternal. It is immortal in that it can survive beyond the mortality of the body. Just how far it survives depends on how it is potentialed and energized to go further, and also upon how much it is purposed to go further. The personality is an expression-point of the soul, of *some* forces and aspects from the soul, and an experience-point for the soul, making contact in actual active living experience first in the physical realm of being and then in the beginning spiritual realms of being.

So the personality can continue to be used insofar as it is an able expression- and experience-point, and insofar as it is purposed to be used. Every personhood is different. Not all of the soul is incarnate at any one time but only selected aspects of the soul, because there are certain purposes that this incarnation is to accomplish, other purposes for the next incarnation, and the soul takes its experiences of earth and of the excarnate realms, too, in a series of personalities, each one especially designed, tailor-made, with a recipe, a formula, for its own particular purposes.

It is the soul that is potentialed for eternity. And I use eternity and immortality not as synonymous. Perhaps technically in earth usage they would be considered synonymous, but I use them in this particular way: The personality is immortal in that it is possessed of life beyond the mortality of the body. But the soul is eternal in that it can progress beyond the span called 'immortality' of the person.

So there is a second death. For those who do not go beyond the lower astral realm, that is where the second death, the termination of the excarnate person, takes place. For those who go beyond that, as Matthew certainly will do, the second death lies much further in the future and after he has, as a person, gone beyond 'Post-Mortemia' and 'Over the Mountain into the Land of Lights.' I am using phrases here from our book *Diary After Death*, to which I refer him to understand these; and that book may reward several readings, for much is there, put in simple language but with a meaning that probes deep and goes high. Yes.

Now what is meant by the second death or the death of the personality? Incidentally, I happily acknowledge that the term 'the second death' has different meanings for different religions, different teachers, different systems of thought. I am using it here in the sense of the termination of the personality, even as the death of the body is the termination of the physical, material body as an active, knowing, living organism. The death of the body means the end of the body except for a brief and shadowy carryover, which is somewhat akin to but usually lesser than the carryover of some of the lower animals, into an astral period of existence. But the death of the personality is far different. It is an *expansion*, not an end. The person is limited to the consciousness which it has and has developed in personal expression. As you know, conductor, I have been bringing through elements of teaching as to the nature of the realm of consciousness for the past year or so and there were some introductory teachings in the earlier readings of the past twenty-five years. But this is something which I am permitted now to bring in fuller detail in these latter days as the New Age comes from early dawning into ever brighter light.

The personality is limited to the nature of consciousness of the person. Now this can grow intensely. Education expands it. Experiences which are assimilated into wisdom expand it. Studies expand it. But nevertheless, it is the nature of the person's consciousness, and there are other levels of consciousness, so at the death of the person—the second death as I use the term—that person-consciousness can expand into soul-consciousness.

The Orientals, who have a rather mystical approach and some understanding of spirituality and its primacy, despite their hanging onto primitive teachings and methods of spiritual knowledge which have been surpassed by the Occidentals' approach involving objective observation and study to ascertain the facts, knowing that facts are the truth of God—the Orientals have a phrase, 'The drop of water rejoins the ocean.' They have hold of a basic truth here. The personality does not actually cease, it expands. It no longer is limited. It can enter into the consciousness and the beingness of its own soul.

Now this is not 'rejoining God.' This concept of union (or reunion) with God has a certain value to it but it has quite a factor of misleading most students as well. God individuated the soul. He begat the individual souls with an eternal purpose. He did not want simply to absorb them once again, as a parent does not care to absorb into his own being the children whom he begat and reared. Rather, God wishes to have companionship with His children, and ever greater companionship as the children mature. As the children grow in their person-nature and person-powers, they are more compatible with and companionable with and partners with their parents. And so as God's children grow in their God-nature and their God-powers, they become more compatible and companionable with God and co-creators, partners with Him, which means a great deal more than any of us as yet know. The infinity of God extends beyond both eternity and immortality.

So the second death understood in this way is like the bursting of the seed pod. Well, it is more than that. It is the bursting of the bud that the flower may come through. It is the bursting of the cocoon that the butterfly may emerge. It is all of this and more, as the personality's consciousness and beingness enter into the soul's consciousness and beingness.

Now the soul has been learning from and, in a sense, contributing to and drawing from the person's consciousness and beingness all along, particularly as the person is a good instrument and grows. Some persons are not very good instruments for growth. Some souls are not very good souls, either.

It is his own soul, the Individuated-God-Being, that the person joins when his 'drop of water rejoins the ocean.' Or another statement attributed to the Eastern religious philosophers is that the person is drawn back into 'the seed atom' of his beingness, which would be the equivalent of what we understand as soul.

So the second death is a tremendous expansion. The first death is the end of that which dies then, the physical beingness. The second death is an expansion. For those who haven't gone very far, it can be the ceasing of the personality beingness on a rather low level. Then that which was good is drawn into the soul but there is not enough to really appreciate the great expansion of beingness and consciousness into which it enters. And so it finds its place, it is more absorbed than expressed or expressing in that merger, let us say.

The second death of the personality is actually an expansion into the soul. It is not the union with God, for the soul is expected to grow beyond the soulhood stage into the stages above; therefore it would not accomplish anything if the personality—or the soul, for that matter—rejoined its forces with God. Souls and other beings begotten by God as His children were created to be companions of God. Souls are the young God-children He wants to continue growing, to continue to be His companions as we develop in our God-nature. And in the earth realm, it is the spiritual element that increases our God-nature, an intelligent spiritual element which encompasses both the facts and the values of this realm. When the personality is spiritually open, the second death is a tremendous blossoming—a beautiful new beginning.

Dr. John continues Matthew's life reading by explaining that the spiritual studies must begin in the earth realm, since there is no spiritual starting point in the astral.

Dr. John: Entrance into spiritual studies by a person must be begun upon earth, for if there is no beginning while incarnate, there is nothing to connect with, there is no starting point for further spiritual development, in the excarnate personality.

When there is this beginning in the incarnate phase, as Matthew has begun, there can be many frustrations, there can be glimpses without full sight, there can be momentary whiffs of a fragrance without the great experience of inhaling deeply the wondrousness of the other realms, there can be brief tastes flitting over the tongue without the full savoring of that which is so tantalizingly tasted.

However, the start is there. The first taste has been had. The first smell of the fragrance, the first opening of the eyes. And this is tantalizing because the human consciousness is limited in what it can achieve in this way simply because it is on the incarnate plane as a human earthbeing. It can be frustrating. However, let me say, 'All things in their own time.' If a flower bud has started to form, it may take in some flowers much time to become ready to open and the bloom to appear. And if an impatient gardener were to assist it in opening, he would not find the flower within and he would destroy that flowering bud. Now, Matthew is not going to destroy the flowering of his spiritual consciousness by wishing that he could do more, but let him be content with doing what comes to him.

Now what is it that 'comes to him'? Well, whatever does come to him of spiritual door-opening, of spiritual studies in which he finds himself challenged, in which he finds growth of consciousness, let him enter into it. Let him push himself slightly to understand it, but let him not chide himself if he senses that there is more than he now can possess in full consciousness, for I assure him, there is more than any incarnate being can possess in full consciousness. But this taste, this glimpse, this whiff of a fragrance, is the beginning point from which, when the excarnate phase of life comes, he can make great progress.

The—well, perhaps it is time for me to sum up what I have been bringing, which is a teaching, but a teaching that is applicable to Matthew. The teachings which I bring in these readings are an important part of and reason for these readings, but each one is applicable to the person getting it. The teachings I and the team that works with me bring are not brought in the framework of a philosophical system. They are brought in terms of life principles, spiritual life principles, which apply to specific individual human beings right where they are, and this matter of the growth of consciousness is certainly applicable to this living person Matthew.

The soul in its earliest lives carries a certain instinctive spiritual awareness, but then this customarily and almost universally must be dimmed so that the soul can focus on developing within its personhood that consciousness which is native to the human realm of beingness, and this is needed if the human is to survive and also if the person is to gain the mastery, the successful living, of the events and relationships of that human life.

Is this understandable, conductor?

Conductor: Yes, Dr. John. It certainly is.

Dr. John: So there is a period then, in which the spiritual consciousness customarily seems almost lost, certainly clouded, and this is a correct period because there are other emphases. But as the soul gains experience it must reawaken, reestablish within the earth consciousness of its own personhood, the spiritual awareness.

It is in the latter part of the second stage and early part of the third stage that usually the spiritual element of consciousness is reintroduced, and reintroduced with a greater cogency and power than simply the spiritual instinct of the very young soul. Here the spiritual consciousness within the personal phase of living is more robust. It becomes not just an instinct but a wisdom, a knowledge, a power.

This is where Matthew is. This is what the Matthew incarnation is doing in the evolution of the Matthew soul.

Well, I believe that about introduces Matthew to himself,

and we trust this basic understanding will help him all the rest of his life in knowing himself in the job of living and growing, which is within his hands, helped, of course, by the guides and teachers who form his council, of whom four are present and one from the supervisory council.
Now, he must still do the growing. He still must find his answers. He still must seek. It is not that God ever gives to His children all the answers and says, 'Look, here is the manual. Here is the blueprint. Here is the final word. Now just simply follow it.' Because part of the growing is to discover what God is like, and we discover what God is like to quite an extent by discovering the God-nature and the God-powers within ourselves. This is true on up the ascending ladder of the growth of the God-child. (A815:2-9)

When the spiritual opens for the soul it is an ascending ladder as the soul discovers the values of God in all the planes and realms the soul enters, and gives the personality the "wings" to travel far and wide. The spiritual rebirth provides a greater understanding of "what God has His heart set on for the soul." And it is a flower waiting to bud and bloom when the time is right.

SOPHIE

Sophie had heard the name "Leiadel" in her meditation, and asked what this meant.

Conductor: She asks, 'What or who is Leiadel?'
Dr. John: Leiadel is one of her council. As the name is mentioned, a rather tall—well, let us say an entity that gives the impression of being tall, but it may be simply because she is slender. In other words, tall in one generation for a woman might be four feet ten inches. In another generation it might be five feet ten inches.
But she was, for her time, slightly taller than most, and slender and quite willowy, quite graceful. She is speaking to me: 'I was with this one in an ancient, yet not so ancient, temple life in the civilization of Egypt in the period before the Master was born as Jesus of Nazareth. We as girls were chosen to receive training for work within the temple. Our parents agreed, and we ourselves were happy for the training.

We were not separated from our homes, although we spent nights in the temple as our training progressed. We were not among those who were terminated early in that training. We were continued in the training. We had certain abilities of the psychic nature and were developed by the occult methods then used in our mysticism, our touch with other realms. We became seeresses within the temple, or practicing psychics who could bring psychic insights into the personal problems and relations brought by those in the area for which this temple was responsible, and some such as teachings to the priests for the teaching sessions.

'We had a closeness together then which has enabled me as the excarnate person from that time—that time was in a later period rather than an earlier period of Egyptian history, the 300s B.C. or so, 400s B.C. maybe—but our work and our spiritual development then has enabled me to become a spiritual guide, and the closeness with this one enabled me to be chosen as one of her council of guides and teachers for this incarnation. I feel honored by this. It is an undertaking of happiness on my part. I hope she will not feel that I am some far-off strange being. I am her friend from a pastlife. Now my soul has had other incarnations since then, but both of us in those personalities created a beingness which could go on a long way, and this is why I exist now and can come in this capacity. I cannot bring her all that I know, for she does not have in her present personality earth consciousness the receptacle points, as it were, for receiving all that I know or all that the continuing excarnate personality of herself at that time knows.

'But I can bring much and I do bring a personal contact with her which itself is valuable in spiritual guidance, and which is a source of sustainment as well as of guidance, of companionship. She and I can again companion as she opens up more and more to me personally and opens up also psychically, and I would hope and suggest to her that she, at the proper time, look into your method of psychic development. It may be that this would be that which would help to open her spiritual doors a little wider, and if not yours, then other methods would be brought for her to try, yes.

'I bring her love, the love we knew before, and I would say again—do not think of me as some far-off angelic or occult being. I am her friend from a former time. In that relationship I can bring her more than if she would put me on some cloud or pedastal.'

Well, she got through very well, didn't she.

Conductor: Oh, thank you, Dr. John, because this was of great concern and interest to Sophie and it was a great need.

Dr. John: How does Sophie spell the name of her friend?

Conductor: She spells it L-e-i-a-d-e-l. Leiadel. She's not sure of the spelling, but this is as near as she can get. Is this close?

Dr. John: Oh yes, it is quite phonetically adequate and that is the important thing. I do not know how Leiadel would be spelled in English. This is certainly quite adequate. It's rather hard to translate ancient Egyptian into modern American English. This is very fine. (A1411)

Leiadel has existed as an excarnate personality since 400-300 B.C. and is now a guide for the Sophie person. This gives us a glimpse of the life of the excarnate personality operating in the etheric realms. The book *Diary After Death*, written in story form, gives further insight into the astral realm.

As Dr. John has said many times, there is plenty of work to do on the other side. An excarnate personality does not sit around on a cloud playing a harp. And Dr. John usually adds, "Unlike earth, there is plenty of room at the top," meaning of course that responsibility increases as the personality learns—another exciting concept of growth for the soul. There is also evidence in the life readings that existence on the other side is not all work and no play. Occasionally Dr. John will follow a past personality and report back that he/she is "romping the star lanes." Or two people who had a special love in their life are sending back the sweet fragrance of their continuing and growing love and joy.

Even though the astral and etheric realms are somewhat a mystery to us, there is a small opening into the "hereafter" through the life readings. And these messages send the signal loud and clear of not only life after death, but also of a joyous and rewarding afterlife.

This does not mean we should seek the astral while on earth, because there is nowhere else for the soul to learn what it can learn on earth. This plane is unique, even though sometimes a demanding existence for the soul. And one to be treasured. But let the spiritual, which is a true component of our human beingness, be instated and well-guarded in our soul and person consciousness during our incarnational experiences and growth.

God's values augment in the soul's beingness the "moreness" of life on earth and beyond. For a soul first opening to the spiritual this is the beginning of an exciting adventure.

CHAPTER SEVEN

SPIRITUAL MISTAKES

"Mistakes are a part of growth," says Dr. John. "To be able to look back at something in your past and say, 'That was a mistake, I would do it differently now' is to show that you have grown since then. If you had not grown, you would not now be seeing the better way to do it. And if you look back and find nothing you would do differently now, you have not grown." This is most comforting. We need not be conscience-ridden and memory-haggled by past mistakes.

We make spiritual mistakes as well as earth-material mistakes, and they, too, are a part of our growth, our spiritual growth. As we would expect, our spiritual mistakes are really mistakes of our soul. In thousands of life readings and tens of thousands of pastlife recalls, a present life shows how what was done in a pastlife was not the best way to handle a situation, and we would do it better now. Profound spiritual growth requires the reincarnation framework, if for no other reason than to set our mistakes in perspective. Our personality framework of mistake-correction-growth is of course of our present life only, but our soul's framework of mistakes-corrections-growth is multi-lived.

In this chapter we see how the balanced growth of the soul, through both masculine and feminine incarnations, is so very important. Seeking the values of God must be an intelligent endeavor. It cannot be obtained with the shortsighted approach of understanding God from the narrow scope of only one gender, or one church, or the knowledge gained within only one lifetime. Therefore the soul experiences lives in all major religions, philosophies and cultures, and must gather this knowledge and shape it into an intelligent interpretation of God-values.

The values of God must also encompass the facts of God and of man's God-given role within the universe. The soul, in its endeavor to comprehend the values of God, sometimes leaves out the facts and misconceives God's way, God's truth and God's desires for planet earth, and ends up with mistaken and twisted answers.

Since the facts of God have been majorly the province of the masculine half of the soul, it is necessary for the soul to have sufficient masculine strengths and accumulated wisdom to make intelligent spiritual decisions. The misunderstanding of God-facts can lead to degrading experiences for the soul. Calling God's name ten thousand times does not change the prescribed formula of an intelligent path to God's values, no matter how sacred the religious order or the religious ceremonies practiced by the personality of the soul. Intelligence and the eagerness to follow God's way for planet earth are the keys to a joyful communion with God.

Presented in this chapter are some of the soul's spiritual mistakes made during its journey in discovering God's values. Since these and other misinterpretations are often deeply implanted in religious thinking, mankind needs a better understanding of the facts and values of the Creator. It is in this century that science has lifted mankind to a new level of discovering God's facts, which really gives this spiritual quest a new boost.

Even though the souls discussed in this chapter have been misled in their interpretation of the spiritual, they are experiencing the karma of growth, not retributive karma. Opening to the spiritual is a process of growth just as strenuous for the soul as learning to handle the material body.

RACHEL

Sufficient masculine strength is a major prerequisite for the soul before it opens to the spiritual, particularly major spiritual lives. The personality can become too emotional, or too submissive in its spiritual practices, or misled in any number of ways, if the masculine strengths are not ingrained in the soul beingness. In the unusual case of Rachel her feminine soul has stayed in the feminine for the last thirteen incarnations, much too long. Therefore her soul's concepts of the spiritual are based too completely on the feminine approach and her last two spiritual lives were not an intelligent interpretation of God's values.

Rachel's previous councils of guides and teachers were at fault for letting her soul stay in the feminine so long, and they have been replaced. A new set of guides and teachers has been assigned for her soul, and her next incarnation will be in the masculine. In fact it will be the beginning of a long masculine cycle, probably focusing entirely on the facts of God and taking material masteries. With the change of guides and teachers, Rachel is being guided more carefully and firmly than before.

The immediate pastlife is brought out in the preamble of her life reading and illustrates the lack of needed masculine strength in a spiritual life:

Dr. John: The first thing that becomes apparent as I study her records is that this soul has stayed too long in feminine expression in its earth incarnations. I believe the past thirteen lives, and this making the fourteenth, have all been feminine.

Now an interesting thing has happened here. There has been a change, a major change, in her council of guides and teachers. In fact, the guides and teachers have been somewhat chastened for allowing this soul to become so 'awash' in femininity, and not to have laced it with some of the masculine qualities and with some masculine development in this period.

I do not quite see why the guides and teachers of this soul allowed it to stay so long in the feminine. Doubtlessly they had their reasons, but apparently the reasons were a bit wrong. Why they were allowed to continue it, I don't quite see, as I have said. But there has been a change, particularly with this life. I believe one of the old council remains, probably a minority voice before but on the right track and so retained.

Souls working in the role of guides and teachers, which is a particular role and usually exercised through a personalized expression, must learn, just as learning takes place on all levels of Individuated-God-Beingness and of life. Even God learns and grows, and wouldn't it be very dull being even God if He could not increase in various ways!

The council looks to me, because the council does not read the akashic records. This is a rather specialized service. Several of them are really quite shocked that the past thirteen incarnations have been feminine, and this the fourteenth. The next one is to go into the masculine, of course.

Why was this one allowed to stay this time in the feminine? It was felt that were it to jump immediately from the prior lifetime, the immediately prior lifetime, into a masculine life, it would be too much of a jump, and it would bring too much inadequacy and pain to the person. So instead, the soul was kept in the familiar feminine this one more time but is being given quite a wide range of new experiences, being shaken out of its lethargy of acceptance of typical feminine roles and values, and brought into many new experiences which will make this life a bridge to the masculine next life. There will be a masculine cycle-of-three. Then possibly again into the feminine for a bit of reassurance, as it were. Then back into the masculine for a more major cycle of development, because this soul truly does need and is ready for the development of masculine values and masculine strengths: the strength of body, the strength of determination, the strength of will, the strength of mind, and such.

The immediate pastlife was as a nun in Italy. This nun was such a nunnish nun as to evoke the pride and the despair of her sister nuns and her superiors. Some of the sister nuns, particularly some of the younger ones, thought this nun who had absolutely eschewed anything of personal opinion, even, was quite the epitome of surrender, of humility, of service, even abject service.

The superiors, however, and those who were truly of a larger understanding of life, rather despaired of her because any word they gave was accepted at face value immediately and with such happiness. They could be utterly illogical and it did not meet with the response that illogic should meet. They could be harsh and it did not meet with the response that harshness should meet. They could be wrong and it did not meet with the response that wrongness should meet. It was just such an un-questioning acceptance.

So she said her prayers and she said them fervently and she said them long, and she fasted, and she took the most menial tasks and so forth, and it was just a bit too much.

You see, to jump from that kind of an earth expression into a masculine expression in this life would have been a bit too much to ask of any soul.

Conductor: When was this, Dr. John?

Dr. John: This was in the 1800s. The life ended in the early

1840s. It was not allowed to go on too long. She was born—
she was in her early thirties when she was taken out.

Conductor: Dr. John, you have not yet said whether she is
from the masculine or feminine half of her soul.

Dr. John: She is from the feminine half of her whole soul,
and she is not a beginning soul. She is well-started and should
be coming fairly soon into the third stage. There were some
masculine expressions way back, I would say probably in the
B.C. period, maybe in the early A.D.s. We may find some a
little later.

I think this outlines the placement of the present life, also
the purpose of the present life. Under the more vigorous and
subtly capable leadership of her present guides and teachers,
she is doing very well in accomplishing the broader range of
experience and the greater depth of real personal beingness and
the purposes of this life.

The 1700s also saw her in a nun life, also overly submissive, and
the personality was nearly caught in one of the horrors of former
religious practice—the practice of self-flagellation, of brutally beating
and maiming the body. When Rachel asked about her mother in this
life, we find that the mother was a nun in the 1700s who practiced
self-flagellation and went mad:

Dr. John: This was a sister religious in Mexico in the second
life back, in the middle 1700s, who practiced self-flagellation
somewhat to the extreme, and who had both a masochistic and
a sadistic trait. So she encouraged her sisters to do the same.

The then incarnation of the Rachel soul was a young peasant girl, a novitiate, who fell under the influence of this older
and rather mad—actually a bit crazy or insane, or off-balance,
let us say, mentally off-balance—older sister nun, not a blood
sister but a religious sister, and did allow herself to be beaten
upon one or two occasions. Then in some fright and some good
sense withdrew from it.

The superior didn't quite know how to curb the excesses of
this other one, but did protect the young novitiate and the other
nuns from her excesses. So that the other one was gradually
isolated and really went mad in a rather gory way, all to the
glory of God. But God really is not very well served by mad
people, even when they proclaim His name a thousand times

without stopping, as this one did in her latter stages of insanity—the present mother, that is.

The present mother is making a comeback. The soul had allowed itself to get caught up in the very things that trapped and destroyed that person. I believe this is the next incarnation for that soul, and it is really doing much better. But it came from not too good a start, and it will take another incarnation or two to get that soul back really into more normal, productive living.

I do not see too much reason for their being together now, the Rachel soul and her present mother. They had that connection in the past. It was one good thing in this life for the Rachel person to overcome such an influence from the mother. Of course, the mother was not as strong this time as she was then, and the mother had other things on her mind than simply giving herself completely to her religious practices in her style of devotion.

Have a certain appreciation of the way in which the mother has come quite a ways. The mother has suffered in this life. There has been unpleasantness visited upon the mother, and the mother was given a type of personality that did not respond with happiness to unpleasantness and uncomfortableness. It did not like suffering in this life, and that was very good. Is there a question?

Conductor: Yes, she has several questions in regard to the mother, some of which you have touched upon. She mentions her fear of insanity in the mother. Rachel has had dreams where the mother has attacked her, and the mother has had gory-type dreams also.

Dr. John: I believe I have nothing further to add to what I have said, and I believe what I have said is the probable cause of those dreams on the part of both of them.

Conductor: Thank you, Dr. John. Is this also the reason that the mother cannot stand to see an animal hurt, even on television? In fact, she won't even watch the survival-of-the-fittest type of program.

Dr. John: The mother had been somewhat given a type of personality, given certain qualities, which very actively oppose the qualities which were expressed and accepted before, and this is the general reason.

Even though Jesus suffered and died for our sins on the cross, imitating His suffering through self-flagellation does not serve the purposes of God. No one is redeemed or benefitted by denying his own body the right to live its life well and happily. Souls do have martyr lives, but they are incarnations that profit good and God, not lives that serve evil and darkness such as the mother experienced. The mother soul is making a comeback, but it will take another lifetime or two before this soul is solidly on the right track again.

The comeback for Rachel's soul began with the change of guides and teachers. These new guides and teachers were not willing to disclose much about themselves, but they did reveal that a higher being was working with them, guiding them in this corrective process:

> Dr. John: Her guides prefer to remain nameless to her. There are four here, including the one who is a carry-over. But they say there is an angel—not exactly an angel, but a spiritual being higher than they—to whom she can call with reverence. They do not want to be approached with reverence, but this other one can be. This one is Raphael or Rafael. Letters are only means of approximating sounds. His name is Rafael, and she can approach him with her prayers. He somewhat makes his wisdom known to her guides upon occasion.
>
> He is one of those who had quite a hand in the shakeup of her council, so he is the one that she might turn to in her thoughts and in her devotion. Turning always to God and to the master Jesus, of course. But this one is of the spiritual level.

Therefore, Rachel is an important incarnation for her soul, and her guides and teachers arranged some interesting experiences in this life. She is living her feminine incarnation in a manner that will help ready her soul for the upcoming series of masculine lives, adding sinew to her soul beingness. All the people brought in to put a little "grist in the mill" are incarnations from loving souls, but with some unusual twists added to augment her soul's growth.

Rachel's twin sister is a cosmic family member who has had several masculine incarnations and agreed to be her twin and a wayshower in this life:

> Dr. John: I must chuckle with this, because here is a cosmic

family member of a very different nature, who with her consent, although it took a bit of doing, was born as twin to bring to Rachel two things: one, as a cosmic family member, an attachment which would be unbroken; two, as being of a very different nature, providing vinegar in Rachel's diet of this life, and sparkle and drive and some goads, and certainly as a wayshower of a quite different type of life, and some of the qualities which to some measure Rachel should be developing in this incarnation.

Likewise, Rachel has some qualities which the other needed to observe close up and to absorb osmotically to some extent, and consciously accept to some extent. The two are quite good for each other in their differences.

They are acquainted on the cosmic family level, but this is the first time they have been together in earthliving. Frankly, the other twin wasn't quite sure how she would put up with Rachel. But they are working along very nicely. We hope they will have increasing adult companionship. Not that they will become very much alike, but that they will like each other. Is there a question?

Conductor: She says, 'We've had a few flare-ups between us, but we've had lots of good times also. Why does she feel she always has to give me advice as if I don't know any better?'

Dr. John: The soul rather felt that of this soul that was thirteen times in succession in the feminine expression, you see. The other one has tasted of the strengths and the delights and the joys and the achievements and the problems of masculine living, too. Although both of them are feminine souls, that is, from the feminine half of their whole souls.

In her adult life Rachel has had two unconventional love relationships—different from society's mainstream. First is a homosexual relationship, which has a feed-in from a pastlife.

Dr. John: They were together in the late 1400s, coming into the 1500s, but not very far into the 1500s. This was in northern South America. Close to Central America but not quite. This is quite interesting. The other one was in the feminine at that time but then was going into the masculine, and I am shown somewhat a trail, as it were. Not the other one's akashic records, but a trail, reaching from that time to this time. I see

this because Rachel, whose records I do have before me, was present in both. But the other one had a masculine trail in between, and the last feminine of the former cycle and the first feminine of this cycle are with Rachel. I do not see precisely why.
Conductor: Well, Dr. John, her friend is very masculine, and they have had a homosexual relationship for about four years.
Dr. John: This will expand experience for Rachel and help get her ready for the masculine cycle up ahead. Let me probe further here: They are cosmic cousins, and the Rachel soul understands something about the other and has quite a compassion for the other. But, of course, Rachel has her own life to live, and is doing so. That was good too, I see, that she did not simply in an excess of feminine surrender and sacrifice give up her own selfhood for the other. Not just her own pattern of this life but also her own selfhood, you see. And that was very good.

So the relationship has been good. They will be together probably in the very next life. Yes, Rachel will be in the masculine and the other will be in the feminine, a little more completely in the feminine, and I think the other will be a younger sister at that time. The two will have instinctively and perhaps consciously quite an understanding.
Conductor: This is a very important person in Rachel's life.

The second love relationship is also outside the norm of society. Her present boyfriend is black. Mixed relationships are becoming more common, but still not entirely accepted by society. In the case of Rachel and her lover, there is a close cosmic bond. They are twin souls. Love relationships between soulmates, cyclemates and twin souls can breach even society's patterns.

Rachel and her lover have had several pastlives together going back as far as 300 B.C. They have been brother and sister, mother and son, and sisters. We will not present the pastlives, but include here the comments and advice given:

Dr. John: They have had pastlives together and they will be together in the future. In the present they are very happily met again, and they will share now on the earth level what they have learned and what they are learning, and each can progress better because the other is present in the lifetime. Now, does this mean marriage? It very well could be. If so, it should take place despite objections. You see, Rachel is to develop a little more independence, a little more of a mind of her own, a little more sureness in following that which she wishes to do, which she decides is right for her to do. She will be guided. She will be better guided and more firmly guided, more wisely guided, by her present council than the soul had been before. These two have a rich fabric of life which they have woven and are weaving together. Just precisely what it all will mean I do not see. That is not my purpose. My purpose is to read the akashic records and bring that contribution. These two are quite happily met.

Conductor: Yes, indeed, they are. May I present to you some of the questions she has here in regard to this great attraction?

Dr. John: Yes.

Conductor: In this incarnation her love comes in as a black, and a very beautiful, beautiful person.

Dr. John: That's fine.

Conductor: Their attraction is very strong, of course.

Dr. John: And was immediate, probably.

Conductor: Yes. The way she expresses it, 'We both feel that we dreamed each other up.'

Dr. John: Yes, but they really are very real. (A4131:2-6,9,10,12,14)

Three souls are assisting Rachel in this life to bring her soul into a better understanding of God's facts and values. Her experiences have been difficult as well as rewarding, but from the standpoint of her soul's progress, they have provided the necessary stretching and soul knowledge to point the way to a greater understanding of God's way.

Rachel has a spiritual outreach in this life, opening a number of doors and examining several different philosophies. She has a special friend who became a nun and Rachel wanted to join the same convent. Luckily her new council of guides and teachers was able to successfully turn her in a different direction, since repeating that pattern for a third time would certainly have been wrong for her. This is a very important incarnation for her soul and Rachel is living it spiritually with greater success, blending a more masculine approach with her deep spiritual commitment.

CLAUDE

Intelligence is required of the God-child, the soul. There will be purposeful incarnations when the personality is rather stupid, but even then the soul is to grow in its knowledge and wisdom.

Claude has had several incarnations where the level of life was low and the religious practices strict and limited in their understanding of God's values. This incarnation—Claude—is to lift the soul out of its previous unintelligent spiritual concepts and his soul is to experience a spiritual "hatching." In the early part of Claude's life reading, Dr. John speaks of thesis, antithesis, and synthesis. In this case the thesis refers to one strict religious thought in one part of the world, then the soul traveling to a totally different culture and religious viewpoint—the antithesis, an opposite spiritual incarnation. This life is to be the synthesis for the soul, bringing together these former religious teachings, all spiritually unintelligent, and integrating a more intellectual approach to the soul's previous interpretation of the values of God.

Claude is from the masculine half of his whole soul and in the third stage nearing the centerline:

Dr. John: The particular purpose of this life is the intellectual expansion of his view of cosmology, of philosophy, of the 'science of all things,' and the method being used is that which has been called 'thesis-antithesis-synthesis.' This is a very good method of learning.

It begins with a particular thesis, a certain substance of knowledge, a certain content of understanding which is considered to be true. The second step is that some element of experience or teaching comes in, which is beyond that of the first view of the universe and quite possibly contrary to it. The very fact that it is beyond is a contrary item. So this is the anti-thesis or antithesis.

There are those persons, and behind them their souls, which when faced with an enlarging fact which goes beyond that which they have accepted and hence 'known,' will reject that

new element of truth. This is all too prevalent in religion today, and it is usually masked by some high-sounding emotional
term such as 'fundamental' or 'conservative'—as though either
of those terms has any meaning in the sight of God.

The third step is to find the *synthesis* of the first known truth
with the second known truth which appears to be contrary to
the first. This, of course, requires a larger framework of
understanding of truth. It is hoped that as the soul goes through
this sort of a process, perhaps not the first time but somewhere
along the route, it will learn that truth is bigger than we will
ever comprehend and contain fully.

Hence, the sooner the God-child learns that it does not have
the full comprehension of truth, the sooner it is the more open
to the learning of new truth. Since the whole progression is
from the early individuation of Godhood—not even knowing
itself very well, and certainly with undeveloped God-nature and
God-powers—into a fuller and fuller development of God-
nature and God-powers, its inherent spirit beingness into a
higher and higher level of Godhood, as you might say
legitimately, the question may come, what about the One God,
the Creator God?

Well, He is so far beyond and He is still growing Himself,
that none of the God-children will catch up to Him, let alone
surpass Him. So do not worry on that score!

Now back to our friend, Claude. This soul has had some
fairly recent incarnations when it was quite sure it had the truth.
The philosophy usually expressed in the religion of the personhoods taught that the system of religion or philosophy of
that culture, of that locality and time, was *the truth*. Hence
the Claude soul had become somewhat crystallized, in a way
that would limit it. Since growth goes on and there needs to
be new stages of growth, it was somewhat in a shell and the
soul needed to hatch again, break through the shell into a new
level of life.

That is not too bad an illustration. There is life inside the
shell. The little bird, or whatever, inside the shell is alive and
there is growth, but it needs to break through the shell in order
to reach a new level of life and of expression and of learning.
That process of breaking through the shell is called, I believe,
'hatching.'

Spiritually, the God-child must 'hatch' many times. And this is a 'hatching' life for Claude, particularly in the area of the comprehension of God and truth. There have been comprehensions of God and truth in his present life, I see, as well as in his recent pastlives, which were quite vigorously sure that they were the truth and hence did not encourage their followers to hatch again.

Every undertaking, every major undertaking in any major field of knowledge or action, has its own particular pitfalls for the unwary, its own particular testings, its own particular nature. The true path must be found within it and through it. The characteristic pitfall, at least one of the major characteristic tests and traps of the philosopher and the religionist—and the religionist is a philosopher, a philosopher that includes God in his philosophy—is that he can so easily be tempted to feel and to proclaim that he has THE truth.

In dealing with God, is he not dealing with ultimates and absolutes? Yes, but his understanding of the ultimate is far from the ultimate understanding, and his knowledge of the absolute is far from being absolute in its content and scope of knowledge.

Most philosophers and religionists, being human beings, are unaware of that fault of inadequacy, are ego-tempted to assume that they are quite adequate and really infallible because they are dealing with the ultimates and the absolutes of life and of existence, and as the spokesman for God they feel they have the final truth and sort of the complete volume of the Book of Truth.

This, of course, is silly. It is silly to have that dogmatic doctrinaire conceit in any branch of knowledge. For, believe me, conductor, it is hard to find a single branch of knowledge in which all truth is yet known to earthlings, or to those of us on other planes as well. Certainly the knowledge of God, of what God has done and what God is like and what God is doing and why, is far from being completely known by even the most advanced of the God-children, those far beyond your stage and my stage and into the stages above us.

Meanwhile, back to Claude and his present incarnation: This is the incarnation when the thesis is challenged by antithesis and in which then he is to achieve synthesis, a larger knowledge of God, of reality, of truth.

But let me warn him: His new synthesis becomes in turn only a thesis. As more is learned in this and in future lifetimes, there will be new antitheses, and he must again and again reach a new synthesis as he reaches upward and outward to his God.

Therefore the synthesis reached in this life will become another starting point, another thesis. The Claude soul will be raised to another level of understanding God-values. He certainly will not have the whole truth, but his soul will have another thesis of God's values— a more factually-based one.

The last three lives of the Claude soul are important to an understanding of the thesis and antithesis pattern Dr. John presented in the preamble. All three of these lives had a spiritual outreach but without a great deal of appreciation of God's values. The 1600s life was presented when Claude asked about his grandfather:

> Dr. John: Here is a pastlife association going back three lifetimes. This is in the 1600s primarily. The then incarnation of the grandfather soul was in feminine expression. The then incarnation of the grandson was in masculine expression. This was somewhere in Central Europe. The culture was not very advanced. The heredity of that particular area was really dominated by the inheritance of genes and chromosomes that didn't carry much mental ability.
> They didn't need too much. They worked with horses; they had agricultural work, and something else with horses. I believe they bred and raised horses and sold them to people who came particularly for the horses. They knew horses. The traditional knowledge of that village—well, it was more of a valley than a village; there were several villages but they worked pretty closely together—knew horses, particularly the kind they raised. They were work horses, not really riding horses, although they were ridden at times. They were good horses, and that was that.
> The religion there was somewhat syncretic, but not intelligently so, not recognized as such. It had quite a background in the rather broad-scope Druid heritage, into which—well, this is interesting, conductor—had come some infusion many centuries before of the invading barbarians from the Orient. So some of that had been impressed upon the religious structure of their valley. Then, of course, the Christian overlay became the most dominant characteristic.

A student of the history of religion would really have had quite a lot of fun unravelling the rather tangled lines of their belief to find the source of each. But it was a religion and they were quite content with it, because they were quite sure it was right. It is interesting, conductor, that so often the human being who is the more limited in intellect is the more sure that he is correct. It takes a certain expansion of the mind, and this expansion has its dangers as well, to view the larger ideas and to accept them.

If the people, the denizens, of this valley really had been faced with new ideas in their whole concept of life and reality, which of course was summarized somewhat in their religion but also in their culture, and expressed more in their culture than in their religion—if they had been faced with inescapable facts quite contrary to what they knew and had been taught and had lived for generations, many of them simply could not have taken it. The general reaction would have been to close their minds to it and with an emotional fervor, often mistaken as religious faith, to have attacked those who brought the new, unsettling ideas, attack them as heretics, attack them as persons forcing unwanted new thinking of which really those people were not capable.

Well, no such ideas really came. Some of the traders who came for the horses knew more and would drop an idea and discuss a little bit and get nowhere. Then the traders might chuckle among themselves, or might go back to their more enlightened cultures with the good horses and report about how stupid the people back here were who believe there were spirits in trees and that one must placate nature spirits and so forth, and whose religious rites and rituals and ceremonies were somewhat different from those of the superior traders on the outside.

I have been looking to see what the relationship of these two was and just what was the position of the then incarnation of the Claude soul. He was not a religious leader. He was a strong man, recognized as a fine member of that society. He knew horses. He bred and raised horses. He helped others do the same. He likewise was capable in the other livelihood pursuits and endeavors. He was a jolly man in the society at that time, although jolly did not necessarily mean smiling very often. But he was contented, he was satisfied. He was happy, although, as I say, usually without a smile. But that was the custom then and that was all right.

This was the first life in the thesis-antithesis series. In the next life the Claude soul went into an entirely different setting and experienced the Mohammedan religion—an antithesis. Again the general life experience lacked spiritual illumination or an elevated view of the values of God.

This 1700s life was brought out when Claude asked about his present life brother:

> Dr. John: His brother was in the life in the 1700s. Again, the then incarnation of the Claude soul is in masculine expression. This is in North Africa; not in Egypt, not a black race. More of an Arab race or tribe. It is a rather fierce tribe in which the men throughly dominate, although the women do quite well in their own ways if they don't confront the men. They are quite fiercely Mohammedan. Some particular sect or cult of the followers of the prophet.
>
> They really have a higher opinion of themselves than would have been deserved. The men think they are very strong and very fierce, and they are more or less. But it is a fairly small group. They do not dare, really, to challenge a larger group, and they are not all that smart. They make up for it ego-wise by a very fierce allegiance to their religion and to their mullah, who teaches them that they are the true followers of the true prophet, the chosen of God, and so forth.
>
> Their religion actually is or has quite an element of compensation for their social inferiority in the world. They are not rich. They have some camels, they have some animals. They have their own village, several villages. They have their agriculture. They have their oasis or oases. They have their area which they fiercely patrol and protect, although if any large, armed band of travelers comes along they do not molest them. The band goes through their area, but the inhabitants get their possessions out of the way so that they themselves are not robbed.
>
> He is not a holy man but he is one of the strong men of that small group. The fact that they really are not as strong nor as intelligent nor as enlightened as some of the others simply

strengthens them in their own self-esteem and in their fierce faith that they have the true religion of the true God, and the true shadings of religion. Because a few miles over, fifty miles away, there may be a group of a different sect of the Mohammedan-umbrella religion. Is this clear?

Conductor: Yes, Dr. John.

Dr. John: How the religion is used as compensation for a subconsciously acknowledged inferiority?

Conductor: And forms the basis for significance for that group.

Dr. John: Yes, definitely, for the group and for the members within it.

After the second incarnation in this thesis-antithesis series of low-level religious concepts, the soul was becoming crystallized in its seriousness toward life on planet earth. The joy of living was nearly squeezed out. Therefore, the guides and teachers brought the soul into the feminine. Again the 1800s life had a limited spiritual concept and the group thought they had the whole truth, but the feminine incarnation allowed the soul not to take this life as seriously. The step-grandmother in the present life was a sister in the 1800s life, and was a joy in both incarnations:

Dr. John: She's a love. She was in the immediately prior lifetime, which was majorly in the 1800s. She was in the feminine. The then incarnation of the Claude soul was likewise in the feminine, although this is interesting. At first, the patterning of that soul's progression had been scheduled to come into the masculine in a rather purposeful lifetime. But it had had purposeful and rather heavy lifetimes, and it was decided by the soul and its council of guides and teachers that it would be better to ease up in that lifetime the seriousness of the progression a little bit and come into the feminine, and let the next serious lifetime be what is the present incarnation as Claude.

So there is this feminine incarnation next. This was in the United states, in the Middle Atlantic area. The girl ended up rather serious, but she didn't have responsibilities of leadership, being in the feminine. She was in a group, sort of a community, that had its own nature. The people of that group had come majorly from Scotland, I believe, and it was not too open a group. They had rather fierce loyalty to themselves with their own members and among themselves, and were really suspicious of others; born out of rough experiences from the border wars with the English, which had exacted fearful toll of the Scots. Conductor, those days were so cruel. There *is* a progression in compassion in this day over that day. So this group in the mountains, probably of West Virginia, really formed its own community and was somewhat ingrown. The blood lines were ingrown, and the ideas were ingrown, and they were really not open to ideas from the outside. This was more of a cultural matter than religious, but the religion, of course, was right in line with that culture. The religion was a Protestant Christianity, but of the same nature as the people whom it served.

It did not really challenge them, except to be a good member of their community and an obedient child of God, as they conceived God to be, which had quite a lot of sternness in it and some fear, which they took as part of the warp and woof of life. They did not go about being very emotionally involved in that fear, but it was part of the general pattern of their lives. They were dour. (A258:2-8,11,12)

The present incarnation, which is again seriously searching for God's truth, is a soul synthesis of these three former lives. The soul is to gather the previously learned spiritual concepts, drawing from each religious thought, and elevate the past with a more enlightened present-life knowledge of God's facts and values. This will lead to another thesis of spiritual understanding, which in turn will probably be countered by an antithesis, then another synthesis. By this method the soul learns. For if Claude's soul should continue within such limited concepts—both facts and values—it could become crystallized in a low mentality and limited spiritual understanding which would slow or could even block the soul's growth. Therefore this life is very important for his soul, a spiritual hatching.

HARRY

The soul needs to raise the curtain to the spiritual at the proper time. When a soul opens to the spiritual before the soul has mastered its earth body, the result can be a setback for the soul. The personhood is a combination of the spiritual, the soul, and the material, the body. The whole process of the spiritual soul taking mastery over the material earth is primary in the early incarnations. To miss this important fact is to misinterpret God's plan, to the detriment of the soul.

Harry is from the masculine half of his whole soul, a rather young middle soul with approximately 18-20 lives to date. The present incarnation is the fourth in a series of spiritual lives. In the two previous spiritual lives the personality went mad, since the soul was not properly oriented in the material and had not built sufficient soul individuality to hold the incarnate personality intact.

Successful spiritual strength must be built on a solid material basis. Without development of the material forces, the soul's beingness is not capable of handling the rather mystifying forces of the spiritual. This may seem unusual, since the soul is spiritual. But it must be remembered that the material realm presents the facts of God which can be put into a formula, can be written on paper, can be touched, can be seen, while the spiritual is the nonmaterial. These spiritual forces are felt with an inner knowledge that cannot be measured by any precise formula. Therefore the masculine strength of the soul needs to be strong enough to handle the nonmaterial and mysterious spiritual forces, otherwise the personality may fall apart one way or another. In the case of Harry, the last two personalities went mad.

Harry is an important incarnation for the soul. He is an ordained minister in this life—this being the fourth spiritual life—but the person of Harry must maintain his stability and keep his personality intact. Some interesting relationships have helped to steep the personality in the materiality of earth.

In the preamble Dr. John traces in the three most recent previous incarnations of this soul:

> Dr. John: We find quite an interesting background for this one in that a number of his previous lives have been devoted to religious pursuits, or the spiritual-consciousness pursuit. The immediate pastlife is as a nun in Italy, in Rome. The girl was very enamored of the church, very impressed by religion.
> From her early years it became her single interest, almost to the point of a monomania. Had it not been a religious interest, people would have thought her unbalanced, which of

course she actually was. She read stories of the saints. She listened with five ears, not just two, as it were, when the sisters told her of saints and their sufferings and their visions. She was tremendously impressed by the story of Jesus. She would, as it were, cross herself three times and fall prostrate whenever His name was mentioned or whenever she thought of Him. She entered the convent really at the age of nine.

Now she didn't really, but she started going to the convent, not simply to the sisters for school, but going to the convent at the age of nine to see if there wasn't something she could do for them.

She was a sweet child and a quiet child, and she was capable of certain things. So they let her run errands. They let her help wash dishes and prepare food. The convent really became her home.

Her parents were somewhat mystified by it all, but were assured by their priest that this was a religious dedication and was a good thing and they were honored. So they did nothing to interfere.

The little girl was a bit of a nonentity at home. There were various other children before and after her and this was a quiet one who didn't really seem to belong, so she wasn't too missed. From that early start in the convent it was just natural for her to transfer her lodging there and to enter it as a novitiate at the earliest possible moment.

The Mother Superior was quite impressed. This one was absolutely obedient, absolutely dedicated, had no other thought in life. As we say, this was a monomania, but a rather constructive one.

She became a contemplative. The order encouraged and led to that. She worked through the tasks within the convent, doing every one with a starry-eyed idealism that this was work for Jesus.

She was psychic and it was all pointed in the one way of visions, religious visions. Her visions got quite ecstatic and the convent authorities saw it was not really right to tell outsiders and they cautioned her not to speak of them except to about three people, two of the older sisters and the Mother Superior.

She would come and kneel before Mother Superior once a week and tell her her visions. The Mother Superior recognized them as being certainly a spiritual outreach but not really within the realm of reality. But she encouraged the little thing, whose mind was really going.

The two older sisters were a little concerned and conferred some with the Mother Superior, who conferred with the town priest, who was the priest for the convent. And they saw it as God or Jesus or the saints or heaven gradually withdrawing this sister from the earth realm into the other realm. They knew of some of the saints for whom this had occurred, and they saw the possibility that this one would become a saint. But no miracles occurred. This one did no healing. There were no visible apparitions. No bells rang out. No light appeared. And so this one at the age of thirty-nine was wasted away. When she stepped over there was quite a little work which had to be done with her on the othe side, because she was so caught up in this consciousness of what we would call psychism, religious-oriented psychism, which was not very clear because the mind was really deranged.

It was a harmless life. She didn't hurt anybody. She certainly contributed a great deal of prayer, and the prayer was quite useful in that it was thoroughly well-intentioned, and it was always in the name of the blessed Jesus. It was always offered to and through the saints whose statues adorned the convent and whose spirits guarded the convent.

So there was this sort of a life. Now this was the culmination of several religious lives, religious-psychic lives, in a row. This was in the 1800s and ended in the late 1800s, was in Rome as I have said.

We will go back to the several other lives that led to this one, for this was sort of a climax along a path that got deflected from the main path. We go back into the late 1600s and early 1700s, which was a life as a monk.

This monk's life began in Germany. He was a simple-minded boy, a peasant farmer boy before he became a monk. He too was quite assiduous at the religous training in the parish church. He attended all the masses that were required and then some more.

He accepted everything the priest told him. The Roman Catholic view of life and then death and hell and heaven. He was frightened by hell, scared of his unlikelihood of getting into heaven, became a monk, did menial work.

But his mind was not too bad. It was sort of an average peasant mind. His devotion to the church structure and of course to the Pope was unquestioned. He was very outraged at Martin Luther and all that had sprung from that heresy.

He had a gentleness about him which would not harm the heretics, but he was greatly, greatly disturbed by them. In this disturbance his being, not just his mind but his being, experienced sort of a cleavage, because there was this gentleness to him.

When he was on the farm he had taken care of the animals. If an animal was hurt or sick, they let this one attend to it, and there was more chance then of the animal getting well. He extended this loving care to people, although he did not have too much contact with people in the monastery.

So he had this loving concern for people on the one hand; on the other hand he had this absolute conviction that the Pope and the reality he had been taught were utterly true. So here are some of his friends who are heretics.

He could not bring himself to pray against them. He could not bring himself to consider them utterly black and evil. So his mind, instead of resolving the conflict, divided itself. He began to imagine the dark things he had been told, the dark forces which were supposedly at work in the heretical movement, began to imagine them, to think about them, to let them gradually take more and more place in his thought until they became quite real and frightening.

He kept himself mentallly away from them, on the side of heaven, but the task became really too great. In a rather frenzied moment he took his own life. He didn't quite intend to, but he didn't quite know what to do and he banged his head on a stone wall, and it just happened. It dislocated a vertebra and pinched the spinal cord. He was paralyzed from the neck down.

He was found, although not right away, and the story he told was, of course, that he had been attacked by dark evil, by devils from hell, but he had withstood them. The paralysis extended to all body functions, so within several days he was dead, but he maintained that steadfast consciousness that he had withstood the devils of hell and he would be received by the angels into the light of heaven, which of course was pretty much what did happen as he was taken over.

In each of these cases, you see, the person had become an

instrument that was not really of further constructive use to the soul or to the world, and the soul had not been able to control the person. The soul was not in as close touch and is still not in as adequate touch with the person as it will be in the future.

The soul is well-started, really a young middle soul, with perhaps about eighteen or twenty earthlives so far. And the soul is not too far along in its own individuation, either. Cosmically it is no further along than it is in its earth journeyings.

Now before this 1600s to 1700s German monastic life, this one had been in India, and it was here, in a way, that the difficulty started. This was in the early 1600s. The person may have been born in the very late 1500s, but the life was in the early 1600s.

In this life the person became a fakir, a holy man. We say the difficulty started here. The boy was quite open and was taken in hand by another fakir, who saw the chance to develop the psychic abilities of this boy and add him as a second to his act, which he did, and taught him psychic abilities.

Now the teacher was an older soul who had had several lifetimes in this, knew how to control himself within the psychic field. The boy did not, but the boy was an apt student and learned many of the psychic things, and psychic abilities that the teacher knew and the ability to establish rapport with and work with the elemental forces of nature, not so much the forces in plants and living things as the forces in what we call inanimate things, the wind, the stones, the processes of nature, some of the 'little people' as we call them, of the less spiritual sort. So he became a fine performer. But the boy had a genuine spiritual streak which the teacher did not have. The boy in his psychism merged more towards the spiritual, the ethical, the mystical.

His teacher was not of that nature, but to the teacher's credit he recognized the boy's finer nature emerging and rather quietly encouraged it so that the boy in time left the trade of being a public entertainer using psychic and nature forces, and went more into seclusion as a true holy man.

Now he did not become a guru. He withdrew rather. He did not take students. He was a student. He was more and more in touch with mystical forces and spiritual forces. So he withdrew into the wilderness.

He was gradually absorbed into the spirit, as it were. He did not lose contact with the outer world to the extent that he did not appreciate his sustenance, and he had a reputation.

Although he withdrew, he was not too far from some villages, even a small town, and some of the people knew of him and they would come to sit in his presence. A man who could sit quietly without moving for four or five or six hours must be truly a holy man, and some of that holiness might rub off on them.

Also if they had a sick child or a sick adult, they could bring the sick one to this one and this one would sort of stir out of his isolation when there was a sick one and he would look and sometimes would reach out a hand to touch the sick one, or place his hand over the area of the pain or the illness, and quite often there was an alleviation of the illness and the pain, a minor healing, sometimes with minor ailments a complete healing.

Why then did not this one's fame spread so that hundreds and thousands flocked to him? Well, there were not hundreds and thousands around him. There were hundreds, but in hundreds not all are sick, certainly not at one time.

So he was a healer for some years for this small constituency, and they brought him his food. He ate sparingly. He was a spare person, but he was healthy. He lived to be sixty-two in this service, really quite withdrawn from the world, excepting in the reaching out to be helpful to those brought to him. So there was this progression, you see.

But the progression got worse, as it were. So a break was brought in with the present earthlife. A person was generated which was not in this stream, was brought into a busy setting, and in America, was brought into a setting where religion was not the chief focus point, was given a personality which did not go into the contemplative practice of deep meditation, was put into a home where very definitely the human relationships within the home kept the personality stirred up and involved in the day-by-day events. Then he was brought into early life in a time of serious material depression within the country, was put on his own to keep the person interested, keep it absorbed, in the activities of daily physical life, was given a very active life, which continues.

Now the spiritual interest has reemerged, yes, and with it this time a better grasp of reality, a better balance, a better mind tool, certainly, than the nun had in the immediately prior life, and certainly there will not be the break with reality that the monk had in the 1600s and early 1700s.

This is the background and this is the essential framework of the present life. Now this is a person from the masculine half of the soul, and we have already shown the soul age. I would go back one time more, and farther back, before we get into his life pattern of relationships and questions and such.

This soul has a religious nature. It is from the masculine half, but the whole soul, you might say, is colored more by the feminine than the masculine—so far, anyway—colored more by the feminine quality of devotion to God, which is a fine quality.

As the soul comes into its own individuation, it must develop, of course, its own competence. As it comes into earth it must be able to take mastery of the basic earth experiences here. This soul may take more rather than fewer earthlives to accomplish its earth journeyings.

This is not to say the soul is slower. This is to say that this soul will learn more from earth than some will and will need earth learnings a little more. Whereas some souls may, for instance, take their earth journeyings in 80 earthlives, this one may very well take 120. As we have said, 100 is a good enough rule of thumb. This one probably will take a few more, rather than a few fewer earthlives.

Now this soul is a very interested student, but not yet a very wise student, of earth history. The soul has reviewed earth history insofar as it could, and has done so somewhat on its own by looking back into history at various periods. It has some knowledge, but not too much, of how the Elohim experimented with the human life on earth, how they took over when life had already been established on earth, experimented with the human form.

Now what does this all mean for the person of Harry? It means that this is a very important transition personage within the varous incarnatons of the soul. It means the transition is being made away from the undue religious interests which overbalanced the two immediately prior lifetime personalities, which were simply not able to stand the strain of what they undertook. It means that this earthlife or person is a man, a good man, who has the ability to land on his feet, as it were. It means also there is the reawakening of spiritual interest which needs to be handled in a very practical way. The emphasis must be on practicalities. The emphases must be actually on this world rather than on the next, as long as this person is incarnate. It means that the spiritual needs to be understood in a practical way and integrated with practical living. It means that the actualities need to be discerned from the fantasies.

The sweet little nun was deluded. The earnest peasant monk got in over his head in several ways. Harry must do neither. He must protect himself from being deluded. He must not get in over his head. That amount of spirituality that he takes must be as carefully as possible grounded on actuality, on facts, and integrated into practical living.

It is not for him to be a contemplative. He is not one to go into deep meditation. He is one to keep practical. He is one to stress involvement with actual living. Now within that framework he can be helpful to those who come to him because so many today have little or no interest or knowledge of the spiritual.

This lifetime can set the soul back on the right track. It is *not* in the cards, as it were, for this soul to go into incarnations of spiritual emphasis, of spiritual centrality, of a central spiritual interest, for a number of lifetimes now.

It has that nature, and it will come back to it, but now it needs to master earthliving as earthliving, you see. This is an important person, an important incarnation, and his task is not done, and in fact as we see it there is still concern, some concern that as the spiritual has been reintroduced, it is not yet set firmly within a framework of factuality, of objective truth.

There is yet work to be done in this area by the person, you see.

Harry's soul simply did not have enough soul individuality before it was led to open to the spiritual. And the practice of meditation is not always good for a young soul. The soul is simply not strong enough to withstand the mystical experience of reaching into the other realms, until it has a deep understanding of the facts, the masculine, and the values, the feminine, of earth. Earth is an important cosmic school for the soul and its feet must be firmly planted in Mother Earth before reaching too high toward Father God.

This is an important transitional life for Harry's soul. In the relationship portion of his life reading we see how several people have been brought in to bring Harry down to earth, stabilizing him before he opened to the spiritual in this life.

First the father:

> Dr. John: There is no pastlife between the two. There may be a future and there may not be. It is not patterned, and the present life relationship of the two has not really contributed continuing forces or purposes for bringing them together in the future.
> This was a person who was of this earth, earthy, in not an altogether admirable way, but this is one of the realities of life with which the Harry person was confronted quite early in his incarnate experience.

Putting this spiritual soul with a very material father would seem a mismatch, but one way to build strength is through difficult relationships. His father represented the earth, earthy, and the Harry soul needed to learn the earth, earthy. Therefore his father, who was not cosmically related and did not have a pastlife feed-in, worked as an abrasive force to pull his son's soul down to earth. This method of honing a spiritual person is not unusual. Often very spiritual souls will choose to incarnate in an earthy situation simply to be sure their feet are well placed on terra firma before rising spiritually.

Harry's mother was mentally disturbed. This was the result of divergent forces feeding into the personality which the person could not resolve. As Dr. John points out, this was a warning to Harry's soul that it needed to keep its balance. Even though Harry as a person could not understand why his mother was mentally unbalanced, the soul knew it was observing what could happen to itself:

> Dr. John: Here he was confronted with another person who was in a sense disoriented in reconciling areas of divergent

forces. Now the little nun was unsuccessful in reconciling divergent forces and the peasant monk was. So was his mother. Now he could watch it in another.

With her the divergent forces were not spirituality and materiality. They were other divergent forces within her. I am not shown just what they were. They may have been conflicting streams of masculine and feminine forces. They may have been a conflicting karma with the husband. They may have been any one of several things. They may have been a background of ease and affluence from which the soul was unable to make the transition to a more humble and harder working life. But whatever it was, there were unreconciled differences which led to the destruction of that person.

This was an example, you see, for the Harry soul to observe, and the soul observed it. The person didn't quite know what was going on, but the soul was shown and was quite sobered by it.

There is no pastlife between them, and it is not expected these two will be together again in the future. They will meet on the other side and the Harry person will be glad to see that the mother has been restored. Yes.

The mother person will not continue on the astral side of life for very long. It will for a while, and then it will be absorbed into its own soul, for it was not potentialed to go far or long, nor into the higher spiritual realms.

Conductor: Yes. He mentions she would have been only twenty-nine years old and she took her life at that time.

Dr. John: Well, this fits into the pattern. The little nun did not take her own life by an act of her own will, which was in a way a little more of a victory, a little less of a defeat, Yes.

A stabilizing person was brought into Harry's life, his stepmother. She is a cosmic family member who had been the mother to both the Italian nun and the German peasant monk. These two souls had several other incarnations together, including a life in Palestine during the time of the Master. His stepmother had been his mother in that life and they had heard Jesus speak upon occasion. This close cosmic family member ushered in a happy interlude in Harry's life.

When Harry decided to become a minister and open to the spiritual once again, another person was brought in to warn his soul that it needed to keep its balance in this spiritual life—his ex-wife:

> Dr. John: Well here is another person, another disturbed person, brought into his present life experience simply to, as it were, warn the soul to keep itself whole, keep itself together, because this other one had disruptive forces. No, there is no pastlife between them and it is not seen that there is any possibility of a future life together. They are separated, and it is hoped they remain separated. They are not good for each other. Some souls are good for one another. Some are not. These two are not good for each other.
>
> But it is another warning to the Harry soul and the Harry person, and a warning to consider, now that the spiritual element has been introduced, to keep things in hand, to keep the person whole, organized, to keep the fanciful and fantasy out, to strive mightily to know the truth, for the truth will set him free, and the part true and the part false and the fuzzied things will enslave, could entrap him again. This will apply particularly to his psychism, which can be used, yes, but must be strained and filtered through a mind that is centered upon objective reality.
>
> The psychism is not that to which the mind must bring itself now. The mind, the good mind, is that to which the psychism must bring itself. The mind is the filter. The mind is the determinative point. The psychism must give way to the objective reality of a good mind that is centered on truth and factuality Yes.
>
> Conductor: Yes. He has no questions in regard to this, but he does say, 'We tore a big hunk out of each other's lives.'
>
> Dr. John: It is a warning not to tear 'a big hunk' out of aspects of his own life. (A1819:1-12,16,17)

This has been a life without a lot of frills and practically devoid of helpful, loving people. But Harry is definitely a turning point for his soul, which will need to build more firmly its own individuality before it undertakes future spiritual lives.

God has a very loving nature, but He also demands that His children grow in compatibility and companionship with Him. He cannot have children who will divide themselves and fall apart, no matter how spiritual they are. Therefore Harry is a very important person for his soul, and obviously he is doing a good job.

SADIE

The joy of earth is an experience and a concept sometimes overlooked by people in spiritual lives. This is a mistake. Each incarnational experience is an original experience for the soul and one to be valued and enjoyed. To dispossess earth and think of it only as a place where evilness dwells, would be seeing God as unloving, distant and withdrawn from this dreadful place. But earth is His creation. Although evil is a part of this realm, the soul was begotten from the Beingness of God to learn and to grow. The cosmic school of earth is strenuous at times, but it is not devoid of God and His love. And the very evil we face can accelerate our soul growth considerably.

For Sadie the doom-and-gloom philosophies became a part of her soul's spiritual understanding until her soul nearly became crystallized in thinking of earth as degrading and evil. Her soul had a series of lives humiliating the spirit and the body. In the 800s the soul incarnated as a woman living in an impoverished atmosphere, and the dour, sad religion of that time pulled the woman down, instead of lifting her out of the situation. In the next incarnation, the soul experienced a life as a monk who died of self-torture and starvation. Therefore the soul had to break out of this gloom and doom, change the feeling that earth and the body were evil into the realization that earth, too, possesses love and joy.

The first correctional life was in the 1000s, with a different spiritual structure. The religion referred to earth as Mother Earth and God as Father God. The present incarnation, Sadie, is the second corrective step in elevating the soul's value of earth, this time through the love of nature:

> Dr. John: Well, she is from the feminine half of her whole soul. She has come through the just-getting-started and the well-started stages of soulhood and has entered but has not progressed very far into the third stage of around-the-midpoint, so oh, perhaps 30, 25 to 30 percent of her incarnations are through and she's coming into the area where the introduction to earth has been completed. She is oriented to it, accustomed to it, and now some of the significant growth ex-

periences can take place. The present life interestingly enough picks up quite significantly and even majorly from a lifetime in the 1000s A.D. so I will go·into that picture. For several lives prior to the 1000s there had been quite a religious emphasis of a dour nature with the emphasis that is sometimes found in religion, usually regrettably, on turning from earth, earthy as being sinful and turning to God as being the good, with God being separate from earth.

This, of course, is a mistake because God created earth and earth is the habitat for His children, the Godchildren who are souls, that is, in the early stage of their developing Godhood; and the earth is also the 'far country,' as I have brought out before, for those of His beings who need a place of sustenance until they are redeemed and brought back to the Father's house, which is spirit.

Now there is a real foundation for the dichotomy between God and earth in that earth is in the material realm and God is in the spirit realm. The very word spiritual means essentially nonmaterial. It is the way in which the human being can differentiate between the spirit realms and the material realms. Spirit is nonmaterial and the basic meaning of the word spiritual is nonphysical, nonmaterial. So there are these two basic realms of being which must be recognized by the enlightened human being and by the soul—the realm of spirit, which is exceedingly real but which is not material, and then the realm of matter.

Now religion has somewhat sensed this at times and come up with a dichotomy which makes matter evil and nonmatter good. Well, there is some reason for that because it is in the realm of matter that the 'far country' exists and that is earth, and this is the provender place for the prodigal while the prodigal is being sustained (really by the great Father) until he, of his own wit and will, realizes that his proper place is the realm of spirit and is in his Father's house and the Father's line of purposeful values and development. Yes.

So there is a certain aspect wherein matter is evil and earth is evil and heaven is good and spirit is the good realm.

But to make a hard and fast cleavage here is certainly inappropriate and inaccurate.

Now let us apply this to the incarnation of Sadie. This incarnation comes from a time when there had been several lifetimes (I probably may see them pretty soon and delineate them) in which religion had been teaching the then incarnations of the Sadie soul that matter was evil and that she must withdraw from it, must subjugate the body, must not take enjoyment in earth and earthliving but must 'turn to God' in very somber tones, yes indeed!

This has a certain validity to it when put in the right perspective and balanced with other factors. But this soul was getting a bit crystallized in that consciousness. And so it was brought in the early 1000s A.D. into a very different life. It was put into a little village in the south of Italy where in one respect religion was not very important. However, this had been brought about partly by unseen forces; partly by the customs, the long momentum of that little village which was somewhat hidden away, was not in any main thoroughfare of commerce or civilization; and then partly by a tradition of priests there who might be called quite liberal. These priests—and this was a very definite thing brought about by spirit forces for they wanted a village such as this, an environment and experience-framework such as this, for souls that needed it—these priests had a great joy of living in themselves. They had a concept of Mother Earth as well as Father God, and of incarnate humans as being children of Father God and Mother Earth. They would point out in their preaching and teaching that Jesus lived upon earth and earth could not be all bad. Earth had its joys as well as its sorrows, and the teachings of Jesus—which they would select carefully out of the Bible which they had and the parishioners did not have—the teachings of Jesus of joy, of faith, of confidence, of the acceptance with full heart of earthliving, these were the teachings they selected and taught.

This combination of momentum and teaching and fine purpose produced a setting in which life had quite a bounce to it and quite a happiness to it. The then incarnation of the Sadie soul was in the feminine expression here. The soul had this gloomy quality but in a sense the soul was almost detached from this life. Now the vital cord of life was there but the person was taken almost away from the soul. The soul was allowed to experience a person whose life and whose personality were really produced and directed by others. The soul was certainly not then a good guide for its incarnations, as it was becoming crystallized in the gloom-and-doom aspect of religion.

So here came a very corrective life, you see, in which Mother Earth was known as good, in which Mother Earth was thought of almost as the mating spouse of Father God to produce God's children, the human beings upon earth, yes, and the animals and the plants as well.

This quality was not only a corrective quality for the soul— and the soul got the point there, it was corrected in its misunderstandings of religion—but also this quality did produce a happiness, you see. After all, the human being must remember that it is of earth. Yes, it is of spirit. The human being is an interaction phenomenon of spirit and matter, of the non-physical realms and the physical realm of earth. This must be understood. This is one of the great realities and it must be appreciated, for if it is not understood and if it is not appreciated, then the individual does not have the correct understanding of what God has done in making an incarnate soul, a human being, in bringing that about here on planet earth.

Is this clear, conductor?

Conductor: Yes, Dr. John. Thank you.

Dr. John: So the Sadie soul began to feel there from the happiness of the personality of its then incarnation the correctness, the rightness, even the divinity of being a child of earth while incarnate as well as a child of God, that the child of earth is a child of God. There is not a split parentage. There is not a bastardization of the spirit when the soul incarnates and produces a human being, you see.

Now the soul is charged with keeping the bubbling happiness that was there. But this was something really quite new to it and so it was allowed time between incarnations and it was allowed also other incarnations between the 1000s and 1900s that did not come into this general area of development.

Now the will and the way of God for planet earth includes joy. It includes pain. It includes grief, for loss is a factor. This is a realm of original sin in that this is a place which before the soul came into it was the far country, the provender place for the prodigal. The soul incarnates and comes into it as a redeeming agent. It is a great test for the soul, a marvelous development place, and a place of really divine and holy service as the soul likewise develops its own God-nature and

God-powers.

But it is likewise a place to be appreciated for what it is, because even though the prodigal son came into this far country, the far country has its own nature. And for those who are awake to it and alive to it, it is a beautiful place speaking in many tongues, and particularly in the voice of quietness undisturbed by human cries.

So the Sadie person is an incarnation in which the bubbling happiness of earthbeingness, of earthliving, temporary though it be, is a part of the experience of this incarnation. This goes back to the 1000s life in southern Italy, as I have said, and in this present life it is hoped that this happiness, this quality of joy for planet earth and love for Mother Earth, is so well set within that soul as to become an eternal part of it.

Even though earth is the realm where the prodigal sons find their energy source when away from their Father's house, it is the provision of God that His children grow through a series of lifetimes in this demanding atmosphere, without being caught in the clutches of evil. (Our book *Destiny of the Soul* gives more details.) For young souls this may seem like walking a tightrope, since they do not yet fully understand what is God's way, God's truth, for planet earth. But to become encased in the gloom of earth or in fear, is to serve evil rather than God. Therefore the soul needs to learn the great joy of God even in a realm where evil dwells. For Sadie this is being accomplished through the artistic touch of God in nature.

In the 1000s life her soul was observing rather than participating in the life. In the present incarnation the Sadie soul is more involved in the personhood, draining away and releasing the old pattern of gloom-and-doom, as brought out in the relationship portion of her life reading. The present-life mother was mother of the 900s monk who starved and mutilated his body. We begin with that life:

> Dr John: They are cosmic family members. She was in the 800s, majorly 800s and some early 900s A.D., in a life with the then incarnation of the Sadie soul. The Sadie soul had come into the masculine. This was in Italy, was north of Rome. And the Sadie soul at that time had joined a religious order which was a rather small, somewhat perverted, offshoot of monasticism with quite a sense of the torturing of the body.

The body was evil. It was to be subjugated. It was to be tortured. Any enjoyment of the body was not only suspect but was sure to be evil, was condemned before it even appeared. This meant that the poor brothers there would search themselves to find some way in which they enjoyed the body just so they could punish the body. And so it was a lifetime of the development of strength back of this idea that the body is evil and spirit is good, that earth is evil and God is good, and one must reject earth and the body to know God.

As I say, it was a perversion and not a very intelligent approach to life or to spiritual understanding. But such it was, and this was the predominant factor in the lives of those who came into that group.

The then incarnation of this soul came in at the age of fourteen, by eighteen was a full member, and twenty-two was dead from the excesses exacted by that person from the body. It had had a good body, which it destroyed. Starvation, beating—I do not like to look at it. It was not good even though the initial impulse had some good in it.

The present mother was the mother then. She did not approve of this order. She was a very devout Roman Catholic Church member and, of course, when the son went into a religious order, she would not question it. At first she had a certain pride in it but secretly she did not approve of it. She questioned it. She talked with her priest about it some, and the priest was rather politic. He would not criticize another order of his church. So he was not much help even though he did not encourage the excesses of this other order, and pointed out that he as a priest had not joined such an order.

The pastlife prior to the masochistic monk life was brought out when Sadie inquired about a special friend, Janice:

Dr. John: They were together, my goodness, this is in Italy again, in the life preceding that ascetic self-torturing religious. This would be the 700s and the 800s. They were in a village in Italy, both in the feminine expression and this village, interestingly enough, had a tradition and priesthood very different from that of the southern Italian village of which I spoke into which they came in the 1000s.

Now the church superiors would not really recognize this too much. These were somewhat subtle things, although they did set the dominant tone of life there. But here the priests were strict. Here the land was rather poor. The climate was difficult. It was rather high in the mountains. The winters posed problems of warmth and of keeping the animals and of providing food for the animals as well as the humans and such as that, the milking of the cows. So life was more difficult. The village was culturally disadvantaged, let us say, and the priests were part of that disadvantage. They were sour individuals themselves and rather believed that sourness was the proper taste of religion and so they promulgated it. These two women had that attitude. They were friends and they'd come together and they'd bemoan this or that or the other thing, then try to find out how they could scratch another small coin out of their household expenses to give to the church and to send down to Rome for Mother Church and such.

These two were together then and I suppose maybe that is one reason they're being brought back together now. Can you tell me something about the relationship or about the person of the Janice one?

Conductor: All right. Well, Sadie has many nice things to say about her. She loves to travel. They enjoy each other. Probably the only thing of a negative nature that she has to say is, 'Janice has a tendency to see the dark side of things.'

Dr. John: Yes. Now remember they are two different persons than they were a thousand years ago or more, and many forces have entered into the growth of these souls and the development of each person. But when we find two coming together who have shared an experience, a lifetime of a rather predominant coloring, very often the purpose of their present relationship grows out of that which was when they were together before. And so if Sadie can help to relieve the pessimism of the Janice one, this would be helpful.

Actually, if this gloom-and-doom aspect is understood, she can transcend it to a significant degree. Every step up and out of that into the larger understanding of God and of earth and of matter in relation to spirit is of two-fold value: (1) it will bring greater ease to the present life; and (2) it will add to the spiritual growth and understanding of the soul.

It is a matter of understanding what is God's way for planet earth and for incarnate soul life upon earth. What are the facts and what are the values, what are the purposes, of God? Well, the great philosophers have characterized the values as being truth, beauty, and goodness. This is not a flagellation of the body nor of the spirit. This is not the denial of such elements of goodness as are upon earth and available to people in earth-living. So the correction of the theology, the correction of the philosophy, is a step forward. This can happen through logic, also it can happen through seeing examples of successful living. Sadie's example of joy and of the successful melding of joy into her religious philosophy, her understanding of God and of earth life, is a contribution to this other one.

In the monk life Sadie's soul experienced the degradation of the body. In the previous life the soul experienced the degradation of the spirit. Both downgraded the God-child. Showing Janice how to understand the facts and values of God's way for planet earth would be a plus for Sadie, since they both need to be lifted out of the gloom and doom of their previous incarnations.

The last person presented from Sadie's life reading is Marshall, a special love. Dr. John reported that he is her soulmate. Since Sadie is from the feminine half of her soul, her soulmate, Marshall, is incarnating from the masculine half of the same soul. When soulmates come together in a love relationship, it can be a joyful union. Since joy is the growing edge in Sadie's life, Marshall can certainly add another genuine aspect of understanding God's love and God's way for this realm.

> Dr. John: Partly Marshall is here because this is a time when the bubbling happiness, the bounce, of that 1000s person is being brought back, with the person of Sadie really having more depth and more substance to her than the person of that other incarnation.
>
> It is in the Sadie person, the Sadie lifetime, that this element of joy is being rejoined with the spiritual quest. The spiritual quest is cleansed in this way, although not without inner conflicts, as Sadie may be aware of, may not be. But in the subconscious there is an inner conflict between the element of joy and the element of asceticism, between the love of Mother Earth and the love of Father God which had been set against each other before.

The Sadie incarnation is really a very important incarnation for this soul, not so much for what it accomplishes outwardly but for what it accomplishes inwardly as, in effect, she reconciles and heals the divorce of her parents, Father God and Mother Earth—this divorce having occurred in her experience, not in their experience.

I will let it go at that because Sadie can put it together. Sadie has a lot of thinking to do on this and a lot of healing and a lot of feeling and this other one—what did you say his present earth name is?

Conductor: Marshall.

Dr. John: Marshall. Let the two of them find all that is there for them for which they are ready, for as long as they will. Yes. And if that be for all of this life and carrying over into the excarnate phase, that would be most appropriate and most valuable and could be most good for them. Yes. (A4301:2-5,7,10,16,19)

Sadie is experiencing a spiritual quest in this life, but it is tempered with a love of nature. Some special people have been brought into her life to help shape her understanding of the joyful marriage between Mother Earth and Father God. The reintroduction of the spiritual combined with the joy of life on earth will bring light into the darkness of her soul's previous religious incarnations.

CHERYL

God may be served at any stage of our spiritual development, and it is always a spiritual mistake to believe that our way is the only way or the best way of serving God. Human history shows a variety of ways of supposedly serving God—from ancient Baal-worshippers throwing babies onto a fiery altar, to young Khoumeini-followers in twentieth century Iran throwing themselves in human waves at entrenched machine-gun positions of the Iraquis. In the fervor of high religious feeling an uncritical person so often has accepted ideas from the church or culture of this time, or from his own cult leader or close companions, without realizing they are not true or even good.

No matter what the influence, it is still the soul's own spiritual mistake. Cause-and-effect have been fundamental to the structure of God's universe since before humanity appeared, and will be for untold ages yet to come. No one can grow for another person, and we cannot pass off onto another our mistakes. When a person or a soul errs, no matter how misguided it may have been, it is responsible for the mistake, a wrong way that must be corrected and the better way learned.

To judge others in terms of our own understanding (or misunderstanding) is a rather popular form of spiritual mistake. In Cheryl's case we find this taking the spiritual form of praying and agonizing for others, that they may forsake the error of their ways and come to her way. Her life reading must have given Cheryl a bit of new understanding when it revealed to her that this had been her attitude in her immediately prior two incarnations. She needed to be reminded what the great prophets and seers have always taught—that there is One who judges and judges rightly, One who wishes His children to grow, and it is His law not her opinion which ultimately prevails.

The Cheryl soul has the habit of entering each incarnation with the idea of living only for the purpose of that incarnation, without incorporating the strengths gained from its previous lifetimes. During a series of religious lives, Cheryl being the third in the series, her masculine soul has interpreted the feminine as feeling. Therefore she is living this spiritual life with too much emotion—hurting and suffering for those who do not follow in the right path, her path.

This is not an intelligent understanding of God's values. If God suffered with the same measure as she, He would be pained beyond endurance. But in His wisdom He allows each soul to grow in the path it has chosen, from one lifetime to another, stumbling sometimes and walking tall other times. And His love is a consistent force which is regulated by a cause-and-effect structure. God's love is not an emotional, impulsive love, which would be fluctuating and undependable in its nature, but rather a stable, detached love.

Dr. John: The Cheryl soul wants to plunge in and immerse herself completely in whatever it happens to be that she is swimming in, as it were, in this or that incarnation. Thus, in the present incarnation the psychic field is recognized as feminine and so she will plunge into that.

Even more than that she will plunge into the spiritual emphasis of the feminine. Now this is rather good because she recognizes that the touch with other realms is more the touch with God who is spirit than it is the touch with psychic communications and faculties and experiences, and so this is good. But even this will be tempered as the soul gains more maturity, and perhaps it can be tempered a little bit in Cheryl's lifetime by a little more mature comprehension of God.

I would suggest to her that she do some reading in the field of science. The current science magazine which my channel finds most rewarding is 'The Scientific American Magazine,' but there are others. Cheryl can discover a great deal about God by reading of the discoveries by various scientists of various aspects of what God has done in His material world. Yes, this is coming from their background which is usually starved pathetically of anything spiritual. But then they are quite happy and very busy and very productively employed in discovering parameters of reality which in essence are the descriptions of God which go so far beyond those held by humanity in past generations as to be very inspiring.

The masculine soul of Cheryl is quite capable of this understanding, and Cheryl herself has a good mind. I think she would be really thrilled, inspired, enlightened, somewhat matured and definitely more balanced, if she will give more of her attention to the factual nature of reality and a little less emphasis to the spiritual. Yes. Her emphasis upon the psychic is as yet not an over-emphasis and it is an interesting aspect of her being which she can certainly pursue just as it fits in with the total reality of her beingness and the normal living of her days.

Now another thing the soul knows is that 'masculine is thinking, feminine is feeling.' This is a metaphysical understanding of a difference between the masculine and the feminine members of the human race. But the soul has once again gone overboard in plunging into the feeling nature of woman with quite some abandon, let us say. Now remember, as she matures she is more and more both masculine and feminine. Let the thinking be co-equal with the feeling, and let the richness of the feeling nature be within a good framework and hung upon a good skeleton of intellectual comprehension. In other words, of thinking.

Yes, God is love, but God also is every fact, every truth, every reality of existence. God is impersonal as well as personal.

God is justice. God has so ordained the universe that judgment is inherent in truth, and so whatever is not true—truth being' what God the Creator has created and has ordained—has a falseness to it which will bring a judgment upon it. This is something upon which she might cogitate a bit because this is as factual, as impersonal, as non-feeling as mathematics, and there is this aspect of God. Those who would only buzz like honeybees to the love of God will really miss quite a bit of the nature of the God-experience.

So the soul plunges into whatever it's doing, in certain lives particularly, particularly this life, and in a way that is good. It certainly is getting the experience of what it is experiencing in this life and doing a very good job of it. It is intense in its feelings. It is intense in its spirituality, expressing itself, the soul, through the person of Cheryl and, of course, thus influencing and bringing about the events of her life as well as shaping the nature of her beingness. But she needs to learn and to love consciously within the total framework of God's creation, God's truth.

In her reading I would not suggest that she go primarily to the mystics. She's gone a bit overboard in that aspect, you see, although not yet badly so. It's really a very fine experience in this life. But as she matures, as the Cheryl soul grows in its Godhood, its God-nature, its God-powers, as the Cheryl God-child grows in compatibility with God, she will come into more of a balance, more of a maturity from which she may look back on some of her 'feeling' and 'spirituality' experiences with just a wee bit of embarrassment as having gone overboard. Now I do not wish her to feel that way, and her council, who— well, there are at least three here of her council and one from their supervising council—have helped to bring up this matter for me to bring out. I see from the akashic records and they see it more from the aspect of the life of their protege. The remaining years of her life, of which there should be quite a few yet, can come into a greater mellowness, a greater maturity, the greater maturity of beingness bringing about the greater mellowness.

She may think to herself, 'Then should not I feel so deeply? Should not I care so much?' Exactly. And she will find that she is more of a God-like God-child as she does control her feeling and caring. Then she may ask, 'Should I not seek God so intensely?' Exactly. She should seek God more casually, more certainly, rather than in the intense peak experiences. She should know God in such a way that a very quiet day, a very quiet week or month, could be spent just as much in the companionship and company of God as a week of peak experiences. Well this is what lies ahead. This is what the soul will be doing as it goes on from this life. But this is what the Cheryl person can be doing as well, and actually she probably would be quite surprised and certainly extremely pleased at the result. Well, that is the introduction to Cheryl. She is a very fine person and a very fine soul. This which I bring is just that she may be finer still. Yes.

Is there a question?

Conductor: Very, very good, Dr. John. Yes, there are several questions. One of her important questions has to do with the fact that she has involved other persons in her life, particularly when she feels they are on the wrong path. She has very acute pain and anguish and emotional suffering for them. Is this really caused by her soul's intensity?

Dr. John: Yes, it is. And actually the soul and the person of Cheryl feel rather virtuous at feeling agony and pain when others are making mistakes. But goodness, Cheryl, if God felt that way, He would be in agony and pain all the time, wouldn't He. God the great Parent, the great Father-Mother, allows His children to make mistakes as they find their own way, as they find His way, and she must do likewise.

And she must have a certain impersonality, which she can gain as she learns more about God through science, because that which God has ordained in the universe is that which science is discovering, and it turns out to have a stability about it which is far above the personal approach to beingness which Cheryl has stressed and is stressing.

Let her study this last sentence and I think she will see what I mean. Now she may reject it. She may say, 'But I have been taught that to love God supremely is an emotional thing. I must bring all of my being and pour it out before Him. I must aspire to ever-greater heights. I must drop all vestige of unworthiness. I must be burned with a celestial fire,' etc. Well, this is all right, and mystics who are emphasizing that in their mystical incarnations will encourage this sort of an approach.

But the point is, this is an over-emphasis upon one thing,

and Cheryl has come to the point, the midpoint of progression through incarnations, soulhood, when she needs to go beyond that stage. She needs to come to a greater maturity, a greater balance, a better perspective of truth, and all of this will be a better understanding of God and a greater compatibility with God and a greater development of her God-childhood, her Individuated-God-Beingness, her own God-nature. And she must do this because until she has a better control of her own nature, she will not be given the greater God-powers which are the heritage of the developing soul. Yes.

The emotional nature of the feminine is not an all-wise interpretation of the spiritual. Cheryl's masculine soul has experienced strong masculine lives, but it does not yet grasp the importance of integrating the masculine with the feminine in its spiritual lives.

When Cheryl asked about her sister in this life, two previous spiritually-oriented incarnations were presented:

Dr. John: Yes. They are cosmic family members. They are quite close. They are taking a course of growth together for a number of lifetimes now. They are not cyclemates but in a way they are cyclemates for a small cycle. Yes. Including the present, I see three lifetimes they have had together. Let us trace them back. They are all in a row here. That's handy. (Chuckling)
The immediately past one was in the 1800s. They were caught up in a revival movement in the present country. The sister was in the masculine. The then incarnation of the Cheryl soul was in the feminine. This was a great revival sweeping the country, or at least a portion of the country. The sister was then a minister, was not one of the great leaders of the movement but one who supported it. He was not one who was a spellbinding orator for God but in his own parish he not exactly imitated the spellbinding orators for God, the leaders of the revival, but he, let us say, utilized some of their thinking and some of their methods of presentation, and it was good in its way. It did strain his basic nature just a little bit. But he was a good parish minister of a fairly large parish in upstate New York or in southern New England, possibly Boston.
The then incarnation of the Cheryl soul was a sister just less

than two years younger, very close to the brother, partly because of the cosmic bond, partly because of the small cycle they were sharing. She had married and then been widowed and came into her brother's home where she was not a disruptive influence. The brother's wife was rather sickly but the Cheryl soul had the maturity and the graciousness to know that this other one was the wife and she did not in any way infringe upon the wife's place with her brother, the wife's husband. But she was of great helpfulness in managing the house and the children and it was with the wife's full blessing that the sister participated in her brother's ministry in some ways, nurturing him, going with him to services when the wife could not, and helping to lead some of the subsidiary meetings, the women's meetings and such, and speaking out vigorously as well.

There were no children for the then incarnation of the Cheryl soul herself. She helped raise her brother's children and this was all very good.

Now the background for this goes back into the 1700s, is rather interesting...it is in a different religion. The then incarnation of the Cheryl soul was a Hindu-Buddhist priest in the area that used to be called Indo-China. I will not try to find out just what portion of that area by the present name of the nation.

Here the fervency for God was a strong factor. Some of the Buddhist priests had that. Others had more of a casual self-assurance that they were thinking and doing and teaching and in their various practices in self-disciplines they were developing their own return to God and expiating any karma and imperfections and such.

But this one had a sense of the presence of God. The religious rites and rituals and teachings had a warm blood flowing through them for this one. And he in his teaching emphasized the God-aspect and a certain companionship with God, an appreciation of God.

In short, there was in this life really quite a bit of the quality that the evangelists and the revivalists of the next century, half the world away, were to express within the Christian framework. (A3751:3-8)

This is a fine soul, simply lacking maturity and understanding of both the facts and values of God. In its future incarnations, this masculine soul is bound to learn that there is always more to understand about God and His way for planet earth.

A mature spiritual approach could help her husband in this life. He is a younger cosmic family member who has a rather narrow interpretation of God's spiritual pattern and rushes with zeal from one cause to another in the name of God. Often younger souls feel they have the whole truth, when they have only the truth within a limited scope. Young souls are working with one aspect, one piece of the puzzle, but often think it is the only piece. Cheryl will be a better wayshower for her younger cosmic brother husband if she matures and helps channel her husband's spiritual energy into more productive pursuits instead of accompanying him in his adolescent spiritual zeals.

LAURIE

This century has provided a number of interesting break-throughs in human thinking. Scientific discoveries have shed light in areas previously surrounded by darkness. Public education has added another dimension. Better communication is certainly a step to opening new doors. Psychology gives man a better understanding of himself. There has been a tremendous emergence of intelligence, particularly in the last half century, our own generation and the past decade. The explosion of knowledge and intelligence continues to expand.

The spiritual has also emerged with considerable new enlightenment. Universities offer courses in religious history, studying the roots and general beliefs of a number of religions. Books have been written on many different religious philosophies and are now easily available, which would have been forbidden in the past. New spiritual ideas are taught from the pulpits of many different churches. People are less inclined to think their particular religion holds all the keys to understanding the spiritual, all of God's values.

A number of souls who have been misled spiritually in the past, have incarnated in this century of enlightenment to seek a more advanced spiritual understanding. Laurie's soul experienced a life as a priest in the 1700s. He was not a good priest, did not try to bring the rather dull people out of their misery and fill his parishioners with enlightenment. Instead he added to their wretchedness by preaching hellfire and damnation.

As Dr. John explains, the karma to be experienced by Laurie in this life is not retributive karma, but karma of growth. Really the priest was teaching what was acceptable, only he went overboard. To bring some balance to the soul it had an incarnation of ease and comfort inbetween, then thought it was ready to attack the problem created in the 1700s lifetime:

> Dr. John: Laurie is an incarnation from the feminine half of her whole soul, so she is in her native gender expression. She is a soul that is in the third stage, as I have divided the soul's progression through incarnation into five stages. She is around-the-midpoint and really probably around the centerline of that. This means the soul is getting into some of the more significant learnings. It means it has problems—or learning experiences—which are more involved, more complicated, with stronger forces actually, that the younger souls have. She is a middle soul.
>
> Now let us go to the second previous life. The then incarnation of the Laurie soul was masculine. This soul, although it has had masculine incarnations, has not developed the skill, the well-rounded capabilities, of the masculine as well as it has of the feminine. so the soul did not bring a great adeptness to that life.
>
> In that life the soul was a Roman Catholic priest in northern Italy, sort of north-central Italy. He was not a completely happy man. He had been somewhat ambitious to rise in the hierarchy of his church, but he was stuck for most of his life, for at least thirty years, in a rather small village parish where the people were rural rather than urban. They were not very well educated. They were not very artistic and such. He rather resented his people actually. He would not have said so, but subconsciously he did, and it broke into consciousness at times when they came for counsel on some difficulty into which they had rather stupidly gotten, and he would call them stupid, which of course they were.
>
> But they were acting in their own intelligence. their intelligence was not very high and they needed a priest who could

help to guide them in terms of what they were and in terms of the problems of the life that they lived, and the problems they actually met.

This priest fancied himself to be of a higher intelligence and personality and character than he actually was. His superiors, after he had been an assistant priest somewhere and then a priest in a small early parish—and then there was a second trial period where he had been stepped up to become an assistant priest in a rather large city church—his superiors judged him correctly as not really being of a caliber they themselves wished to associate with very much, nor of a caliber that could successfully handle the more sophisticated urban parishes.

So they thoughtfully placed him deliberately where he was, and they kept him there. So his ambitions got nowhere, and this led to a certain bitterness within him, as well as his bitterness at his parishioners whom he had judged to be below him, which they were, but to whom then he did not truly minister in terms of their own needs, but used his post and position somewhat to express his own ideas and his own inner resentments.

He had been taught a religion that emphasized hell. People were good in order to get into heaven after their physical death, and if they were not good they went to hell, and the hell he preached was quite uncomfortable, let us say; much more than that, of course. He took out some of his own inner bitterness by emphasizing this, and he laid heavy guilt upon his parishioners. This was one way he could feel himself to be superior, for he had no doubt that he was saved.

He was preaching the theology he had been taught, but the emphases he put on it were, as I have pointed out, pretty black, pretty heavy, pretty condemnatory, very highly demanding. Because in his own person he did not have much of an uplift of joy and happiness, there wasn't much of that in his preaching.

He was preaching the acceptable theology of that day, but he was also expressing some of his inner resentment at being where he was, as I have pointed out.

Now you see why, conductor, and I trust that Miss Laurie will see also, the skip was made to the present century where some new understandings of God and God's relationship with man and the right way for man to live, are coming about. To this, of course, must be added new understandings of the death experience and of the life beyond death. Really, it is only in this half century that there is being made available to an increasing number of people, even though still a small percentage of the population but yet much more than in previous generations, the new understanding of the spiritual components of man and the universe.

The new understandings of the physical portions of man and the universe really are quite new, having been brought by science and being increasingly brought by science. The new understanding of the psychological portions of man is really quite new. And the new understanding of the spiritual portions of humanity and of the universe is also quite new, and even newer than the understanding of the physical and the psychological portions.

This is understood and with a great deal of appreciation by those who are in New Age groups and such. There is a new light upon the path. There is a new shining light upon the spiritual nature of man and the understanding of man's relationship with God, and the understanding of God and God's will; a light of enlightened knowledge, and also the light of discovering the greater goodness of God, which expresses itself in what He does because of what He is, but which expresses itself also, and very particularly, in that which has been set up in accordance with God in the matter of guides and teachers and the channeling of the purposeful flow of forces from God into individuals' incarnations and everyday living.

That probably should be reread and studied a bit, for I have said a bit; there is much in it.

Now with these forces feeding in, you can see that the Laurie person will know certain turmoil, because many of these forces are from inside. You see, that priest took advantage of his position. He was preaching the acceptable orthodox theology, but he was also doing it as a way of asserting his superiority and of getting out some of his subconscious resentments at being where he was, his resistance at ministering to these dolts his parishioners who were not his equals in intellect and education and such.

Thus it was to his advantage, as it were, to lay guilt upon them. It asserted his superiority. But now there must come, and through her own experience, a realization of what this did to his parishioners. Because it set up many fears in the minds of many of them. There were not many there who were strong enough or bright enough or self-sustained persons enough to go against this priest, to say that his concept of God and his preaching of what they should do in life and of what they were and such, was wrong. There were not very many that could stand up in the confidence of their own beingness against the pattern which he laid upon really all the people in his little parish.

Some would think that this would bring an extreme karma upon the soul of that priest. No. He was a child of his time, and his parishioners were children of their time. So this was more a matter of needed learning for his time and for those who have come through it, a needed learning of the various souls that came through that experience, to discover that God is more, and God is different and God is light and God is good.

So the disadvantages of it, the evil in it, must be chalked up to the nature of the times. The answer is human enlightenment, particularly in the area of the spiritual understandings of man and God and the universe, the relationship of man and God, you see. So the karma which she is now expiating, as it were, is more a karma of growth. (A4000:2-5)

Laurie was raised in what she referred to as "dark Christianity." Her mother had been one of the parishioners to whom the priest taught "dark Christianity" in the 1700s. Therefore Laurie, as a person, received in her childhood some of the medicine to help heal the 1700s incarnation. It took her a number of years to rise above the strict, gloomy religion of her home. This was the process of the soul learning. The new knowledge available to people in this enlightened century has aided her and a number of other souls to climb out of the darkness surrounding many religions.

It may seem that religion has been responsible for downgrading humanity. This is not the case. Dr. John has been asked questions concerning "dark" religion a number of times. He usually responds that generally religion stayed ahead of humanity. If religion seems to be behind humanity in this New Age of man, it is only temporary.

Dr. John chose to bring his teachings to earth after science had been well established. He spent 4000-plus years learning to read the akashic records in order to combine the facts gained through science with additional knowledge of the values of God, the spiritual. Religion can establish its own scientific research and take its rightful place in this Age of Science, hopefully before the end of this century. The spiritual mistakes of the past are, when rightly used, steps of growth. **Karma, the great teacher, makes sure of that.**

CHAPTER EIGHT

LIMITED LIVES

Seeing disabled people can make us question whether there really is a God. How can a loving God allow such suffering? Soul growth is generally the answer. When we examine incarnate life on earth from the standpoint of each life being a part of the soul's growth, disabilities take on a different meaning.

It is the responsibility of the soul to guide several of its incarnations through limited lives—limited socially, or physically, or mentally, or economically, etc. This is one of the requirements of the soul. But a wise soul will combine this requirement with another general purpose. Perhaps a soul has several pockets of negative emotions and fears in its beingness that it is itchy to cleanse from itself. The soul can create a mentally unbalanced personality and drain off these pockets of negativity, thereby combining the experience of a limited lifetime with a second purpose. Dr. John sometimes calls such an incarnation a "sewer" life.

Other reasons for disabilites are simply souls learning to cope with incarnate life. If the soul did not handle a previous incarnation well—such as accept an accident, or a war injury, or disappointments of one kind or another—then a similar situation can be visited upon the soul in a future incarnation. Often the problem is then greater because the soul did not face the situation the first time.

Mental and physical disabilites can be the result of negative karma, yes, as the soul brings upon itself what formerly it brought upon another. Or such personal limitations can be a soul proving it can do a good job with an inept mind or body. The reasons are numerous, but the primary purpose for a limited lifetime is soul growth.

JENNY

"If life gives you lemons, make lemonade." Earth with all its wars, diseases, and accidents is not a place where each incarnation can be lived as the soul planned. It is the soul's responsibility to guide its personhood through, around, or between life's problems, even if one of its personalities is unexpectedly crippled or disabled. Should the soul get caught up in the suffering and pain of the incarnation and not effectively direct its personality, the soul will have to be given further instruction and then face a similar situation in another lifetime.

In the case of Jenny her soul did not adequately direct its 1800s masculine personality through a war injury. The original life pattern included marriage, children, and life on the family farm. But when he was wounded in the neck during the Civil War and left speechless, the 1800s personality retreated from the original pattern and lived a hermit-type existence. The soul did not take the lead in that life and so has now been given another personality with speech problems.

Jenny has had difficulty speaking all her life. As a youngster she had trouble putting words together to make sense. She withdrew within herself. With some special help in school, Jenny restructured her speech pattern and learned to talk. Then in her early twenties, Jenny contracted spinal meningitis, losing her memory and her speech. She had to relearn how to talk. Often, if a problem is not overcome in one incarnation, the dilemma is compounded.

> Dr. John: This is a rather unusual lifetime. It might be called a restart lifetime because the progression of the soul came somewhat to a stop in the immediately prior lifetime. Now, not really. This soul is a good soul. It is a very positive soul. It is well established in the ways of God. It is going right along. But the flow of experience planned for it came up against a decision of the soul in the immediately prior lifetime.
>
> The Jenny incarnation is from the masculine half of her whole soul. The soul is well into the third of the five stages into which, for the sake of convenience, I have divided the progression of the soul. Here most of the earth incarnations are taken, fifty to sixty percent. It is here also that the incarnations become more meaningful. The problems become more difficult, the achievements correspondingly greater, for the

middle soul.

The immediately prior lifetime was as a man in New York State. He was nineteen years old. He was engaged. This was in the 1800s, the mid-1800s. He was born in the 1840s. He was a farmer. That is, his father was a farmer and he expected to become a farmer too. He worked with his father and learned farming, and he liked it.

Then the Civil War came, and he joined the northern army. He was with it for almost two years. He still wrote back to his home and to his girl, and twice on furlough visited. Then in a fairly minor skirmish, he was hit by a rifle ball in the neck. It was a rather grazing blow. It did not break any blood vessel, it did not break the breathing tube. But it grazed the voice box and he never talked again.

I am trying to look at the wound. It smashed some of the delicate bony structure and the anchoring of the vocal chords. Were that to happen today, I believe it is quite possible that careful surgery could restore the voice or at least a voice. But in those days such knowledge was yet far in the future.

He was discharged from the army. He was retired or whatever, and went back home. His girl was very faithful to him. She really loved him and loved him all the more because of this that had happened. She was quite willing to go ahead with their marriage. She saw no reason why not and was planning to. But he said no.

In effect, he turned his back on the pattern of that life. Had he continued with it, he would have had a very fine experience of overcoming limitation and proceeding to accomplish the purpose of a life, fulfilling that pattern. But since he could not speak—now he was quite normal in every other way. His body was not otherwise affected. His health was good. But his mind became somewhat set in sort of a monomania, if you will, around this limitation that he could not speak, could not say words, could not make a sound.

It could have been a lifetime of overcoming limitations and going on to fulfill the pattern of that life. He could have married the girl. She was there intentionally for him. They could have had children and he could have been a farmer. Someone else could have done his speaking. There could have been happiness, a happy family. But he withdrew.

After a matter of some months, he left his home communi-

ty and went north into New England, where he had heard fac-
tories were needing workers. He felt that to become a factory
worker, all he need do was learn the procedures of whatever
machine he would undertake, and he would not need to speak
with anybody. And so it was.

That really became his life. It was quite introverted, it was
drawn in upon himself. He had a room in a house, and then
he had a small house, a very small house, one room or maybe
two, of his own. I see he bought a little tract of several acres
which had sort of a small shed on it. Then he expanded the
shed into a little two-room house. The shed, I believe, became
his little bedroom, and the part he built became his kitchen
and living room.

He could hear well. If there had been radio and television
in those days, his life could have been quite full of that communication. But he withdrew from society. He read, he read
the Bible a great deal. He brooded. He overcame his disappointment but he locked himself into this aloneness.

It was the doing of the person, primarily. He had met such
a shock of a disappointment. But the soul, instead of taking
hold of the person and saying, 'Nonsense, this is not the way
to handle this'—the soul was too sympathetic. The soul was
too caught up in the feelings of the person. The soul identified
with the person too much, and the soul accepted this deviation from the intended pattern.

After that life ended—and it was not too long, it did not
continue into old age; I believe he was about twenty-nine, not
quite thirty years old when the life ended—he discovered as
an excarnate entity how shallow, really, was the limitation. He
regained his voice, of course, and realized that he could have
communicated in many ways without the voice while incarnate.

He saw his girl, who had married someone else and had a
happy home, but with a strain of wistfulness, of unfulfilled
loneliness, in her. She was a cosmic family member, or cosmic
cousin soul, who had incarnated to be his wife in that life. She
accepted a substitute pattern and did well with it. But whereas
with him she could have had at least ninety-five percent of the
happiness which they had planned, even without his voice, with
someone else it was more like seventy-five percent, simply
because it was not the one she had come for.

The soul was somewhat chastened to find that its sympathy

had been mistakenly applied. That instead of being so sympathetic with the person of the young man, the soul should have been more firm. Firmness, not a harsh but a kind firmness, would have been the loving way in which to work with that incarnate person. The soul could have brought the person over the hump of disappointment.

Is this clear, Conductor?

Conductor: Yes, Dr. John, yes, and most interesting.

Dr. John: So the general pattern of progression for that soul through a number of lifetimes was blocked by this detour, this dead end. It was not completely a dead end, because the young man coped with the situation in the second best way, perhaps. He also got into the mechanical end of things. He made the progression from the agricultural to the mechanical, the industrial, mode of living.

He did a lot of thinking. Unfortunately, the thinking was not too clear, because the thinking began with the limitation and how to live with the limitation rather than the surmounting of the limitation. So the limitation was accepted too much.

It was a plus life, but still it was a stop life, and the present life is the restart life from that. It was felt that it would be better to take the present life into the feminine, because the feminine has natively a greater acceptance. The lot of woman in human history, and the nature of femininity as well, has more resiliency. Woman has had to cope with more things from outside, more conditions, more restrictions. Woman has had to find success in living within more restriction than the man, in general.

This is not the first major feminine life. This soul is rather well-versed in both masculine and feminine, although better in the masculine. But it was brought into the feminine, and there would be certain carry-overs, certain karmic carry-overs, and then there would be certain things to happen as well, certain events to test the soul again with unexpected limitations which would stop its looked-forward-to expectations. Would the soul now, in kindness but in firmness and strength, carry the person through the unexpected limitations with a positive attitude to make a success of life, whatever the details of that life would be?

So that is the nature of this life. As I can see from the imprint already upon the akashic records, this life is being successfully lived. There has been a restart of the program of its progression.

That is the identification of the nature and purpose of the present lifetime for Jenny. (A3324:2-4)

Making the best of any situation is a good policy, no matter how uphill the job may be. Incarnate life on earth is not a place to vent irresponsible notions or self-limiting emotions.

FAYE

Often people who have heard of reincarnation will fancy a disabled person as someone who was a miserable character in a pastlife, the "hiss-boo" villain of the old melodramas. Our research has not upheld this theory. Negative-karma-related physical and mental disabilities more often stem from the soul not living up to its potential, than a really bad character of the past. Therefore Faye is the exception rather than the rule.

In the 1700s a cruel, mean personality from the Faye soul was a sailor on a slave trading ship. Fortunately for the soul, he did not live too long. Her feminine soul was aghast at letting one of its incarnations get so out of hand. Since the feminine carries the values of God in its beingness, it is the duty of the feminine to nurture and love, not kill and maim. Hence Faye's soul is taking this present corrective lifetime very seriously.

Even though Faye is considered handicapped, she has not let her illness keep her from working as a practical nurse. Her disability is a blood-related disease. The capillaries are extremely fragile and she will bruise severely with very little pressure. Faye is relatively young but she looks old—the disease marking and scarring her badly.

Faye did not get a life reading, but a friend asked about her, wanting to know why this helpful, loving person was burdened with this terrible disease:

> Dr. John: This was a sailor on a ship that plied the slave trade in the early 1700s. This is an incarnation from essentially the feminine half of its whole soul, but in that masculine incarnation it gave in to some of the vices of masculine living.

It enjoyed its own strength, it enjoyed its own position of superiority, and a certain amount of sadistic pleasure crept into the treatment of these others.

It was partly a way of saying, 'See, I'm a strong man, you are a weak person.' The fact that these weak persons were held in chains and were in no position to retaliate gave the sailor the opportunity to feel a false strength and a false superiority. He was cruel upon more than one occasion.

That person got quite out of hand of its soul and of its council. It was not good at all, what he did. In a number of instances it was quite bad. He took the life of one who was a rather fine young man, a young black. He imposed himself upon several of the women. He was gotten rid of by losing his grip and falling overboard in a storm, and it was good riddance. So it wasn't very many trips that he had made with this sadistic, rather sly behavior.

The soul was utterly shocked that it had allowed one of its personhoods to get so out of hand. Now the soul has almost gone overboard to produce a compensating life in which there is no pretension to superior strength. There is an assumption of physical liabilites and hurts, and a commitment to service despite disabilities.

The Faye person deserves much spiritual appreciation. This person is working whole-heartedly with this soul, in what is truly a cleansing lifetime. It is expressing a very positive, outgoing forgiveness as it reaches out in this aspect of service, and as it takes upon itself these limitations. This is a karmic expression of forgiveness, outgoing forgiveness, in which the soul itself is forgiven and cleansed and strengthened. The strengthening is a very important element here.

That soul will never again find one of its personhoods going off on an evil tangent of cruelty to others. This life is the seal of that element of its spiritual growth, truly of its salvation. (A106:22,23)

Valiant Faye has brought healing to her soul through the efforts of this lifetime. Any life well lived is a plus for the soul. But when the person is starting way, way back behind the usual starting line and still wins the race, this is a mark of a good soul. Faye's soul has learned through failure—the hardest of all five ways of learning, but it can be effective.

SARAH

A disabling disease can be the result of a nervous soul. Sarah's soul has not lived several of its pastlives to their potential, becoming disillusioned or simply giving up. Since her soul has reached the centerline, where the lessons are more difficult, it must tackle these incarnations with firm commitment. The past failures have built quite a bit of anxiety within the soul's beingness and Sarah is living an incarnation (1) to strengthen the soul by living this life well and (2) to dissipate some of the soul's anxiety.

A more advanced soul would not have allowed itself to become so upset. This is also a learning experience. A comparison example could be a person who has to give a speech. In the back of his mind, he remembers several times when the words got mixed up and the speech was a disaster. Before the next speech he is nervous, can't eat properly, does not sleep for two or three nights. Many years and speeches later, the same person can give even an impromptu speech without fear. Sarah's soul needs to get past the sleepless-nights stage into a greater spiritual maturity.

The anxiety—the sleepless nights—have come out in Sarah in the form of multiple sclerosis:

> Dr. John: There is a good deal of disturbance on the part of the soul which effects into this personality and this has, in a sense, a double significance for the soul in that the soul itself must learn how to deal with anxiety as well as learning how the conditions of the soul, its emotions and its thoughts, affect its personalities, its incarnations.
>
> There are quite some anxieties in this soul at present. I might add that this is the feminine half of its whole soul and is around the midpoint of its soulhood learning and of its incarnations. It is by no means a young soul but it is, likewise, not an old soul. It would not be as perturbed if it were an old soul. In fact, the ability to become perturbed as this soul is perturbed must be overcome and the ability to remain unperturbed established before it can be considered in either of the latter two of the five stages into which we divide the soul's experiences from just-beginning to well-started; then into the largest single stage, around-the-midpoint; and finally into well-along and

nearing-the-end. The last two stages would somewhat qualify a soul as an old soul as that term is generally understood. Sarah is a middle soul.

The question naturally before us, and which I imagine will have arisen in Sarah's mind by this time, is 'What has caused the soul to become anxious?'

The answer lies primarily in its earth experiences of recent incarnations. The soul is not anxious because of demands upon it from other realms; it feels it has understood that which it is taught in other cosmic schools, and is not anxious therefrom. And it is not anxious from feeling that it has lagged behind the requirements of its progression, and thereby is in danger of being recycled. Its anxiety comes from certain disillusions and disappointments in fairly recent earth experiences and from its own reactions thereto.

Now the particular purpose of this life grows out of this particular problem of the soul, a certain anxiety which has developed primarily from the soul's possibly too great identification with its incarnate and excarnate personhoods. It is developing the quality of personalness quite well, which is a very essential part of the development of the sense of individuation or the knowledge of its own individualized integrity. But it has not distinguished sufficiently between itself as a soul and itself as a person, it has not developed the impersonal—which not contradictorily but in a complementary fashion, is an essential counterpart and counter-balance to the development of personalness.

The anxieties go back through several past lifetimes. In its immediately prior lifetime this soul incarnated in the state of, I believe, Mississippi, yes, Mississippi, in the American South, shortly before the Civil War. Its father was a plantation owner. It was in feminine expression and she, the then incarnation of the soul, married the son of a neighboring plantation owner. She was married really quite young, at fourteen, which was not unknown in that period. The parents and, of course, the husband, as son of his father, had plantations but not great plantations. They were cotton raisers. They lived the 'good life' of the American South, their field hands were negro slaves, their social life was that which is characterized by that which is known of the social life of the upper-class whites of that period of that time.

By the time she was sixteen, well, into her seventeenth year, she had two children. She was managing them all right and she and her husband got along very well together—both were products of the time and place and neither had been put under undue stress. Each had been brought along by her and his own parents in good preparation for their role now. And of course she lived in her father-in-law's house, which was quite large enough, and the mother-in-law took a kindly and beneficent and intelligent interest in her daughter-in-law. There was no friction there.

But then came the Civil War and her world was destroyed. Her father, who was still a young man, and her husband were among the many men of the area who went off to war and did not return. They were not all killed at the same time. Two of them, her husband and his father, were, however, killed in battle within about a two-week period. I do not know if her own father was killed before or after this. But there were these three shattering blows. Plus the fact that her whole way of life crumbled.

Upon the proclamation that the slaves were free, and without the plantation owner and his son there to enforce discipline, the slaves became somewhat truculent and certainly less productive. There was some sabotage of the work that was accomplished and, of course, the market for cotton had been quite disrupted. Some cotton bales, even after they were baled, were left where they got wet, possibly they were under the roof but some leaks mysteriously developed in the roof over the cotton and the water got into it, deteriorating its quality. This was discovered and was a cause for concern for the mother and daughter-in-law, of course, although they did not quite know what to do about it anyway.

There was a young man, white, who became the foreman. His father had been the foreman of the husband's plantation. The young man had a clubfoot, I believe it was, something about his foot which made it impossible for him to go to war. But he was strong and he remained and he kept things going. Secretly he was in love with the young woman and stayed for that personal reason, his interest in her, as much as from any sense of loyalty to the plantation and its ownership family, although there was that element also. And as the war approached its end, he definitely dared, as it were, to have beginning thoughts of some day marrying the young woman. Which would have been a very practical thing and an element of salvation for all concerned, because certainly to salvage what could be salvaged and bring things back to some kind of viable condition required a strong man with some knowledge of the local situation and he was the only such one left in the picture.

The mother-in-law went into a decline, reeling from the excessive shock she underwent. And there may very well have been a small stroke or several such, I do not see for sure, but there could very well have been because the shocks could very well have increased the blood pressure. Anyway, the mother-in-law lapsed into a condition where she was barely able to take care of herself and was of no real assistance in managing things.

So here is this young girl, barely into her twenties, with apparently the responsibility of the remaining household upon her, with her world and the expected life to which she looked forward completely gone—truly 'gone with the wind, and the place thereof shall know it no more'—and two children, small children, as well. She appreciated the interest and helpfulness of this young foreman, but did not realize his personal interest in her and that she and he together could have made a home and at least successfully raised enough food and somehow found a way to continue living for all of them.

Now with the end of the war there came unscrupulous and some very, well, they were called 'carpetbaggers,' from the North, opportunists who were not attractive. There were demands made for taxes and such. The slaves had mostly left the plantation and gone North, but these northern scallywags—and scallywags they truly were, really disreputable types of human scum but shrewd in their opportunism—so different from the courteous gentlemen type of man she had known—came and made demands and even suggested advances.

In a particular low point she took her own life, leaving all the anxieties unresolved, and the opportunity with the young foreman—who was older than she and who would have pulled them through satisfactorily certainly, although not in the manner to which she had become accustomed, which was now gone forever—and leaving behind her two children as well, who after some difficult experiences were adopted out. They were taken over, I believe, by some relatives, although not before they had experienced anguish and anxiety at their mother's loss. It was one of the children or both of the children who discovered the mother's body. I believe she had taken a rather quick-acting poison which caused a great deal of pain even as it worked its death upon the body.

So there is one source of much anxiety, and several other lives of the recent past contributed disappointments as well, all of which added up to the soul becoming unsure of its ability to handle earthliving in the experiences now being given it. When a soul comes into this stage of being, around-the-midpoint, it is not given the kindergarten lessons of incarnations but the more difficult ones.

The present life is the beginning of the way up. In the present life the turn has been accomplished. The soul's anxieties reflected in the personality but the soul has been given quite a lot of teaching and it is being carefully watched and assisted by its council of guides and teachers, who have confidence in it but know there is a real job to be done. So the present person is plagued with some circumstances which can very really be called karmic, not that the soul brought a hardship and suffering upon other persons in pastlives for which it is now paying a debt but rather that there is unfinished business, there is incomplete mastery of earthliving.

This element of unfinished business, of incomplete mastery, brings what could be called afflictions unto this personality. Or one might say that the anxieties of the soul have placed some almost intolerable strains upon the physical body of this incarnation. In this sense, it is an injustice that the person is suffering. But in the larger sense, this person, this incarnation of Sarah, is a venting point, a learning point, one of the 'saviors' of its own soul, a cleansing through the person of disabling anxieties from the soul.

This process will not be achieved completely by this person, because the soul itself must achieve for the soul. However, the essence of it is being achieved by the soul in the reflection into the soul of the valiant spirit of this person. Because even as this person experiences much negativity in its makeup, and this negativity I see extends into the body, as is a common thing when there is much negativity, so also there is a counterbalancing quality of valiancy, a quality of being valiant in adversity, which is enabling the person to endure the afflictions, to achieve the clearing for the soul, to make a good life under difficulties.

This certainly bodes well for the future even as it gains a high mark for the person in this present rather difficult incarnation, and represents a turning point for the soul. Is this clear?
Conductor: Yes, Dr. John. I do have one question that she has asked which could be connected to this 1800s lifetime.
Dr. John: Please, yes.
Conductor: She has multiple sclerosis. I take it that you were saying this is from the disturbance of the soul?
Dr. John: Yes, this would be. It could have come out in various ways but this is a very logical way in which it could come into the body. There were other ways as well also, even before the the multiple sclerosis developed.

Now, this is a rather harsh and somewhat extreme way, of course, but it is a way which allows the quality of being valiant to express itself mightily also. If she had simply had a small affliction, oh, say a twitch in her little finger, then there would not have been the opportunity for the same amount of valiancy in meeting it, you see.
Conductor: Yes.
Dr. John: She has the opportunity now for much of this quality of being valiant.

There is an impersonalness the soul must retain in its earth incarnations. To become overly caught up in any lifetime can be to the detriment of the soul. It must learn to guide its personalities with love and care, yet maintain a detached, unemotional interest.

Another lifetime when this soul experienced a partial failure was in the 1400s. The then personality of the Sarah soul became disillusioned with the church to the point that it refused to enter into the afterlife, the excarnate state of personal life. This incarnation was brought out when Sarah asked about her present-life husband:

Dr. John: They were together as mother and son back, oh, better than 500 years ago, in the 1400s, in France. Well, interestingly enough, here is another lifetime leading to some of the anxieties in the soul of which I have spoken, for which the present life is a corrective force.
The mother was, well, quite spiritual in the way in which

being spiritual was expressed in those days. She was a devout Roman Catholic lady. She honored the church as being the expression-point of spiritual aspirations. She could enter into the mystical reality of the mass. She entered into the rituals. She honored the Virgin Mary. She prayed with her whole heart. She lit candles. She was honest when she went to confession and she was greatly uplifted by the absolution she received from God's appointed agent, the priest. She wished she could have become a nun herself, but that was not her life; she married and had children.

The present husband was one of her sons and he delighted his mother's heart by choosing to become a religious. He entered, well he did not become a monk, he did not go to a monastery, he went into regular seminary training, which began very early. And he fit into it quite well. He had the type of mind that fit into the training given to produce the type of person that the church officials then wanted as priests and as church officials.

Unfortunately, the state of religion then in the church, within the church officials and the church administration, was not as high as the state of religion within those parishioners who were such as the then incarnation of the Sarah soul. And her son, instead of becoming better, became in her eyes worse—well, the ethics and the morality and the spirituality of the priesthood at that time and place were not such that the church would now tolerate, let alone be proud of. So the mother became quite disillusioned and bitter and this added to the anxiety of the soul, for if you cannot trust the church which is the expression of God upon earth, then what is there left to trust? Well, of course, there is God Himself or God Herself left to trust. But, nevertheless, the blow went very deep and was quite disruptive.

The son somewhat pulled away from his mother because he recognized the honesty of the mother's commitment and spiritual reach and he realized that he, who had been given the opportunities of spiritual studies and the spiritual life, had failed her expectations. He just simply did not want to face this and he did not face it. That meant he had to avoid her, too.

The excarnate personhood of that 1400s incarnation was a bit hard to reach. She had lost faith in the church which had taught that you live after death, and so she did not really open up to the life after death. There was an excarnate life for a while, but even after death she kept the doors closed to the more spiritual life and kept herself more in earth terms and would not be reached. So that person was allowed to run out. Its energies were expended without being replenished and gradually its vitality and its very life ebbed away, with the consciousness which had been impressed upon that person remaining just where it was. (A2040:2-7,11,12,14,15)

Even though both of these lives were difficult, giving up is not advantageous for the soul. In the 1400s life the soul gave up on its faith. In the 1800s incarnation, it gave up life altogether. The present incarnation is a demonstration of the redeeming valiant nature of the soul expressing through the Sarah incarnation. By her courage this life will help cleanse the soul of its anxieties and demonstrate it can carry through a lifetime of difficulty.

MELISSA

Another example of a person suffering from a disability is Melissa. Her budding career as a dancer suddenly ended when she injured her hip and could no longer dance.

Her soul had willfully entered this incarnation through a series of intricate cosmic maneuverings. In the immediate pastlife the soul's personality was a dancer and it wanted now a second lifetime to carry on in the same pattern. The arts are an important soul evolvement, building over several lifetimes, but not often in a series. It is necessary for the soul to develop intellect and strengths between artistic lives for the art form to grow in its expression.

Melissa's lifetime was cosmically arranged with the help of the soulmate and help from the unsuspecting father. When Arnold asked of his daughter, we find that she is the next incarnation of his mother, who died four months after the birth of Melissa. Since each half of the soul can have only one incarnation at a time, the soulmate provided the soul touch until Melissa's grandmother (the former dancer) died, then the grandmother-granddaughter soul was free to take over the personality of Melissa.

This intricate story and the willfulness of the soul needs to be unraveled from Arnold's life reading. When Arnold asked about an older brother who had died after only two days, Dr. John brings out that they are the same soul—Arnold and his dead brother—and the mother's resistance to motherhood caused his soul to pull out the first time:

> Dr. John: This was Arnold. It's the same person. He wasn't scheduled to die. Of course, earth presents many physical realities. You say he did die. He came right back again because he had a very purposeful life already patterned. Other souls were patterned for incarnation to mesh with him such as his wife, and others, and he very purposefully and quickly came back.
>
> The mother was not completely committed to motherhood at that first time. She may have thought she was, but there was something about it that she wasn't. It may have been a physical thing but I think it was even a soul thing.
>
> The father knew that this son was to come. In a sense, on the soul level, or on deep subconscious levels, or something of that nature, the father prevailed over the mother in this regard. Of course, the soul of the son likewise prevailed, and so he came and so he is.
>
> Conductor: His question is, 'What is the meaning of the very brief visit?' And in this case you have already answered it.
>
> Dr. John: The meaning had something to do with a certain element of resistance to motherhood in general—not resistance to him in particular but motherhood in general—on the part of the mother soul in this incarnation.
>
> She was richly rewarded in accepting motherhood by the son she got. So her resistance to motherhood was respected, her own self will as a soul. But the purposes of God are much more important and more strong than some particular purpose or fancied purpose or chosen purpose of a soul. So she did have motherhood, though it was not repeated, and she had a very rewarding child.

The mother's self will was respected by the Arnold soul the first time, but he had his purpose for this incarnation, therefore he came back a second time. He was an only child.

In order to continue unraveling this cosmic tale, we present the continuing story of the mother, who died in 1956:

> Dr. John: She is still present. It may be she is simply strong-
> ly present on the astral realm, but that would not be too logical,
> for she did not have that much of a connection with her son.
> I think she is again incarnate. I think that soul has again taken
> human form; someone within their perimeter of life, someone
> of their acquaintance. I could not guarantee this, but I am quite
> certain of it.
>   This, of course, is not so much in the akashic records as in
> the feel, the present reality. Whether or not they will be together
> in some future life I think is not yet patterned. There is still
> a question mark here that perhaps will resolve itself as we go
> on in the reading. If not, I shall go back to it, and if I do not
> remember it, conductor, simply remind me to come back to
> this matter of the mother.

Indeed the mother was still within his perimeter. The mother soul
in its next incarnation came as his elder daughter, Melissa.

The soul's choosing to return to the same family is an honor to
Arnold. Since he is an artist and a fine man, the mother/daughter
soul realized he would be a good father for its next incarnation: (1)
He had the artistic genes the daughter would need to be a dancer,
and (2) he was a fine strong man who would provide a good home
for Melissa. But God is not deceived by a willful soul and has His
ways of handling one who schemes and maneuvers.

The picture falls into place when Melissa is asked about and Dr. John
recognizes her as the next incarnation of Arnold's mother's soul:

> Dr. John: I rather hope she does not know her father is get-
> ting a life reading, so that he is not committed to sharing with
> her the portion about her. Yet, having said that, I realize this
> which I see in the akashic records can be of great helpfulness
> to her. So the sharing of it is in their hands.
>   In one sense, she should not have been born. She is the next
> incarnation of the mother, but the mother was not supposed
> to come back yet. For the mother there was an insistence upon
> the part of the soul to continue the life she had known in the
> mother incarnation, to carry it further. There were ambitions

unfulfilled, there were forces really of her own self will.

I have mentioned how there was a resistance to motherhood within her, which was overcome, at least to get Arnold born twice. To get him born once it took two tries to get him into incarnation. Likewise, she insisted upon this life, this new incarnation. This insistence was allowed, and her own soulmate took part in it, whether of his agreeing with her or whether of his being allowed to as part of the learning process which is coming to that soul and hopefully will be accomplished in this life, of accepting the counsel of its guides and teachers, of making its own wishes known, yes, and they will accept those. By accept, I mean listen, consider the suggestions, the wisdom of others. Not that one's own wish and will and wisdom is overridden, but that one realizes that one's own wisdom is insufficient and then does not cause one's own wish, the forces of one's own will, to ride inadvisedly forward along a path for which true reasons have been brought to not take it. Conductor, I think my grammar is slipping, but there is something to be expressed here.

So the mother soul arranged for a physical vehicle, a conception of incarnation, to be brought about even before the former one was relinquished. The soulmate provided the touch of life with the new vehicle, the present daughter of Arnold, until the mother soul took over, which she did within six months, or perhaps four and a half to five months, after the transition of the other personality, the mother.

Likewise, that other personality has remained somewhat close to earth, somewhat earthbound by its own wishes and will, to almost overshadow the daughter in beingness. However, since that beingness comes from the same soul, it is not a possession, even though there is an undue influence from the excarnate entity of the former incarnation.

Now, I must ask for more details. I see the big picture. I see the forces at work. Now how did they work out, conductor? Or do you have that information?

Conductor: I think I do, Dr. John. The mother, although she was a good and caring mother, was a fine dancer in her early years and a well-known teacher of dance for many years. This was her real passion and could be the reason she hesitated about having children. The daughter is a vivacious, goodlooking young woman—was a dancer until a hip injury stopped...

Dr. John: Wait a minute at this point. I want to ask, did the mother have some point of limitation or discouragement?

Conductor: The mother, in the dancing?

Dr. John: Yes.

Conductor: Well—

Dr. John: This is somewhat academic—let me outline it: If she had a point of definite discouragement, there might have been the creation then of a strong desire to fulfill the desires, the career, the life and nature of it. On the other hand, if she did not, it could be a desire simply to continue, you see, and hopefully to reach even greater heights. Which is a legitimate desire, but usually there can be an intermission of several incarnations if such seems wise on the other side, to allow for other developments and other qualities to come in before coming back to the particular area in which the desire is for a greater fulfillment, a higher achievement.

The great artists, the great achievers, the great scientists, the great inventors, the great political leaders, the scholars, and the great psychics also, reach their greatness not in one lifetime alone. There may be a period of several incarnations working toward the development of that quality to a peak expression. However, within the development there must be a more well-rounded soul development. The soul is beloved of God, and God is not going to let it just fritter itself on one area.

Likewise, to achieve in one area there has to be a growing maturity which involves other areas. So if there are to be, say, a half-dozen lives to develop a good musician, they usually will not all come right together, definitely not. Because there will have to be some lives in which other basic experiences are had, and lives in which qualities of patience, or perhaps social achievement and such, maybe even physical strength or mental development, in order for the peak musician to be reached.

So the mother, either through some disappointment or through a self-willed resistance at now taking one of these corollary lifetimes, let us say, was pushing on. But what does this do for the girl? Well, it's rather unfortunate, isn't it. But it gives the girl an opportunity to in her own right create something else as her own personal achievement, of course for that same soul.

It can be a certain correction for the soul, but it can be an achievement also of certain qualities. You said the girl had a hip injury?

Conductor: Yes. She was a dancer, and the hip injury stopped the performing, which devastated her.

Dr. John: The will of God will have its way with us, won't it.

Conductor: Yes. She does teach dancing, but she has always been driven to be a great dancer and did show great promise.

Dr. John: The drive came from that former incarnation.

Conductor: Arnold also says that his daughter is a striking, almost exact copy of his mother, almost alike in face, figure, movement, temperament, and talent.

Dr. John: It would seem as though the mother was quite pleased with herself, wouldn't it.

The hip injury reminds me, and I hope it reminds you too, Rev. Conductor, of an item from the Old Testament. There was a character back there named Jacob who had exercised his own self will and had thereby taken a certain inheritance away from his brother, Esau. His brother was not too smart, and really the inheritance was better used in Jacob's hands than would have been in Esau's hands. Nevertheless, there was a certain amount of skullduggery involved on sort of a semi-cosmic scale by the mother soul insisting upon and arranging this self-willed comeback.

I might also add that the comeback is a tribute to her son, as she saw this son would make an admirable father for the kind of daughter that she wished to become to carry on, you see.

So as Jacob was coming back to his homeland and to his destiny, there was a night in which, as it were, God appeared and wrestled with him. The story, which is both physically real and symbolic, is that God touched Jacob upon the thigh, and after that he had a hip injury and he limped. But he went on to his own destiny and Jacob became Israel, the chosen people.

So rather quickly we can see where this is in line with a great cosmic principle of turning limitations to spiritual advantage, to spiritual growth, and the great cosmic principle of, 'All right, let's see what you as a soul will do with this now when this great change comes into the life you had thought was to be in this personhood.'

So the daughter person, on her own, can now build her contribution to the soul. She may not be too happy about contributing to the soul, rather than to her own nature as a person. *In a sense, the hip injury freed her from being her grandmother over again.* I hope the transcriptionist will underline that. Well, let me repeat it: In a sense, the hip injury frees the daughter from being her grandmother over again.

Many good things came from the grandmother, admittedly. The love of this form of art, the past history of achievement in it, these are experiences and forces which are good and which are hers and which no one can take from her. But in a particular way what Melissa does with her life from now on will be her achievement, her doing, her prize. If it be to teach dance, that is very legitimate. That is not just simply carrying on the grandmother, you see.

The touching of the hip by God, literally, that is by the forces which God has ordained through agencies of His ordination, frees the daughter from being the grandmother over again and allows the daughter to begin her own life as she overcomes what would be the devastation, the double devastation—the devastation of her own being and the devastation of her grandmother. That girl, that woman, really has something to work through there, the cloud from the soul as well as the cloud on the person. But to work through that and to become something on her own is her chance of real achievement, you see, in this lifetime.

Most interesting. I certainly wish her well, and the guides and teachers, who are different from the guides and teachers of her grandmother, are working with her with confidence, and already with a certain assurance and also a certain pride on their faces. (A151:9-15)

As stated by Dr. John, Melissa was freed to be her own person after the hip injury. She is guided by a different set of guides and teachers than her grandmother, and they appear to be directing Melissa with strong, loving care and wisdom. Hence it appears that there will be a happy ending to this intricate cosmic tale. It is bittersweet, but can become a major spiritual achievement.

GERALDINE

Hereditary diseases are one of the causes of both physical and mental disorders. Science has studied heredity in animals, where selective breeding is common, breeding out the weak genes and building the strong traits. However, people who carry disease-bearing genes are allowed to have offspring, since humanity is not ready to consider the problems created by heredity beyond treatment of its various debilities.

All through her life Geraldine has suffered from fear. She has been diagnosed as a paranoid schizophrenic. Although the soul has dealt with the problem admirably and used the diseased mind to cleanse it of certain fears, the mental disorder is hereditary. As Dr. John brings out in the preamble of the life reading, "In one sense she should never have been born." This is a rather strong statement, but people who are known to carry both physically and mentally defective genes still do bear children. A good strong soul like Geraldine's has wisely used this incarnation to its benefit, but a younger soul would be less adept at handling this situation.

For people who have hereditary problems, adoption might be a better way to have a family. As reincarnation is studied from the standpoint of the cosmic relationships, karma, and the soul, humanity will become aware that cosmic arrangements can be made to bring the right child to the right adoptive family. The understanding of cosmic principles helps us resolve both social issues and individual choices. However, religion is one of the major proponents of childbearing as a God-given exercise not to be tampered with. How humanity faces the problem of defective heredity is still in the future.

Dr. John introduces Geraldine to herself at the start of her reading:

> Dr. John: This is a lifetime for the soul of coping with problems. We hope—that is, her guides and teachers assembled here with me, and I—that this simple statement, as we elucidate upon it, will give her a new peace within herself as well as guidance for this life.
>
> It may seem completely unfair to the person of Geraldine that this be a lifetime in which the soul is coping with its problems, using her as a laboratory. That is not fair! And of course it is not fair to the person, if you would see the person in the perspective of being the only thing or the only life involved.
>
> But persons, or incarnations, are first of all the expression-points and experience-points of souls. Now the person is loved by God, the person has an integrity of its own, the person has

its own psychological or personal forces, the person hurts and laughs and cries, the person has ambitions and desires—but the soul is much greater than the person, and the person must come to see itself in this secondary role of serving the soul. We expect the problems to ease up a bit, although the general nature of this incarnation of the soul is the dealing with and coping with problems. But as the soul learns how to cope with problems, it should be able to ease the burden upon its person, its incarnation as Geraldine.

If Geraldine can become a little more lighthearted about it, even find some ways to joke about it, she will be able to step aside from her own sufferings from the problems. And she has a right to do this.

Now the soul really is learning how to cope with this sort of problem. And there is another great advantage working for both the Geraldine soul and the Geraldine person now: the advance in the human understanding of many problems, including the particular type of personality and mental disturbances which are the problems plaguing Geraldine, the problems with which the Geraldine soul is learning to cope and hopefully to master in this lifetime.

In past centuries, in past generations, the knowledge possessed by humanity in this area was far, far below that which is possessed now. The knowledge is still insufficient, but souls must learn how to handle persons in lifetimes where the general level of knowledge of humanity is insufficient for meeting those problems. Does this mean that there is a failure in meeting the problems? From the person's standpoint, yes—as is evidenced every time a person dies of cancer, or heart trouble, or suffers from personality and emotional disturbances, or dies in a war, or any such thing. Yes, there is failure in that the person, the incarnation, may suffer and die. But there can still in any generation and in any culture and in any situation be victory for the soul, as it learns how to handle as best possible its personhood in that situation, as it manages to hold itself above giving way to certain temptations presented it, as it develops the strength which it can develop in that incarnation experience.

Let me further say that there will be a cleansing of all the emotional and mental and personality disturbances after the death of the Geraldine body. In other words, the Geraldine *person* is not condemned to handle these problems eternally.

Death, the passing from the incarnate to the excarnate part of her personal life, will be a freeing.

I shall have a little more to say about that very soon, but the point now is that the Geraldine person as it leaves the body behind will be freed from these disturbances. Now this freeing will not be immediate, but it will be accomplished quite quickly. The problems have entered into Geraldine's consciousness, and the consciousness will be cleared of them when the physical basis for the problems is cleared.

And here we come to a further understanding of the body element in this matter. In one sense, Geraldine should never have been born, Geraldine should never have been conceived. We definitely look forward to the time when persons with inherent and inherited and inheritable problems such as her parents had, will be restrained from having children.

The human race has learned a great deal about the advantages of careful breeding with animals. In time, this knowledge should be used to improve the lot of the souls taking incarnation as children in the human race. Let us simply put it in that way. It does not mean that some souls will be denied incarnation, because some children born to some parents will simply not be born. Rather, it means that there will be fewer second-rate births which must be taken—for every human birth must have a soul attached to it to provide the life factor—and thus the conceptions offered to and available to souls for incarnation will be improved.

Conductor: Thank you!

Dr. John: For those who may have ecclesiastical or doctrinal objections to what I have just said, I can only say that I trust their souls will have sufficient second and third and fourth and fifth and sixty-ninth rate incarnations to come to a more enlightened view. And in the grand scheme of things, they probably will.

If Geraldine can keep these difficulties out of her consciousness, she will benefit both now and in the hereafter. This may seem like a tall order, but very simply, Geraldine, does not this make good sense? I speak directly now to you, Geraldine: If you can keep the *real you* in a sense above the mental and emotional and personality disturbances, you will have a greater tranquility. It will take quite a bit of figuring to learn just how to do this, but the rewards are worth the effort. Likewise, this clearing of your consciousness, of your real self, now, will facilitate the cleansing and readjustment of the person as you enter the excarnate stage.

Remember, the basis of this difficulty is physical. It is in the inherited genes of your present incarnation. Knowing this, see what you as a person can do in living above the difficulties. As you refuse to enter into these difficulties—and there is a way and a degree in which you can refuse to enter into the difficulties—you will be on a better plateau, and this without disturbance to the personality; in fact, this can bring a greater degree of integration to the disturbed personality. It is a challenge, it is something to be discovered and learned and undertaken and accomplished. But there can be helpfulness, Geraldine, in this approach.

All souls must learn how to handle their personhoods, or personal expressions, in all of the major types of human experience upon earth. The improvement of the overall human condition of course will lessen some of the difficulties which souls have had to face in incarnations in the past; and this is a very legitimate improvement, just as legitimate as indoor plumbing and antisepsis and the better transportation that the modern automobile provides over the old-fashioned ox cart.

As the Bible says, when God created the human race God instructed it to *take dominion over the earth.* As man does obey God, man does come into a finer level of living and higher level of achievement, satisfaction, fulfillment, and comfort. So the attainment of the understanding and mastery of the mental and emotional and personality disturbances such as Geraldine and thousands of others now suffer from, is one way of taking dominion and of coming into the greater comfort which is available as the children of God learn how to leave some of the errors and difficulties and pitfalls of physical earthliving behind.

The guides and teachers remind me that both they and I have neglected as yet to 'place' the Geraldine soul. It is around-the-midpoint, which means it has enough experience in pastlives, both feminine and masculine, to undertake the rather difficult lifetime it has now. Now this type of lifetime is not the most difficult that a soul must undertake, but it is certainly one of the more difficult ones, and not undertaken—usually, that is— by a soul which is in the just-starting or only the well-started divisions. Geraldine we trust will gain some confidence, extending into her day-by-day thinking and living, knowing that her soul is quite a competent soul, and is carrying along pretty well. And if Geraldine feels still that it is unfair, then let Geraldine think of herself as serving her soul, as all that she endures really is accomplishing more than only for herself. Yes.

So the problem created by her heredity—the paranoid schizophrenia—will be relieved when Geraldine enters the astral realm. Although the consciousness will not be cured immediately, there will be this healing. This does not diminish her present situation, but it must be comforting to know the mental disorder will not last forever.

Even though Geraldine is well educated she has trouble holding a job because of her fear of people. Unable to cope with pressure situations, she has suffered several nervous breakdowns, usually job related. Since her soul is utilizing this incarnation wisely, it is draining certain fears and misunderstandings from its beingness.

In the relationship portion of the life reading, it was brought out that Geraldine had a life in Russia when the personality died around ten years of age. The young girl had a special affection for her father in that life, but he in effect ignored her. This is one of the situations the soul is draining off in the present incarnation. Now Geraldine has a favorite sister who turns out to be the reincarnation of the Russian father who rejected her love and attention. This was purposeful, because the childish desires of the little Russian girl need to be released:

> Dr. John: The present sister was a father to Geraldine in a past incarnation. This takes me into Russia, the Russian Russia. This was in the early 1600s A.D. The little girl lived to be, well she lived to be ten years old but she did not reach her eleventh birthday.
> The father was a horseman in the military service. He was a strong man and a rather fierce man. The daughter really admired him a great deal, and wanted to claim him. Daughters very often develop a love affair with their fathers in the early years of their lives. And to quite an extent this is good, if the father is a good male-role model.

In this case, however, the girl did not grow old enough to make the transition of placing her love with another man, first in the outreach of dating and courtship, and then to her husband. The little girl was stricken quite suddenly with a disease—no, not so much a disease as a quick ailment. It caused a congestion in the lungs. The father was home, and lent his strength and his real love to his daughter in this period. But really she died in about, well it was several days, with a rather intensive period of eighteen hours. During this eighteen-hour period the father stayed with her constantly.

The mother was there also, but it was the father who took her in his very strong arms and carried her, and kept her warm, and held her close to his own strong body. The little girl's outreach of love was thoroughly awakened by this very real kindness on her father's part. And the fact that he had not really given her such attention, such concentrated and intense attention, very much before, only heightened this love that she felt for him.

So that life ended with this great and rather possessive love of the little girl reaching to the father. And in some odd way there is a carryover of this now towards the sister.

This is perfectly natural, given the background—but it is an unusual situation between sisters. And it is further complicated by the fact that the emotions and the mental processes of Geraldine are not under the usual control of a physically well-ordered and healthy body and brain.

I am interested in following through the person of that little Russian girl after her death. The consciousness and the will—the quite strong will—of the little girl held her very close to the father. She simply refused to look at others on the excarnate side who had come to take her into the other realms. So after three or four or five years in earthtime of this, which of course did not seem to be that long to the little girl, it was seen best by its own soul to withdraw. The soul conferred with its guides and teachers, who quite agreed that this was the only thing to do. The person of the little girl was no longer a constructive and positive and useful instrument for further expression of the soul or experience for the soul.

So the soul withdrew, and the little girl as it were sort of closed her eyes and collapsed on the excarnate side into sort of a nothingness, and that personhood was ended. So the forces were given another opportunity to reach out now, although of course in a much modified way and without the energy and substance they had before.

Of course, the sister did not incarnate only for this. She has her own purposes and destiny as well. But this is one of the reasons why she came into the same family.

Now what to do about it? We would suggest—and her guides and teachers suggest this quite strongly—to Geraldine that she let this relationship as it were subside simply into a present-life sister relationship. Drop the inner forces and the greater forces which she will see from what I have said, coming from almost 400 years ago. Those were understandable forces, but are neither appropriate nor legitimate in the present-life relationship. Let there be simply a normal sister relationship, and all concerned will be happier and better off.

These two will *not* be together again, unless Geraldine can in this life put the relationship on the more normal basis.

Psychological forces were set up in that Russian life. In this lifetime Geraldine has a very possessive love for this sister and a need for her approval. Until the reading she could not understand why the sister rejected her love.

Even though Geraldine has a spiritual outreach, she has a deep fear of God, and wanted to know what caused this reaction. Dr. John was able to trace her fear of God to another pastlife:

> Dr. John: Yes. She was a young boy victim of a religious warfare in India. This was in the very late 600s A.D. She was I think in a Buddhist sect, and the other sect had more of a Moslem cast to it. Whether it was allied with the Moslem religion or whether it was just more warlike in its religion even as the Moslems are, I do not see. But these fierce, wild-eyed, scimitar-swinging others came and they were shouting about God. They took over and terrorized this area. And it was all in the name of 'God'!
>
> The unwarlike people of the then incarnation of the Geraldine soul in a sense didn't care all that much; their concept of God was much more eclectic and broad and flexible. But these 'God' warriors were of course really in the grip of an evil blood-lust, and this little boy who was about seven—

well, he was in his eighth year—was ridden down in the street, struck by one of these curved swords. It cut very deeply into his shoulder right at the neck, and rather quickly he bled to death. His assassin rode on, and the boy's family retrieved the body when they could do so safely, which was within a few minutes before the boy died, so that the boy died in his mother's arms, and she was of course weeping.

But the consciousness of the boy was of this horseman riding him down and striking him with this sharp curved sword and shouting the foreign name which the boy had come to know all too well as being their name for God.

So God really got a bad name with that boy!

Now in the excarnate realm, much healing was accomplished. There were those who met the boy, who ministered unto him. But there were so many casualties in that area as these religious assassins, these inhuman fired-up raiders, did their deadly and despicable work, that there were not enough really on the other side to do a completely effective job with those who came over so many so quickly.

The young boy was soothed in the excarnate realm, and eventually simply allowed to go more peacefully asleep. But the momentum of this 'God' association with fear was not completely spent. So it did carry over into this life.

If it were not that fears in general were quite activated in the Geraldine person, this fear of God probably would not have surfaced, because it really is not all that important. But since this is a lifetime in which many fears have surfaced, and particularly fears that have engendered rather than being surfaced out of the past, it was all right for this fear of God to surface and be expressed and run out, as well as the other fears. (A3194:1-5,10-12,18,19)

Geraldine's soul is productively living this incarnation. The fears the soul has accumulated over a number of incarnations are being drained from its beingness. This is one of the purposes of mentally disturbed lives—to release the unwanted garbage from the soul. This cleansing is important because future incarnations of this soul will not have to face the monsters she faces now. Although the mental problem is hereditary in nature, a strong, wise soul can turn even such a human problem into a serviceable incarnation.

MASON

Another service of diseased minds and bodies is to benefit humanity. The final two life reading excerpts in this chapter tell of incarnations of souls who are serving humanity in general.

First is Mason. His father got the life reading for his son, who suffers from a disease diagnosed as tuberous schlerosis, a rare disease characterized by tumor-like masses of certain nerve cells scattered throughout the brain and by warty growths on the cheeks which grow progressively larger involving the whole face. The average life expectancy of sufferers from this condition is about twenty years, but at the time of his life reading Mason had lived seven years past that average and was still going strong.

The disease showed up when Mason was about five months old and after he developed epileptic seizures. The family took care of the child until he became so abusive they realized he needed outside care. Since the age of eleven, Mason has been in special homes for the mentally handicapped and in outside family situations where special trained attention can be given him.

Mason's father is a doctor and he wanted to know why his son suffered from this disease. Dr. John explains in the preamble that this incarnation was purposely planned by the soul. Because it wishes to be a doctor in its next incarnation, the son's soul wanted to experience firsthand what it was like to have a disease-ridden body and tortured mind:

> Dr. John: This one is not to be pitied. It is a strong masculine soul-person, especially designed to be expendable in a special project.
> As background, I should get into the matter of healing. As you know, I have not had earth incarnation for some four thousand years, so I think my request for the next one will be honored. It might be of some interest to the father to know that I have requested that my next incarnation be as a doctor, a medical doctor of health. Why would I do that?
> Because the understanding of the human body and the restoration of it to a state of health when something has gone wrong somewhere in the intricate, the very complex and inter-

woven processes of it, is not an easy thing. The people who speak glibly of spiritual healing are often speaking in hope and ignorance more than in practical reality. Although there are, of course, psychosomatic factors, where the mind influences the body, and what we might call pneumasomatic, where the spirit influences the body.

There also are karmic factors. There also is the fact that the human flesh is a very intricate machine subject to 'a thousand slings and arrows of outrageous fortune' or something of that sort. It is also true that knowledge comes about by learning, and the knowledge of healing is not exempt.

Yes, the Master could and upon occasion did bring miracle healings, far beyond the understanding of those around Him, but not beyond His understanding. But He is the Master. He is the most advanced God-child, or the most spiritually pro- gressed Individuated-God-Being, now associated with planet earth. The consciousness He had was gained, the knowledge of it, bit by bit; the understanding of it in outline of the large and knowledge of the details of the intricacies involved—all had to be won.

There is nothing in consciousness that is not put there. The very earliest beginning consciousness in the soul stage, the beginning soul stage, has something put there from the animal body and its instincts. Wisdom must be solidly built by the knowledge of truth and then by the ability to use that knowledge, along with the character and commitment to use it aright.

I might mention three aspects of this growth in the ability to heal: The very first I would mention is objective knowledge to ascertain what the facts are. It was not more than a century ago or so that the facts of the skeletal structure and muscular structure and the circulation of the blood were first discovered and traced out. The knowledge of the neural structures is still in its very early stages of objective ascertainment.

This is pretty much the job of science. In other words, the method of science is the best tool available now and the best tool of which I know for ascertaining objective realities.

The second aspect of increasing healing knowledge is sub- jective. What is the experience like? The first question is, 'What are the facts?' and the second is, 'What is the experience like?' Here is where Mason is a volunteer, a brave and courageous volunteer. Some would call him foolish but I would not call him foolish. For that soul volunteered and in a sense constructed the plan himself, with the assistance and the permission of his council, who conferred with their advisory council, to come into this life where he would experience a very serious disease of the physical system, the animal body with which the soul must incarnate.

This was not karmic. However, karmic forces can be released in this. As I trust you have noted, God endeavors to get the maximum return out of every effort, every experience, every period of existence of His children and, we suspect, of Himself as well. I believe this probably represents a certain aspect, a characteristic, of God's beingness.

So the Mason person is a—well, to use the illustration of the amoeba, with which Dr. Evans is probably familiar: Likening the soul somewhat to the amoeba, this person is a pseudopod extended by the soul to encircle and draw into itself something which it perceives within the environment to be a nutrient—in this case, a source of information, of knowledge.

The third, and in a sense a still future and by far the largest aspect of learning healing, is to learn how the human body was brought about. The amoeba was the creation of intelligences and abilities of beings who are so far beyond us now that we have no contact with them except through this that they have done. The amoeba, that strange collection of chemicals which has been endowed with life and some consciousness, is only the beginning.

I would like to meet some of these beings of millions of years ago who—exercising levels of God-nature and God-powers beyond that of anyone I know except possibly the Master, and I have not asked this of Him—brought about the appearance, the evolution, the emergence, of life as it is known now upon planet earth. This is not the only place or manner of life at all. But this holds so much of that which has been done which is to be learned by those who would understand what God has done, as it were, understand this area, this plane of existence of life, and understand how to bring helpfulness and health to their brother men and to themselves.

It is an awesome thing to contemplate, a magnificent adventure to undertake. I trust the good doctor will understand both why he is a doctor and why I have requested to come back as a doctor of health; and, even more important, what his son, Mason, is doing.

The son is working, of course, in the second of these three things. The good doctor has worked in the first to ascertain objective facts and the reality of certain aspects of the human body. The son in this incarnation is getting the subjective experience. The matter of learning how it all came about essentially lies still ahead for all of us.

It is doubtful if any of us will be able to, as it were, talk with the architects of life who brought this all about. We must learn what they did from what they have done.

This is the basic introduction to this interesting and courageous soul and person. I might speak further on the matter of how a situation like this can be used to vent negativities gathered by the soul in past earth experiences: When the intelligence and the self-control and self-knowledge is limited, inhibitions are down. Certain forces which would be controlled, and the expression of which would be denied, by a person more in control of himself, can flow out.

In a sense, in this capacity the son is acting not only as a noble pioneer, of whom his father and mother can justly be proud—and they were honored in being selected to be his parents—but this son personality is also acting in what I have sometimes called rather inelegantly a 'sewer lifetime.' However this is a quite mild and distinctly secondary factor here. (A937:1-4)

The soul, through the lifetime of Mason, is gaining knowledge of the human body by experiencing a dreaded disease. This insight will equip the soul with special awareness. All knowledge must be gained—one experience developing upon another, one life upon another. The incarnation of Mason is an important type of knowledge for the soul.

Also, the soul is dumping some of its garbage through the personality of Mason. This is again wisely using the "sewer" incarnation. Negative forces which are held in pockets within the soul beingness, can be released through the uninhibited personality of Mason. Therefore, this incarnation serves a dual purpose: (1) The experience of a diseased body prior to becoming a doctor, and (2) releasing pent-up negative emotions and fears and cleansing the soul.

MAUREEN

As a growing edge a soul may create or be given personalities that require extra skill to lead through a lifetime. Maureen's soul is strong and wise, but intentionally built a mentally defective mind tool, then placed the personality in a deprived family situation. The soul wanted to experience leading a mentally unbalanced personality out of the slums into being a productive citizen.

Maureen has been diagnosed as a manic-depressive. She was the tenth of eleven children. Since the family was poor, she was deprived of many necessities of life, including a proper education. She has not only survived, but has been well guided by her wise and strong soul, surmounting many problems, even pursuing spiritual understanding. As Dr. John points out, many souls do not bring their personhoods to spiritual seeking in a normal lifetime.

What this soul has accomplished adds to the reservoir of goodness of all humanity. Maureen's soul did not have a garbage-karma to release through its personality, but it took on some of the garbage of the world. The Faye soul we studied in this chapter had a lifetime as an evil slaver in the 1700s, which is the reason the present Faye person started her present personality incarnation way, way back behind the starting line and still comes out ahead. The lifetime of Maureen also started way, way back behind the starting line and won the race, but it has no past wrong-doings to make up.

In the Jesus-lifetime of the Master, He shouldered the sins of the world. The great love He expressed was used as an instrument to defuse evil. Returning good for evil weakens the grip of evil on incarnate life. Maureen's soul understands this principle. Therefore, following the example the Master set, her soul is taking on some of the karma of the world.

Dr. John gave Maureen's life reading special attention:

> Dr. John: I was advised by her advisors that her reading was coming, so I have had opportunity to study her akashic records ahead of time. I am very happy that she was brought for a reading, for I believe the reading can bring her much help. It will not bring the ending of some of her difficulties, because

the difficulties are interwoven with the purpose of this life. But it will bring the ending of some other difficulties, difficulties of understanding why she is having a life such as this. This is not a young soul. This is a middle soul that is well into the third stage, the around-the-midpoint stage, as we define it in our readings. The soul incarnating now as Maureen is the feminine half of its whole soul, because to take this difficult assignment in its native gender is more easily done than to take it in the non-native gender. This soul has more than half of its earth incarnations behind it, perhaps 55-60 percent, which means it probably has had forty-five to fifty pastlives, not counting some that ended in miscarriage or in very early years, which really had no significance for the soul.

This is a life of limitation. Every soul must be able to guide several of its incarnations through lifetimes or partial lifetimes of limitation. This limitation can come in various ways. The physical limitation is perhaps the most prevalent and best known; and there are various statuses in human life, social, economic, cultural and so forth, which might be called limitations.

This is a life with a certain compound of limitation for Maureen, because the basic limitation is in the mind equipment which as she knows brings limitations to opportunities and outlets to some extent. Likewise, and appropriately, the life was set in a setting of limitation—the birth, the family into which the soul came in this incarnation.

There are not too many in her life who have pastlife acquaintance with her. There are several, but not many. This sometimes happens, and usually by the soul's own choice. The soul has had happy and successful experiences—experiences of achievement, experiences of congenial temperament, experiences of a real happiness and love relationship. It may prefer to take a limited personality lifetime not really among its close friends. This is the case with Maureen.

True, at other times a very close friend or a number of them will be brought in to help sustain the person through that lifetime, and in so doing to help sustain the soul and help it guide its person through such a lifetime. But the soul of Maureen is a competent one with quite a bit of confidence. Its guides and teachers are confident of it, too.

The net result is that the soul was given the opportunity of guiding its personhood expression, its incarnation in this lifetime, in other words the Maureen person, pretty much itself, with its guides and teachers helping it.

It has done well. Not that the person has experienced ease and comfort as a continual flow, but rather that the soul has brought the person through the experiences without letting this mental limitation—which, as Maureen knows, is an affliction which occurs, rather than being a low ceiling placed on the mind—without letting this deny the person really some quite basic experiences of incarnate life.

So the soul has guided this person through this incarnation really, as I have said, quite successfully, and in that has achieved many of the purposes of an incarnation.

The achieving is not over. The soul has not allowed the person to slump into the acceptance of despair and defeat, and the soul has not taken the experience in this way either. A younger soul might have done so, and many young souls when faced with an experience such as this do throw in the sponge and give up. But not this soul.

Moreover, the soul having led its personhood, Maureen, through experiences of successfully growing up as a person, despite the difficulties, and through marriage and motherhood, is now bringing the soul into a spiritual quest. For some incarnations the purpose does not include this, but in general—not always, I repeat, but in general—a soul that includes a spiritual quest within the earth lifetime of its incarnate personality has achieved a greater fullness for its incarnation, for the person, the earth-being it is directing and expressing through and experiencing from.

What about the outcome? What can I suggest to ease Maureen's bouts with discomfort and suffering? Here the human ignorance is still rather large, since what causes this sort of a recurrent mental fluctuation is not quite known as yet. Human minds are working on it, and the great tool of science researching in this area is bringing greater understanding, as it has brought in every area in which it has been used.

I believe, however, that there are those who would suggest certain dietary aids to human beings enduring difficulties that Maureen has. I believe there are some suggestions in your literature of natural foods. Possibly the use of the wheat berry is included in some of these. The wheat berry is actually simply whole-grain wheat, not ground. This can be slowly steamed or left in hot water for many hours. Not being boiled, although the water may simmer occasionally, but let the wheat be softened and, as it were, cracked in this manner. This then might be eaten once a day, perhaps with a little honey on it, or something else if wanted to add some taste to it. Likewise, if this is eaten with a form of legumes, some kind of bean, the total picture of the amino-acid nutrients, the essence of proteins, is secured, and secured together, which has a definite advantage. But whether or not the beans are taken with the wheat in this way, I believe there are those who might suggest to Maureen that a small dishful of this wheat about once a day might have several helpfulnesses.

In addition, a general emphasis upon natural foods might be helpful. The wheat berry certainly is a natural food. Natural foods may be eaten raw or they may be cooked, depending upon the food. But I believe this has been suggested by some human beings, and I would suggest to Maureen that this may have helpfulness for her.

She has noted probably, even as we have, that when a human being or a particular group of human beings get hold of one good idea, they may expand that one good idea into a degree of goodness that it does not really possess. Thus, there have been some people who thought that electricity was the final great key to the universe, only to discover that there are other great keys as well.

So let her use good sense in considering and utilizing any of these suggestions I have made, or suggestions that others may make. It could be that some chemical element needs to be diminished or needs to be augmented within her dietary intake. I believe that the eating of bananas has been suggested, and possibly substituting for potassium, or sodium, or augmenting the potassium within the body among other things. This suggestion might be interesting for her to try. Not eating a dozen bananas a day, but in general increasing her intake. This can be done, we understand, without medical prescription and without a great expenditure at the grocery store.

Then we would suggest a psychological approach which may be of helpfulness to her. This psychological approach we have called the 'pack-mule technique.' Since I work with concept banks within the mind of the channel I use, as a general rule, for this is much the quicker and more efficient way of transmitting information, I go back to an illustration which was brought in a reading and then transferred into the concept banks of this, my channel, many years ago:

In the United States armed services at that time and possibly at this time, certain elements of equipment issued to an army unit are considered non-expendable. These must be accounted for. If they wear out, the old must be turned in to get the new. They are not considered used up in normal usage. In time of warfare, of course, these items may have to be abandoned or jettisoned, and hence the responsibility of that unit for them is ended.

In long terms of peace, however, some of these items naturally disappear in one way or another but may be carried in the inventory of that unit, even though they cannot be produced upon demand. The unit then hopes that some event will take place within that unit which will justify dropping those items from its inventory, as though the event had caused their disappearance or abandonment.

So we understand that a certain army unit which had been stationed in the Philippines—this was before World War II— for many years had lost certain typewriters and other pieces of equipment, for which no excuse was provided in the standard manuals. So their inventory sheets showed that these missing bits of equipment were still with them. They were waiting for an event which the manual would justify as a write-off event.

This occurred one time when they were on maneuvers in the mountains, and one of their pack mules fell from a cliff and was killed. It was clearly too dangerous to descend the long distance down the steep mountainside to rescue or salvage anything that was left. So there was an event to write off their inventory, that which the particular pack animal had been carrying.

So the items of inventory which they did not have were charged off as having been carried by that pack animal and thus lost. It so happened that an investigation was made, however, of the items, and it was discovered that supposedly that pack mule had been carrying about twenty tons of equipment!

I do not know the rest of the story, as far as that army unit is concerned, and I'm not even sure that this story is accurate, but I am quite sure that events such as this have happened in many army units and other organizations which go by a manual of set procedures and rules.

My point is that the use one can make of this 'pack-mule technique' is very sound. When there is something happening anyway of somewhat a loss nature or a disagreeable nature in one's life, in a human being's life, one can, as it were, load on all the things one wants to dispose of and let them all be thus disposed of in the loss or discomfort sustained.

This is a rather practical way of achieving some of the results spoken of spiritually in such terms as 'washed in the blood of the Lamb.' Now here the somewhat facetious tone of my former several paragraphs gives way to a very deep and serious spiritual tone.

What Maureen has gone through and occasionally goes through is entering into the sufferings of Jesus in a way, in that this is a result of ignorance and evil not her own, which causes her to suffer. We know that Jesus suffered for the sins of others, that He truly was sinless in His own Being, that He did not deserve from His own conduct nor from His own karma the discomforts and the suffering that came upon Him.

So His sufferings were helping to carry the general ignorance and karma of humanity and of this earth. Thus, He suffered redemptively. Maureen can suffer redemptively in this suffering which she does undergo. She can know that as she undergoes it, when it comes, without a great emotional rebellion and with a certain patient acceptance of that which cannot be avoided, she is being 'washed in the blood of the Lamb' and made clean.

The soul incarnated as Maureen is not a young soul. It is not an inept soul. It is not a rebellious soul. It is a wise soul. It is a strong soul. It is successfully accomplishing this incarnation, and its success shows, at least in part, by the success Maureen has made of living a life despite this limitation, and is now coming into the spiritual quest.

The concept of reincarnation brings a different framework of thinking to one who is caught in a particular lifetime of limitation. That limitation is seen as belonging to that lifetime, and the lifetime is seen as being only one chapter or even a small paragraph of the total story of its many lives.

This reduces the importance of the afflictions, as it places them in perspective. It helps to make what is seen as a mountain back into a molehill. Or maybe more than a molehill, but still only a hill and not a mountain. There is a great difference in a hill that a person is asked to climb, and can climb, and a mountain which is insurmountable for that person in that particular lifetime.

Emotionally, I am sure, she has been given certain good counsel, such as when she is feeling good to 'not spend it all at once.' If she has a habit of swinging like a pendulum, then remember that if a pendulum does not swing as far in one direction, it will not swing so far back in the other direction. This has a certain amount of valid comparison with her state. I'm sure she has had that suggested before, which might be phrased as 'don't spend it all at once.' Meaning that when she is feeling good, don't expend all that good feeling at once but let part of it go 'into the bank.'

The foregoing paragraph is sort of a precautionary introduction to what I would suggest to her as a combination spiritual and emotional exercise in the use of our Directed Consciousness Method. Please send this to her. The particular thing I want her to do is, in the use of the affirmation, to really experience the feeling of being happy. The third sentence of the mantrum I quote: 'I am happy, buoyant, and a radiating center of buoyant happiness.'

I want her to use this and establish the feeling of it. It will not be hypocritical to say this and to enter into the feeling of happiness at a time when she is not happy. For one minute, let herself be happy. As she establishes this, it becomes somewhat the habit of feeling to which she can refer back and reestablish in times of unhappiness. It is a creative center in the midst of discomfort, let us say, and it is a good comfortable feeling.

This is a creative center, because this feeling can grow and help to convey any other good and desired feeling. Nothing that I have said denies the reality of her difficulties. But I trust that at least several of the things I have said will help her to diminish the difficulties by increasing her ability to live through them and to live above them.

In the spiritual quest, she will be further guided by her soul and by her council of guides and teachers. Also, as her experience of living increases and it has—give me her birthdate again. I believe she is around fifty or so years old?

Conductor: She was born in 1933, so she is forty-six.

Dr. John: She is approaching the fifty mark anyway, and she is over the half-way mark of the three score years and ten. As an earthbeing increases her framework of reference, many things find a changed significance in her thinking. This is part of what often is called mellowing. Likewise, certain physical conditions can, as it were, subside. This also is a part of the mellowing that we often find.

As Maureen increases her peace in every way possible— perhaps with diet, perhaps with spiritual exercises— psychological exercises, certainly with understanding and certainly with an increased continuing spiritual quest which has led her to Religious Research, which has led her to the concept of reincarnation, which has led her to the knowledge of life after death, and can lead on into fields she hasn't even approached as yet—this too will be helpful.

As she studies the nature of the death experience, and particularly the continuity of life through the death experience, she may wonder if her personality will have to carry with it the difficulties of the incarnate phase of existence to the excarnate.

There is some cause for thinking that it might, because the difficulties have been so much a part of the incarnate experience. However, the difficulties have come from certain anomalies, certain mix-ups, certain irregularities, in the physical system. Since the physical system dies in that process you know as death, the transition process, these difficulties will not carry over for Maureen. Rather, the valiancy of her own spirit, the way in which her soul has held her and she herself has held to constructive purposes, purposes and convictions and faith, the way in which she has succeeded and prevailed—these will carry over.

As it were, there will be perhaps a little band to meet her, playing a victory march as she comes onto the excarnate plane of her personal experience. There she will not be within a family of physical limitation. She will not know hunger. She can 'eat of the Lord and be filled.' She can drink of the joy of our Lord and be filled and fulfilled. She can discover that having been 'washed by the blood of the Lamb' she is 'white as snow.'

The excarnate phase of the Maureen personality will be one of much greater happiness than the incarnate phase has been, with much greater fulfillment, and be truly more significantly in keeping with the spiritual level that she as a soul has attained, the spiritual level which the soul really has held to faithfully and firmly in the direction of this earth incarnate personality. Is there a question?

Conductor: You have mentioned the Directed Consciousness Method and have gone into some detail on that. Do you have any other suggestions as to spiritual studies that would help her?

Dr. John: This is what we have. I would caution her, although I believe the caution is really not needed, to not 'go off the deep end.' As she comes to where she opens the Guarded Doorway to other realms, she will have certain spiritual insights, visitations, visions. But these are natural and are brought about in a realistic manner. These are within the realm of what a human being is as a spirit temporarily within a body.

We know she will not think she is a Joan of Arc to call the nation to follow her. But she will rediscover herself as a spiritual being and experience aspects of her soul and of the company her soul keeps, and aspects of her Master, Jesus the Christ, whom she serves and whose she is. There will be guidance, and there will be a certain guarding of her, that she will see. There will be direction and protection, and she will see how she is loved and how she is moved and how she is used in constructive ways.

We also hope that the time will come when she will see how she has entered into that experience which St. Paul, who suffered much himself in the physical, could summarize by saying, 'If we suffer with Him, we shall also be glorified together with Him.' That glorification will come more on the excarnate side where the sufferings can be truly dropped. However, she **does not need to wait for death, for the beginning of the glorification, the happiness of being with her Master.**

Maureen is one who has suffered without bitterness and without defeat, some of the karma which is not hers personally but is of the world, and she has undergone some of the attacks of evil without returning evil for evil, and by doing thus she has weakened evil rather than reinforced it. (A4654:1-10)

Diseased bodies and minds can be part of a magnificent purpose, serving humanity as well as soul growth. Both Maureen and Mason are accomplishing soul advancement in these limited incarnations.

The basic purpose for physical and mental handicaps is soul growth, whether the soul is an inept young soul which did not create a good body or mind tool, or a soul meeting retributive karma, or an older soul that is meeting the more difficult experiences of incarnate life.

The rest of us cannot judge, for we do not know the reasons. We never know when looking at a diseased or crippled or mentally retarded person, whether his/her soul is paying the karmic debt of past misdeeds, or is on a noble adventure, or is simply trying to keep up with God's mandate that His children grow in compatibility with Him through the stage of soulhood and beyond.

When we understand the many important good things being accomplished, we look at the limited persons in our midst with new respect.

CHAPTER NINE

RESTING-LIVES

After a sequence of strenuous incarnations, the soul may be given a "resting-life." In such a life the person does not rest all of the time but is given generally favorable and easy circumstances of livelihood, relationships, culture, etc. Not that the person must be lazy, for a resting-life can be one of happy excitement and productivity. But the personality is less pushed to accomplish, relatively comfortable and living pleasantly at ease, with little negative karma and fewer major hardships or demands upon it. There should be growth but in general less is required of the soul because it is primarily rebuilding its fabric and energies after the heavy expenditures of several difficult and possibly traumatic lifetimes.

There are several reasons for God's provision of the resting-life. A major purpose of the cosmic school of earth is to educate the soul. In education punishment may be used to train the child, but reward for good behavior encourages learning even more. The resting-life is a reward for the soul's hard, good work. Also, without recess school children become fatigued and function poorly. So it is with the God-child in the cosmic school of earth, and a resting-life is somewhat a recess from the classroom.

Of course the soul can rest and recuperate on other planes between incarnations, but it is appropriate and even necessary that some of the restoration come in the same plane as the effort was expended. In God's goodness every realm of beingness and plane of expression has its own integrity and its own learning program. Therefore, the plane producing the difficulties must also produce the answers to these difficulties in order for that plane to keep its honor. Since the soul must take mastery of every realm and plane of soulhood, any hardships encountered should be counteracted majorly in that same realm or plane. This is a natural part of the total picture of taking mastery.

In addition to respite for the soul, there is also the element of adding more quantity of experience in earthliving. But the resting-life emphasizes restoring the soul.

The life readings demonstrate how this operates in the cosmic school of earth:

PHYLLIS

Phyllis is a happily married young woman who has no major problems. Her life reading indicates that she is in a resting-life. Early in the reading Dr. John explains Phyllis' purpose:

> Dr. John: This is a feminine soul approaching the midpoint in its earth journeys. In this particular life it has a rather simple purpose, mainly just to live this life well.
>
> In the book of incarnations of every soul, some lifetimes will really stand out, and some will provide the basic continuity. This is one of the basic-continuity lifetimes.
>
> It is also somewhat of a resting-life as we have called it. The soul has had three rather strenuous earthlives preceding this one.
>
> Now some persons could well ask, 'But cannot a soul be rested and refreshed on other planes after strenuous earthlives?' Yes, and this does take place. However, there is a necessity as well as an appropriateness for the relaxation after effort to come in the same plane as the effort was expended.
>
> This is not merely psychological. The psychological significance or necessity of this would be rather obvious, I believe, in that a soul could develop an apprehension, a quality even of fear and pulling back, if too many of its earth experiences were in succession of a very difficult or disagreeable nature. This would hold true of its experiences in any realm of being and in and on any plane of expression within any realm of being. None must be only difficult or strenuous.
>
> The resting-lives thus need to be within the realm and upon the plane where the difficulties were experienced, so the quality of withdrawal and fear of that realm or plane does not develop in the consciousness of the soul.
>
> But even more than this psychological consideration, is the consideration that each plane has an integrity of its own. Thus

the plane that produces difficulties must also produce the answers to the difficulties, if the plane itself is to hold its own integrity within the goodness of God.

Also, the individual, in taking mastery of any plane of expression within any realm of being, must find the antidote to that which has been a poison or difficulty to the soul in that plane.

With this explanation—which we trust will find its way into the teachings drawn from these readings—we say that this is a resting-life for this soul.

We are ready for relationships.

Conductor: She first asks about her mother (name, birth given).

Dr. John: Yes. The mother was an older sister in the 1700s A.D. in this country, and it was a difficult life for both of them in a number of ways. There was need for a lot of work to attain the physical basis of life, the food, the shelter, the clothing. But more than that, there was an intense ambition in these two, and in their family. They had come over from another country, from a section of northeastern France.

They had a sense of being good and able people, and they had been quite unhappy with the limitations placed upon them where they were. They came to this land of freedom determined to show others how good they were, and to attain to not only quality in a general way but whatever superiority they could express.

They thought of themselves as being superior people. Which they were, actually. They had good minds, and the parents had a tradition of education within the family. So these good minds were trained. They were trained in their own effective usefulness, as well as in the general knowledge of the day.

For the boys this meant going off into professions, which would have been denied them in the somewhat caste system of the old country from which they fled.

This may have been in a Germanic area of France, there in the northeast portion of France.

For the girls, this meant an intense striving to be the finest women they could be. The girls had good minds; they had good education, particularly in the use of their good minds; they had good business sense; they had good psychological understanding so that they somewhat understood and could manipulate people around them. And they understood enough of the feminine-masculine interplay to make themselves the finest, most attractive marriage prospects they could be in order to get the finest husbands they could get.

This energetic life required much effort from the soul, and we can see how it would be one of the strenuous incarnations which led to the present resting-life. Later in the reading Phyllis asks about her husband and we learn that he is a cosmic family member. Then Dr. John describes a pastlife with him which was also difficult:

> Dr. John: They were together in the 1600s, he in the masculine, she in the feminine. This was in Russia. He was in government employ and didn't have to work very hard. He had a superior social status, he had a very comfortable physical living, and he rode with it. But it did not really represent as much 'gut accomplishment' as the present life will for him if he accomplishes the purpose before him.
>
> This 1600s Russia incarnation was a much more intensive life for his young wife, the present wife. She was in a frail body, which the husband did not comprehend as much as he might have. He was caught up in the uniforms and the glitter and the social activities, and even though he loved his wife and was considerate of her, he did take her along as much as he could, even if she did cough and feel weak.
>
> Childbearing further weakened her. She produced two— well, she had six long-term pregnancies and reared two of the children.
>
> The childbearing, as I have said, further weakened her already frail constitution. But she had a determination, partly from her husband's insistence, to live an active and a full life to the fullest extent possible.
>
> It was an intensive life. The soul did a good job. The person stayed with it, and even survived to be—well, she was forty-one when she died. To live forty-one full years in that environment and in that social system and with that frail body, and to keep a positive approach and to keep her health and strength as good as it was, was a very real achievement, a very fine life accomplishment, after which the soul really deserved a good rest.
>
> Now it got a good rest after that life, but also the rest is partly

in this life.

None of those of whom Phyllis inquired were in her immediately prior incarnation, so Dr. John presents it separately near the end of the reading:

> Dr. John: Let me go into the third of the intensive prior lives: It was the immediately prior one, in the 1800s, when the then incarnation of the Phyllis soul was a southern girl, caught up in the Civil War. She married a young man whom she truly loved, who went to war, was away some years, and came back wounded. He was wounded in body, and also pretty much broken in spirit by the defeat and the wipeout of the life they had known in their area of the South. The book *Gone With the Wind* rather describes what happened to them as well.
>
> His young wife was a very needed element of strength in that picture. If she had gone flabby, disaster would have overtaken them both, would have undermined their marriage and their lives. But she remained strong and positive, and encouraged him, and he did come back as far as could have been expected, and they made a good life. But the life which had begun in happiness and gaiety and color and fine clothes and laughter and parties, because of the war went into a much drabber, more demanding type of existence. It was strenuous. They did have two children which she raised; lost several more. It was a third in a row of strenuous lifetimes, strenuous physically and strenuous mentally and emotionally, as you see.

The active 1600s Russia lifetime definitely stretched the woman with the frail body. The intense striving to be the best she could make of herself in the 1700s, and then to experience and rise above the 1800s American Civil War devastation, earned for the soul the reward of a resting-life now in the 1900s.

Phyllis is not idle this lifetime. She is learning and growing. But Dr. John stresses the importance of ease in her living patterns:

> Dr. John: She can choose what she would like to do, and interestingly enough the one requirement as it were is that it not demand a great expenditure of her. This life is to restore the balance of life on this plane as the soul experiences it, as

I have pointed out.

So that which she wants to do and can do with a certain amount of ease of competence, is that which would be indicated. This can be quite satisfying, and quite fine. It is not a retreat nor a withdrawal at all, but it is a safeguarding of the quality of being comfortable and pleasantly at ease upon earth, even though there will be times she will expend quite a bit of energy and thought upon something.

Conductor: Would this, then, be the final word for Phyllis?

Dr. John: Yes. Along with the word from her guides and teachers and from me to regard this easier life as a gift from God. It is not 'goofing off' at all. It is very seriously purposeful, as I have pointed out.

And it is a gift, from the God who so created life and living for all of us, that after exertion there can be rest. After a hard day a good sleep, a restful night. Yes. God bless. Her guides and teachers say she is doing very well. Good afternoon. (A4083:1-5,8-10,12,13)

It is a loving gift from a wise God. The significance of Phyllis' resting life should not be underestimated. Without it that God-child could not progress in a balanced, productive way.

CANDACE

Candace, now a middle-aged woman, grew up in an unhappy home. Her parents' constant fighting was interspersed with tense silences. To escape her home she left high school for marriage and was never able to get the education she so much wanted. Shortly after the marriage, her husband left her. She felt quite rejected and unwanted. Later she married an older man and found some happiness, but all her life Candace has been plagued with extreme depressions and constant fears.

Her immediately prior life was a resting-life. In the 1800s she was the child of affluent parents, the darling of an art colony whose inhabitants were proteges of her father. Then she was steered into a good marriage. If the soul had been allowed to skip the 1800s incarnation, the strain of the present life could have overwhelmed her.

In her life reading, Dr. John gave the placement of her soul and then went into the last three lifetimes:

> Dr. John: I would like at this time to trace in the three im-
> mediately prior lifetimes for the Candace soul. I'll go back to
> the 1600s: She was in the feminine expression in China and
> one of those in her present life was there with her, I believe
> as a sister. I see a sister whom I believe is carried over.
> It was perhaps a repressive life because the role of woman
> in that particular society was quite well defined. It was a life
> also that required strength. She worked in the rice fields with
> her husband and they had quite a large family, many mouths
> to feed. So she worked from dawn till dark and ofttimes she
> waked before dawn for work within the home, and stayed up
> working after the dark had come. The husband had a true com-
> panionship with his wife, as they were in this together. They
> loved their children, especially the first half dozen or so; after
> that they accepted the children and they gave what love they
> could but the love had to be divided between more and the work
> took more of their time and energy and strength, leaving less
> to give directly to the children. But they saw to it that the older
> children shared with the younger so that the division of paren-
> tal affection and care was undisturbed, to be considered quite
> equal by the children in their experiences.
>
> This was in a village in mainland China. It was not on the
> sea and it was not on one of the great rivers. It was in the south
> central portion. The land was fertile and well watered and so
> they did not know the poverty of starvation. They were able
> to produce enough of what they did produce to trade some of
> it with the traders who brought in sources of extra protein, such
> as fish, strong-smelling dried fish (chuckling)—you, my dear
> conductor, would not have called it very appetizing, but those
> people knew that it gave them greater strength and health and,
> 'necessity being the mother of invention,' it was quite appetiz-
> ing to them and was much appreciated.
>
> They must have been healthy, especially the mother but the
> father also, because I see nine or ten or eleven children there
> who survived and grew up. They did not experience as many
> of their children dying as would have been the condition with
> a less healthy wife or a less strong wife. This was in the latter
> part of the 1600s.
>
> From that she came into a feminine life in the 1700s in the

U.S.A. It came rather quickly. Here the quality of strength was continued within the feminine expression but the experience-framework allowed for a little larger expression of life. A good person can make a fairly good life within a socially restricted framework as a general rule, but as the experience-framework expands, experiences can expand.

This girl was born in the mid-Atlantic states. It was in the Virginia area. She was a strong girl. She had large legs but the legs were not flabby, they were muscular. She was a very gracious person as well, with an engaging smile, although she was not smiling all the time but only when appropriate. And it was contrived and brought about that she met a very particular young man from upstate New York, north of New York City but not so far north but that he knew of the trade that there was for those who lived within, say, a day's journey of a big city. Of course, the big city of New York of that day had perhaps 20,000 population.

Some way or another this particular young man of New York very purposefully met this girl from Virginia. The two recognized each other as souls. They quite fell in love with each other as persons.

The boy stayed, won the approval of the girl's father and mother—won their quite honest and complete approval—married her and then, having laid plans carefully and also with some funds on hand, for both of them had worked and had saved some money, they went west of the biggest metropolis of the young country, which was Philadelphia. But not too far west. They did not go out to the frontier where there was danger, and they stayed within a day or a day and a half travel distance of the city. They explored and picked their location carefully, purchased the land, started to raise the things that the young man knew could command good prices from the traders who took these things to the city, essentially foodstuffs.

So they were into agriculture and small animal husbandry; they could process the animal meat so that even in those days of no refrigeration, the traders who had horses or horse-drawn vehicles could take the fresh meat in to the city of Philadelphia, and the traders who perhaps had only oxen-drawn carts could take meat which had been treated in some way so that it was dried or cured or preserved for the journey for sale in the city.

These two also had carefully and with a bit of luck chosen

to put their place of residence and business along a road which they rightfully figured would be an avenue of travel. More people would be going a little farther out and some more people would be coming and settling close by. The need of the city for foodstuffs and for the things produced in this way would grow, making for more trade. So they added to their production of foodstuffs and a few other items, some rooms and some beds and meals and had, in effect, a small inn facility.

They had their family, children who were raised with affection and diligence and taught upright principles amongst which was diligence. And that was a good life.

Then in the next century (because these lives are running pretty much on top of one another), in about the middle of the 1800s, we have a much different type of life. It is still in the feminine expression but she was born to a rather wealthy man and his wife in southern Italy.

The man was a bit of a bohemian—he ate well, he drank well, he grew to where he weighed rather close to two hundred pounds although he would periodically bring that down. He was a strong man, he had a voice and liked to sing but it was not of truly top caliber.

But he was a good money-maker. He had inherited a family business which was productive and lucrative and he did well with it. He expanded it and became, with his wife's enthusiastic approval, a patron of artists.

Now he was not able to find a Leonardo da Vinci or a Michelangelo to sponsor, there just wasn't anybody of that caliber among the artists, among particularly the young artists, who gathered to live in the somewhat dormitory arrangement he had for them and to eat from the common table where he supplied most of the food.

But they were a gladsome lot. Glad to be eating and glad to have a roof and a bed. And in their bohemianism their inhibitions were struck down, plus the fact that they fancied themselves to be and really were in the stream of the artists. They did some fairly good painting. There were many pictures given to their patron and places were found for them, although if a member of this little art colony left, his pictures might disappear within a week or two leaving place for the pictures or the sculpturing or the molding or whatever of some new resident artist.

The then incarnation of the Candace soul was born as a daughter into this family. She had just had two difficult lifetimes, lifetimes when strength and endurance were needed, and she was headed for this 1900s present life which has difficulties of other sorts which we'll get into later in this reading. So she was given this 'hyphen-life' as I call it sometimes, or a 'resting-life,' in between. She was a happy young girl and she was well fed and she partook of her mother's rather generous feminine endowments of body, let us say. Now even if she had been ugly and dull, the little art colony (the group members came and went) would of course have made much over her because she was the daughter of their patron. But she was pretty and she was a happy little thing. Her mother dressed her well, her father loved her much and saw to it that money was available, she was given a few simple dancing lessons, she had a natural grace and rhythm, she had a rather thin voice but a pleasant one, a sweet voice. And so her picture was drawn in chalk, in oils, in water colors, in charcoal, in every media they had; it was full length, it was a bust picture, it was profile, it was full front face; and she was quite the center of attention when she would come around.

Her mother saw to it that she was not around this rather Rabelaisian group of artists too much of the time. She also had serious schooling and very serious churching. She even thought of becoming a nun, but that thought was rather quickly and effectively scotched by her parents, both of them. So her religious interests were firmly rooted and held throughout her life. She married in that life, not one of the artists who came and went, although a number of them professed their love for her, including at least one or two of the young women artists who would gladly have extended their physical love to this comely wench, the daughter of the patron.

But she was steered into marriage with a man more like her father, more serious, more capable of earning a good living, more established. And then she was not within the little art colony there so much, although she would visit it, but as she grew older she was not so much the darling of the group anyway. She was then a married woman and not the young daughter of the patron and patroness—oh, she was still the daughter but she was in a different status, you see.

These three prior lives have led her to the present life with its more sober load of learning, let us say. (A281:2-6)

Any mother can appreciate the energy needed to cope with the large family in the Chinese lifetime. Add to that the work in the rice fields and one sees a most strenuous incarnation in the 1600s. Then the 1700s found the Candace soul in an industrious farm life in early America. So she deserved her 1800s "recess" as a darling of the little art colony. That recess refreshed the Candace soul so that she could handle the present difficult life. It was well provided.

DORINDA

A life of serious limitation can take a heavy toll which in turn can produce the positive karma of a resting-life. In the 1800s Dorinda was a hunchback. This situation had been birthed by a 1700s personality who had refused to accept a broken leg and had turned quite bitter. The negative karma of the 1700s was met exceptionally well in the 1800s, bequeathing to Dorinda the present happy life. The excerpt from Dorinda's reading begins as Dr. John is telling her present life purpose:

> Dr. John: With this incarnation the pleasant and capable soul has a pleasant and capable person-expression, and this is a happy occasion. Now in a sense this is what we call a resting-life. Dorinda may chuckle at this, because this life has not had much of what she might call rest in it. That is true. She has been a very busy person, a productively busy person.
>
> But this happy life comes after several lifetimes which were quite strenuous; strenuous in their limitations, and productive of a certain amount of unhappiness. In the 1800s this one was a hunchback. Moreover, this one was then in the feminine expression. The half-soul from which Dorinda is an incarnation is the feminine half of her whole soul. So the feminine is the native valence. But this one has known very fine feminine expressions. This one values a fine feminine expression-point, a fine feminine personality.
>
> So to be a hunchback was a very distinct limitation, and really was a 'grind' of a life for the soul. The soul did not exactly grit its teeth and see it through, but the soul felt the limitation throughout. Had the soul been an old soul it might have accepted that limited life a little more easily. The soul actually

in its earth journeyings is at the midpoint and a little beyond the midpoint. It is in the advanced midpoint stage, as we divide the age of the soul. It is a little farther ahead in the cosmic learning.

So it knows much of the other realms, and it knows the lessons which are to be learned. Then of course it comes into actual earth expression, into incarnation, as into a laboratory, to demonstrate its mastery of the lessons, to really make the lessons its own.

This hunchback was in England, which really was an act of mercy because there was a certain amount of civilization in England. The hunchback in some primitive tribes might have experienced early death. The tribes in some primitive areas could not afford to have individual children born with serious limitations. They must expect a pretty good standard input into the tribe from every member for the tribe to survive, for the tribe to remain healthy, let us say. So it could have met death, it could have been simply abandoned, in some of the other cultures.

In England there was a little more civilized approach. But on the other hand, this prolonged the experience as well. The soul, had it been given its choice, might have preferred that the hunchback life end in being abandoned as a child or even as a baby. But such was not to be. This was to be a 'grind' lifetime. The soul was to be held to this condition of beingness. The person lived to be almost sixty-one. She was glad not to see that next birthday because every day less was one day less of that karmic life.

There was physical suffering involved. The conditions of the spine which produced the hunch in the back also meant physical pain. The person did not starve but she had to work. She had to continue with her employment, so she had to keep going even though the body was often in pain. There were pain-free hours, yes. But there were very few pain-free days. There was an easement, and she learned how to bring to the body a certain easement of the pain when she could, but she could not escape it, and only death ended it.

She had to continue her work. She could not retire just to nurse herself in her pain or her condition, you see. There was of course no marriage. In her own home she was protected by the mother, who was an older soul and a cosmic family member. We do not mean an older soul than this one is, but any soul that is at the midpoint and around there and beyond is one of the older souls, as we use the term here. The mother loved the little girl, and the mother's love was really the brightest point in that whole life. It was the point at which light entered into that existence.

The family accepted the little hunchback girl—she was the third child born and there were others who followed—because the mother did, and the family took its cue from the mother. So the family was kind to the little girl. She did not experience too much contact with her peers, children of her own age, and those with whom she did come into contact were more on an individual basis or a few at a time, so there was not the competitive element whereby another child to put itself forward would put her backward.

She did have some friends who became good little friends, little girl friends. She had friends throughout that life. Not many, but some. No love interest from the boys, and this was good because there are always some men and women whose sexual impulses become twisted, and there are some who look to the grotesque for sexual stimulation. She was protected from any of those.

It was a life of physical pain, although not great physical pain excepting at certain hours. It was a life in which this feminine soul could not express as a happy feminine being. Many things are gained in such a lifetime, and this soul gained them. But it was very glad to be through with that life. As that person went through the gate of death it was in pain, and it was put to sleep as it reached the other side. The mother was there to receive her, and she came into the relationship to mother that she had known when she was a tiny being, and the mother, as it were, rocked her to sleep. Not exactly with a lullaby, she didn't sing very much, but with the care and love that a mother gives to a baby.

I won't go further, other than to say that gradually the consciousness of being a hunchback was removed. Of course on the astral plane where the mind is more immediately creative than it can be on the physical plane, the hunch shrank and pretty soon was no more. This was a gradual process in the consciousness of the excarnate woman. The back straightened, the woman straightened up and years dropped from her. The years were stricken from her by the mother taking her again into the early stages of her life. She became an erect, smiling, happy, fine woman creature there on the astral realm.

This is good, and this has helped feed into the present life. The being that she became on the astral side became in turn the major portion, a major portion, of the astral person which was then brought into incarnation as Dorinda. This does not usually happen but it can happen, and when it is purposeful, it does. It was purposeful in this occasion, of course, in this instance. This is one reason that this is a happy life and a resting-life from that previous one.

Now we go back not too far beyond that, into the 1600s and the early 1700s, in the Arabian area. Here this soul was in masculine expression as a boy, and it suffered from an accident with an animal. I believe it was a horse and I believe it was a kick from the horse. It could have just as well been a fall from a camel, as far as the purposeful element was concerned. Because what happened was a break in the leg. It was in the right leg and in the upper leg.

The boy was in his twelfth year. He had not yet achieved his full growth. The break was serious and it was not set, it could not be set by the knowledge they had at that time. It created a crippling, a certain drawing over a bit. The right thigh did not grow as much as the left thigh from then on. So there was this limitation of physical growth, this somewhat grotesque formation, although not as grotesque as a hunchback. So the boy could no longer grow into strong manhood.

In this case the boy became quite bitter. He had the same mother that the girl later had, this cosmic family member. She endeavored to keep the boy on the bright side, looking at the bright side of things. The economic status was such that the boy could be cared for and did not have to become a major man in providing for his family. The father, who worked well with the mother in that life, worked with the boy to teach him some of the aspects of business in which the crippled leg would really not matter, and by means of which the boy then could have his own family and provide for them, you see.

But the boy refused. He became increasingly bitter. Allah had not been kind to him. He became anti-religious in a way. His own unhappy estate caused him to turn against the magnificence of the universe and of the Creator. This has hap-

pened to many and many a person. The soul somewhat entered
into this. The soul thought it had been dealt some bad cards,
had been given a raw deal in that incarnation. So the soul instead of protecting itself from the bitterness of its person let
the bitterness of the person enter into the soul, and the soul
in turn reflected it back, and the person became even more
bitter.

So the soul was responsible for the depth of bitterness of
this one, and this one went on in that renewed bitterness to
deny himself what he could have had in life. He did not marry.
Any woman could have told him that any man with even one
leg can find a wife. But he refused to. He did do a little work
to provide somewhat for his own maintenance, but he became
a bitter, introverted, sour prune. I do not know actually that
prunes go sour, but he was a sour prune of a person, I am told.

He died when he was twenty-seven. The guides and teachers
kept working with that one. The soul pretty soon came to where
it wanted to pull out entirely. The guides and teachers kept
working with that one to hold him in, to see if the lifetime could
be redeemed, if the personhood could triumph over the disappointment and the physical limitation. But he did not, and the
soul was wanting to withdraw from about the age of, well, from
the teens, the later teens. Finally, the guides and teachers and
God allowed him to.

But the soul then was given some pretty strict teaching on
the other side. The soul had denied its basic beingness as a soul.
The soul had denied its basic learning of spiritual light and
truth. So the soul was given some very strict teaching on the
other side, and then brought back in the 1800s into the English
hunchback life in feminine expression.

In that life the soul saw the life all the way through and
without bitterness. The soul did not set its light on a hill, as
it were, to shine forth a great deal, but the soul kept the light
going within itself. It endured the pain. It endured the ig-
nominy, really, for a soul of its establishment to have a person of such non-establishment and dis-establishment. The soul
really rectified its mistake, cancelled out the negative elements,
and came through quite well.

It is in the light of these two immediate pastlives that we say
this life is a resting-life. Its major purpose, if you will, is to
experience happiness once again within the earth framework.

You might ask why should a soul have to come back to earth to be happy, when the other realms are potentialed with great happiness, as they are. Well, if any one particular realm of schooling becomes associated too much with negativity, then that is a dark spot in the universe as far as that soul is concerned, and the soul must clear up these dark spots wherever they are. This is a manner of speaking, you see. Do you think this will be clear to Dorinda?

Conductor: I hope it will. If not, I'm sure she'll ask.

Dr. John: So this life in one sense does not have any great purpose, and yet its purpose is a very sound reason for coming: To be happy in earth once again. Not to let earth carry the darkness of unhappiness in the soul's experience. (A3720:2-7)

If earth presented a dark picture to a soul, that soul might become hesitant about incarnating again. Even if it were forced to return to the school of earth, its enthusiasm would be dampened, thus its willingness to learn decreased. Through the Dorinda personality, the Dorinda soul is erasing the dark spot put on its universe by the previous two lives.

It is interesting to note that this resting-life was given also as reward to Dorinda because of her acceptance in the karmic hunchback lifetime. That soul had learned well the lesson it had failed in the 1700s. God-values teach more than punish.

LEE

During any major gender cycle, a soul will have some lives in the other sex to prevent crystallization. After several very difficult non-native gender lives, there may be a resting-life in the native gender. Lee is from the masculine half of his whole soul and is in a major feminine cycle, so his present masculine personality was formed to avoid the soul becoming crystallized in feminine living. But the present incarnation is also serving as a respite, a recess, for this God-child.

For the young soul and for the middle soul, functioning in the non-native gender is usually more strenuous than life in the native sex. Before the present incarnation, the Lee soul lived two lives as a pioneer woman. The rigors of a pioneer life take a large toll even when in the native gender, and incarnation as a woman added stress for him. So the Lee soul needs this resting-life to replenish his strength.

The excerpt from Lee's reading begins with the identification of the soul:

> Dr. John: This is an incarnation from the masculine half of his whole soul, but he is in the midst of a feminine cycle. This is really a resting-life, or perhaps relaxing-life would be a better term in this case. It is more than a hyphen-life, it is more than simply a resting-life although the past two lifetimes have been particularly strenuous. More strenuous than the present, certainly.
>
> The soul will be going back into the feminine cycle with the next incarnation, for there are several—I believe about three— feminine lifetimes scheduled for this cycle yet ahead. It is in a major feminine cycle. There have been probably four feminine lifetimes in the past in this particular cycle, and I believe one other respite-life in the masculine. So of a total of nine incarnations in sequence, seven will be in the feminine and two in the masculine.
>
> Why are there these non-cyclic lives within a cycle? To keep the soul from getting too crystallized in any one strain of earth experience. Likewise, especially when the cycle is in the non-native gender, to give a certain respite to the soul. Because the non-native gender incarnations are a bit more strenuous until the soul really has gained the full mastery of them.
>
> This soul is in the third of the five stages into which, for the sake of convenience, I have divided the soulhood experiences and incarnations. It is around-the-midpoint wherein about half of the earth incarnations, the significant ones, take place, as a rough rule of thumb. This soul is close to the centerline of this midpoint stage.
>
> I may disappoint Lee in not being able to tell him, yes, there is a turn ahead in his life program into a very purposeful avenue of endeavor and expression. There may be such, but if so, it will be of his choosing, because the purpose of this life is a resting-life, a respite-life, a change back into the native gender and without strong experiences. The two immediately prior incarnations had quite strong experiences. They were both in this

country and both as pioneer women. I will get into that shortly.

The present life, of course, is another type of earth experience with its relationships, its experiences, its framework, adding to the soul's total expression within earthliving and gaining a mastery within another experience-framework. Simply because it is a respite-life does not mean it has nothing of value or consequence or no real purpose to it. It had that. And this purpose has been accomplished.

The pattern has largely been run, of the purposeful endeavor, the output of energy required to accomplish the particular purpose. It would be quite all right for him to retire and simply find that which will—well, I am tempted to say 'amuse him,' but I should say 'interest him.' Perhaps go into a retirement settlement, a colony, a senior citizens establishment. There are many such.

There would be much that would help him to pass his time away. The establishment of new social contacts, perhaps entering into new social activities. Some in this stage and in this pattern will take up square dancing, golf, bridge, a hobby craft, travel, and such.

I repeat, this would be very permissible and right in line with the essential purpose, the central purpose of this incarnation. However, it would seem quite probable that Lee is not willing to settle for this. He would not have gotten a life reading really if he were happy with going this route.

This soul has a strong element of purpose within it, so that whether or not the pattern of an incarnation has a continuing purpose, this soul will put purpose into his life after the original purpose has been accomplished. Sometimes we characterize this as 'living two lifetimes in one.' That would hardly be correct in this case, however, for to have that as the picture would require that there be a pre-planned additional purpose, a turn into another chapter that had been planned from other realms.

The more correct characterization of the remaining years of this life, which can be quite a few if he so chooses, would be as a certain extension of the present life. It would not be marked by a right-angle turn but more perhaps as a gentle, although perhaps sweeping, curve in one direction or another.

He might ask me what I would suggest in this regard. I am sure he would, conductor. I would suggest that the curve be, as it were, neither to the left nor to the right but upwards—

that there be an increase in the use of his time and energies in the pursuit of spiritual knowledge, spiritual factors, spiritual associations, spiritual groups, spiritual ideas, spiritual writings which he can read, things of that nature.

He is a very capable man, conductor. You picked that up?

Conductor: From his material, yes.

Dr. John: Fine. I pick it up from watching him and seeing his life to date before me, which it is to some extent.

Let me get into the immediately two prior lifetimes, which were both in this country. Well, the second one back did not begin in this country. It began in one of the Slavic or Slavic-neighboring countries. It would be north of Italy and somewhat east of Switzerland by the present mapping. The person came as a girl with her parents to this new country. The coming over was in the mid-1700s, before the American war for independence.

They were not particularly caught up in that war. They came as part of a small movement from their area. There may have been only ten or a dozen families involved in it. I do not see exactly what it was that brought them. It was something rather unusual. There may have been a dislocation in their own area, forcing them to migrate. Then the migration may have turned into an emigration from Europe to the Americas.

The girl was about nine years old in this process, and became ten years old, because this process took some months. I believe they were forced out. They were not Jewish. It was not an anti-Jewish pogrom, but it was something that forced them out. It may have been simply economic need that forced them westward from their place in Europe and then led to their coming to the Americas.

Or, more likely, I believe a commercial enterprise in this new world was looking for laborers, non-slave laborers, and came across this rather small group who were very good prospects and who then, not immediately but after due consideration and arrangements, came to the new country.

The girl was quiet. She was a bit large for her age. She reached her tenth birthday about three weeks before she landed. It was on the ocean voyage, and there was a little commemoration of her birthday by her family and friends, because the whole group was rather close-knit. But also, she spent time on the deck of the ship near the rail on her birthday, feeling that the tenth birthday was quite a milestone in her life. Now she was leaving behind all that she knew and coming into a land which she did not understand. Her parents had chosen it without really consulting the children, although they were a close-knit family.

So it was a major experience for her. She came to the new land when she was old enough to join in the work. It was agricultural work. I was thinking it might have been in the tobacco fields, but it was a little north of the tobacco country of Virginia. It was more the Maryland area in which they landed. Then they went west, possibly into southern Pennsylvania, and were put to work in a farming enterprise which was specializing in some particular crop.

The crop was not labor-intensive, but still it took quite a little personal care, and this girl came to spend rather long hours with a hoe. The sun was not too hot and the work was not too hard, and the supervisors were not harsh. But it was work. She was strong and rather large of build, and she developed the muscles she had and some new ones as well.

She married within this little group, a boy she had not really noticed romantically much, but there was not much romance in the marriage. There was not much chance for romance as it is now understood and appreciated, in their lives. This boy, who was almost seventeen—sixteen but going on seventeen when they were married—was reaching the time when it was just generally understood that he should marry.

He had been looking around somewhat, but the parents did more of this arranging. The girl was fifteen. They were both strong, they were both a little larger than the usual size, and that made a good match. So they were put together in marriage. They had their own family.

The members of this group, as they worked off their indenture for their trip over, split. Some of them stayed and made a place for themselves within the commercial enterprise for which they had worked as indentured servants. But some secured nearby land of their own. It was not more than five miles away. When a piece of land became available, a good piece, they had saved their money and they purchased it themselves. They were still dependent upon this commercial enterprise for the merchandising and really the other arrangements of their work: the seed, the tools, the merchandising of the crops and such.

But they did establish themselves independently, owning the land, even if the others established themselves independently somewhat leasing the land on a rather long-term arrangement; and both ways worked out all right.

That was the essence of that life. It was a life of a good deal of hard work. The cultural and medical care was somewhat sparse, but better than they had known before. The land was better, the living was better. They all agreed that the hand of the Lord, which had seemed heavy upon them, really had led them to a much finer land and living than they had known before. So they appreciated it.

They were not caught up in the American Revolutionary War. They were too far west in Pennsylvania—it must have been what is now Pennsylvania—to be caught up in the feelings and the emotions of the war. They did not really have a patriotism for the new country, although they were very good citizens.

The next life was in some ways a little more strenuous. It came rather quickly and, in a way, it was a continuation of that 1700s life. This is unusual. This is interesting. The soul came back rather quickly as a new-born child within the same community, but by some means became a pioneer woman. Well, she married outside of that community. This was done by then, even more than before, and there was a neighbor boy not of her particular historic background.

There was a little more of romantic love. The two gazed upon each other and found the other attractive, appealing. They talked, they found a camaraderie, they were congenial. They had more of an outgoing nature than the girl had had before. When the time came that a small group, a caravan of, I believe, nine families, with wagons and some cattle. They had some sheep. This is odd. They had the sheep to provide wool for their spinning, their weaving, their cloth-making. That was primarily why they had the sheep. They didn't need too much money, didn't have too many sheep, didn't need too much wool.

Nine families went, majorly young but at least two older ones, under the careful tutelage of a guide who knew what he was doing and who had worked in this way before, taking small groups farther west, into Ohio, to establish new land. The establishment of the new land had some new experiences, new responsibilities, new difficulties.

They had a while when the livelihood was rather rough. This was when they had two children. Something happened, some event of nature, possibly a flood—I think it was a flood—almost wiped them out. The whole community banded together. Each one was responsible for his own work, of course, and his own livelihood, but they helped one another. They survived and they did not have to leave their area, their land. They later protected themselves someway, possibly by increased — well, I see them digging a big ditch, almost a small canal, to carry off water should another flooding come.

I do not see just how this was effected, but it was. They certainly would not spend their labor to that extent if it were not practical. They were intelligent. After that their land was not flooded. They took due precautions. This was a fine thing intellectually and spiritually in taking mastery over life.

This woman bore nine children and there were two miscarriages, where the fetus was perhaps five or seven months along. So she really had about eleven births. Luckily, she had a strong constitution, but this was a drain upon it. Of the nine live births four grew to young adulthood. One died at the age of seven to eight. They thought they had brought her through. But they did bring four into young adulthood and to adulthood.

That was the nature of that life. As you see, there was real attainment in it, real attainment of earth mastery, real attainment of self-mastery, to undergo the disciplines of hard work, responsibilities, and the learning of survival values and the development of survival skills involved in those two experience frameworks of earth.

So the present life is a respite-life from that. The next life will go back into the feminine for a different type of feminine experience. I do not see the nature of that. It will not be in the way of such physical work and physical demands for survival as the past two. But it will be a rather strenuous feminine life, in that there will be marriage and children and the requirement for meeting a certain type of experience in a different framework.

I say strenuous, but not in any way to raise feelings of apprehension. The soul is ready for this, the soul is prepared for it, the soul will do a good job of it. It is another type of earth experience to be added and over which mastery is to be taken. It is to be successfully directed, you see, by the soul, this next incarnation in that framework.

So the present lifetime of Lee is essentially a respite-life. This is the purpose of it and this should be maintained. It would be quite wrong if he were to develop a feeling 'life is real, life is earnest, I must be up and doing every minute' now. That would lessen the goodness of this life for the soul, you see. The soul needs to, as it were, have certain qualities within it, certain energies extended to earth, rested. It needs to have a different type of experience in this life so that its consciousness of earthliving will not be so heavily freighted with responsibility and hard work.

Is this clear, conductor?

Conductor: Yes, Dr. John, very clear, I believe. Though he doesn't ask why he doesn't have children, I would think this is the reason. Is it, Dr. John?

Dr. John: He has no children?

Conductor: Correct.

Dr. John: That soul has had children before and will have a number in the next lifetime, too. I believe only three or four, but sometimes three is a handful. A handful of fingers is five, but a handful of children can be three or four or eight or ten.

As the reading progressed, it was found that Lee's parents and his wife were cosmic family members with congenial past relations. All of those who were of significance in Lee's life showed pleasant pastlife connections. There was no one with whom Lee was having any real problems. Dr. John explains why:

Dr. John: A student of this reading in some future time might say, 'My goodness, it is very unusual for a person to have so many congenial people in a lifetime,' and I would quite agree. I would also remind him that this is a respite-life for the Lee soul. This is not a life when there are to be greatly problemed relationships. This is not a life when there is to be a greatly burdened livelihood. So it is quite right that from the thousand or more souls with whom there has been pastlife acquaintance or some relationship, the choice be made now of a setting with those with whom there are close and friendly bonds in past experiences. (A4286:1-3,5-9,15)

For Lee, this is a lifetime with compatible people and without excessive demands, but yet with purpose and growth. The resting-life is one of God's great provisions to renew the soul and its dedication to growth in the cosmic school of earth.

We have examined four souls and how they earned the right to such a respite. Without this resting-life each one would function below par or perhaps fail in the next incarnation.

As we study the life readings we see the goodness inherent in the system set up by our heavenly Father. There is reward for a job well done, there is rest for the weary.

CHAPTER TEN

SECOND-CHAPTER LIVES

Sometimes the present life of a soul is so strongly tied in with a pastlife that it is really a second chapter to the prior incarnation. Although the setting may change, the God-child will have the same purpose and similar circumstances of life. And some of the same souls will be present in both lives. When this happens we call the incarnation a second-chapter life.

One of the advantages of reincarnation is that the soul doesn't have to do everything or be everything in one life. Often it takes several incarnations to learn one major lesson. For example, to become a good woman may take a masculine soul a half dozen lifetimes, or more. Integrating the spiritual into earthliving also cannot be done in one incarnation. The proper application of some of God's laws is a multi-lifetime project. In a progression of lifetimes devoted to mastering some line of development, the incarnations usually will vary considerably in details. But at times one life will be almost a repetition or continuation of a previous one.

In addition to the requirements of multi-lifetime projects, there can be other reasons for a second-chapter life. The soul may fail and be forced to try again; or events can cut the life unexpectedly short; or the soul may discover the inherent goodness of the new achievement and want to examine it again, more fully. Since the soul is individuated, no two souls learn in exactly the same way. What is easy for one may be hard for another. Children who fail a class customarily improve the second time around, and the same is true for the soul. The knowledge gained in the first life, even if that life was not a success, can provide the needed background for the second chance.

A shortened life-span often is the cause of a second-chapter life. Accidents do occur on earth. Just because a certain life pattern is purposed does not mean it must happen. Earth contains many uncertainties: disease, war, disasters, the free will of man, to name a few

Each of these can cut short an incarnation. If the soul has a destiny which cannot be accomplished in another lifetime, the person will be protected. But if the same scene can be set at a future time, God's laws prevent intervention in the normal course of affairs.

The second-chapter life is a useful tool for the education of the God-child. We share with you now two illustrations from the Loehr-Daniels Life Readings. Mortimer is repeating a life because of failure; Randolph is continuing a life which was cut short by war.

MORTIMER

Mortimer is a young man in his mid-thirties who has a deep spiritual thirst. He is single but has fathered a daughter who is precious to him. The mother—we call her Doris—was unhappily married when Mortimer met her. The two became very close. Mortimer wanted to end the relationship before it went too far, but found he could not abandon Doris. Two months later the child was conceived.

When Doris left her husband, she did not marry Mortimer. For several years it was a most difficult time for him. He did what he could to help his daughter and her mother: bought their home, paid their taxes, moved nearby to share parental responsibilities. At the time of the reading, Doris had found a good man and Mortimer was celibate, but content.

In the life reading for Mortimer we find that he is in a cycle of lives purposed to develop spiritual qualities. But he detoured in the immediately prior incarnation. The detour precipitated a failure life. So the forces of this incarnation were set up to be a second chapter to the former one. The details emerge in the following excerpt. The conductor has just given Mortimer's name and birth date, place and time to Dr. John:

> Dr. John: There is quiet pleasure in this one, among his guides and teachers and in the spiritual realms close to earth. Mortimer is an incarnation from the masculine half of his soul, and that soul is about three-eighths of the way through its earth journeyings and its soul journeyings. This will place it beyond the just-started and the well-started stages, in our five-fold division, and well into the around-the-midpoint third stage, a mid-

dle soul. Since approximately forty-five to fifty-five percent or more of the actual incarnations occur in this around-the-midpoint classification, where the major learnings of life are undertaken and hopefully achieved, the Mortimer soul is now into the serious business of experiencing life as an earthling and not only coping with it but taking mastery of it.

In this process, of course, he is developing certain spiritual qualities as well as earth abilities. This particular stage, and this involves several lives now with this emphasis, the soul is undertaking more of a 'religious' development on earth. Souls come from God, and in a manner have more of a spiritual nature as they just begin earthliving than they have around the midpoint. This is not simply that they lose their spirituality, but that the momentum and the focus of their consciousness *must* be placed upon earthliving for quite a while majorly, in order to achieve mastery of the lessons of that school.

If one is taking serious courses in college, one cannot very well spend a great deal of one's time and attention and effort on something quite extraneous to those course.

This emphasis began in the second prior lifetime, which was in the 1700s in the masculine valence and set in Germany. Here the young boy was brought up in a Catholic family, and his church and religion was taken rather perfunctorily. But the influences to a deeper spirituality which were prevalent in some of the Protestant movements, especially the rather mystical movement, caught and stirred him.

This was purposeful. The soul and the guides and teachers of the soul had planned to put that personal expression-point of the soul, that incarnation, into that setting for that purpose. So religion became more important to the young man. He was rather sensible about it, and did not become a 'flaming evangelist,' but did talk with his parents and several of his siblings of his new-found discoveries.

By this time he was approaching his twenties, so it was not simply as a child but as a young adult. He had good rapport with his parents and with his siblings, so they listened. Thus the break with the family did not take place. Several of the siblings came with him into the new church affiliation, and even though his parents did not, they shared as he spoke with them of some of the deeper spiritual realities, particularly in the actual living of their lives.

As I said, the young man was not a rebel. He married and raised his family. He was a solid citizen and earned his way in society. But he was also a rather staunch member of the Protestant group to which he belonged, which had a certain pietistic quality but was not solely centered on that.

The next lifetime was in the 1800s in India, again masculine. Here the setting had been chosen by the soul and its guides and teachers to advance in a more personal and more devotional manner this general spiritual urge. The young man here, at an earlier age was exposed to a quality of devout living. His parents had it, and the young man chose at an early age to become the disciple of a 'holy man.'

This decision was not a climactic single experience, but an experience that extended over the period from when he was around seven years old to thirteen or fourteen. Then there was a break in that development. As I have reported, there was not a strong psychological conversion experience, no peak moment in his decision. This proved to be somewhat of a weakness as well as a strength.

At fourteen he realized the developing biological urges within him, and rather swung away from the idea of becoming the disciple of a holy man. He began noticing the girls. Well, he had been noticing them, and this is what stirred the forces within him, the vital life forces, which swung him away from his first purpose.

Sometime in his sixteenth year he became married and fathered a daughter. But something went wrong in that experience. Actually, of course, the thing that went wrong was that he had swerved from his real soul purpose in that life. This was not a soul purpose of great intensity, but it still was the major purpose for which that soul had incarnated at that time and place. The soul, not being fully wise and adept at handling a person of its own incarnation, did not manage that person well enough to keep it from that detour.

But the zest, the zing and tingle, of married life departed. The soul was able gradually to regain control of the person, and to reinstate on deep levels the forces moving toward the coming into the religious student state. So when he was about nineteen, he did withdraw from the marriage. He did not do so with the utmost of grace and honorableness. He really abandoned his wife and child. This did bother him, and it also bothered his guides and teachers and his soul even more. It also bothered his family, who helped the abandoned wife and child, and really turned against their own son.

In short, it was a mess. Turning back to the original purpose was a good step, but the situation was really more than that with which the soul could cope at that time. Also, the progression, the spiritual progression, had been flawed. So upon the serious counseling of the soul with its guides and teachers, who were quite understanding both of the dereliction or rather the detour and the good step taken in reestablishing the major purpose, counseled that the soul withdraw from that life.

The abandoned wife and child were being cared for, and rather than continue and try to recover from the false start, it was counseled and decided, and accepted by the soul, that it 'cash in its chips' on that one, and undertake the purpose in the next life. So he died. Which brings us to the present life.

This is what I see and what I am shown as to the nature, the placement, and the purpose of the present person in the sequence of incarnations of this soul. Have you a question, conductor, at this point?

Conductor: Not as much a question as an amazement. What happened in the 19th century is so similar to his present life.

Dr. John: This will be interesting as we get into the relationships. The present life is, as I have pointed out, the wiser reliving of the immediately prior incarnation.

Conductor: Dr. John, does this often happen, one century following the next century like this, a replica?

Dr. John: I believe we could say it happens occasionally. 'Often' is a word of various connotations. But in one sense it can be said to happen often. Probably not more than a few times in any one soul's total incarnations, but within a general framework the repetition of a pastlife purpose can take place either to further a progression that has been begun and can be continued in a similar life pattern, or to provide a correction for something which has gone sour or cut off on the wrong track in the former life.

These are not necessarily immediately successive lifetimes, but usually are.

Conductor: Thank you very much. That's a good clarification. We will go to his person sheets at this time. Mortimer first asks about his mother (name, birth data given).

Dr. John: She is a cosmic family member and has about the same degree of soul progression. She was a sister in the 1700s in Germany, and she volunteered to be the mother in the India life, and was. She likewise volunteered to be the mother in this life, and is really quite a fine and supportive person. Of course, her being with Mortimer is only one of various factors in her own incarnational picture. She has the personal progression and various forces and relationships and experiences of her own, of course. Mortimer will understand that and appreciate it, and really prefers it that way rather than that his mother came only or primarily to be with him.

Conductor: Will they be together in future lives?

Dr. John: Not immediately, but somewhere up ahead, yes. She helped—well, the home into which he came, not just the mother—to establish a religious setting for this life and get him started on a religious track. Of course, in a sense the home life in India did as well in its own way.

It is expected that this cycle, this small cycle emphasizing spiritual development, will be completed with this life. This does not mean, certainly, that this life will see the whole spiritual development that this soul will ever achieve on earth. Not at all! But it should achieve in this life that degree of spiritual development and integration of the spiritual and philosophical components into the material framework of earthliving, for which the soul is now ready.

This also, of course, will be good basis for the spiritual development considerably up ahead, in other ways and other cycles and other lifetimes and other progressions.

Conductor: Thank you, Dr. John. Mortimer next asks about Doris, the mother of his only child.

Dr. John: There is a very interesting picture here. This soul had an incarnation in the 1800s in India as the sister to the then wife of the then incarnation of the Mortimer soul. The then wife was much too angry to come back now, and quite possibly will never again be in the Mortimer soul's orbit. Her anger is her own problem, and can help to hold her away, and well it be so.

But there was a karmic debt incurred, and the sister instead of the wife is here collecting it. She also was angry at the young man's desertion of her sister, but, of course, that anger did not have the roots nor the intensity that the abandoned wife herself had. Also, the sister was of a little different temperament. So things worked around and forces intermeshed to bring her in now, not simply to collect the debt but to use that factor and the forces of that background in an interwoven way to accomplish certain good experiences in this incarnation for both souls.

They probably will be together in a future life, quite possibly in a very, very happy marriage relationship. The abandoned wife, in her anger and turning away, has abandoned this possibility for herself, but the younger sister may very well win it and find it quite good. In the present life, I am told, they are handling the relationship quite well.

Reactions to events can determine future life patterns. The wife in India, because of her extreme anger and lack of forgiveness, will not collect the karmic debt owed to her. And she has also forfeited the right to a happy future life with the Mortimer soul.

We return to the reading as the conductor brings Mortimer's questions on his relationship with Doris:

> Conductor: His question: 'Any suggestions as to how I can best be of help to Doris in this particular life?'
> Dr. John: In this particular life he is drawing into the expression of a religious life, which has a great deal of the framework of the 1800s India life, and really the major forces in this life's religious development come from that. However, there are also forces from the 1700s Germany Protestant Christian life and from the present life. So this is his life purpose. But within the accomplishment of his life purpose, he can be kind, he can be honorable, he can also find a real pleasure in the proper attitude toward and association with this other one, even as he goes along faithfully into his life purpose.
> Conductor: He says, 'We are cooperating in the raising of the child.' He is furnishing the home, but he does not live in the home. They are within walking distance of each other and doing very well.
> Dr. John: The Mortimer person is an incarnation of a wiser soul than the 1800s India lad, and is a more capable personality as well. He is doing well.

Conductor: He next asks about the daughter.

Dr. John: This little one is the daughter who was left behind in the last previous life. Now that little girl did not have the feelings against her daddy that her mother had against him. She was young when he left, and she was well cared for and did not know want as she was being brought up and for the rest of her life.

But she was made aware that her father left them and had gone away, and she used to wonder really what he was like. She quietly picked up such information as she could about her daddy, and rather fantasied him as really a pretty nice man, and wished that she had known him. So the forces were set in motion for them to meet again, and to have a very fine relationship. Of course, the Mortimer soul is learning that there can be the inclusion of human ties, and human happiness in those ties, in a religious life.

Actually, the eastern 1800s version of the religious life and religious development, while it is a fine pattern, is itself undergoing certain changes in this twentieth century, and the Mortimer soul's initial commitment to it is undergoing a few changes as well. Even though it finds its major life purpose has brought him into this pattern at least for now.

Other lives were brought out, but these three were the only persons that Mortimer inquired about. However, a few of his questions reflect forces from the past in his present life:

Conductor: He next asks the question, 'About half of the people I am presently most closely associated with are dark-skinned. What are the karmic reasons for this?'

Dr. John: None, particularly, aside from what I have already pointed out. His interest is pretty much in the Indian framework of spirituality, you see. This is a factor, a magnetic force, if you will, in helping to bring this about. Likewise, he is at home with them.

Conductor: 'In a lifetime of strikingly good health, I am having some skin trouble and seasonal sinus problems. Any karmic reasons behind these relatively minor health problems?'

Dr. John: Yes. The soul was uneasy about what its 1800s incarnation had done. This uneasiness of the soul has come out apparently in some of these conditions. As the soul attains greater ease now, particularly from having made recompense for leaving the wife, and having found the daughter and brought to her what the father could bring (and gaining from her the delightful love and companionship which a daughter can bring), the soul force is abating in this uneasiness. What effect this will have on the physical condition now, I do not know. I suggest, of course, that he keep abreast of any medical development in this line.

As long as the daughter and the mother remain in this sinus-conducive area in which they all now live, he should stay there also. But the time may come, when the daughter is grown and the mother is well established and his own work has developed and such, that he could come to a less sinus-conducive environment.

Conductor: His last question: 'Although I am most interested in any previous association with the Paramahansa Yogananda soul, I realize this may be an out-of-bounds question.'

Dr. John: The Yogananda soul was not the soul that would have been the teacher of the Indian youth, but the Yogananda person is, of course, a well-known example of that kind of Indian religious teacher. Likewise, he was a very attractive person in his own spirituality and his personhood.(A3091:1-10)

In Mortimer's last life, the personality was to become a "holy man" but married instead. Three years after the marriage he left his wife and daughter to pursue his original purpose. But it was too late, for to forsake responsibilities is not God's way. The soul was in a mess and was counseled to pull out of that incarnation.

The present lifetime finds Mortimer following his spiritual quest, with the same mother who instilled this interest in the last life. And he is fulfilling his obligations to the previous wife and daughter. In this second-chapter life the Mortimer soul is repeating the class that he failed and passing it now with flying colors!

RANDOLPH

Randolph was a war casualty in his last lifetime. War has stolen so many lives. But God, with a tear in His eye for the pain He sees, must also chuckle. For He knows that anything taken from His children can be restored in full and overflowing measure. Of course there are many ways that restoration can come. Randolph is but one example.

The present life finds Randolph a successful, happy pilot for a major airline. From an early age, flying was his major love. As he was learning to fly, Randolph found that he already knew many directions before the instructor gave them. Others commented on how quickly he picked up the lessons, and he wondered if he had flown in a pastlife. Because he was born in the 1930s, it seemed unlikely. But his life reading showed his soul's immediately prior incarnation to be as a Japanese pilot, training for the war which was to come:

Conductor: We are here on behalf of Randolph (name, birth given). Where would you like his reading to begin, Dr. John?

Dr. John: So he's forty-eight years old. That is quite a bit longer than he lived in his immediately prior lifetime. The previous time he was born, I believe, in Hokkaido or near Hokkaido, a city in Japan. He was then masculine. He is an incarnation from the masculine half of his whole soul, and is a fairly young soul. He is in the second stage of the five stages into which, for the sake of convenience, I have divided the soul's progression through incarnation, the well-started stage, and is verging toward the around-the-midpoint stage. He has fairly recently come from a serious cycle of feminine earthlives.

The immediately prior lifetime was cut short. He was a casualty of the war you know as World War II, although he did not actually live to see the war. Let me explain this, because this is quite an interesting picture:

He was one of the young Japanese men, and sixteen or seventeen, when he really started in serious training for aviation. The militarists of Japan had taken a good look at Germany, and they were aware that airplanes would in some way or another have an important part to play in any military undertakings of their country. They were not limited as was Germany for a while to simply gliders. They started training a few of the young men in powered planes, although the power was quite low, of course, at that time.

This one was selected because he came from a good family, a middle-class family. He had somehow come to the attention of someone who could recommend his selection for this training. In his early tests it was shown that he had fine muscular coordination, excellent reflexes, very fine eyesight, and so he was selected for this training. He progressed rather well in the training. Then something happened that caused the crash. I think it was some mechanical failure. As I look at it, I cannot tell if it was some engine failure or a failure of some control surface or linkage or something. Anyway, he crashed and was killed.

But because there was this fascination of the personality with flying, he was allowed to continue, as it were, but on the astral side. For a while he did not realize that he was on the astral side. He just knew he was once again flying, and there were the planes and the instructors and the commanders who set out his training missions and such. But pretty soon it was borne in upon him that he had progressed into a higher echelon of flying, from which he actually became one of the spirit instructors of the growing Japanese Air Force.

From the astral side, he rode along with many of the young pilots, and upon at least two occasions he probably saved them from a serious crash in their training. They simply knew that somehow thay had gotten into a particular situation and they did the right thing or something happened and they came back and landed all right.

He liked this very much. When war actually came, he was continued. But an interesting thing happened. He was allowed to experience death in the crash of a Japanese plane. It was in one of the sea battles, a very large battle. There were many planes from various carriers, and there was a lot of flying and a lot of fighting. He was that particular day assigned very closely to one of the Japanese flyers who was shot down, and it was allowed that there be such an identification with that one he was flying with and guarding that he also experienced death, 'the second death,' the termination of the astral personality, the excarnate being of that incarnation, you see.

This had some very definite purposes back of it. The next incarnation of that soul had already begun. It was begun within six months of his physical death, maybe five. The new incarnation was approaching puberty, and the new personality had already shown an aptitude mechanically, in reflexes, in coordination and interest in such things, and a keen interest in flying. This was fed in.

When the Japanese pilot crashed, the soul was free to take another incarnation. But the pilot could continue in the astral realm even though the next personality of the same soul was on earth. And when the "second death" of the Japanese man occurred, his forces could be fed into the young boy with his love of and abilities for flying.

Dr. John: But now the full force, as it were, of the developed personality of the Japanese young man was fed in. It was fed in in means appropriate to a twelve or thirteen-year-old or so; ten or eleven, in that area. Which means that it could be fed in gradually. It could be held there for even a year if need be and fed in at some propitious moment. For time can be utilized on our side in some manners at variance with the restrictions on the utilization of time on your side.

So the present life as Randolph is a continuation of the prior lifetime, even though they are two different persons. Many of the forces are the same. The former person was a rather happy-go-lucky person. He 'walked easy.' He was on good terms with life. He thought well of himself and, having been one of the early ones selected, he thought more than well of himself, and rightly so. Although that quality was based primarily upon his having been selected to be one of the early ones to receive training, rather than upon an over-all superiority of beingness, you see.

This is quite an interesting case of overlap, conductor. This sort of thing can happen. Not frequently, because usually the excarnate personality will go on. But this excarnate personality was terminated there in, I think it was 1943, maybe 1942 or 1944, or in that time span. It may be that as Randolph looks back over his life, he may find some rather distinctive happening when he was about eleven or twelve or thirteen years old in the present life, which really could be attributed to the influx of qualities, abilities, forces, nature, from that former incarnation, which in a sense is the first chapter of the present incarnation.

I have taken longer for this than I usually take, as you know, in introduction with a specific prior lifetime, but this specific prior lifetime in this case has unusual tie-in with the present. I think Randolph was selected by his guides and teachers and by whoever does the selection of the persons to get a reading, partly to bring us a very interesting and unusual example of overlap and of the packaged feed-in of forces from a past life into a present life.

In a sense, this particular case is more in keeping with what some of the popular ideas of reincarnation are. Whereas the reality usually is that each personality is quite a distinct and separate entity, as you know, and that the person does not reincarnate but the soul has a new incarnation. In this case the person would almost seem to have reincarnated, the Japanese person, and yet it not be true. The forces from that person, not *in toto* but in a selected manner, comprising the essential forces that were wanted to be continued—these were fed into the present person, and really quite smoothly. I would compliment his council of guides and teachers, and I do so as I turn to them.

There are four present, incidentally, and one from the supervisory council, and I sense one or two others possibly. I do not know who they are. It may become apparent before the reading is over and it may not.

I compliment his council on the smooth operation that was conducted and completed there, a real transition.

The purpose of this life is in one sense to continue and to complete the purpose of the former life. The rather happy-go-lucky, rather handsome, rather debonair, somewhat swashbuckling, young Japanese man, still in his teens but a man, had developed a real passion for flying, and a very real ability for it as well. So this force, rather than being cut off to be fed into some later century, and rather than being left within that personality of the prior person, this force was deemed had better be expended now, be given its chance for fulfillment, for fruition, so the present life is doing that.

Aside from that, the person is capable, but it is a young soul yet, possibly about eighteen past lives, counting some of those that did not have too much significance. So the bulk of its learning, its development as a soul, lies ahead. As the soul gains more experience, its incarnations have more of the 'grist for the mill' type of human experiences. Much more lies ahead than behind for this soul, in the way of incarnations. But that is no reason at all for any concern in the present life.

In the present life, the concern needs to be that all of the experiences of this life are lived with understanding, with compassion, with growing mastery feeding into an increasing beingness of the person, and hence of the soul itself.

Is there a question at this point, conductor?

Conductor: No, Dr. John, no question. However, I would like to read you something in his material that bears this out if I may.

Dr. John: Please do, yes.

Conductor: He says, 'At the age of six I had my first airplane ride, and that day I knew I wanted nothing else but to fly. Everything I did, read and worked for was to that end. Making rubber band models at first, then the gas engine ones, to the real ones and lessons when only sixteen.'

Dr. John: Now he can understand why, can't he.

Conductor:Yes. That was one of his questions, too.

The akashic records are soul records, so Dr. John doesn't necessarily have access to specific details about the personality. This is why the conductor brought this information to his attention.

In this second-chapter life Randolph is continuing and completing the purpose of the young Japanese pilot, so cruelly cut off by war. In addition to his successful flying career, Randolph is carrying through with some of the relationships of that past incarnation. Several of the souls in the Japanese life are with Randolph now. First the present mother:

Dr. John: This is a cosmic family member, an older soul. She's in the around-the-midpoint bracket, where forty to sixty percent of a soul's incarnations usually take place. She is probably approaching the midline of that, too. She is the sponsor soul for her son.

She was either a grandmother or a great-grandmother in the Japanese life. It was not known then that there would be the death. You may say, 'Does that mean that there are accidents?' Yes, it means just that. There are many uncertainties upon earth. Had this one then been in a life which had a real destiny it could have been protected. But since there was no real reason aside from the gaining of the experience, the young flyer was not given the supernatural, 'miraculous' protection.

So the accident of flying, which was not a part of its fate then, not a part of the pattern, but certainly was recognized as a very real possibility, did take place.

The grandmother then knew every one of her grandchildren,

but this is a rather common trait among grandmothers. But in a special way, on the soul level much more than on the personality level, there was the tie between these two because she is the sponsor soul for this one.

The grandmother in Japan was very proud of her grandson who could take to the skies, although she did not know he took to the skies until she was on the astral side. She died when he was still a youngster four or five years old, probably.

Let me go back a bit. The grandmother in Japan was probably a great-grandmother, and it was from the astral side that she watched him. When he came into the astral part of that lifetime, she in a sense was his family. She was the one who helped him to realize gradually that he was not in the physical any more but on the astral. She, being an older soul, knows about this on the soul level, and so helped to bring him into that stage where he could from the astral side really continue his incarnate pattern. This took a bit of skill and understanding on her part, too, you see.

This is quite an interesting episode all through.

The excarnate personality of the great-grandmother to the Japanese pilot functioned as the mother when he came to his afterlife. And how appropriate that her next incarnation then became the earth mother in this second-chapter life! Since she is the sponsor soul, there were of course other lives brought out—which we won't go into—between Randolph and his present mother.

Randolph had requested that the reading focus on his present girlfriend. Several past lives together were brought out, but we will present only one:

> Dr. John: They have found each other again. They were going together back in Japan in the 1920s. They were boy-girl friends, and she was quite impressed when he was chosen for flight training. She definitely had considered him a prospective husband. Her reaction to this death was two-fold: a very genuine sense of loss of him as a person, and this was the major thing. Secondly, a sense of her own loss, that she could no longer consider him a prospective husband.
>
> These two are cosmic first cousins, and cosmic first cousins can be even closer than some cosmic family members, as you

know. There are 'good vibes' between them, which situation goes right to the soul level and has its rootage in several past lives, one of which I have mentioned.

She did not live too long after his death. She did marry, moved, went away from where she had lived. Her husband was in a somewhat different occupation than her father, so that life provided a marriage that expanded her experience occupationally.

I do not see the cause of her death then. She was married, she had a child, possibly two, and then she died. There were many things that caused death in those days, even more than in these days, and something caused her death.

Conductor: I would suppose then there is a good basis here, from what you have said, for a marriage, if they should so decide?

Dr. John: Yes, and I would also say the content of the marriage and its success would then depend upon the two of them as persons. There are good forces here, and each one has good traits of character that can make for a good marriage, if they so choose.

Another who was in the Japanese life was found when a close friend was asked about:

Dr. John: Scott was another young flyer who survived the death of his friend, but who was an early aviation death within two years after that. He did not have the drive that carried him into the astral incarnation of aviation. That excarnate person went on. I do not trace it. But the incarnate came back quite quickly, partly to shift it from the Japanese to the American culture.

That other one had taken the Emperor cult quite seriously, and was in danger of becoming crystallized in a very nationalistic mode of thinking, and might have incarnated three or four times within the Japanese framework, if that kind of setting had continued. But as a correction, the soul was brought into incarnation in the United States with its pluralities, and the tendency to crystallize on a very strict nationalist basis with a theological foundation for such crystallization, was nipped in the bud.

Since that was the pattern, it was nice that the two, who had been friends before, could be friends again, and with an even greater friendship this time. (A2023: 1-16)

Even though the friend's life was also "nipped in the bud," Scott's incarnation now is more for the purpose of preventing that soul's becoming crystallized in the Japanese culture. Since Dr. John was not into Scott's akashic records, we don't know whether or not his death was planned by his guides and teachers.

But we do know that war had cut off the learning pattern of the Randolph soul. And we can hear the chuckle of God as all that the Japanese pilot had and was is restored with overflowing measure in Randolph.

So much is unaccounted for in a one-lifetime framework. Without reincarnation all soul growth would have to be accomplished in one personality and usually in a short three score and ten years. The Mortimer soul would have failed with no chance to repeat the class; Randolph's success would have been halted by war.

But with multiple incarnations no soul has to accomplish everything in one. With their second-chapter present lives, the Mortimer soul is not a failure, and the Randolph soul is not cheated by war.

CHAPTER ELEVEN

SOULS AWAY FROM EARTH TOO LONG

The length of time between incarnations can affect the next earthlife. This is natural. The soul, even though it is that particular Individuated-God-Being intended and formulated for incarnation, is native to spirit and alien to the realm of matter. Therefore, if a soul stays away from earth for an extended length of time, it can take a while for the soul to get settled into earthliving again. A comparison could be an American who was placed in France for several years and had to learn to effectively speak French there in order to survive. If this American were then to return to an English speaking country for a relatively long period, his French could become rusty, he could lose the fine points and nuances of speaking in French, and he probably would have to re-learn certain language techniques. So it is with incarnation and reincarnation, a soul gets "rusty" if it stays away too long from the material realm of earth.

We have found, both in the Loehr-Daniels Life Readings and in the pastlife recall work, that a soul actively participating in the earth experience may incarnate roughly once a century, or six or eight times in ten centuries. But there is no set number. It may be more for a while, it may be less. A soul incarnates when the time and circumstances are right. For example, appropriate parents and environment are looked for to provide the right setting for the soul in its next earth lesson. And since between incarnations the soul attends cosmic schools in the spirit planes, it may be busy several centuries with these lessons.

But once a soul has established itself in the incarnate experience, staying away from earth for a long period of time can dull a soul's incarnational skills and its material sensitivities can be diminished, making the first return life difficult as the soul learns to speak the language of earth again.

STEWART

Stewart has been away from earth the past 1700 years—his last previous incarnation was in the 200s A.D.—and it was expected that it would take at least two lifetimes, possibly three, for his soul to "get in the groove" of earthliving again. So very much has happened in earth history in the last 1700 years! Rome fell, and barbarians engulfed Europe with a thousand years of Dark Ages. Crusades came and went. The Reformation in religion and the Renaissance in learning and art brought intellectual, aesthetic, and spiritual rebirth. Columbus discovered America and Spanish, French, and English settlers established a New World. The Scientific Age was born. The areas of established peace grew from tribes and city states to nations, pushing the evils of war to the international level. Aviation. Two World Wars. Now the Space Age. Stewart is doing well to effect his soul's major re-entry into earth in this incarnation!

Dr. John: This can be called a re-entry life. The Stewart soul has been away from incarnation for 1700 years. The last incarnation was in the 200s A.D. It was in the masculine, ended in the late 200s. It was in India.

This is going to make quite a difference, of course, in the reading, because it makes quite a difference in the life. There will not be recent acquaintances in incarnations with the people of whom he asks. There will be some who have a farther-back acquaintance, yes, and there will be some with acquaintance in the other cosmic schools. But earth acquaintance he has not had for 1700 years, because he has not been on earth. In this life he is very happily getting re-acquainted with earth.

That is the primary nature and purpose and function of this life. I will not be able to bring to him some major purpose such as developing some ability or resolving some relationship or such.

Conductor: That's all right. I think he'll understand.

Dr. John: I think so. Because his soul knows this, you see, and the soul will recognize it, and we trust the person will not be too initially disappointed.

Now, this is a serious lifetime. The extent to which he becomes reacquainted with earth will make the success of this life, and the degree of success of this life will profoundly influence the nature of the next life. It was seen by his guides and teachers, of whom five are present as a council here today, that it might very well take two lifetimes for him to become reacquainted before he really could be very usable in earth again.

But it is quite possible that the essence of it will be accomplished in this one lifetime. It possibly may surprise him to know that he has done a very good job. It may seem to him that he hasn't done much of anything in any profound way. But in the profound way in which this life is important, which I have outlined, he has accomplished a great deal. In the remaining twenty years or so which are expected for his incarnate existence, the council tells me, if he continues this getting acquainted with earth he can very well be in a position to be of quite definite specific use in his very next incarnation.

The getting reacquainted with earth involves a number of things. It involves gaining again a certain sense of ease for the soul to operate with and in and as an earthbeing with an earthbody. This apparently he has done quite well. If he had not, it would have shown up probably in various aches and pains and illnesses and even accidents, of course. It means getting acquainted with the topography of the planet earth, if you will. He has traveled about some. He may travel more if he wishes, and we hope he will. He has had an interest which has made him acquainted with parts of the earth that he has not visited.

Of course, this is so much easier today than it was in former generations, to know about other countries even if one does not visit them, and to see them in travelogues and in motion pictures and in television presentations and in magazines particularly devoted to travel and such.

It also means becoming acquainted with the other forms of life on earth, with what one might call nature, the plant and animal realm. It also means—well, just how shall I say this? It means having a spiritual interest. Now the soul has that, but to bring it into personhood sometimes takes several lifetimes for a soul to accomplish. But if this one, Stewart, can perhaps expand his spiritual depth and scope, this is one area that would be quite helpful in the accomplishment of his life's purpose.

Actually we would suggest that he not push himself in any way, but as his interests may exist, they may be expanded in many fields. We would suggest that he read perhaps a good popular book on the history of medicine and healing. We would suggest he read some general popular book on chemistry and on astronomy and physics, and perhaps agriculture. I think perhaps I have made my point here. The more he becomes reacquainted generally with earth and life on earth, human life and other life on earth, and the developments that are taking place now and the contacts being made with other realms by men on earth, and all the developments that are happening, the more successful this life.

Include the expansion of microscopic knowledge, as well as the astronomical expansions of the physical universe. All of this is part of that general background of knowledge of earth again as earth is now and as earth now is known, which will be background for him as he comes into the next life.

Having spoken quite a bit of the next life, you might ask me or he might ask me what will it be like. That I do not see. There are higher forces, higher than his own council, who will decide just where to use this soul in the next incarnation. It will be used primarily in a specific service, I believe, and not particularly for its own development. Although, of course, its own development will come right along with the experiences it has as it works in this or that line.

He may, for instance, be an agricultural expert, help train the farmers of the future. The farmer of the future will still be raising edible plants, fruits and vegetables and such, but there will be differences, of course; there will be progressions. This one might be one who could travel around and bring to those engaged in this work a direct knowledge, his own direct touch and his own direct knowledge and expertise. Perhaps staying with a farm family for a day, or a farm community for a week, answering their questions, getting to know them, having a regard for them as persons as well as for their work in the fields. In short, a real teacher, helper, personal friend.

This is just a possiblility. I really have no idea whatsoever that he will be an agricultural visiting consultant in the next life. But this is an illustration of what the next life probably will be like in some area.

In a way, the present is a bland life, yes, but the spice of it will come in the next life. In this bland life much is being prepared. The body of the food is being prepared, and the seasoning can be added a little later. But if the body of the food is not well prepared, the seasoning will only accentuate deficiencies.

Is there a question to this point in your mind, conductor?
Conductor: Yes. What has he been doing all these 1700 years?
Dr. John: He has been busy all right. This is a good question. For the first thousand or twelve hundred or whatsoever of these years he was majorly in other realms, and learning some of the things there which he will be bringing in some of his future incarnations to earth.

But he was kept somewhat in touch with earth. He was brought close with a good tutor, really with several, to look at the Dark Ages, for instance; the fall of the Roman Empire and the recession of knowledge. To look at some of the superstitions and really most uncomfortable conditions and lacks then.

Then he was apprised of the Renaissance. Did not have too much tutelage in the Reformation, his religious interests are not in question; but the rebirth of knowledge in the western world and the way in which knowledge had flourished better in the eastern world for a while.

He was given quite thorough grounding in the history of earth, let us say, from about the middle of the nineteenth century, from about 1850 on. So the soul understands quite well, in a way that a soul can understand, the development of the Industrial Revolution, the development of science, the development of nations, the difficulties of the present nation-oriented stage of the human community, and such.

I note that he was born on the day of the Armistice, November 11, 1918, as you have pointed out, and this seems to me to be a good choice. Not only does it place him within an interesting astrological group, but also the Armistice was a turning point, a landmark, a milestone in modern earth history, and this was an interesting time to have him reenter earth. Incidentally, did I report that the Stewart soul is from the masculine half of the whole soul?
Conductor: No. How far along is he?
Dr. John: How far? This may surprise you. He's really in the third stage, perhaps just a bit over the center point of around-the-midpoint, with possibly sixty percent of his earth-lives accomplished. Soulwise—well, this too is interesting—he is a very little bit ahead of his incarnations. One might say, why isn't he much more ahead when he has been concentrating

on that, as it were, for 1700 years? The answer is that the earth incarnations had gotten ahead of the soul growth, so to speak. Now they do not have to go hand in hand, and sometimes there is quite a disparity (with some interesting consequences), and for various reasons and purposes. But in this case the soul had taken quite a number of incarnations in a rush and then was given time to let its soul catch up with it. This is one way of doing it, and it is valid, although that is not the only factor that was at stake.

Perhaps one of the reasons for Stewart's fine success in earth-reentry in this incarnation is the fine welcoming committee he had, some close cosmic family members. Stewart's father is an older cosmic family member who was his father in his last life—a 200s A.D. India incarnation. This fine man was a guiding light for Stewart to follow.

Stewart's sister was also in his last life, as a close younger sister. When the sister was asked about in the reading, Dr. John noted that they are also cyclemates:

> Dr. John: They are cosmic family members of course, and cyclemates, with quite a hiatus in the cycle. So this 1700 years that Stewart has not been around, this other one has been and has had, in a sense, another cyclemate during that period. But she was with Stewart for several lifetimes, as sort of a beginning of a certain cyclemate relationship, and will be now probably four or five times in the next five or six or seven incarnations. They are quite congenial as souls.
>
> We find her in the 200s India life as a rather close younger sister, very close in age. The cyclemates wanted to be close together in that last time they would see each other, on earth that is, for a while. It was also seen it would be good if they were, to carry over the time, and the time did carry over very successfully. That is, the relationship carried over through that time very successfully, kept warm and personal and knowledgeable.
>
> Conductor: He says they are remarkably alike in physical appearance, and also mentally. 'We both like exactly the same things and almost know what the other is thinking.'
>
> Dr. John: As they came back together there was a very hap-

py sort of a rush of the souls toward each other, an expression of reaching out to touch, which would eventuate into something of this sort, and it could and apparently did eventuate in this closeness.

A soul must develop a certain sense of ease with earthliving to operate effectively in the material realm. With Stewart, although he of course had to do his own growing, the close cosmic family members in his present earth family helped him regain this. As Dr. John pointed out, if Stewart had not made a smooth re-entry it would have shown up in various aches and pains and illnesses and even accidents. Even though this may not be a sensational life earthwise, soulwise it is a blockbuster.

DAMON

This incarnation has been quite a shock to Damon's soul and it will probably require two incarnations to become comfortable again on earth. Damon is an early masculine incarnation from a young feminine soul who has been away from earth since the 1400s. Earth has undergone some major changes in the last 500 years, and a soul that has not kept up with these transitions is shocked to find human society in the 1900s so very different from the 1400s. Therefore Damon's soul is not at ease in this incarnation, and the soul's uneasiness is expressed in Damon as mental illness. Actually the soul tried to master two major feats in this incarnation: (1) a masculine incarnation for a young feminine soul, and (2) re-entry into earthliving.

Damon's soul did not have a valid reason for spending so much time in the other cosmic schools. The soul knew it could always return to earth, so it went romping through the other cosmic schools, not paying any attention to what was happening on earth. If his soul would have returned in the 1800s instead of the 1900s, it would have found human society far simpler and more like the 1400s. But the soul is given much free will, and this experience can be chalked up as soul learning:

> Dr. John: This is what we would qualify as a young soul, and it has been away from earth incarnations for quite a while and is having difficulty re-inserting into the stream of incar-

nation, into the stream of earthlife; and this may take another incarnation before it is satisfactorily accomplished. This is one of the nice things about God, the provision of a number of lifetimes, that that which is not accomplished in one can be undertaken again in a later one.

Damon is a young masculine incarnation from the feminine half of his whole soul. This means that, quite frankly, he has several strikes against him, perhaps three major difficulties or challenges: (1) the young soul, (2) the lack of recent continuity in incarnation, and (3) being in the nonnative gender expression.

This may sound gloomy. Within the framework of this one life only, it may be gloomy. But within the framework of a number of lifetimes it is seen that he does not need to do everything and be everything in this life, nor even to accomplish the re-entry completely. The soul already has taken on incarnate form again. The soul already has accepted a masculine body, not for the first time but still being the nonnative expression. The soul already has learned a great deal of what life is like now.

Life now upon planet earth—human life, that is—is far different from what it has ever been before. The twentieth century is unduplicated in human history, presenting so many differences from every other past century. So to accomplish *this* much is really quite an accomplishment and merits a passing grade certainly.

Damon was born into the correct family, where he was loved and received and where there are several cosmic family members. I see two, three—well, both parents, with the father especially; well, the father being the sponsor soul—and the elder brother, who is a cosmic family member. Not the sister.

So much has been accomplished, and if the Damon person feels that this is not yet a full re-entry of the soul into earthliving, he need not let that disturb him too much. He can understand, and the understanding should take pressures off him.

Now the further accomplishment and the betterment of his mentally disturbed condition will be brought about majorly by the person of Damon rather than the Damon soul. The Damon soul is frankly at a loss as to quite what to do, for the reasons I have given.

But the Damon person is educated, has a good mind, and if he will and if he can detach himself from the uneasiness, the restlessness, the insecurities of the Damon soul, the Damon person can make a better life for himself and can help to lead the soul into a better re-entry into earth.

It is a popular notion that the soul knows everything and that the answer to almost any personality problem is to relax into the soul and such. This is not true. Upon many occasions the person must lead the soul. The Damon person is in touch with earthlife. The Damon person is the incarnation. The soul is of a different nature; and so the Damon person can lead the soul.

Now, how can the Damon person be helpful to the Damon soul? The answer is rather simple, and Damon may tend to discard the answer because it is simple. In effect the answer as far as Damon as a person is concerned is to become less introspective, less concerned, more simplified in his living of life.

Now this is more easily said than done, and I hope that saying it will not add to Damon's worries, because what is wanted is to diminish the very quality of worrying, and thus to diminish the quantity of worrying.

There are areas in which Damon does not worry. Damon really feels at home in the universe of nature. This is good. This certainly is re-entry into earth. If the world of people, if the rather dizzying pace of scientific advance and research, is too much, let him find the simpler things.

Now by this I do not mean meditation. Meditation rather compounds the problem because meditation as usually practiced is a looking within and this is what it would be good for Damon to diminish in his life.

There is a verse in the Christian scriptures—I am not sure if it is in the New or Old Testament—which says, 'Let no man think of himself more highly than he ought to think.'— Paul.

This usually is interpreted as advocating humility rather than pride. But there is another meaning to that verse, another use of it as well. If a person becomes too introspective and looks within himself too much to see how he is feeling this morning and how he is feeling this noon and how he felt yesterday evening and to compare how he feels now with how he felt yesterday and the day before and at some other time, he is 'thinking too highly' of himself, perhaps in the sense of valuing his own opinion and seeking his own opinion too much.

Now there is an underlying flow to life established by God, and if Damon can relax into it and not look within himself as much, gradually he can come into a greater peacefulness, and with the greater peacefulness, a little larger productive participation in life.

The knowledge of the working of the human mind and emotions is much greater today than it has been in the past, and there may come some more medical discoveries which could be quite helpful to Damon. The discovery of the balance of chemicals, the discovery of the balance of electrical forces, the discovery of the effect of the body upon the mind and of the mind upon the body, and the spirit upon both and both upon the spirit—all of this knowledge is increasing, and it may be that some further development of some branch of that knowledge will prove quite helpful to Damon in this incarnation.

This is the introduction to Damon of who he is and why. More will come out as the reading proceeds, of course. I am sorry I do not have a cut-and-dried answer to the problems, because that which is to be accomplished is the actual learning and growth of the soul as it comes back into earthliving, and this can be accomplished only by the soul through its own incarnations. Others can help. Others have helped. Others will continue to help. But the growth must be in the Damon soul, and at present the learning edge of the Damon soul is the Damon person.

He has known much of suffering, and for this I reach out a hand of fellowship. Suffering is a part of earthlife. Suffering is one ladder of growth. Every soul experiences suffering and nearly every personality experiences some.

Now can Damon, of his own personal effort, improve his condition? Well, in a way, no, because the condition has been brought about partly by Damon's effort to improve. As such, the condition is somewhat a mark of honor, in that it shows that the Damon person has been very concerned about improving himself, his touch with life, his understanding of life, and his walk through life. In another sense, yes, he can; the result has not yet been really satisfactory, but there is progress there.

Progress always is a step-by-step affair, and progress is certainly not impossible for Damon.

Is there a question so far, conductor?

Conductor: Yes, Dr. John. First of all, you said he is a young soul. The first or the second stage?

Dr. John: Oh, perhaps between the first stage of just-starting and the second stage of well-started. He really is not well-started yet because of the hiatus in incarnations.

Conductor: Do you see the reason for being away so long from earthliving?

Dr. John: Well, the soul got interested in doing other things. There are many cosmic schools which the soul attends and in which it has learnings and experiences. It may have been unwise for it to stay away from earth so long, but it felt it could come back any time it wanted to, so why hurry? If it had come back a century ago, it would have found the earth and life upon earth much more like what it had known. The last previous incarnation was in the 1400s, and the 1400s were not nearly as different from the 1800s as they are from the 1900s. (A511:1-5)

A familiar family situation was recreated for Damon in this life. His father had been his father in the 1400s Italian life, his mother returned to be mother, and his former older brother is his older brother again. Hence these same souls are in the same major family roles as they had been in the 1400s, helping to create a similar family setting. This eased the pain of this re-entry life, but the soul probably will not be on a normal reincarnational pattern for at least another lifetime.

The youth of the soul, the staying away from earth too long without keeping apprised of what was happening here, and the general uneasiness of the soul, have expressed in Damon as mental illness. If Damon can grasp the significance of feeling more at ease and being less introspective, he may relieve some of the mental disturbance. This would help lead his soul through this important transitional life. As Dr. John says, this is easier said than done. The principle must be not only understood but put into practice in his daily living.

Although Damon may feel he is not accomplishing anything in this life, he is the first of two steps his soul will have to take in order to get back in step with earth schooling.

CELESTE

Every soul will vicariously experience some incarnate life from other realms or planes. This can be accomplished by observation. For instance, a close cosmic family member can be going through an interesting or a difficult incarnation while its friend watches the lifetime from the astral realm, even entering into the experience to the point that it can feel some of the pleasure and pain of the incarnation. Other vicarious experiences can be had under the careful tutelage of cosmic teachers, bringing their students close to earth to observe the present, or bringing them up to date by showing their proteges earth history. Soulmates particularly can share in this manner. This is part of the soul's earth schooling.

Celeste's soul has used this means of vicarious living to study the last four hundred years. Getting caught up in just one incarnation when so many interesting changes were taking place on planet earth was too limiting for her soul! It wanted to keep abreast of more than it could have experienced in one body—such as the scientific advancements, and the birthing of the new country America. So since the 1500s her soul has been sitting on the bleachers watching "all three rings" (to borrow circus terminology) of earth progress. This is a rather unusual way to experience earth. But this eager soul did not want to miss any of the excitement by being hooked perhaps in a stodgy incarnation where work could have kept its nose to the grindstone.

Celeste is not experiencing the pains and pangs of a re-entry life since she has not actually been away from earth. But she has had some psychological adjustments now, because sitting on the bleachers and watching is different from experiencing directly the realities of incarnate life. Celeste has survived these minor shocks with no hurtful physical or mental carryover:

> Dr. John: Well, there are five members of her council here. Four are her immediate council which is, I believe, all there are, and one from the council above them, here by request of the four. The older one is sort of chuckling, and I am sort of chuckling, but the four are perplexed. They don't exactly have a runaway on their hands but they have one in whom there is a certain element of impetuosity, but it's all to the good.

It's all for good, it's all an impetuous, somewhat rush nature into that which is good. But there is a little bit the quality expressed by Mr. Carroll in his interesting story of 'Alice in Wonderland' when he comes to one of the knights who 'mounted his horse and rode off in all directions at once.'

The person of this incarnation is in its soul's native gender expression. Celeste is a feminine expression of the feminine half of her whole soul. The soul is emerging from the second stage of well-started, and soon will be entering the around-the-midpoint third of the five stages into which we divide the Individuated-God-Being's soulhood experiences and incarnations. And it is just very possible that this one will make its way through in just about the minimum of time and of incarnations because she does pack a great deal into each, and she has the ability to vicariously experience much of earthliving that she does not personally undergo.

This quality may well have translated in her childhood into a vivid imagination. Between lives this soul certainly does not retreat into any quiet cloister, although it has taken lessons in other cosmic schools with a great seriousness; in fact a great seriousness somewhat characterizes this soul and at least some of its incarnations, including the present one. This great seriousness does not in any way militate against a certain kind of happiness, but it yet carries over into and even expresses within that certain kind of happiness. She tends to live life in high gear more than most people.

Now this makes for a certain attractiveness and it makes for an overcoming of obstacles and it makes for a greater achievement than would have been expected, possibly. It is a good quality. Certainly her council of four would not trade this quality for lethargy or apathy for her. But at times they find it a little hard to keep this quality from a too-quick enthusiasm, a too-quick immersion in an idea, and a certain overemphasis upon some aspects of experience which may open unto this person.

This soul has not incarnated since the time when the Renaissance had become well-established within the British Isles, with the upsurge of civilization involved with that. I find her in the 1500s, the latter part of the 1500s, in England, in the feminine. And I do not find a lifetime in between but (chuckling) this takes a rather careful reading of the akashic records because the soul has accomplished a projection into at least a quasi-personality consciousness which from the astral realms, higher and lower astral, has watched earth happenings with a great deal of identification with what was going on as it watched selective earth happenings, that is, somewhat as the reader of a skillfully told story may identify with one and then another of the characters delineated within the story.

This has the result of a, well, one might call it a false image of other lifetimes upon this one's akashic records. But they are not really false images. They are experiences into which she has entered to some extent and which have affected her consciousness. This is what makes an impact upon the akashic records. This is one of the major forces of such impacts, and this could be read by those perhaps not as carefully schooled in reading the akashic records as being a number of lifetimes, some of them overlapping, when in reality these were vicarious experiences, identifications with others who were having the actual experience.

Is this good or bad? In general, it is good. It makes for certain mistaken identification in which she might herself recall lifetimes which actually she did not quite live, but with which the soul identified itself to a somewhat larger rather than lesser extent. So this can make for a certain fuzziness in the akashic records. This might be called detrimental. I do not so call it, because the totality of it is certainly upon the plus side. She has gotten much of life experience without the soul actually having to send forth the 'pseudopod,' as it were, of an incarnation. Is this clear?

Conductor: Yes, this is clear, Dr. John, what was happening. But as to why—why so long since her last incarnation?

Dr. John: Because the soul is very, very interested in whatever it gets interested in. It has this rather impetuous wholeheartedness. It is very enthusiastic, if something catches its attention, a great 'I want to do that, I want to be that.' It sees and has fully accepted the necessary and the excellent opportunity aspects of various incarnate experiences. The soul understands that if it is to progress farther spiritually it must accept the plan of God that the soul successfully guide persons, its own persons, its own incarnations, the personhoods developed by it and assigned to it, through the various basic experiences that the cosmic school of earth has for it. And so from the sidelines it is almost on the playing field itself, and is getting many of these experiences.

This is why in the four hundred years since its last incarnation it has had the equivalent of four or five incarnations to quite an extent. It has taken a great interest in the new country. It has, well, it did not travel with the pilgrims on the Mayflower for it did not realize how meaningful that trip was to become, but it has lived among the early New England settlers, experiencing some of their strong faith which led them to withstand the hardships there. It has watched with keen interest the American Revolutionary War, and it entered into the development of nursing which grew out of woman's urge to alleviate the suffering of war. This came about later. It has trekked westward with the American pioneers who set out to explore and discover and claim this continent. It understands the fact that America has a large significance in the coming New World. America has not been called the New World wrongly, but truly is the early stage of so much of that which is to be accomplished by mankind in the New Age as the New World truly is built, the true human era upon planet earth.

It—the Celeste soul—was caught up in the early development of science within England. It quite early saw the significance of the scientific approach to gaining information, and so it actually almost sat in, that is, sort of on the bleachers, on some of the early meetings of the Royal Society of England. It watched as the way was found of ascertaining the freezing point and the boiling point of water, and as these pioneer scientists studied the three states, the three material states of matter, the solid, the liquid, and the gaseous of water, for illustration. It was very, very enthusiastic about this new method which got the objective facts of the situations, and saw that in this way this new method was getting truth such as the older methods never did get.

Then it swung back to the American continent during the Civil War. Saw how this new country, this new instrument, was saved from blunting itself, from breaking itself in two, and admired the inspired knowledge of the leader, Abraham Lincoln. It observed the difficulties visited upon a gracious civilization, the South, which had committed itself to ends which were blocking rather than advancing progress.

Interestingly enough, this soul did not become closely

involved with the two world wars. They were too much. Well, of course, the soul was incarnate before the Second World War developed and was fought. But they were a bit beyond the soul to experience fully. Although the soul understood that the historic progress of the enlargement of the human community must take place to where a lawful society of order is established within this area embracing nations, the area beyond which the lawful community has already been established.

Well, with this preliminary picture of this soul we come back to the present life. It incarnated at the present time because it definitely wishes to have a part in the spiritual progression that is now being made. The material progression was necessary to free many persons from the necessity of giving the bulk of their time and energy and thought and work to attaining the material basis of a secure and good life. That material basis having been now more or less accomplished, then the purpose of it, of course, is undertaken, that the spiritual understanding of mankind, the knowledge of himself as a creature of two realms, the spiritual and the physical, the knowledge that he must live by the laws and the values of the spiritual realm and that in so doing he is helping to bring the knowledge and the values and the way and the laws of God into earth-knowledge and earth-operation. In other words, the bringing in of the Kingdom of God on earth. And so this soul eagerly accepted incarnation at this time, having made very good use of the time since its last incarnation.

Each soul is begotten with its own individuality, which is expressed in earth through the personalities of its personhoods. Celeste's soul is filled with the desire to be a part of whatever important is going on, which oddly enough in her case is the main reason the soul sat on the bleachers for the last four hundred years watching history-making events. Her soul also has the tendency to live each incarnation with a great deal of enthusiasm.

We can understand more about the individuality of her soul from its immediate pastlife, which started in Scotland and ended in England. When Celeste asks about her daughter, Dr. John identifies the daughter soul as an older cosmic family brother, who volunteered to be an older sister wayshower in a 1500s Scottish life:

Dr. John: These two have been together also as sisters in—well, it's very close to that English life. There's something confusing here. This soul took an incarnation in Scotland in the 1500s and then decided that a life in London would be a lot more interesting. There were religious happenings in Scotland and they were significant and the soul was interested in this freeing of the human spirit religiously. But the—well, how did this soul by the time it was almost three years old understand that even the Reformation and the early Presbyterianism and Calvinism of Scotland was quite a bit stuffy? Here's a little three-year-old girl, but the soul was very close by and watching and decided, well, yes, this was important but my goodness, it was stuffy and these people were dour and the climate and the conditions were rather staid and did not encourage much of change. So the soul talked it over with her council, who on the whole encouraged this soul to (chuckling) 'go get all the gusto it can' because the gusto is used constructively, and allowed it to pull out at the age of three, as another appropriate home was found in London. And so it jumped.

Now this cosmic family brother had come into that Scottish life as an older sister, to be with his greater experience, his wider experience with earth, a wayshower for the younger girl. She was seven years old when her sister at three pulled out. And so there was a little bit of a feeling of (chuckling), 'I can't completely count on this younger sister. Here am I stuck with Scotland!' But the soul had its own purposes in that Scottish life as well, of course. And with a bit of a rueful smile, it waved goodbye to its sister and said, 'Well, I'll see you again doubtlessly, and I wish you well and have a great time down there in London.' Then it settled in to be a Scottish girl, young woman, woman, mother, meal-maker, grandmother, and corpse—even a Scottish corpse is somewhat distinctive.

The Scottish breed is different as all of life is different in some subtle ways, in some small ways, in some large ways, in the different experience-frameworks that earth has.

In this life there is no carryover of resentment. The daughter soul is an older soul as I have said, is possessed in some ways of a greater stability, is not rocked as badly by a changing wind. It has learned to keep a course even in a changing tide. But it appreciates very much the fineness of the mother's soul.

The 1500s English life is picked up again when Celeste asks about her granddaughter, Karen:

> Dr. John: Yes, she was a daughter in the English life and the mother had meant quite a lot to her and the daughter very much appreciated the mother. The father in that life had, well, let's see: The father of the then incarnation of Celeste was a successful merchant with, oh, let us say, a half interest in three ships. He and another successful merchant who respected each other but still had things drawn up in a legal way, decided to go into the trade that involved a ship, a crosschannel ship with Europe, a ship that could venture into the Mediterranean. And the two of them instead of getting a ship apiece, took a half-interest each in two ships, dividing the perils, as it were, in that way. Both ships survived all right and they added a third ship, and they prospered, prospered rather well. Their families had the advantages and such. Now the daughter of this one married the son of the other one and so this pattern of life was extended. The daughter being the then incarnation of the Celeste soul. The present granddaughter, what is her name again, please?
>
> Conductor: Karen.
>
> Dr. John: Karen was their daughter.
>
> It was a good life. It was a life of many interests and a lot of gusto, and the father and mother had a great love for each other and a very robust way of living life.
>
> When they had roast beef, for instance, they really had a great round of beef and they would settle in and they would have friends in and they would eat ten or twelve pounds of a round of beef, maybe more, maybe fifteen or eighteen, in three days. They just did things with enthusiasm. They traveled some. They went to France and they visited Paris, some of the entertainments of Paris. They did this in company with a number of other Englishmen and they had their ladies and they did it with enough gold coins and retainers, strong men servants, that they had a great and safe time on such a visit.
>
> In short, it was a very interesting life and their children were privileged and, on the whole, entered into the same type of enthusiastic living of that life. Yes.

The impetuous nature of this soul and its robust zest for life is illustrated in the immediate pastlives and the last four hundred years of vicarious experiences. But incarnate life has its problems. Celeste's sister was injured from a fall and left crippled. This was an unexpected incident that shocked the Celeste soul, though it handled the situation well and learned from her sister's plight:

> Dr. John: So here a crippled person was brought into the actual family experience of this eager, enthusiastic, impetuous young soul and she probably has presented some unexpected problems, some unthought-of problems, to the Celeste person.
>
> But the council shows me and I see upon the akashic records that Celeste has handled this constructively, is learning from it as well as gaining a better-than-passing grade in that experience.
>
> Will the two of them be together again? Well, certainly in the excarnate portion of their present personhood life they will come together and there the restrictions upon the consciousness of the sister will be broken through, will be so much shaken off, broken and peeled off, that there can be a greater expression of equality and appreciation and sharing and love between them.
>
> They will be together in some future earthlives, not just one but several, because that which is being built between them is good, represents forces that can be used. Now the Celeste person did not necessarily see all of this to begin with. Its impetuous wish to advance the coming of the Kingdom and to have a part in this extremely interesting age, did not quite see at first or accept that this experience of a crippled sister was a part of that. She was expecting other things with more excitement, more band-playing, as it were, more noble work to be done. But the Kingdom of God is built brick by brick, stone by stone, person by person, and with the clearing away of rubble and overlays of impediments. Yes.

An illustration of her frustration of incarnate life was expressed in one of her questions:

> Conductor: Let me read this one: 'Who was I to have been so filled with the love of God all my life, to feel I have sat many times with great teachers, to want to share all of this, and yet feel so limited and to have so many times turned my back?'

Dr. John: This is the enthusiasm of this soul, as I have spoken, and it has learned much, and it has sat in on classes of great teachers. But it is a young soul, and to become a great teacher itself or a great worker for the Kingdom, it's going to take more experience and a certain greater stability. However, in this life the quality of enthusiasm and impetuousness is attaining much good, bringing it much experience and much of good.

I suppose the simple answer is a greater maturity, which may (chuckling) sound like a dash of cold water but really is not. It's bringing in the stabilizing and strengthening factors which will enable her to be the kind of person she wants to be and to do what she wants to do. Yes. (A2853:1-9,14)

Each of these souls had its own purpose for its extended stay in the other realms. The soul's learning experience is more than just earth and the astral realm. It is a combination of earth, which is the laboratory where the spiritual principles are put into practice, and the other cosmic schools where the spiritual principles are taught. Whereas most souls keep their cosmic schooling and earth schooling in balance, occasionally a soul may wander off, as in the case of Damon; or it may simply get ahead of its earth schooling, as in the case of Stewart; or it may experience earth vicariously, as in the case of Celeste.

So the karma—the results—of staying too long away from earth teaches the soul to better pace itself, balancing the lessons learned in the classrooms of other cosmic schools with the practical, personal mastery learned in the laboratory of earth.

Karma, the great teacher, warns us not to stay away from earth too long, once we've started our incarnations.

CHAPTER TWELVE

JUMPING INTO THE WRONG INCARNATION

If a person takes a trip to a far country, he usually prepares as carefully as possible ahead of time, especially if it will be a long stay. The same is true for a soul. When it comes into incarnation with the expectation of spending a full human lifetime, there are certain preparations the soul needs to make. The parent souls should be carefully selected, consulted prior to the incarnation and their agreement obtained. The soul may also want to know who will be the prospective siblings, what cosmic family members and cosmic cousins will be in the family or incarnating at the same time in close proximity. The country, the timing, the culture, the opportunities and other requirements are all of considerable importance, and the wise soul plans carefully with the help of its council of guides and teachers.

But sometimes a soul takes a diving leap into just any incarnation, most unwisely. The parents of the intruder might have been expecting another child, or no child at all. The courtesy of accepting or not accepting the child might not have been extended to the parents. If any of the important details were arranged, it may have been done haphazardly and the incomer may not have anyone prepared to meet him.

Louella and Dolores are examples of souls who jumped into the incarnational pond willy-nilly, helterskelter. The results upon their own personhoods, the incarnate Louella and Dolores, are quite educational to their souls, and give an insight into the cosmic significance of planning ahead.

LOUELLA

Sometimes a soul will throw a temper tantrum if something doesn't go the way it planned or if its guides and teachers suggest one thing and the soul wants to do something else. Temper tantrums have detrimental results for souls as well as for persons. Louella's soul threw a temper tantrum and jumped into the first incarnation available to it, thumbing its nose at the guides and teachers as it dove into the incarnational pond.

The incarnation that had been planned for Louella's soul was slow in developing. The next incarnation was scheduled to be a masculine lifetime in England with a birth to rather affluent parents. But the mother and father had not even married yet, and other things were happening that did not appear to be right for this incarnation. Hence the guides and teachers suggested they begin to draw up an alternate plan. The soul became miffed and simply jumped into the next available incarnation, not looking where it was going and not really caring.

The soul woke up and found itself in a feminine body, which was a bit of a surprise. Instead of an affluent home, the situation was poverty and shame. Louella's parents were not expecting a child— the father was ill and died shortly after Louella's birth, the mother was mentally ill and was committed to a mental institution. Therefore Louella was raised by a great aunt and uncle. They were not expecting a child on their doorstep, either. It was an unhappy home life—the uncle molesting the child and the aunt ignoring her.

The soul soon realized the mistake it had made, but it knew the error would be compounded if it pulled out and requested another incarnation. This was where it had landed and the soul realized it had to accept the consequences of its temper tantrum:

> Dr. John: The soul did something that was quite foolish and did it really in sort of a momentary pique, yes. It was not a peak experience but rather a fairly sad experience of being piqued.
> The soul had a plan set up for incarnation which it thought was really quite good. It was coming in to a rather influential family in England. One of the gentle folk and not a 'common folk' family. It had the agreement of its guides and teachers, but while the whole matter was still in a tentative stage—for instance, the prospective father and mother had not even married yet, had not started their own home—it was felt that it

might be wiser for this soul not to enter there, not to have thaι particular earth experience at that time. There were reasons and they were good reasons, though it was not really definite. It might have been that the soul still might have had that experience. But the soul, in a moment of pique, said, 'All right. Take your old pattern and do what you want to with it'—and the soul simply jumped into an incarnation.

Now what it got into has been quite a learning experience for the soul. This soul is the masculine half of its whole soul. It's not a very old soul but it is in the early part of the third stage and so was really old enough to be smart enough not to do something like this. When it did do this, it is learning a rather strict lesson, a rather hard lesson, for when it just jumped into incarnation without real preparation at all, it found itself first of all in a girl-body, which it certainly had not bargained for, and found itself in a social status and a family situation certainly not to its liking. We will find as we go through the persons, conductor, probably we will find that there are not very many relatives in that family with whom there is past life association or even purposeful connection.

Now the soul was in a quandary when it found out what it had done to itself. It was not allowed to pull right out again and it somewhat came to its senses and realized that if it did pull out again that it would simply inherit a life such as this because of its choice, its foolish and quick choice but its choice, and so it had better stay with the present and see it through. Now this is good. This was an act of maturing. In fact, this choice was an act of maturity even as the pique and the jump had been an act of immaturity, and the experience itself is providing certainly some quantity of learning.

But even this would have been lost if the personality had not swung into the positive approach, into making constructive best use of what it did have and, of course, that is the secret of success in the reincarnational framework and the soul framework of any life—to make the best of what one has and the experiences one meets. Yes.

The mellowing, if one might call it that, the turning to a constructive approach, took a while. Yes, it took place and it has taken place, but in terms of an earthlife it comes through as a somewhat gradual development in that it does not appear right away, and here there is an interesting spirit teaching point, if you will. The soul can come to a better attitude, a sober realization of its mistake, a certain contrition, for it did feel sorry that it had done this stupid thing, and set about doing the best possible job and this can take place as an event from the spirit side. But the translation of the event into terms of the progressive life-span of the person involved, the incarnation and the translation of the event from spirit time, if one might call it that, into earth time, which is a steadily moving point along the linear dimension, the line of time, you see, is a process in itself. And so even though the event of the soul making a good spiritual decision took place rather early—oh, it might be said within the first four years of finding itself in this incarnation—the translation of that, or one might say the feeding in of the force of that decision and that attitude, would be a progressive, a gradual thing rather progressively influencing the nature and the behavior of its incarnation.

So one would expect, and I think the life of Louella will reveal, that the thing of which I have been speaking has been a process and coming quite likely into fairly recent manifestation in the flow of time of her existence, her life. Yes.

Neither the mother nor the father had any cosmic relationship or any pastlives with Louella. She was born among strangers, and strangers that were not prepared for her coming.

It was the great aunt and uncle who reared her, and they treated Louella like the unwanted guest she was. But they were not incarnations from particularly good souls. So Louella and her soul had their hands full at a very young age.

The great uncle presented the most problems:

> Dr. John: No pastlife acquaintance and no cosmic relationship. He was not exactly a plum but when she jumped, when the soul jumped, it didn't know if it would land in a plum orchard or a nettle patch, and this is what it got, which was quite a sobering experience, the whole thing, to the soul. And during its upbringing, its young years, it had quite a little job on its hands—well, mind, attention—to protect the personhood it had and the little girl's body and to bring it along. Once the soul had decided to accept what it got and make the best of

it, it had a job to bring a certain social environment protection around the little one, and it worked at that. The adults were not really conducive to a good environment, a good early childhood and youth of the Louella person. Yes.

The great aunt was a little more sensitive, but simply was not advanced soulwise sufficiently to shift with the winds and greet this child with open arms:

>Dr. John: Well, the same picture holds here again. This little girl was a totally unexpected event in her foster home as well as in her physical home. That is, the incarnation of this particular soul was. It was not simply that the child was unexpected but the soul was a stranger, and so no preparation had been made for it. There is no pastlife acquaintance and no cosmic relationship with this one. There may be a future as there was a certain amount of maternal outreach by the great aunt. And so that is a bond which can be used and I believe probably will be, but certainly is not patterned as yet for use in a future incarnation which they would share in some form of acquaintance. Yes.

Since this lifetime was not planned there were not previously arranged husband prospects for Louella. Although she did marry, the marriage did not last. Cosmically Louella and her husband were distantly related and they had had a pastlife together, but as Dr. John indicated, his life pattern did not include her, so the marriage was only temporary.

Two children were born to Louella and her husband before the marriage broke up. One came in to help, the other was another soul who had jumped into incarnation against the advice of his guides and teachers.

First the elder son:

>Dr. John: Yes. This is a cosmic family member, one who diverted his course so he would come when he saw what had happened to his good friend. He's from the masculine, too, so they are cosmic brothers. When this one saw what happened to his good friend, he did not exactly dive into the swimming

pool to rescue his friend and swim to shore, because that could not be done. But he came in as son with his own life pattern and life purpose but cast in this role. There was time, you see, for this to be undertaken and planned and it is a good relationship and a kind action.

Louella and this cosmic brother had had several pastlives together. The last incarnation they shared was in America in the 1600s when Louella was a devoted father and her present son was a son. This cosmic brother knows the Louella soul to be a good soul, only it took a wrong turn. Hence there is a closeness between them.

But the second child is a different story:

Dr. John: Well, this is rather interesting, conductor. There is no pastlife acquaintance. There is no cosmic relationship. But this is a karmic relationship in this way: The soul of this son pushed through unwisely, against advice, and against the purposeful flow of God for it, pushed through into this incarnation for reasons different from the Louella incarnation. But the Louella incarnation inherited this other one as a son—not exactly in retribution, although there is a certain element of justice in it, but even more in sort of a wry expression of learning.

She drew this other one to her in this way, you see: her soul's rash jump set up a certain resonance with another one who was pushing to come in precipitously and against good counsel and against logic.

So she inherited this younger son and his problems, for I see he has had quite a problem-plagued existence.

So this is a karmic associaton, and as she learns from watching this other one who came in against good advice, she as a soul is learning again and again the lesson that it must not come in again against good advice. Yes.

Meanwhile, of course, as mother and son there are certain forces between them simply in that relationship. These were met in terms of the two persons involved. Forgetting for a moment that each is a soul, they are persons and their interpersonal relationship was the dominant factor of their relationship, not a soul relationship, you see.

The son soul is, well, it has its problems, or let us say its council has their problems with him—the different members of the council having, as it were, different particular responsibilities. Yes, they have their problems with that one, and I do not really wish to look into it too closely. The other one is not established, it's not well established yet as a God-child, a soul, in its own right. Yes. It may well be recycled, and soon.

This son has been a continuous problem for Louella and a trouble-maker all his life. He is now institutionalized for drug-related insanity and is not expected to be released.

In her life reading Louella asked about a number of her friends. None of them had any cosmic relationship or pastlife with her. Her cosmic friends would be looking for her in an affluent family in England rather than in the poverty stricken life she landed in. So her cosmic acquaintances are in another part of the world and their life patterns follow along a social scale far different from Louella's. Therefore Louella has felt alone most of her life. One of her questions in the life reading related to this loneliness:

> Conductor: Louella says, 'I've always been alone even while I was married. Why am I to spend my life alone? Is this karma or a lesson to be learned?'
> Dr. John: Well, there was no mate, there was no marriage picture prepared for it. Even the two children were, as I pointed out, somewhat last minute arrangements. The elder son very defininitely coming in purposefully. The younger son being drawn by that rather odd karma. The fact, too, that Louella is from a masculine soul and the fact that it had unfortunate experiences of helpless femininity as a child would militate against an easy marriage.

Also Louella suffers from various ailments, which have plagued her most of her life. Although Dr. John usually does not give medical advice, he can sometimes look at the akashic records or the life purpose and give what he sees from that standpoint. In Louella's case, there was rather an obvious reason for her minor disabilities:

> Conductor: She has several physical problems, Dr. John. The first one she asks about is, 'Why do I suffer from headaches and blood circulation problems?'

Dr. John: Well, there will be physical reasons for this which an earth medical doctor can tell her about much better than I can from the akashic records. The soul experienced a bit of a headache when it jumped and, as it were, landed head first in a dry swimming pool. Because she had not been expected, the water had not been turned on to receive her. I would hope that her headaches will diminish. But the major key is that these are physical things to be physically handled by physical experts, the medical doctors of her time. (A2237:1-4,6,7,10,12,13,19,20)

The jumping into the dry swimming pool also affected her mental agility. Louella has difficulty writing and speaking, and is regarded as mentally slow, though not retarded. Most of these physical and mental situations can be related back to making a running dive into an ill-advised incarnation, particularly since the soul had put together masculine forces rather than feminine. And certainly the environment in which she was reared would influence her mental faculties.

There seems to be an underlying current of anger in Louella, which is natural. She was almost an alcoholic until six or seven years ago when her attitude started to change and Louella began a spiritual seeking. Since her soul realized its mistake and has known contrition, the soul's new position regarding this incarnation gradually seeped into the personality of Louella. She is expressing her soul's change of attitude by altering her life style.

This is not a bad soul. Its impetuous nature most likely has been curbed by this lifetime. Louella's soul probably will never again thumb its nose at its guides and teachers, impatiently jump when it should just go off and pout for a while and then listen to the good advice of those working closely with it. Just as people have personality, souls have individuality. The soul individuality needs to be developed over a period of lifetimes before the soul is sufficiently accomplished to be a diplomat. Even though the person, Louella, seems to be resting near the bottom of the human barrel, she as a soul has the potential and now the impetus to do much better with life on earth. This lifetime was only a sidestep in the incarnational pattern.

DELORES

Other cosmic schools the soul attends help prepare it for its various incarnations. Certain principles and concepts are studied by the soul, which it will put into practice in the laboratory of earth. Delores' soul is an eager soul that has not learned to carefully plan an incarnation after its cosmic schooling; therefore it tends to jump too quickly into incarnations.

The last cosmic school it attended taught her masculine soul that the feminine was the natural vehicle for experiencing the spiritual on earth. So the soul simply wanted a feminine incarnation. Spotting a possibility, the soul jumped. Actually another soul had planned to come into this incarnation, but Delores' soul pushed ahead and claimed the conception—unprepared for the consequences.

This has been a rather difficult life for Delores. Her mother was not expecting this child—a child perhaps, but not this child. And even though there was an expression of a mother's love for her child, it was not a complete commitment. Since the father did not stay around long enough for Delores to know him, she was orphan-bound. At eight years of age her mother left her at a Catholic-run orphanage, and did not return for fourteen years. Loneliness has been a companion for Delores:

> Dr. John: This is an eager soul, a rather impulsive soul, a soul that will learn a lesson in one of the cosmic schools associated with the cosmic school of earth, and when it gets the point it may jump full tilt into earth to try it out. So the soul learned in a cosmic school before this incarnation that the spiritual development of a soul in incarnations is accomplished more successfully on the feminine side, as a general rule, than upon the masculine side. The masculine side is designed primarily for making a success of earthliving. The feminine side, on the other hand, is designed to keep touch with the realms other than matter, other than the physical realm, for the true nature of the human being is as a child of God, a soul, and that is a spiritual rather than a material being.
>
> So the soul jumped very enthusiastically into a feminine life this time. This is not the first of its feminine lives. The others were more just getting started in femininity, however. In this one the soul very much wanted to reach the spiritual side of its nature while in earth expression. It wanted to develop the

earth consciousnes of its beingness along the spiritual aspects. So impulsively, eagerly, not completely wisely, it just took a long run and jumped right in, landing with both feet in the feminine.

Now it did not choose its home very well. It rather thought that almost any feminine incarnation would allow it to explore and develop the feminine qualities. To a certain extent this is true. But as with all incarnations, masculine or feminine, there are some environments, some homes, some cultures, some times which are better than other environments, homes, cultures, and times. It was not particularly choosy.

And its council of guides and teachers really didn't have much to say about it. They suggested a greater caution but the soul, in effect—being a young soul—said, 'Well, feminine incarnation is what I want, isn't it?' And they said, 'Yes,' and the soul said, 'All right, I'll get it.' So, just about the first opening that came along, it took. And human beings with their uncontrolled breeding habits give a lot of opportunities for incarnation, as you know.

But the result has not been all bad. Not at all. In fact, the soul's interest and determination, its pluck and native drive, have carried it quite a way. However, I must warn Delores that she as a person will not be able to fulfill completely the soul's desire for complete spiritual enlightenment. It simply takes more time than that.

But this life is accomplishing a great deal in this direction. Whereas I do not want her to feel that she is a failure if a really impossible reach is not attained, I do want her to feel that she is a success for the considerable progress she has made and will make towards this goal. Yes.

As expected, Delores and her mother were not cosmically related and did not have any pastlife acquaintance:

Dr. John: No, there is no pastlife acquaintance of Delores and her mother, and there is no cosmic relationship either. When the Delores soul jumped into incarnation, it did not really see where it was going to land. It just saw a light, as it were, that went on suddenly saying 'feminine baby being made,' and it jumped right in. Actually, there was another soul that had been intended for that conception, but Delores got there first, claimed it, established the vital life attachment, and so it was.

But such obstreperousness usually meets with some rebuff. I would imagine the relationship with the mother may have been somewhat incomplete, may have left some things to be desired.

Or possibly the mother would be an older soul who could accept with greater equanimity such a happening, such an intruder, really. But I do not believe the mother soul was an old soul. So, there were ways in which the over-anxious, over-zealous Delores soul did not have a complete and satisfactory relation as daughter to this mother. Is this correct?

Conductor: Yes. When Delores was eight years old, she was put in a convent run by nuns for orphans. She was there twelve years and did have academic preparation, you see. The mother moved away for fourteen years and then returned.

Dr. John: Well, this is quite understandable, and it is hoped the Delores soul will learn to be a little more prudent and to at least ask permission—as it usually does, but this time did not—before it plows into any future incarnation.

No real harm has been done.

This means the Delores soul got the pattern of living it did in this lifetime. Actually the pattern is certainly not all bad. There was not the closeness of mother and daughter that could have been had otherwise, had more careful preparations been made and permission asked and introduction achieved. But the Delores soul is genuine in its commitment to God, and its quest for the spiritual aspects of life and for spiritual development is genuine and it is honored; so alternate provisions, as it were, were made for it.

There is no reason for the mother soul and the Delores soul to be together in any future incarnations. It might happen, but nothing is patterned and there is no reason to.

Unlike Louella, Delores' soul had a purpose for this incarnation. It wanted to experience spiritual seeking while on earth. Once she began her life purpose, cosmic friends were brought into Delores' life and the loneliness she experienced as a child was replaced by the companionship of close friends.

One of these friends in a pastlife helped to awaken the yearning for a spiritual life in the Delores soul. That 1700s life is feeding directly into the present life, helping to build a bond between them as they seek spiritual understanding together:

> Dr. John: Yes. They were together fairly recently. Now, this is interesting. There is a direct feed-in, and yet it was two centuries ago but not in the 1800s; it was in the 1700s and sort of the mid-1700s, in Italy. The then incarnation of the Delores soul was in masculine expression, its native gender expression. This other one was a sister, a blood sister. The two were close in the family. The brother was about a year older. There was no sibling in between, of course. They are cosmic cousins and rather close on the cosmic level. And this produced a bond between this brother and sister. Also they were middle children— there were several older and a number smaller, younger—so these two were a natural bracket of age and interest and congenial likemindedness within the family.
>
> So they discussed many things. Both of them had good minds. And they got out into nature quite a bit. This, as I have said, was in Italy. It was in a part of Italy that had mountains. Their father had a farm so it was natural for them to follow the cows out into the pastures or to go for the cows, and the mountains were a source of unfailing interest to these two. They would discuss the mountains. Their family was devout Roman Catholic, so they had a lot of religious teaching about God and angels and supervisory spirits and so forth. This gave them a lot to talk about together.
>
> Now if the two had not been brother and sister, they might very well have married. There was that kind of a happy closeness.
>
> The sister became a religious, a nun, entered a convent. The brother was quite impressed. This particular convent was of an order that stressed the mystical, the concept of seeing God in everything. She was allowed visitors—not all the time but, oh, let us say, on Sunday afternoon her family would come. And this brother would come even if the rest of the family did not come. He was mature by then. He would come and she would talk over with him what she had been taught during the week or the month or so, and some of her experiences in prayer. This helped to awaken in the Delores soul the desire for spiritual awakening in earth consciousness which led to the action in the present life. (A1511:2-6)

There is a happy ending to this story. Other cosmic friends from that incarnation have come into her life, forming a small circle of people on a spiritual quest. And for Delores they are closing the gap of loneliness she experienced during her childhood.

Dr. John does warn Delores that her soul may not be satisfied with the outcome of this life. Its eager nature wants complete spiritual enlightenment in this lifetime. It is not possible for any soul to reach the heights of spiritual understanding in just one life. It must climb the ladder of any knowledge step by step, one incarnation built upon another. Hopefully though, her soul has learned not to jump into incarnations, seeking its purpose in a rush. The consequences of a zealous nature can sometimes result in loneliness.

The Delores and Louella souls are "party-crashers." The unhappiness they experience as persons, the lack of cosmic and pastlife friends who so often are the greatest joys of a new life, the misery of their childhoods, the long years of wondering why so many things were going wrong, the lack of prepared husband possibilities and children—all these and more are ways in which karma, the great teacher, lets us experience the results of our sometimes impulsive mistakes, learning from them a better way for the decisions and the lifetimes up ahead.

CHAPTER THIRTEEN

THE HEALING OF WAR VICTIMS

Man has attempted to solve many problems through war. So often the justification was meager, senseless, but still battles raged, and so it will be until the Kingdom of God is established on earth. Evil pushes for war because in battle Satan has a field day, as bodies, persons, and many souls suffer wounds not easily healed.

It often has been said that war is hell, and the hell that is war devours many innocent victims. Where is God during this hell? He is there, but He will not interfere with man's free will even when it promotes idiocy. But the Creator can heal the casualties and return unto them that which was lost.

What happens to the soul whose personality is ravaged by war? This depends on the nature of what has been done to the person and also on that soul's wisdom and strength. In general, the older the soul, the less it is detrimentally affected.

A soul, particularly a young one, may bring fear into itself because its personality is so very frightened during wartime. Or sadness can descend on the God-child, a sadness so strong that earthliving is rejected. Perhaps the soul will puff up with righteous indignation at such treatment of its person. Physical problems, psychological problems, even severe mental illness—all of these symptoms can stem from war trauma.

God has established many means of healing, and this too is individual. There is restoration on the other side. But there must also be remedy in the earthplane, where the hurt or loss was experienced. Negative forces in the soul have to be released, the God-child must be reassured. So the circumstances of the healing life will be carefully planned by the guides and teachers. This chapter presents six individuals who were victims of war, what happened to them and how their healing is taking place.

SCHUYLER

War strife can make a soul uneasy. Schuyler came into his present incarnation with two recent pastlives in war-torn areas. Both lives were fraught with fears, some of which did not materialize. But as a result his soul, not yet old enough to feel confident, is apprehensive.

The Schuyler incarnation, now in his early teens, is purposed to instill more confidence in his soul and to release much of this built-in anxiety. The story begins as Dr. John identifies Schuyler's soul:

> Dr. John: Well, he is an incarnation from the masculine half of his whole soul and he is into the third stage of soulhood and approaching the centerline in it, so he is getting good experiences and the soul is undertaking and being given personalities and incarnate lifetimes a little more difficult than the young souls get. Of course, this is good because here the lessons are more significant and more advanced. It is like going to seventh grade instead of fourth grade or first grade.
>
> But the soul is a little apprehensive. The soul is not too confident of itself yet. Now this is not a serious trouble, but it does give Schuyler an extra opportunity: As he develops confidence in himself as a person the quality of confidence will build in his soul. All incarnations are expression-points and experience-points for the soul. And so the soul can express a portion of itself through that person, but also through that person the soul can receive, can experience, and can gain as a soul the results of the experiences.
>
> So as Schuyler builds a rather quiet self-confidence, as he can and as we think he will, he will be adding this quality to the soul. In fact, the Schuyler personality, I see, has been deliberately brought in with a certain lack of confidence so that he can develop confidence. If you develop confidence from a percentile, say, of 20 to 50, that is a 30 percent gain on the scale of 100, and so it is as much of a gain as if someone came in with a 50 percentile confidence and built to 80.
>
> The very fact that the Schuyler personality came with a certain lack of self-confidence was purposeful among other things and other reasons as well, but it was purposeful so that he could build a goodly amount of confidence from that beginning point.

Is this clear, conductor?

Conductor: Yes, Dr. John, and most interesting. I don't believe I've run across this.

Dr. John: No. This I think is sort of a different point. Every person is different. Every reading of the akashic records that I do interests me because it is different. God certainly gave the quality of individuality to His children when He individuated portions of His own Beingness to become His children.

The present life stems also from the immediately prior life, which was...well, let's see...the prior life ended...well, prior to 1880. I do not pick up the precise year at present. Maybe I will. It is not too significant.

In that prior life, the then incarnation of the Schuyler soul was in masculine expression and was the son of a fine southern white man who had a small plantation and a nice house. But the man, the father, was called to the Civil War. He was capable. He was an officer in the infantry. He went with the major body of Confederate troops. He was in on their greatest penetration of the North, which was stopped in the very costly battle of Gettysburg. So many men lost there, dead, wounded, maimed in that fierce fighting. It is too bad that war is still the final way of settling disputes. That will change.

Now, the boy was too young to get into the war. He was about, he was probably about five years old when the war broke, because he was about ten years old when his father came home. His father was not killed. His father was not wounded. His father lost his horse and that was a serious loss because the animal was needed for plowing and such back home. They had a small farm and...well, here I go looking for other horses! I mustn't do that, conductor! I could see that for some reason or other, the loss of the horse was significant. Well, it may have meant that the man himself was confined to slower travel, had to walk home.

When the Northern troops made their great drive into the South, the march through Georgia, they separated the Confederate groups and they walled some of them off so that those Confederate troops could not be in that battle against them. This man was walled off. He was walled off to the west. Actually, his home was in western Georgia. His home was not in the path of the march so it escaped destruction. However, in some ways the people who were close but escaped, heard stories that were worse than actually did happen, if possible. And so this young boy had a great fear. He was a sensitive person. He was a compassionate person. He feared for his father's welfare. He then feared that their home might be destroyed, and everything they had taken or destroyed. But also he had a deep compassionate sense that the people who were getting these killings and such destruction were—well, he felt very sorry for them and he identified with them.

Now this shows a very fine quality within that soul. I repeat, this is a masculine soul, not a feminine soul. But it has some of the outreach of sensitivity and of caring for others which provides a certain nurturing, which is found more quickly in the feminine soul but which the masculine soul is to develop as well during its course of 60 to 100 significant incarnations.

The father came home, life picked up. We cannot say it resumed because it was of a different pattern and more difficult and less privileged. But the young boy...well, let's see. The young boy died at thirteen. He lived only three more years. His concern over the destruction that had taken place and the loss of life, the destruction of people as well as their homes and all—well, that continued to weigh upon him. The return of his father relieved the worry for the father, yes. But the boy himself was still weighed down by the sense of the enormity of what had happened, and his father was quiet, too. The father had been through some very serious experiences.

Whether or not this contributed to the boy's death I do not see. Something occurred. Some event, I believe it was an accident of some sort, which injured him and within about two and one-half days, sixty hours, he died.

This means that the forces which had been aroused within him of compassion and concern and a lot of just plain worry had not had time to resolve completely in that personality, you see, so there were certain forces as 'karma on the doorstep' when he came into this present life. Now these can be very constructive forces, as mankind is in a period when a different way of living together must be established so that the old way of killing and destroying is not the final resort. And we think this will happen within Schuyler's lifetime but it will be dependent upon the coming of the Lord Jesus to initiate and guide the reorganization of human society which will follow. But Schuyler will be a very happy observer of this and co-worker with it as a better way of living develops, and a better way of handling disputes is established. Yes.

The worry and concern during the Civil War are forces that were not resolved in that lifetime. These energies feed the soul's apprehensions, but the knowledge gained through his reading can help Schuyler to understand and release the fears.

Later when Schuyler's grandmother was inquired about the other war-time life emerged:

> Dr. John: They had a rather peripheral acquaintance in the 1600s, which interestingly enough is a lifetime that had some of the same qualities of violence and turmoil as the 1800s life. This was in what is now known as Germany. It was the time when that unhappy land was being trampled over and torn apart by wars on almost flimsy reasons, reasons supposedly of religious belief or political ambition and such.
>
> This meant the common people could be seized and dragged from their homes and their work at almost any time. It did not happen all the time, of course, but there would be an army raised and given a small amount of training and sent off to war. There was a great deal of carnage, of death and destruction. The wars were not well led, they were not well planned, they were not well fought, and they did accomplish a great deal of destruction and death.
>
> These two, the grandmother and the grandson, were not related. The present grandson was a friend of someone from the present grandmother's family who was caught up in those wars. They marched and fought together at least once, probably twice or more. And so the two knew each other but not really closely.
>
> The major thing is that that was another time to instill sensitivity within the Schuyler soul, present him with a problem, because as long as war and destruction are a part of life, it is something that must be dealt with. The 1800s Southern boy did not really deal with it completely, you see. The 1600s German boy, there wasn't much he could do. He was a rather stolid peasant. In one sense the war never ended during his lifetime. This or that skirmish or war would end, but the war kept going on in one way or another and one place or another, and

so he was vulnerable until he was too old to be called upon.

He was not killed. He did receive a wound but it healed. It took about six months, about half a year to heal, I see, but he did heal from it. He was not maimed or physically limited from it. (A4451:2-4,6,7)

Two lifetimes of concern, unrest, and destruction by war! No wonder the Schuyler soul feels apprehensive.

Because his sensitivity can best be handled in a powerful but peaceful nation, Schuyler incarnated in America. His family also was well chosen. In all families there can be problems, but for the most part Schuyler's relations are loving and good. And they live in a high desert climate with beautiful pine trees and clean fresh air.

In addition, there are strong pastlife influences for Schuyler with two family members, his mother and his sister. The present mother was grandmother in the Civil War lifetime. She was quiet and strong, a stabilizing influence on the then incarnation of the Schuyler soul. Her presence in this life helps to reassure the soul. Schuyler's sister was with him as a friend in an island lifetime set between the two war lives. Their relationship now brings forth the pleasant forces from that previous incarnation. But the major healing for the Schuyler soul will come as he himself grows and develops more and more confidence.

MYRNA

When a person is killed in the horror of war, the next incarnation of that soul hopefully is well-planned. The individuality of the soul and the circumstances surrounding the death determine the setting. But a protective home, with tender loving care, is usually chosen.

At the time of her mother's life reading, Myrna was nine years old. A very timid child, she did not make friends easily and she still depended heavily upon her mother. As the baby of the family, Myrna received much attention and enjoyed every moment of it. The mother was mildly concerned that they were spoiling her daughter. When Myrna's name was given to Dr. John he replied:

Dr. John: I see her as a little girl, pre-school but pretty close to what would be school age, say, around five or five and a half, as it were trampled under foot, as an army with big boots comes through. This was quite recently. This was in the early days of World War II. She was in the area of East Poland. It's interesting I see the big boots, because this is what she saw as the Russian soldiers came in with a ruthlessness, killing and pillaging.

She lost her life in some act of brutality. The little thing couldn't understand it. She didn't even know the more brutal things that happened to her mother and to her father, who likewise were killed, and it was good that she did not know. She just knew that these big men with the big boots came and she was crouching in a corner; not exactly a closet, a corner. Of course, being crouched, the boots were higher than she was. They would have been anyway almost.

She was killed. I do not see exactly how. I don't think she was kicked to death. It may have been a shot, a bayonet. But in that orgy of cruelty, what did her life mean.

I do not know whether the mother should tell this daughter that or not—possibly later on as the daughter becomes more firmly established within a world which is not doing that to little children any more, at least not where she lives.

She came to the mother because they do have a cosmic cousin relationship, second cousin, I believe. The mother was prepared for this in a school of preparation for the next incarnation, before incarnating. It was the mother's consciousness as a person, for the person had been, as it were, gathered on the astral level before the birth of her as a child on earth. It was not only the soul. The soul was involved but it was also the person who knew of the little one who would come with this particular background and the need for a mother who would be compassionate and protective and understanding, and a father as well, a home that would be the right home for the healing of this former experience. And such it has been—the mother, the father, the country, the culture, the home and the healing.

The healing is still proceeding but it is taking place well. After all, the little girl was young. The experience was quick. The trauma did not go deeply into the forces of the soul's experience, which, of course, would need finishing, as it were.

I would have expected that they would have been introduced in a former life but I do not find one. They will be together in the future. Yes. (A2320:14,15)

The family is not spoiling Myrna; their tender, loving care is helping to heal the soul. In such a protected and warm environment, Myrna can discharge the fear of the tragic little Polish girl.

NORTON

In Myrna's traumatic war experience, death came quickly and her soul was not deeply wounded. A family's tender, loving, care will make her whole again. However, with a prolonged episode of suffering, the soul may not heal so easily.

In the 1700s Norton was a Canadian war refugee who came to New England. He had lost his family and all his possessions; he wanted to earn a grubstake and return to Canada for a fresh start. However, his efforts were rewarded with the American Revolution and death in that war. In sadness, the Norton soul turned its back on earth for two hundred years. Through the masculine soul's interest in science, his guides and teachers gently coaxed him back into twentieth century America. The excerpt from the life reading begins when Norton's name is given to Dr. John:

> Dr. John: Here is a soul which did not want to begin this life. Its unfortunate experiences in the immediately prior lifetime left it with a sadness, and the soul turned its back upon earth. If that sort of thing could happen on earth, not only to it but to others, to a number, and not just accidentally but of human design, it really wanted nothing more to do with planet earth. Nor could we blame it.
>
> So its interest had to be caught and stirred in somewhat of a different way to make it even half-willing to return to earth. Its interest was caught by the fact that it is a different kind of earth now into which to come. You have a saying, 'No man steps twice into the same river,' and certainly the river of earth has changed very, very much in the several hundred years since this one was here.
>
> This is essentially a masculine soul but a gentle soul with quite a good development of the feminine in pastlives, and a good integration of the feminine qualities into the masculine soul. But it still is a masculine soul and it was caught by masculine

interests of intellect, in what was happening in this new earth so different from the earth of several hundred years ago, even though the same locale was chosen. The same locale was definitely chosen to help to overcome the rejection of earth, which was a very strong force in that pastlife.

The soul still was withdrawn. As it were, it would reach out a hand and touch life with a timid finger or reach out a whole arm and touch it at arm's-length. It did not really want to be in close contact with the earth. It wanted to hold back a bit, to have its own privacy. Norton will recognize that this was not a good thing, this withdrawal. The soul must undergo a certain amount of earth experience. If it does so reluctantly it does not get the full experience and it wastes time, its own time and God's time, and will be slow in arriving at the further reaches of its development after earth has been surmounted.

So it was allowed two hundred years on the other side, and on the other side it was reunited with loved ones it had loved and lost in that prior lifetime. This assuaged the grief, the hurt, the sadness, to quite a degree. It still did not eradicate the fact that the soul was being asked to return to a place where hurt and grief and sadness had taken place and had been very poignant, and where poignant hurt and grief and sadness could still take place.

But by dint of quiet training and the quieting of forces, and concealed cajoling, such as sparking a masculine interest in the new developments of the new day, the new century, which are largely gathered up in what you call the age of science—he was not interested primarily in the age of woman or the age of metaphysics or the age of enlightenment or the age of psychology, but the age of science, a deeper and truer knowledge of facts, of truth. So this which we call concealed cajoling was used to bring the soul, not against its will—against its surface wishes but not really against its will—into incarnation once again in this quiet way.

Now the re-entry, as it were, could have been accomplished in several stages. There could have been a brief lifetime and then another. But instead there was this lessening of the impact of earth, you see; lessening of the impact of incarnation, cutting it by, say, half, so that in a sense it is a half lifetime and yet a whole lifetime. This is fine. It is quite all right.

So the Norton person has been the direct expression of the Norton soul in the coming quietly into incarnation once again, and coming into the same general portion of the world, the northeast United States, in which it had been before. With a different interest, without close human ties, to help assure the soul it will not have such grief and loss and sadness this time. The soul is finding it is doing all right. It has come to where it is really willing to undertake a little more experience this time.

And that essentially is who this person is and why he is where he is and why at this time he has been brought by his guides and teachers and loved ones on the other side to get this reading. This is what I am shown, and his guides and teachers are taking quite an active part in enabling me to understand Norton in this way. Of course, then I can be their spokesman when I read the akashic records for him as I have so far in this reading.

We are ready for relationships.

Conductor: He first asks about his father (name, birth information given).

Dr. John: This is a cosmic family member, an older cosmic family member, an older soul. The Norton soul is rather newly into the middle area. It is well started into the middle area. The father soul is well into the midpoint, maybe a little over the centerline of the midpoint. They have been close friends on the other side. The father likewise is a masculine soul, and having the advantage of perhaps an additional dozen or so lifetimes more than the Norton soul has had, it has the basis in experience for understanding the reaction of the Norton soul to the sad experiences it went through in its prior life, of inhumanity of man to man, of innocent sufferers who had no part in bringing about what was visited upon them.

So the father was one of the souls who was a teacher of this son on the other side, and incarnated to come as the father with quite an understanding of what the pattern of Norton's life would be this time. The father of course had other purposes in incarnating. That is, he made it a very fine life experience of his own. But this was one of the reasons why the father soul cast the father person, brought it together and put it into its present incarnation, and then the Norton soul was brought into incarnation as a son.

They have had three pastlives. In the 1700s, the mid 1700s,

in New England, both were in masculine expression. The father soul was a town leader in Massachusetts, I believe it was. He was a stalwart man, rather quiet, rather taciturn. He did some farming. He did some craftsmanship work—you might call it manufacturing of small articles—and he was in business. He was not exactly well-to-do, but he certainly was very comfortable economically. He had a nice family. He and his wife had a good rapport. He was the dominant one and she was quiet. Well, he also was quiet.

It was a good marriage, and children. I see several daughters. The then incarnation of the Norton soul came into that area as a refugee from the north, a war refugee from, well it was not Maine, it must have been some portion of Canada. This was before the American Revolution. But this one was a war refugee. This one had been separated from the rather close-knit community or group of which he was a member.

He was a man of about the same age as the then father soul. He was a good workman. He got work there. Any good workman could find or make a job, so he helped in a blacksmith shop, among other things, and that was quite a bit of his work. He also could farm and milk cows and such. He was quite quiet and withdrawn and very sad. The sadness really reached the heart of this one who is now the father. They took this one into their home, really. The other one had had a home of his own, a wife and several children, all of whom apparently had died. I do not see them. It was understood that this refugee wanted to go back to his general home area when he could. Conditions were not conducive to it at that time.

Also, he wanted to get a grubstake so that when he did go back he could establish himself again in a livelihood, a small farm or something, and perhaps establish a home there or find somebody he knew there. He wanted to return, you see. So this was the general idea, even though it took quite some years. Then this war refugee was killed in another warlike act before he ever got back home. This was the last time the two of them were together in a pastlife.

Dr. John brought in two more pastlives that Norton and his father shared (before the 1700s life) and then said:

Dr. John: So we find these three pastlives, and they will be together again. I do not see what relationship, but it is quite possible the Norton soul will be a father or an uncle or a benefactor in some way, or a teacher maybe. Because the Norton soul has an appreciation of the father soul and would like to come sometime when as a person it can be of assistance to the other one, even if that assistance is only to provide the daily bread while the other is young.

What was the father's work in this life? Was it associated with science?

Conductor: The father was an aviator from 1927 to 1957.

Dr. John: Yes, that would be associated with science and the scientific developments of this time. You see, the son was brought in by an interest in science, and you tell me that the father's livelihood, the father's life work, was in that general area too, quite appropriately, and I am not surprised.

Conductor: After he retired, he taught in science, mainly physics in high schools, for about fifteen years.

What a perfect father for Norton! A cosmic family member, present in three pastlives, a teacher in other cosmic schools, and now vocationally into science.

Here the conductor read from a letter she had received from Norton, with a most interesting confirmation of Dr. John's statement that his 1700s stay in America had likewise gotten him into a war activity from which he, an innocent bystander, perished. Norton writes:

Conductor: 'When I first came to Connecticut back in 1955, I had a strong feeling of having been here before, a feeling which has never left me. I have come to regard my present life in Bridgeport as a continuation of a previous life in Norwalk which abruptly ended when the British burned the town to the ground and scattered the population. This happened in July of 1779.'

Dr. John, this goes back to your mentioning that area.

Dr. John: His guides and teachers are nodding their heads and they are looking very wise and rather smug. 'Yes, yes,' they are saying, and somewhat as though they have put something over on me, which is quite all right. I have a good camaraderie with the guides and teachers whenever I'm working. They are nodding their heads yes, and this would fit in, wouldn't it.

Conductor: Oh, it's so close that I could hardly keep from interrupting. But I wanted you to fulfill this picture as you were developing it. He asks, 'Could Dr. John confirm and describe this life?'

Dr. John: He was getting along in years, that is for then, at that time. He would not be considered old now, but he was, let us say, grayhaired, between forty-five and fifty, maybe into the early fifties at that time. A very quiet and rather sad person, rather resigned, but still sad.

Conductor: This letter continues right along and dovetails in with what you have said: 'I have a close affinity to things French and French-Canadian, although my ancestry now is three-quarters German and one-quarter Irish. Wine is my daily drink, and I dislike beer. Montreal is my favorite city and I visit it when I can. Very vaguely I seem to recall a life as a French-speaking Arcadian farmer, driven out of Nova Scotia by the British in 1755. I was a young widower then with two small sons. Could Dr. John confirm this?'

Dr. John: Yes, only he lost the children. He lost the children some way. I think they died or were killed some way. I think it was more than simply a separation. Anyway, they were not with him when he came into the New England area, where of course he got away from the British enemies in Canada, in that part of Canada.

Conductor: He says, 'There is a possible link in that I could have come to Norwalk as a refugee, only to have to flee again in 1779. I think I tried to make my way back to Montreal.'

Dr. John: He had wanted to go back, but he was killed in—I think there was a bombardment. I think it was some cannon fire from a distance, that a cannon ball plowed into some kind of a small building where he was. And death was very quick. But his sadness had been very long. He did not re-establish a home there. He kept looking forward to going back, and he never got there.

When some happening is both close and traumatic from a pastlife, it is usually near the surface in a person's subconscious and can be relatively easily brought to the person's awareness. Often something occurs to trigger the surfacing of such memories. In Norton, a second life near the same town in which he was killed in his last life, could have brought forth his awareness of this past incarnation.

Norton was born in the 1930s and he inquired about five children from one family, all of whom were born in the late 1950s and early 1960s. One of these children had been an acquaintance in the 1700s life, but there was no pastlife or cosmic relationship of Norton with the others. He had felt a closeness with these children and a love for them. Dr. John gives the reason:

> Dr. John: Do you know what has happened here? Do you see what has happened? Norton in that pastlife, the then incarnation of the Norton soul—I believe his name then was Phillippe or the French equivalent of Philip—was looking for a family. He was looking for his family which had been destroyed, but in a sense the soul was looking for a family. Now in coming into this life the soul was withdrawn so that it could not have a family, and yet a portion of it—well, there was a carry-over of looking for a family, and he found a family here.
>
> Without being really close to it, you see. Without being closely enough involved to be hurt, although he would be hurt now if something happened to one of these.
>
> Conductor: These are one-half French Canadian, this family.
>
> Dr. John: That is appropriate, isn't it. He did find a French-Canadian family, two hundred years later. Thus this can answer that seeking aspect of the soul. The search can be ended, and then the soul is more free to go on afresh and directly and have its own family in future incarnations once again.
>
> If he wishes very strongly, there could be a father-child relationship with any one of these children in an incarnation up ahead. It is not patterned as of now, and we rather suggest that he simply accept them for what they are now and as being a somewhat muted answer to his long cry of the heart. Then not try to hold onto these individuals. Appreciate them now, yes. Be whatever he is to them now, but let life bring in those who would be his children in any future earthlives.
>
> He will have children. He will again have a lovely home with much love and happiness within it. As the Good Book says, 'The Lord shall restore the years the locusts have eaten.' In the future earthlife he can have a home with five children in it if he would like, of his own. But let them be those souls which

would be appropiate to him, you see, in whatever that new situation will be. They need not be French-Canadian, because that aspect of his yearning has been answered, has been met. Let life bring the appropriate ones. Do not try to bring one of these, fine though they are, into his future plans.

Soul qualities can express as physical problems. Norton is deaf and wants to know the cosmic purpose of his deafness:

> Dr. John: Ah, so he is deaf. This is a direct manifestation of the soul holding back. The soul did not want to enter fully, it did not want to—well, one might say, it did not want to hear the sounds of earthlife or feel the feelings or see the sights too completely. This is a way of expressing that the soul wanted a certain amount of privacy, and also was not willing to enter in fully because he had been hurt before so badly, and of course this hurt had continued so long within him.
>
> Yes, his deafness is karmic in that respect, as having that pastlife rootage. It is not karmic as a punishment. He did not cause loss of hearing for anyone else in a past life. (A957:1-10)

The present personality of Norton is helping in the healing of his own soul, one who suffered so much in the 1700s that it turned away from earth for two hundred years. Future lives will be happier and filled with closer family ties, including children. "The Lord will restore the years the locusts have eaten."

WALLIS

Fear is not the only negative emotion that war produces. Righteous indignation and hatred can plague the soul of a war victim.

In her last life Wallis was a victim of the bombings in England. She was a woman of forty, most active in the war effort, and worked in the civil defense. Two sons fought in the war; one had been wounded. As a person she was filled with anger at the Germans. When a bomb exploded near her and cut short her life, the feminine soul was furious. She insisted on another incarnation in the twentieth century.

Her council advised delaying until the negative forces could be better dealt with. Against their advice the soul jumped into a life as daughter to cosmic friends; but God will always have the final say. A rebellious soul is not long tolerated, and the guides and teachers managed to have the baby girl adopted out. The new family was carefully chosen as one to help Wallis' growth. But the switch in families also told the soul that God is in charge—not the young God-child.

Since the age of ten Wallis has been most difficult to live with. Her mother—we will call her Mrs. Atkins—requested a life reading for this fourteen-year-old adopted daughter who has given the Atkins family so many problems:

> Dr. John: She is an incarnation from the feminine half of her whole soul, so she is operating in the native gender expression, which has certain advantages and, in a sense, allows the forcefulness of the soul to come through more clearly into its incarnations, especially this incarnation.
>
> She is not a young soul. She is in the forepart of the third stage, of around-the-midpoint, and actually has probably about thirty-five percent of her soulhood experiences behind her. On the whole, these have been quite successful. She is making good progress, is not under the censure of God's agents.
>
> This particular incarnation was not advised. She met death in a bomb incident upon London in, I believe, the latter part of 1943, in World War II, the German bombing of London. She was a civilian woman and at the time about forty years old. She had raised several children and had two sons in the service. She was very active in the civil defense. Well, she was very active in anything she did, and that included just about everything which she could get into and which interested her.
>
> One of her boys had been rather severely wounded in the earlier stage of the war. He had been in the hospital quite a while and then home, but had not fully recovered yet, and there was a question whether he would fully recover the use of his body; some portion of the body, I do not see just which. She was filled with righteous indignation against the Germans, the Nazis, as a loyal Briton and as a sensible and good person was in those days. Also, she had the emotional content of really rather hating them for what they had done to her fine son.

She knitted, and she saved everything that could be saved, for the war effort. She was a USO hostess. She was a civil defense person. The air raid siren sounded and she was getting those for whom she was responsible into the air raid shelter when a bomb exploded very near by, almost upon her. She was a bit careless of her own safety, but it was in the line of duty and not in any frivolous way. She was one of the casualties, one of the martyrs of the war. Her work did contribute to victory and did save lives by getting her people into the defense shelters.

It would have been good had the soul waited a century or so before returning to earth, to allow some of the strong forces within that personality to round off a bit, to mellow into the overall pattern a little more. But this soul wanted to get back. It very definitely wanted to have another life in this fascinating twentieth century.

The soul is rather steamed up about incarnations in one way. In another way it is not. It does not care for the preparatory stage of a new person. It wants to get into life very actively and fully as an adult participant. This makes for difficulties during the childhood years. A soul with that eagerness—well, it is commendable in some ways. Certainly a council with an eager and enthusiastic soul considers itself much more fortunate than a council with an apathetic soul, a lethargic soul.

But such a soul is 'rough on kids,' meaning hard on the early stages of life of its various incarnations. These are the formative years of the new person, and thus are necessary. This is the way God has ordained it, and those who work with God and within God's patterns, that there be a formative period for the new person which has new tasks, new experiences ahead of it; fulfilling another portion of the total experience-picture of the soul.

Rightfully seen, the childhood stage is not one to be rushed through. Actually, the person will become of age soon enough. But the young soul of enthusiasm may not see this.

The Wallis soul forced its way in this time, of its own will, against the advice of its guides and teachers, its council. Incidentally, four of them are present here, and two from the supervisory council are here, the council that supervises the actual council of guides and teachers of Wallis.

The council is reminding me that a crisis is made up of two

elements, danger and opportunity; and that very often the most
growth and some of the best growth takes place in a crisis situation within a human life. The early life of Wallis has been
somewhat a crisis situation for the soul and for persons around
her, and, of course, for the Wallis person herself.

The outcome should be good. What will she do since she
is in? The pattern was not very carefully drawn. In fact, there
are many blank spaces in the pattern. She wants to have a part
in this new age. It represents, for one thing, a greater opportunity of expression for those in the feminine valence, for
women. It also represents an explosion of new knowledge,
usually characterized as science. She might go into science. She
might find some particular phase of science that really interests
her.

She might like to go into business. She might like to go into
business management where she would work with people, or
some other aspect of business where she would work with people. She has a good mind and a quick mind. She could very
responsibly direct twenty or two hundred people underneath
her. She might become a factory foreman in some manufacturing enterprise.

She might go into some phase of the arts, possibly with some
aspect of being a performer, but also with some aspect in the
production department or the merchandising. She might
become a member of the organization which will buy a play
and produce the script for the actual performance, hire the per-
formers, advertise the play, get it established, take it into other
cities, and things such as that.

In other words, she has pushed in. The pattern is not pre-
set for her, but the very forces which led that soul to push itself
in can lead it to discovering and creating a pretty good pattern. Its council will work right along with it.

Its willfulness was checked rather neatly in the fact that
although that soul pretty much was anxious to get a body, any
body, in this time, it had managed to slip into a particular conception, and thought that that man and that woman would be
its parents. But its willfulness was checked and they were not
its parents. Then she was, by the processes of society and not
the processes of her own devising—for as a baby how could
she devise the processes of the selection of foster parents—she
was adopted into the Atkins family and found herself willy-

nilly, not of her will, in a home not only not of her choosing, but really not of her foreknowledge.

This was a rather neat trick and did have a certain salutary effect, letting the soul know that it would not get by with just anything and everything that it might attempt. This, of course, did not completely enlighten the soul. It must still learn that, as you, conductor, said so well in the opening prayer, 'the way of God is not just the best way but is the only true and lasting way.' The God-child, the Individuated-God-Being, of which soulhood is the early stage, must discover what God has done and what God is still doing, and then learn how to operate within that framework.

It is a far better framework than any framework that the individual soul, let alone the individual person, could ever devise. Eventually, and possibly in this life, and possibly through the personhood of Wallis Atkins, the soul may learn to seek not simply to be doing a lot of things of its own devising but to discover the way of God, which is the most efficient way of progression and is the only true and lasting way, as well as the best way.

I have rambled a bit, I fear. This is a very interesting picture that the akashic records reveal of this highly energetic, capable, willful, enthusiastic, stubborn soul, now incarnate in a quite lovely female body in twentieth century America. A pleasure and a trial to those who take a responsible affection toward her.

Is there a question so far?

Conductor: Dr. John, you have at least touched on three of the questions. Could I at this time offer them?

 Dr. John: Let us do so, yes.

Conductor: The first question you perhaps have answered, because as I understand it she did not choose the Atkins for her parents. The question is, 'Why did Wallis choose to come to our family by adoption rather than the natural way, and not knowing her natural heritage and family?'

Dr. John: The high ones who work for God chose the Atkins as the home for Wallis. Wallis didn't.

Conductor: That was the way I understood it, but I wanted to make sure. Quite often children come to adoption by choice though, don't they, Dr. John?

Dr. John: That is true.

Conductor: Her next question has to do with career. Wallis is very interested in singing and dancing. She plays in the band at school or did play in the band at school, and is the lead gospel singer where she is now. The mother's question is, 'Should Wallis' work-life lie more in the arts?'

Dr. John: I have a question. You say she is a gospel singer?

Conductor: Yes, Dr. John, and this leads to the third question and I will give you the background.

Dr. John: I am surprised.

Conductor: I will give you the background on it. When she reached the age of ten—puberty, an early puberty—she began to rebel quite a bit and gave them considerable problems: boys, almost men, older boys, sex, marijuana, drinking, just considerable problems.

Dr. John: This would be a way in which these forces from the soul could work out in the person. It is sort of too bad, and yet it is a capable person and a capable soul. It is not damned by this but it certainly was getting off on the wrong track. What happened to reclaim it and make a gospel singer out of this mixed-up, rebellious young person?

Conductor: Last summer her father was moving, changing jobs. The mother was staying at the old home to sell it. He took the children with him for a while. Wallis ran away from him, was gone ten days, and when she was found she refused to come home. She was placed in a couple of foster homes. Finally they found a place that seems to really just suit her, a particular institution (name given). It has a semi-family situation, with parents in each home and ten children. There is a lot of love there, but also very strict discipline. It is the hell-fire-and-damnation type of religion.

Dr. John: Then it is a religious-oriented institution?

Conductor: Very much so. I believe they have devotions every day. She has become the lead gospel singer. She has been converted to this religion. In fact, she has even tried to talk her mother into this. It appears to be genuine, because this has been six months now.

Dr. John: She might become an evangelist!

Conductor: She very well could. Mrs. Atkins' question was, what motivation was behind Wallis in putting herself in this situation, and I believe you have covered that.

Dr. John: The forces had to be given a direction that had

quite a lot of emotional content back of it and expressing in it. This is fine. Possibly the parents may be a little worried that the girl may be getting a rather inaccurate and limited view of God. But don't worry about that. If at this stage this is how she is being swung into a constructive use of her energies and thought and time, fine. She has a good mind and she will make her own life and her own life pattern, along with her council, of course, and with the supervisory council taking a more than usual active interest.

The supervisory council is made up of individuals who are wiser than the actual council of guides and teachers, who are in turn wiser than the person who is their protege. As a general rule, anyway. (A2612:2-6)

The problems with Wallis have dramatically decreased since she has found an emotional outlet, and the family breathes a sigh of relief. Mrs. Atkins is especially happy to know that Wallis' rebellion expressed some of the soul's anger, helping it to heal.

MONROE

Eighteen-year-old Monroe has always been fascinated with fires and sirens. At one time he was a volunteer fireman, but he also has been arrested for calling in a bomb threat and for setting fires. He attempted suicide twice and has been in mental health clinics. But no amount of psychological delving into his present personality—outside of pastlife recall therapy—could unlock the secret hidden in his soul. For in his last life Monroe was a victim of a fire bombing.

The story unfolds as Monroe's mother asks Dr. John about her son:

Dr. John: This is a cosmic first cousin but, as it were, a young one as a soul, for whom the mother has more responsibility than for the son previously mentioned.

And yet his major pastlife was not with her. He was born in Japan in the late 1930s, and I see him—I think it is in Tokyo during the latter stages of war there, in perhaps 1944 or 1945, when the fleets of American planes were bombing with fire bombs from high altitudes and the Japanese defenses were so inadequate.

He was just seven years old when death came in one of these

raids. There is an interesting fixation upon this soul's consciousness from that experience. There had been deprivation. The food was not too plentiful. The war was going against Japan. The parents were concerned and would talk about it in the privacy of their home. There were several children, and this one particularly was open to the then mother (who was not the then incarnation of the present mother soul. The present mother soul was not there.) So there was an abnormal psychology created in the consciousness of the youngster.

When the fire bombing came, and came their way, there was a certain fatalism, but there was a certain gathering up of meaningfulness in life. In fact, as it were, the meaningfulness of all the youngster's life was pretty much gathered up in the catastrophic ending. This produced over a period of several days a very, very profound effect upon the consciousness of the person.

The soul, which is young, was unwise enough to be drawn too close to its own personhood in this. A wiser soul would have pulled way back so that the consciousness of the person going through this experience would not have affected the soul so much. This soul, partly in the desire to protect its personhood but even more in a rather morbid curiosity as to just what was happening, was drawn into a rather close identification with the person, and so experienced the catastrophic events of the fires for three days and three horrible nights, and then death.

Is there a question?

Conductor: Thank you, Dr. John. Yes, a couple, but let me first read you what she says about this son: 'He has no memories before his seventh birthday, and he remembers a fire then, fire and excitement. Sirens. All had a tremendous fascination for him. He was arrested in 1977 for calling in a bomb threat, and from 1980 to 1981 he was arrested for setting fires. But he was also a volunteer fireman and would help put them out. It has been quite a year for him. He attempted suicide twice and was in the mental health clinic.'

Dr. John: She can see how events of one life can carry over disproportionately into another, particularly when there is not much time inbetween for the alleviation of the forces on the other side. Also, she can see how when a soul does allow itself to identify too much with the consciousness of any one of its

personality incarnations, it has set up certain problems. It has
certain forces then which must be handled.

She also is having experience in how she herself can be
helpful. There is no magic word to cure these. His life will have
to bring a certain amount of curing to this, and hopefully this
lifetime will accomplish the essential curing of the trauma of
the immediately prior lifetime for him.

She can be helpful. She can learn, and in her learning from
this, as from all present experiences, she can be of greater
knowledge and helpfulness in future service lives.

Conductor: Would there be any good in this one being told
of this pastlife?

Dr. John: No, certainly not at present. The person does not
have the maturity for this, and it would probably only exacerbate the force—increase the force of the past in the consciousness, and exacerbate the results of it in the present life.
(A3447:10-12)

An older soul would not have been so deeply wounded, but the young
Monroe soul just did not have the background to cope with this
experience.

The mother's responsibility for Monroe is a heavy one, but the healing of his soul is gradually occurring. His mother wrote that the
understanding she received from her life reading fills her with pride
to be chosen as Monroe's mother. She is a good mother, a good
person and a good soul.

JANE

A wound to the heart can bring more pain than death. In the 1500s
Jane was a mother who agonized over the slow destruction of her
son. The invading conquistadors enslaved him, and the mother
watched in helpless frustration as her son's life forces ebbed away.

In this lifetime Jane is a wife, mother, and part-time secretary. Her
boss is not too easy to get along with, but she has felt a compulsion
to help him succeed and a joy in his accomplishments. Other
secretaries had left him, but Jane seemed to see only his good points.
The answer to her strange attitude toward her employer came in her
life reading:

Dr. John: This is another cosmic cousin, but almost close enough to be called a cosmic family member. He is a younger soul, has not been in incarnation since the early days of the Industrial Revolution in the British Isles. Of course I am not working with his records and I must not go into them as I must stay with Jane's. But this one has come back with the same kind of fierce determination to make a success in masculine living as her husband has. And this time instead of being in the working class he has come into the professional class.

They were mother and son in the 1500s—Jane was the mother of course—in the late 1500s and coming into the 1600s in Central America, and were victims of the Spanish conquistadors.

The son as a young man was usurped by the Spanish to be a servant and to carry some quite heavy loads. This happened when he was still in his teens, and he was not all that strong. I use the word 'usurped' because the Spanish, you see, stepped in and took over the purposefulness of life for that one, usurping his own kingship of his own being.

The boy did not live very long under this load. He was harshly treated. He survived only about four to five and a half months of this kind of treatment.

The mother was fiercely angry but was unable to do anything about it. Her protest was laughingly and brutally turned aside and there was nothing she could do really, although she did visit the boy surreptitiously at night several times with additional food, with some healing potions for sores, with great love and tears.

Now there is a certain healing to the anguish of that life in seeing that son now really succeed. And this has been a strong factor in their relationship. However, as it is brought thusly to her consciousness she can see that the boy is all right, and that she does not need to stand by. She has been again somewhat of a mother in her inner dynamics in this relationship. She has fiercely seen to it as best she could that her erstwhile son succeed. But he is a success now, and really she is free to go elsewhere if she wishes.

This is rather odd, but her council tells me that she will understand. Is there a question?

Conductor: She had felt at times almost indispensable to his work. She had left and she had come back and she wonders

what the attraction has been. You have explained this. It has
been a very perplexing situation to her and she wonders how
she should deal with it, if it is purely fantasy or imagination
on her part. But I think perhaps you have relieved her feeling
in regard to this great strong attraction to her employer.

Dr. John: I have brought the reincarnational picture, the
pastlife factors and forces involved.

It is quite possible and probable and I believe intended that
they will have future incarnations, at least one, together, but
in it they will meet as equals, or quite possibly with the present Jane being a bit of a superior, as perhaps the leader of some
project in which the then incarnation of the other soul is also
working, or something of that nature.

She will not 'lord it over him' as this is not what she wishes,
and her soul is really beyond that. But there can be then a better expression of the realities of their equality than there can
be now, and I believe she will see this and accept it and know
that in the large picture the seeming bumps and inequities of
a small part of the picture are smoothed out. All is now as it
should be, and should be left that way. However, as I have
said, as she understands this and allows the inner structuring,
she will be free to look elsewhere and go elsewhere if she wishes.
The ties with him have been accomplished. The purpose of—
well, I have brought what I have to bring. (A4517:12-14)

So the heart wound of the 1500s mother is healed as Jane observes
her employer's success. The son of four hundred years ago has
returned and is living a successful, productive life.

Without reincarnation where would be God's justice for the victims
of war? However, through reincarnation God can balance the scales,
using various stages and actors. With the multi-life framework the
wounds of a life scarred or cut short can be soothed and cured in
another incarnation. But the methods will vary, for each soul and
each injury is unique.

Schuyler is now learning the confidence to still his soul's apprehensions. As Myrna is "being spoiled," her fears are melting away. With
his deafness protecting the soul, Norton's aversion to earth is being
overcome through Science. A loving family and a fundamentalist
religious group are transmuting Wallis' anger and indignation into

an expression of love for the Creator via gospel singing. Though the disturbed Monroe personality still suffers, his soul's infected wound is draining away its poison. And Jane is watching her son from the 1500s climb the latter of masculine success.

As long as war is on earth, man can at least be thankful that God has provided reincarnational processes of healing for its victims.

CHAPTER FOURTEEN

COSMIC EFFECTS OF BEING
A SOLDIER IN WARTIME

So many persons throughout human history have been forced by war into hideous crimes. Sometimes the causes have been just and even most necessary; sometimes not.

Leaders and issues, not the common soldiers, make the wars. But the question arises as to what effect killing other human beings in battle—whether the cause be just or unjust—has upon the soul of that soldier.

Study of the Loehr-Daniels Life Readings shows that an incarnation as a soldier in wartime produces different cosmic effects and karmic carryovers, all in accordance with individual events and souls.

Extreme guilt feelings may gnaw at the God-child. To the soul who incarnates as an ordinary soldier, whether or not the cause is well-founded is less important than the personality's attitude. More significance is attached if the person enjoys the killing or tortures the victim, for this almost always brings on negative karma.

Even when the personality abhors the violence, a sensitive feminine soul might feel accountable for the death of her victims. Whether innocent or not, if the God-child knows deep guilt, it will incarnate again to be punished and thus cleansed.

When the warrior has acted honorably and the soul finds no fault with its personality's actions, there may be no punishment. But its growth pattern can lead the soul to experience the culture of the former enemy, thus neutralizing the effects of the fighter's zealous attitude against the foe.

Sometimes physical problems arise from a pastlife wound, particularly if this wound resulted in disablement or death. Then the soul leaves the earthplane with consciousness of that injury and this negative consciousness must be cleared in the same plane (earth) in which it occurred. We might call this body-memory or cell-memory and watch how the memories must be cleansed through the healing of a lesser wound in a future life.

When a soul has an incarnation which fights in battle, it risks developing a tendency to violence or aggression. Such forces must be constructively redeployed, often in another lifetime.

These different cosmic effects—karmic results—of being a soldier in wartime are illustrated in this chapter through the following six examples from the Loehr-Daniels Life Readings:

JUSTIN

Not all war victims are actually victims. War displays evil at its height, but God can use even the greatest of evils constructively. Sometimes a soul's growth is best accomplished by a war death.

Justin was a young man of eighteen when Pearl Harbor was attacked. Like so many young men Justin enlisted in the Navy on December 8, 1941, eager to serve his country and to help squelch the cancer of war. Still in the States in 1943, he asked to be attached as a medic to the Marine Corps group which was shipping out. Justin yearned to help but knew he could not kill. While attending the wounded in the battle for Okinawa, his life was cut short by a sniper's bullet.

Justin had a friend, Bill, who received a life reading. Bill was told among other things about his last lifetime as a landowner in the American South before the Civil War. When Bill inquired about Justin, Dr. John reported:

> Dr. John: Yes. Bill and Justin have had a pastlife relationship. Justin was a grandson who then was involved as a soldier in the Civil War and had expected to come back and take part in the management of the rather expansive land holdings, but was killed and was not able to do so.
> The boy was in some savage fighting even before Gettysburg, but in Gettysburg there was very savage hand-to-hand fighting

and not just for the final hour or so but upon several occasions in that battle. In this he acquitted himself quite well as a soldier. He was strong. He was skilled in the use particularly of the knife, sort of a bayonet knife, kind of a carryover from the short sword of earlier century warriors, and in hand-to-hand combat he killed at least three of the northern soldiers. In a sense he gloried in that. He felt the justice of his cause, and, of course, in hand-to-hand combat where the guns had to be laid aside you either killed or were killed.

In the fourth such encounter he did not meet death from his opponent but from someone else from a little distance who shot him. The death did not come instantaneously. The shot felled him. The shot was into the body laterally, sideways. It was a rather heavy rifle slug, rifle ball, tore vital organs, caused internal bleeding, and in some way caused him to lose strength. It may have torn some nerves and he lost the use of a portion of his right side including his right arm and I believe his right leg, and slumped to the ground. This was an occasion for his opponent, then, to follow through with his knife and finish him off, but the opponent was somewhat appalled. He had been scared. He was not as able a physical fighter as his southern soldier assailant was. But instead of following in to bring the kill, he, in his eyes, expressed the appalled reaction at the death of a fine man, and made some gesture even of kindness, of care.

It was in the thick of the battle and he could not do more than that, but he may have thrown the other's coat over him or something, so that the then incarnation of the southerner, of the grandson, the Justin soul, experienced a sudden very dramatic shift in emotion from fierce fighting to helplessness and from not the hate—he was not fighting in hate but he was really fighting with full heart and vigor—to a reversion of feeling, a revulsion, a reverse when he found his antagonist, the hated northerner, showing compassion.

This was quite an experience for that one.

Conductor: A comment, Dr. John. It's rather interesting that in World War II Justin was eager to sign up but he requested to be assigned to the medics because he could not kill. He wanted to help those in the battlefield, and he was killed at Okinawa.

Dr. John: Well, for goodness sake. Well that certainly was

a carryover, wasn't it, of the emotional forces, and in one sense was a healing, quite a healing of the emotional forces within the soul. The soul probably wished for this even though it did bring his death, although the death may or may not have been patterned. (A3054:13,14)

Because Dr. John is not reading the akashic records for Justin, we are not sure that his death was preplanned. But we can observe one way that war—supreme satanism—can be utilized by God to cleanse and heal a penitent soul.

HAROLD

Harold's mother—let us call her Mrs. Concordia—received a life reading a few years after his death. She spoke of Harold as quiet and easy-going, a good student, with plenty of friends. Under unusual circumstances, Harold was accidentally killed. At least this was the official verdict, but the family suspected murder.

In the 1800s Mrs. Concordia's soul had an incarnation as an American Plains squaw. When Harold's name and birth information were given, this came:

> Dr. John: Well, this was a son in the immediately prior lifetime in that Plains Indian life.
> The boy became a fine, strong, young Indian brave. They did rather effective battle against the white man, capturing some, usually killing their prisoners after torturing them, as was the custom. But eventually the white man prevailed. The white man established certain lands that he claimed as his own and claimed them successfully. And the white man also established certain pathways farther west and rather well defended them. So this Indian tribe, which wasn't too big, learned after losing a number of their members that they pretty much had to work around the white man. It restricted their land, which cut into their style of living, and they did not understand why their gods did not keep this white man away from them, this nuisance, this plague. But so it went.
> Conductor: Thank you. There are several questions, Dr. John. Mostly about Harold's death. They think it was accidental. Do you see whether it was or was not, or anything about

the death?

Dr. John: Well, I can see certain lines of force, as it were. Let me probe this and concentrate upon it. All right. I see a white man, a cowboy type, who had been captured along with some cattle. He is the lone captive. He is tortured and killed by his captors and the body is disposed of in a very inconspicuous grave so that the other white men really could not know for sure what had happened to him.

He was not a very good white man. He had a certain quality of slyness and the Indians had reason to dispose of him, and this quality of slyness really got into the soul, the soul accepting it as a way to accomplish what its personhood wants in earthliving. This is evil, definitely. But in this sense, I think, the shooting was very purposeful in the present life, not accidental, although it was not really the purpose of the present incarnation of that soul. It was the purpose of the soul itself. And in this sense it was a karmic debt and not too significant really. The score has been settled and the other one faces his own judgment. And that is neither Harold's nor his mother's responsibility.

These two definitely will be together again, Harold and his mother, as I have said.

Conductor: Thank you, Dr. John. She has another question or two. She says, 'Did I somehow know it was going to happen?'

Dr. John: Well, quite possibly. She's a rather advanced soul, and her soul and his soul probably had the whole thing talked over with them by others before this incarnation, so on one level within her she probably knew, yes. (A3216:18,19)

Harold's murderer will face judgment, for "vengance is mine, I will repay, saith the Lord." But the Harold soul has paid its karmic debt. Of course the Indian had a right to defend his lands, but God will not justify torture, no matter how reprehensible the victim.

The incarnation of the Indian warrior produced a heavy cosmic effect for Harold, his own early violent death. But a good soul wants to experience the results of its actions so that it can learn through karma, the great teacher. Thus the soul of Harold, with the mother's support, planned its own punishment.

JAMES

In a cataclysm such as World War II any allied soldier should have been proud to take part in blocking the Axis forces. This war, with its annihilation of millions of Jews and Poles and its other atrocities, shaped up so clearly as a battle between good and evil. Although other conflicts have been fought for petty purposes, one shudders to think what would have happened had the madman Hitler and those with him not been stopped.

But the taking of a human life is not casually performed by a loving soul, no matter what the justification. A feminine soul can be particularly affected by an incarnation as a soldier in war. James is such an one. In his last lifetime he incinerated several Japanese soldiers with his flame thrower. His young feminine soul could not take this, and guilt forced the soldier to repudiate his religion and commit suicide. The present lifetime is a quick comeback from the World War II incarnation, and James is to experience an appropriate karmic cleansing.

However, God did not require this action of the soul. The feminine nature wanted punishment. Dr. John brings the complete story when James' father inquired about him in a life reading:

> Dr. John: James. Oh! We see turmoil here!
> Conductor: Yes, definitely.
> Dr. John: Going back to the immediate past incarnation for this one, which was not shared with the parents but which we are being shown, the interesting thing is that the turmoil in this one's consciousness was used to bring it into this family where turmoil in consciousness is a factor and is being understood and mastered.
> So as the father and mother learn how to ride the rapids and in time to come onto the raft and float through, they can help the son do the same thing. Now the consciousness of this son, which is producing the turmoil, is a very interesting thing. In a way he did not need to be turmoiled, but he is sensitive. It is a feminine soul, and its holding onto values and human relationships and all got in the way of the more masculine acceptance of jobs to be done in wartime and doing them decisively and without guilt.

This one was an American soldier in the war, in the great war of a generation ago, and was in the Pacific. Among other things, he was one who used flame throwers in the routing out of Japanese soldiers. And brought death, a horrible death, to a number, not a great number, but more than one, more than two, at least three, maybe four or five Japanese soldiers, several of whom emerged from the places they were hiding, in flames.

They were sufficiently consumed so that portions of their bodies were seen to be consumed. This soldier did his job for a while, carrying on in the masculine the expression of being a soldier in war. But the feminine felt, 'Oh!' You see, in feminine expressions this one had been a fine mother and had nurtured the bodies of her children, had protected them, had a value of the bodies. And to see the bodies being destroyed made such an impact upon the consciousness of this one, who has come back early, quickly, before the turmoil in his own consciousness could be assuaged.

It came back to experience some of this. Now this may be—it may be that this son should not be told of this reading. I do not see precisely what has happened. Is the son to be caught in a burning building and burned, badly burned sometime? Something will happen. I want to prepare the parents for it, because something will happen to this boy, which will severely afflict his body. Now it need not have been so, because warfare is warfare and a man knows this. There are times a man must treat other men as enemies because these other men are agents for that which is the enemy of the warrior.

But the femininity, the feminine beingness and the touch with values, the nurturing of life of the feminine soul of this second son, came to the fore, and now it will experience itself an expiation which will cleanse it, cleanse that soul of this force. It could have been taught on spirit planes, and maybe over a long period it might have attained peace. But instead it came, this soul, of its own choice, came to experience some of that which it brought to others, and to expiate this which it felt to be guilt and which it carries as a guilt and a sin, a sin against the values that the feminine side knows are true values.

So this one will experience something which may bring its death. But we think not. We think that as part of the pattern it will be sustained in an experience of severe burns. It looks as though that may be so. And lose some of the function of its body, lose some of the grace and fullness of the body, but live on in that state. I am given this to bring.

It is not a pleasant picture, and maybe this is only symbolic. But let me say that these two parents are honored in being chosen to be the parents for this one in that situation. I do not see any pastlife acquaintance of this child with either parent. But this one has been brought to them that these two may render a very fine, I might say magnificent, service to this other.

The parents, who have a real depth of spiritual understanding, can understand this, can understand how they have been honored at being chosen to be the parents of this other one in this cleansing lifetime. Stand by him. He will have to of his own do the major achievements. But it is a strong personality, this James person, and has been deliberately made strong so as to be able to accomplish this cleansing for this soul, this rapid, complete, severe cleansing of the soul.

When that is accomplished his life may end. It could do so very honorably. As you know, I do not see the end of lifetimes except in rare instances. It is not my function. Or the person may continue and really make a good life, and that in a way would be two stars in its crown. Then let it know through such things as perhaps our book *Diary After Death*, and other books and reports of like nature, that as it goes into the other realms it need not go with any consciousness of physical impairment but can have on the astral side the full, glorious body which it would have earned so well.

And may it know that the Japanese soldiers, whose bodies his flame-thrower destroyed, on the astral side were brought into the consciousness of their whole bodies once again. For some it took some time, but on the whole not very long. They too were honored warriors. They too were committed persons, and they were met on the other side and their honor and their commitment were in turn honored. They were cleansed of the consciousness of the agony of their death.

Which, actually, which agony actually did not last too long. It is a rather quick death. Much quicker and less painful than would appear to sensitive observers. He will not see them. They have gone on in fully restored bodies and so will he when the time comes, whether the time be after a fairly short life or after a long life or a medium life.

Conductor: Before we go into the questions in regard to this son—and I didn't want to interrupt you when you were telling about him—when he was sixteen years old he developed a very, very rare form of meningitis, wherein some of his body, his fingers, his feet—he no longer has the use of them, he no longer has them, some of them.

Dr. John: Then it has taken place.

Conductor: It has taken place?

Dr. John: It was a fire from within that consumed him, wasn't it, so to speak.

Conductor: So to speak.

Dr. John: I see. Well, I am glad it has taken place. Now the parents won't be fearfully wondering. Thank you for telling me.

Conductor: Also, last May, there was a cardiac arrest with this young boy.

Dr. John: He could have gone over at that point, but apparently the decision was made to stay and to achieve some glorious further life. That is, glorious from the standpoint of the soul's growth and the personality achievement through limitations. Thank you, conductor, for telling me.

Conductor: I just did not want to interrupt you because you were just right on line all the way down. Here is one of the questions in regard to this wonderful young one: 'Unfortunately,' the father says, 'James did not want and did not have a grounding in established Christian beliefs.' He wonders how he can help him to find his way in the matter of religious philosphical beliefs. 'And how should we attempt to help him develop his innate psychic abilities? How can I help him with his life's mission?'

Dr. John: The young soldier repudiated religion, ethics, philosphy; had a severe nervous breakdown and took his own life. He was quite a young soldier. He had not gotten out of his teens. But do not worry about this. This one as he comes into a greater maturity now, and is cleansed from the horror it carried, will find his philosophy of life. Do not press for psychic development, let that come as it may, as it quite likely will.

Remember that this one, although a feminine soul, is in a masculine incarnation, and whether or not the feminine opening to other realms expresses in him, I do not know. It may.

It may become quite a feature of his continuing life and person, and a helpful factor. The parents certainly can make these things known, but do not push, do not push. (A2039:13-16)

What a picture the akashic records revealed of the karmic effect upon this sensitive young feminine soul of its incarnation as a soldier in World War II! We can understand its complex sense of deep guilt.

Physical ailments often furnish healing of pastlife emotional wounds, and meningitis is providing a fire within James to burn out the soul's self-blame.

GERARD

James' feminine soul burdened itself with guilt from its soldier incarnation. In general a masculine soul would be more pragmatic. Since the masculine half of the soul was given the responsibility of survival on planet earth, it would be less affected by using force to maintain survival for one of its personhoods and that of its group.

Like James, Gerard was an American soldier in the Pacific in World War II and saw quite a lot of combat. But unlike James, Gerard is from the masculine half of his soul and did not feel guilt. He was killed in action and on the excarnate side of life studied the war from a larger viewpoint. Through astral visits to Japan he realized both sides of the issue and even gained a personal appreciation for the Japanese people.

Because he still wanted an incarnation in America in the twentieth century, Gerard was born in the late fifties. Again he went into the service, but this lifetime he has married a Japanese girl. Dr. John brings us the soul details as Gerard's mother asks about him in her life reading:

> Dr. John: He is a fairly quick come-back. This is interesting. I am shown this even though this does not have a concern or a relationship with the present mother. He was an American soldier in the Pacific area in World War II. He saw quite a lot of combat and was hit by a shell fragment which tore into his body and killed him, not immediately but within less than an hour.

However, the shock produced a certain anesthetization, so there was not a great amount of pain experienced. The young man had a rather robust attitude towards life in the Pacific war anyway, so there was not a great deal of trauma as he did cross the line into the excarnate side.

Then, still wanting to have a life in twentieth century America, he came back rather quickly and was born into their family, and is pursuing a pattern of life which the soul has established for this incarnation.

Conductor: This is very interesting, Dr. John. There are three points here which I think you'll be interested in. When he graduated from high school at seventeen, he went to the Air Force for four years; point number one. Point number two: he married a girl of Japanese heritage and they are very happy together. Point number three: he was born with a deformed lip and cleft palate. This has been taken care of through surgery and teeth straightening, and he looks fine today. She asks, 'What is the purpose of being born with facial deformities and need for surgery?'

Dr. John: This was the healing of the wound. The wound did not heal before, you see. The boy died. This was the healing of the wound, although I cannot say for sure that the wound had been in the face. I do not see that. I know he was hit by a large shell fragment which produced an open wound and a great shock to the system, but which did not put him into a coma. He struggled back to the medic station, but there was nothing they could do for him. So there was no healing of the wound before.

In this life the wound is healed, and that is fine. You can see the purpose of having been born with that difficulty, so that in the much larger framework the wound could experience healing. The consciousness of the wound now carries a consciousness of healing as well. This is quite interesting, isn't it.

Conductor: Yes, it is. The other points also I thought were interesting. Both these young people are interested in police work, and he is also going to college.

Dr. John: They ought to make a good success of their lives and of their life together. The fact that he did marry a Japanese girl or a girl of Japanese ancestry, would be a healing in his consciousness of the divisiveness of the two nations in the war. Coming back to accomplish the healing on the same plane, the plane of physical incarnation, as the division had taken place, you see.

Conductor: You see, he went right back into the Air Force.

Dr. John: He was not in the Air Force before, he was a land soldier; Army or Marines, I do not see which. (A3821:13,14)

Physical carryovers of a war are not unusual. The American soldier died with the consciousness of an unhealed wound. Because of the quick return, these body memories were so fresh that Gerard was born with deformities. Surgery remedied not only the disfigurement, but also, in a very real sense, the pastlife injury.

AUDREY

When there is a traumatic injury to the body at death, cell memories—physical body memories—may retain the consciousness of that injury. One way to clear this consciousness and heal the cell memories is by allowing a similar but less drastic injury to occur in another incarnation. When the lesser wound heals, the cell memories are also cleansed and cured. Since the basic cause of the hurt lies in the memory of a past damage, metaphysical means can counteract the wound.

As a soldier in the Napoleonic wars, Audrey was traumatically killed in battle. In her life reading the story unfolds as she asks about her husband:

Dr. John: They were together in France in the late 1700s, both in the masculine. There is a rather confused picture here. The present husband was of the peasant stock but was a leader in the rebellion against the excesses of royalty at that time. The American Revolution had rather fired many of the French people with the sense of freedom and individual opportunity. This, plus the continuing and increasing decadence of the royal class and government, led to the French Revolution.

This young man was a natural leader in the revolution days. Then when Napoleon came to the fore, this young man found in the leadership of Napoleon that which he sought. He very quickly came to the forefront, swinging local public support back of Napoleon, getting many people to join the Napoleonic forces. He became an officer. He was not one of the marshals, he was not a general nor a colonel. He was not really a captain. Perhaps a second lieutenant or so. These being the modern equivalent terms.

He responded with all his heart to Napoleon's strange ability to offer a sense of significance for those who would endure hardship, danger and probably death in following him. This sense of significance was very important, because what did he have to trade for it? Without that, life would be going back to the pigs and the plowing.

He was quite a devoted young officer. I see him about twenty-three years old. He was in the Russian campaign. At that time the then incarnation of the Audrey soul was in the masculine also and was a younger friend, not quite two years younger. They may have been cousins. They were not brothers. They were from the same village or little establishment.

The energetic older young man enlisted this one, whom he knew and trusted, and made him one of his adjutants, one of his master sergeants or an adjutant or something. As they pretty much raised a small company of soldiers, the present husband was in command of it under, of course, the officers over him, and then the present wife was the first assistant.

The two of them went with Napoleon into Russia with great high hopes and all. But the Russians handled Napoleon. On the way back, the then incarnation of the Audrey soul was killed in a skirmish. It was a battle. The then incarnation of the husband was not killed at that particular time. Of course, I am with Audrey's akashic records so I do not see whether he got back alive or not. I do not know.

His loyalty to Napoleon was still firm, although it had been somewhat shaken. His side was beaten back and his adjutant, his first sergeant, who was also his personal friend—I believe he was also a cousin, a second cousin, which made him even closer—was killed.

This was a personal blow, of course. The officer reminded himself he was a soldier first and foremost, of course, and rallied his company and they fought their way out of that particular engagement, bringing the wounded sergeant with them. He had been wounded by a heavy rifle ball and was in much pain. He was disabled by the bullet. Some of the essential nerve force to some of the internal organs was gone. Some nerves had been ruptured, and quite possibly some blood vessels as well. Death came within three or four agonizing hours, or five or six hours.

The pain was somewhat alleviated at the end by a—not a coma—a bit of a frenzy, in which, however, there was not much consciousness. The body thrashed around. It was more the body's consciousness of its own pain and the approaching end. There is a particular word for this. Something like hysteria, but not with full consciousness. Can you supply me with such a word, conductor?

Conductor: No, not offhand, Dr. John.

Dr. John: Convulsion isn't quite it. I trust I have spoken enough of that difficult situation. However, that having been brought even in this way to the consciousness of the Audrey person may prove to be a bit of a healing to her in some fashion or other. The soulmate is telling me that, or is rather nodding his head on that.

Conductor: Was this a back injury?

Dr. John: It could have been. I do not see for sure. Why do you ask?

Conductor: Because she has had a pastlife regression in which she was the aide to the husband in an army. He was the commander. She did receive a back injury in a battle and lost her life.

Dr. John: He was not the commander of the army but he was the commander of that little unit to which she belonged. If this were a back injury, if the rifle ball hit him in the back and broke the backbone, it could have accomplished this that I have been describing. It might have done that. I do not see for sure.

Conductor: She has had a major back problem in this lifetime that she has healed pretty much, using metaphysical methods.

Dr. John: That is good, because the major back problem may have had its source in the carried-over memory of the trauma from the past, and metaphysical healing is much more effective on this sort of injury than it would be on certain other traumatic injuries. Her father helped on that too.

Conductor: Her father was into metaphysics when she was quite young, so he was one of the influences that started her into metaphysics.

Dr. John: Her injury came after he had made his transition,

did it not?

Conductor: I believe it did, Dr. John. I believe it was a fairly recent injury.

Dr. John: I think he helped metaphysically from the other side. That was good. Because the real cause of the injury in this life was the memory from the past. Yes, there was some physical something that precipitated it. But the cell memories, the body memories, had to be healed, and they were. Her body memory has been healed. (A1076:11-14)

Metaphysicians sometimes generate dramatic cures, but it is a mistake to assume that all ills can be healed through mind power. Dr. John has often said that the subject of healing is not that simple, that there is also the *physical* aspect of healing to be considered. However, Audrey's back problem exemplifies one type of karmic physical injury which metaphysics can heal.

In the excarnate, Audrey's father aids her in cleansing and curing the cell memories of the war injury. What a blessing this is, in its effect upon Audrey. It must be a blessing, also, to the father in spirit, to be able to reach back and still help his daughter.

CLIFFORD

Soldiers in battle can capture or generate negative emotions other than guilt. In the midst of war, troops are aroused to a fever-pitch of violent passion. "Kill or be killed!" is the battle cry. However noble the cause, this frenzy of violence can remain with the soul, especially if the soldier is killed at a time of peak emotion.

Such a tendency to violence can be harmlessly released in another lifetime through physically intense sports or labor.

A good soul may not want to express its inner fury but may find it necessary to do so. Clifford is releasing savage forces in constructive ways but is puzzled as to why he has these urges. In his life reading he asked this question of Dr. John:

Conductor: The first question is about a violent streak he tends to have inside of him. He says this has helped him in his hockey playing and in some of the various jobs he has done, but he's afraid of hitting someone in the face or 'of hitting them with a baseball if I try to pitch the ball. What is the reason for this discrepancy in the use of violent force as it pertains to myself?'

Dr. John: I see two things. One that I have spoken of: the soul does at times feel the urge to express its raw masculine power. This could come out in what he would interpret as a violent streak. I rather doubt if it would need to be called a violent streak. It is a very healthy, active, concentrated expression of this quality. And with Clifford there is another force feeding in, too:

Let us go back to the immediately prior life. This one has been hidden from the Clifford person. It is in the subconscious mind. It is close in time but has been hidden, has been held back from emerging into impingement upon consciousness and thus knowledge.

He was a young German soldier in World War I and was killed. This was late in the year of 1915. So actually the birth probably took place about 1899 or 1898 or so. He was about seventeen or eighteen, possibly nineteen years old when he was killed. He was killed in one of those mass charges which resulted in such a mass murder in that war.

He and his fellow troops had been worked up to a certain emotional pitch so that they charged, yelling and with bayonets fixed, within the midst of really quite a frightening cacophony of explosions. He was hit by a heavy bullet in the chest. It was not shrapnel, it was a bullet, but of a large caliber—well, of a sufficient caliber and with sufficient force that it delivered a very strong impact in foot-pounds, a forceful impact which was felt first as a physical blow which stopped his charge.

It didn't exactly spin him around. It more shocked him greatly and then sort of doubled him up. It did not bring immediate death. There was a rather quick hemorrhage into the lungs which brought death within a few minutes. Some aspect of blood vessel fairly close to the heart was ruptured. It bled into the lungs which produced a very frightening coughing, doubly frightening when he saw his own life's blood coming out in the cough, and then the lungs filling up to where he could not breathe.

Death actually came from strangulation, not getting breath. But if it hadn't come that way in about two or three minutes it would have come through loss of blood in another two or three minutes, or in the stoppage of vital functions in another two or three minutes after that. It was a very fatal blow. But not being an immediately fatal blow, it brought quite an emotional impact to that young man.

He was more seventeen than nineteen and may have been approaching eighteen. The fact that he had been emotionally wrought up to a high pitch by his officers before the charge and by being in the group of his fellows who swept out of the trench and over the top in the charge, this had him already at an emotional high pitch, and so this particular wound and death had an even greater emotional content.

With death the spirit was there with the body for a while. Then he noticed the bodies of his comrades, some of whom he recognized, who had been mowed down in that charge, possibly by a heavy machine gun on the French side. They may have been trapped, not knowing the force they were charging against. He noticed that some of his buddies started to get up and stand and look around. Several of them then seemed to look upwards and smile, and it seemed as though a ray of sunshine would hit them and illuminate them, and illumine him also.

Then someone came over to him, a person in the uniform of an officer, but not anyone he recognized, and reached out a hand and helped him to his feet. Of course this was really an astral being, and this was the method used to get his conscious attention and take him over.

So several of his buddies and he were formed into a little squad and they marched off. As they marched they found the road going upwards but it was not hard to travel. Of course, this took them out of the battlefield into a more tranquil countryside. This was the way in which his transition was made in consciousness to the astral realm.

Once there he was given quite a lot of healing. The emotional trauma was bridged over. But it was to be recalled sometime in earth consciousness, possibly in the present life, possibly in some future one, so that the healing would take place in the realm of consciousness where the wound took place, which was in earth consciousness, you see, and personal consciousness during an incarnation.

Possibly that can happen in the present life if he has a chance to work with someone who is skilled in pastlife recalls and the healing of them. If not, he need not worry about it. It would be interesting, but if not this time he has quite a number of incarnations yet ahead; let us say, fifty or sixty or so, maybe fewer. The healing will take place in one of them if not in the present.

Now where were we, conductor?

Conductor: We were in the questions, Dr. John. Thank you for that. There is a question he has that could possibly be from this death. He asks, 'Is there a special purpose in my hay fever and asthmatic conditions I am experiencing in this lifetime?'

Dr. John: It might be. Since it was the lungs which were so drastically involved and brought death, it could be that the hay fever and asthma are carryovers from that. Certainly the past death is a factor here now.

However, I could not say for sure if they are the main cause. It might be a physical or a psychological something in the present life that has brought it up. Modern medicine knows so much more than it used to about these respiratory matters that I trust he has found methods, medical if not psychological or spiritual, to alleviate this condition, or possibly he is outgrowing it. (A1218:21-23)

There are two possible cosmic effects of Clifford's war experience: (1) A carryover of the war wound through hay fever and asthma, and (2) a tendency to violence because of the highly aggressive feelings at the time of death.

Dr. John feels that Clifford's vicious inclinations are exaggerated in his own mind—that they are not really violent tendencies, but are more connected with the expression of raw masculine power. But he does point out that the war episode increases these feelings. Meanwhile Clifford is constructively channeling the emotions through physical labor and athletics.

SIEGFRIED

Siegfried's mother described him as "very aggressive and stubborn, always in a hurry to do or go (and usually at any cost) without the least worry as to any consequences. He is only six years old but has made many references to being stabbed or shot before. Siegfried acts as though there is something he did not finish, and therefore he is in a hurry now. I feel that he is on a self-destruct path.''

When his mother asks in her life reading about Siegfried, Dr. John replies:

>Dr. John: Well, this is interesting. I see his immediate pastlife. I do not see her in it. Maybe I will see more as I explore this. He was a young German boy who was quite taken up with commitments of almost literally heart, mind, and soul to Adolph Hitler.
>
>In World War II he was too young to get in in the early days, and he chaffed at this. He wanted to get in on the exciting things, doing what he felt was truly historically significant to establish Germany. As the tide of war turned against them, he resolutely refused to see any possibility that Germany would lose or that Germany was wrong or that Adolph Hitler was evil instead of good.
>
>There came a time when fourteen- and fifteen-year-old boys were drafted, given very brief training, and sent into action. He gloried in this, and he was killed just about the first action he got into.
>
>But those forces were carried unspent, you see, and they were such disruptive forces because they were bedded in such a total commitment that really not much could be done with that one after death.
>
>So it was decided by a larger council of councils—with good counselors in on it, and the soulmate also was called in on it— that the best thing would be to have this one born again and work out those forces in a different framework within which they would be given different direction.
>
>He is not loyal to Hitler now. He is not blinded by Hitler. He is not working for the eternal Germany that Hitler was promising. He is simply a young soul filled with a great force of commitment and quite a willingness to give his entire heart, mind, soul and body and life to a cause.
>
>The trouble is he doesn't really have a cause to give it all to now, and he is in a different framework, with a quiet father, with a strong and enlightened mother, with intelligence on the part of both parents, with an older brother who goes the way of non-violence, in a culture which has so much more to offer

than the German culture he knew ever had—so the whole framework is different and the outlets for expression are different. It will have to be a different outcome, you see. It simply will have to be because the old outlets are not there.

The forces were important more for themselves than for the channels into which they flowed. This soul has enthusiasm. It's a young soul. It doesn't have much good sense yet. It will gain that with experience.

I think this one does not have any pastlife association with the mother but does with the father. Possibly the father was involved with that German picture. I do not see.

Is there a question?

Conductor: The mother is concerned about this one. She feels he is on a destructive path, even though he's only six years old. Of course, she had wanted to know about the past and you've answered so much of that, but her major question is, 'What should we work on in this life together and what can he learn from me?'

Dr. John: Well, that's a hard question to answer, and at the risk of seeming to be very inept and short of answers, I will plead that I work from the akashic records. I have brought what I could from them and my suggestion would simply be that what she can do will lie within the framework of her being the mother and him being the son. And in that framework she is much closer than I am to the question, and she can provide answers, for it will need not one but many answers.

But I trust that this that I have brought to her, which is going outside the usual bounds of a life reading because it gets into his records and not only hers, will give her an additional understanding within which she can fashion more answers. Yes. (A3247:19,20)

A young soul. A young boy. Both so dramatically affected by Hitler's charisma that even the guides and teachers needed help from a higher council. God's workers recognize how youth can be entranced by power—even the power of evil—and it is their responsibility to rechannel such cosmic effects. The new environment, with only positive outlets for expression, should transport this young God-child from a path of destruction to a path of healthy commitment.

War has damaged countless souls. Guilt can tarnish the God-child who is caught in a uniform during war. As hatred is stirred up toward the enemy, wrong impressions may be formed. Physical wounds, cell memories, can crop up in another lifetime. Violent tendencies, commitment to an evil cause—these can be karmic effects from lifetimes as soldiers in battle.

But the same God who permits man's free will to result in war also provides and desires healing for His children. Through reincarnation the soul can atone for its guilt and correct wrong ideas. The physical wounds of war can be permanently healed as a new personality suffers a lesser injury, cures it, and cleanses body memories of past trauma. Destructive currents can be channeled to flow into constructive pathways and projects.

In time, perhaps sooner than the world knows, man may see the end of war. The end to man's evil and idiotic destruction of people and property. The end of forcing the soul to inhuman acts. But until that time there is comfort in the knowledge that the Creator uses reincarnation and karma, the great teacher, to heal the effects of war.

CHAPTER FIFTEEN

ARE MARRIAGES MADE IN HEAVEN?

To really answer the question "Are marriages made in heaven?" would take an entire book and then leave a lot unsaid. But a general answer is available from the study of reincarnation and the soul's progression: Yes, marriages usually are "made in heaven" in the sense that there is a celestial or cosmic or soul purpose in them, but—and here's the joker—that purpose is not primarily personal happiness.

The western world has largely dropped the custom of arranged marriages, but marriages often are arranged for souls—and by souls—long before the conception of the persons involved. Purpose flows throughout a life, including the marriage(s) in it. This purpose existed before the person did, but that major aim is not happiness—it is soul growth. Thus a "marriage made in heaven" may be quite different from the usual earth meaning of that term.

This pre-planning of marriage must be qualified in various ways. Sometimes it is not known who the spouse will be, for at times a person is born without his lifeplan containing a certainty of marriage. Even if a marriage is pre-patterned, it does not necessarily take place. Part of the soul's experience in incarnation is to learn how to cope with the unexpected, and there are many uncertainties on earth: accidents, diseases, war, free will of the persons involved, etc. Life on earth is dynamic, not static. Although many events are intended, even pre-patterned, very few are so fully pre-destined that change cannot take place. An intended wedlock can be offset in various ways, and then may be shifted to a later incarnation or abandoned entirely.

But as a general rule, yes, many—perhaps most—marriages are preplanned and do come about as designed.

Marriages are made in heaven—in the pre-personal life-planning designs of souls and their councils of guides and teachers—primarily for the growth of the souls involved, not just for pleasure. The soul is immortal and much more important than the person. The person is an experience-point and an expression-point for the soul and for God's wishes for the soul. Thus, even though the person is considered, first priority must go to soul growth.

In countless ways marriage can produce growth. Squandering the strong force of sex merely as lust, outside of longterm meaningful, problem-solving relationships (marriage or otherwise) is so wasteful, partly because this power of sex can be harnessed for real growth, along with happiness. There may be very specific lessons one is to learn from another, and fine qualities to build, in a longterm give-and-take situation. There may be negative karma to work out, which will only be worsened if one party runs out at the first appearance of a problem. In an early non-native gender lifetime a close cosmic family member may be "sent from heaven" to be the spouse who will understand the probable inadequacies or mistakes of the other. Hurts, pastlife traumas and emotional carryovers, can be vented in marriage, hopefully with an understanding and faithful helpmate who will not hold it against us as would an unrelated soul.

Happiness also is a good medium for growth, and positive karma can bring two people together in wedlock with that true happiness which encompasses mind, body, and soul. An unfulfilled pastlife love or simply good prior relationships can produce such a joyous union.

In short, a marriage made in heaven means a pre-planned and purposeful marriage, but that purpose may or may not bring the happiness usually meant in the earth use of the term. Because the subject is so complex we cannot possibly present here all of the karmic reasons for marriage and its successes and failures. But in the following examples there is much insight as to how and why marriages are made in heaven.

MABEL AND SAM

A woman in her fifties, Mabel has a major problem in her marriage with Sam. After thirty years he fell for another woman and he left

Mabel. Now, about a year later, he tells Mabel he wants to come back to her. Although she loves Sam, Mabel has suffered so much that she is uncertain about a reconciliation. There is also her natural concern that Sam might not really love her.

This marriage was made in heaven for the growth of both parties. By their union the Mabel soul and the Sam soul are learning to rethink certain crystallized patterns of understanding. Because of the importance for each one of them, this marriage should not be broken. Early in Mabel's life reading Dr. John explains the significance of their union:

> Dr. John: Three of her band of guides and teachers and protectors are here for this reading and a fourth will join us for a portion of it. These form her council, as it were, to sit with me as I read the akashic records. And together we will bring this reading, although of course the far major portion of it will be from her akashic records.
>
> She is from the feminine half of her whole soul. If she has read our several books she will recognize this as being what we call a feminine soul.
>
> She is rather in that merging area between the well-started and the around-the-midpoint stage of her earth incarnations and of her general soul experience.
>
> In her case this means that she has had certain experiences which have led to a certain development of her consciousness with certain rather set expectations and rather definite nature. Now this represents quite an advance over the more amorphous state of the very young soul. But it also means that the time has come when the conclusions she has drawn from her experience to date, as it were, are being challenged. They have become a bit crystallized, and these crystallizations must be broken up in order that the patterns of her understanding and the patterns of her expectations may be enlarged.
>
> Her guides and teachers tell me that the challenging of these crystallized patterns has been accomplished by bringing her into long term association in the marriage with another soul not quite as far along as she but nearly, and who likewise has some rather definite notions, as it were, of what is, what should be, and what is to be expected. The ideas of the two are similar in some ways and different in other ways, so each of them is

expected to learn from being placed in this long and close association with another who is very, very similar in having developed certain ideas of what is and what should be and certain expectations, so that each of them really was rather surprised to find that the other had with equal force developed other set ideas of what is, what should be, and what can be expected.

It has been quite a constructive and educational experience. Both have grown from it and both are expected to grow further from it. The council tells me very emphatically that this marriage should continue throughout this life. It is as though they have spent many years in planting and nurturing and raising the crop and they have been picking fruit from it almost from the beginning—fruit of experience and growth and challenge and some change—but the fruitage should increase now as the years become more mature, and really the two lives should come into a little easier period as the persons mellow and the intended results are and have been attained.

This is pretty much the identification and the purpose of this life, and it is, as it were, 'written large' in the akashic records as such. It also shows in the records that really much has been accomplished, that the Mabel soul and person are on time and still going forward, and that the life to date definitely is on the plus side as an incarnation and it is expected that it continue to produce the good fruits along the intended lines.

Both spouses are in their native gender, a factor which makes for differences in their beingnesses. Neither soul is very old, but each has had enough earthlives to form rather definite opinions. When Sam is inquired about, Dr. John gives his purpose as similar to Mabel's:

> Conductor: Mabel next asks about her husband, Sam...
> Dr. John: They are cosmic family members. Both of them are among the younger members. Both are in that same general stage when life has brought them to some very definite early conclusions. Since these conclusions were different, in many ways, and since the conclusions need to be challenged and enlarged, and since there is basically a good bond of love between them, it was decided by their guides and teachers and somewhat by the cosmic family older members in this case,

that it would be quite good to bring them into an incarnation as husband and wife.

He is natively masculine even as she is natively feminine. His ideas of what a wife should be do not coincide with hers. Her ideas of what a husband should be do not coincide with his. Which is right? This is not the correct question. Both are right insofar that to have reached these conclusions definitely shows growth as these young souls are coming ahead. And that both are wrong in that each must learn this time as he does modify his position, either in the incarnate stage—hopefully—or, later in the excarnate stage of these personhoods' existence.

Being cosmic family members forms a love bond between Mabel and Sam, but they have also had several lifetimes together in different relationships. In the 1700s in Italy, for instance, they were to be married, but the then incarnation of the Sam soul died before the wedding. This brief encounter between them set up forces of desire and added love which has been most useful in this lifetime.

Several of Mabel's questions reflect the marriage situation:

Dr. John: Now what question have you, conductor? What question is she asking of the marriage?

Conductor: Well, the marriage is the biggest question of her reading. A year ago the husband separated from Mabel and fell in love with another woman and had intended to marry this other woman. But the time went by and Mabel wasn't prepared for divorce so the other lady decided she liked someone else better. This made a very traumatic experience for the husband, you see. So the question is, shall they go on together?

Dr. John: Well, I have already answered that. It is hoped and intended that they do, and they can reap more fruit of what they have sown and nurtured in all the many years they have been together, if they do remain together.

We do not see any forces within either of them nor within their relationship really necessitating the breaking of that relationship now. The difficulties we see as being primarily precisely along the line I have outlined, leading to a breaking into of two crystallized patterns of what is felt to be right and of what is expected to happen and become.

It has been quite a bouncing experience for the husband, challenging some of his concepts of himself and of the male prerogatives. If he got his fingers burned, good.

Actually, the other woman is not a prime threat to Mabel. Yes it could have been, although we do not think it really would be now, that her husband might have left Mabel for this other woman and established a home with her. He would not have been happy in it. This other woman is rather disturbed on inner levels and is rather opportunistic, so he would have found sooner or later that she was not the completely altruistic love-bringer to him, but that she had certain axes of her own to grind. And this is a good thing for the husband to know. It was a good experience for him to have and we trust that it is over and that he will be wise enough to keep it over.

Conductor: Yes. She mentions that the time while they were separated she could think of only the good things they had done together, the happy times they had together. The husband now says he wants to stay together but Mabel doesn't know how he really feels. I think this you have brought will help her to clarify the situation.

Dr. John: The husband is discovering that life is not as he really felt it was and as he really felt it should be. The crystallized patterns he had of reality and expectations of natural and 'legitimate' expectations, were not too real. Excuse me, they were not too realistic. They were quite real with him, yes—but they were born of partial experience let us say, plus a not-too-wise feeling that he as a man is a superior being and others should listen and he should have his way. Yes. (A121:2,3,11,13,14)

The aim of Mabel's marriage is very closely tied in with her own purpose in this incarnation. She is to break certain crystallizations of attitudes by living with a man who has different biases. Frequently discord between spouses —which is so complained about—represents strong growth possibilities. As two people love each other they usually try to see the other's views, learning much in the process. The love furnishes motivation to grasp the opposite viewpoint. This marriage was made in heaven.

LACEY AND LARRY

As cosmic family members strengthen their bond in earthliving, difficulties of different types can be introduced. The first earthlife together will probably be shared by compatible personalities. But as the souls get older and more adept, antagonisms may be ushered in for the growth of each. The cosmic family bond and the happy relationship of the previous life or lives help to reinforce the love needed to work through the problems.

A couple in their mid-forties, Lacey and Larry had been married more than twenty-five years at the time of their life readings. Although the personalities were quite different and had had many trials to work through, they loved each other and had developed a good marriage. Dr. John brought out that they were cosmic family members, both masculine souls, and then gave their pastlives together:

> Dr. John: They were together rather briefly in the American South in the 1800s in the same roles as the present. But after two years together in the marriage relationship they separated. Which was the way chosen by those two personalities as the way out of a situation in which they were uncomfortable, but a purposed situation which, being short-circuited by the wills of the personalities in the 1800s, was brought into expression for this present lifetime.
>
> They were together prior to that 1800s in the 1000s in Peru, in which they were in the husband-wife relationship but in reverse roles. The relationship began with a very real commitment born out of a mutual love and respect and desire for each other. And the first years of their relationship as husband and wife were very good. But as they went along strains and tensions and pressures were introduced by one or the other, to which on the soul level each responded, in a manner of speaking, as though 'gritting the teeth and bearing it.' They stayed with the relationship but it was a half-hearted acceptance on the soul level which meant that neither soul was really committed to the challenge of the difficulties introduced by the personalities as a way of growth.
>
> When that life was over, and in the review of the experience, and with a greater soul comprehension, there was a realization of the loss, the element of loss in a relationship which is only half-heartedly accepted. And there was a reach on the part

of each soul for the opportunity to have another go-around and to do better. Which is the experience of the present life but in reverse roles, which serves to expand the comprehension on the part of each of the difficulties for the other in the role and adds a certain new challenge from variation of the experience.

Conductor: If the souls had seen, as you say, the elements of loss in a relationship that is only half-hearted back there in Peru in the 1000s, nine hundred years ago, it looks as though the souls have appreciated the good in a relationship that grows more intensive and more whole-hearted as they have come along through it. Let us find out if there is still other pastlife acquaintance or cosmic relationship.

We had a feminine (Lacey) early 1800s, United States South; 1000s Peru, Lacey in masculine. Have they other pastlife acquaintance?

Dr. John: They gave an early earth rootage to their relationship as cosmic family members in a life in Egypt in the 1900s B.C. That was a lifetime simply to give earth rootage to the relationship. It was a husband-wife relationship with Lacey as the husband. And it was good, it was positive and, in a sense, it was complete in itself for the purpose of it. It did not need correction or expansion in continuing lifetimes. It simply served the purpose of establishing a good earth root to their cosmic family framework.

Conductor: Have they other pastlife acquaintance?

Dr. John: We don't believe so. At least there is no feed-in from other lives into the present. (AB3988: 14-15)

Since cosmic family members usually incarnate taking different roles, it would seem strange that Lacey and Larry were married in all three of their pastlives. But the second lifetime actually set up the forces of the third, and the third birthed the present life. Doubtlessly they will be together in roles other than marriage in the future. But this time around they are learning what it means to commit in a difficult but purposeful marriage situation.

JOCELYN AND NICHOLAS

Some marriages seem to have been made in hell rather than heaven. For Jocelyn, this is true of her marriage with Nicholas. She is a very sweet woman who has been wedded to a disagreeable man for more than twenty years. At the time of the life reading he had become disabled. This ladened Jocelyn with an even heavier load but made it impossible for her to leave him.

Early in the reading Dr. John told Jocelyn that there was negative karma feeding into this lifetime. She is a feminine soul and veered off the God-path while in a masculine incarnation.

When her father was asked about, Jocelyn learned that he was her sponsor soul. Several lives with the father were brought out and then Dr. John told of the one which generated the karma:

> Dr. John: We come up into the 1500s A.D. for the most recent one in which the two of them had been together. This was in Italy. She was in masculine expression. The present father was an uncle, an older brother to the father of this one.
>
> This was a life in which some new temptations were to be met: a temptation of physical strength and lustiness, a mind that was not too bright but didn't realize it, a rather hot-tempered temperament that would brook no put-down and not much teaching. The soul must learn how to successfully guide its personhoods, the earth human beings given to it, through all the major basic experiences that earth offers, and guide them successfully. This person was a real challenge to handle, you see.
>
> In this case, the feminine soul was not too successful. It is interesting to see that the soul itself to some extent became part of the problem instead of part of the answer. The soul gave in to the temptation to feel its strength and to enjoy the assertion of its own strength over others in this lifetime.
>
> It was not the smartest person in its peer group, but it usually had its way by its own physical strength and its psychological as well as physical bullying of its companions. This carried over into the home life when the boy married.
>
> The uncle viewed all this with a great amount of concern. He was rather sternly—not exactly Puritanical, that is Protestant; he was stern in a Catholic way. This was his religion, this was his philosophy of life. He held to probity as really almost the touchstone of human living. But his nephew did not do so.
>
> His nephew experimented with some of the girls before he

chose one to be his mate, and finding the taste of lust and sex pleasant and rewarding to his ego, continued with the womanizing after marriage as well. The nephew was not above some small petty crimes when he could get by with them. He did what you now call mugging a number of times, not a great many but some, when he could get by with it. Usually outdoors at night. He did not preplan or premeditate these too much. But with his strength, he rather quickly learned how to appear innocent, and yet with a quick blow render another person on a lonely street unconscious, pull him into some doorway or alleyway and rather quickly search him for and relieve him of any valuables he might be carrying. Then go his way looking very innocent. He was never caught.

Within the home he was a bit of a bully also. When he felt like sex, his wife gave in to him right then and there. It didn't matter if a baby was crying or something was boiling over on the stove or whatever. Of course, his sex didn't take very long and she could be back to the crying baby or the boiling kettle within a few minutes. It happened frequently enough so that she got over the outraged feeling but never got over the lump in her heart that her husband was like this.

She had been rather swept off her feet by his strength and his protestations of devotion to her and such. But she was of tough peasant stock also, so if this was the way life was and if this was the way marriage was, well, that's the way it was and she took it. But she didn't like it.

The children knew him as a provider. There was always food in the house and the roof did not leak. In fact, the house was a little nicer than the dwellings of some of their playmates. They knew their father was strong and brooked no disrespect for himself outside the house or in, and brooked really no disrespect for them outside the house. It was because they were his children and not particularly in the comprehension of their own self-respect that he did this. But within that framework they experienced that life.

The uncle did not approve and voiced his disapproval upon various occasions, and found he made a dent only one or two percent of the way at best. He never did give up letting it be known that he disapproved. But he was an influence only because in the consciousness of his nephew there was the realization that this man who had a kind of strength that the boy did not have, plus the physical strength which the boy did have, did not approve.

This was good. This was in the consciousness of the person as a nagging reminder, but not listened to very much, that some of the things he was doing really were not right. So the sponsor soul performed a good function in that life, even though he was not of much actual significance in really affecting the conduct.

The thought in the conductor's head by this time was, "I'll bet Nicholas was the mistreated wife, and that's why he gives her so many problems now." But when the present husband was inquired about, Dr. John replied:

> Dr. John: He was back there in that Italian life, too, as the eldest son—no, the second eldest, who had a certain streak of what we might call tenderness or gentleness or even of artistry and being interested in beauty. But that soul was not strong enough, experienced enough, old enough, ept enough, to carry that through the unfavorable climate of his father, and so succumbed to the father's pattern. In one sense, he expressed that pattern in the present life.
>
> Here is some of the karma of which I spoke, which in the Jocelyn lifetime is being met.
>
> I do not find other pastlife acquaintance of these two, nor do I see any necessity of future lives if this life finishes up the relationship. They might come together in the future as two different persons, of their own choice. But this time it was not so much of choice as of karmic necessity. The Jocelyn soul knew before it came into the Jocelyn incarnation that this would be the husband, and somewhat of the nature of the life that would be.
>
> Let me point out that that Italian father had certain strengths. His children did not go to bed hungry, and they were not bullied in the streets. In that sense they had both success and protection. So this concept of providing well, at least in a physical way, for the family, for the household, was inculcated in that second son and is expressed now, and it is a good strength.
>
> The things that were missing then and now can be added later. This is one of the nice things about reincarnation. The

soul can add the various ingredients of success as it goes along. As has been succinctly said, 'Don't give up on me, God isn't finished with me yet.' This is quite true, and in that truth there is much of hope and much of the process of what you call salvation, as the soul successfully completes its experiences in this stage of its God-Beingness and then hastens on to a higher stage of its Individuated-God-Beingness.

Conductor: This certainly explains the difficulty in this lifetime.

Dr. John: I hope it will give her certain comfort as well. In a sense, she must do it. But with the price she pays, she really is buying more than she knows. Is buying freedom, for one thing; is buying greater maturity, for another thing. Let her add to this. She can add additional factors that she is buying, more than she knows, as she serves out the last days, the last times, the last period of time of this relationship.

Conductor: This is her other question. She feels that he is clutching onto her now, since he knows he doesn't have much longer to live. She wonders how she can help him to make his transition.

Dr. John: He is not too open to the spiritual approach. I am not sure she really can help him. She can pray for him. If he is open, she can talk with him about how life does go on and is better on the other side. If she can do this, recapturing some of the aspect of love which they have had rather than in a feeling that is in any way negative toward him—not a feeling of 'I'm trapped and I'd like to be free, and you weren't interested in spiritual things before and so you don't understand now that which could be a comfort and a light upon your path.'

If she takes this approach she won't get very far, and I'm not sure she can reach him in any way. I would suggest our book *Diary After Death*, but I do not know if he would be open to it at all. Really, in a way, it would not apply to him and to her, for on the other side their marriage will not hold. If he changes and if she changes, they might find a happy companionship, but at present they are unequally yoked, in a yoke that should continue only until it is broken by death.

On the other side, like attracts like, and these two are not that alike.

There were other pastlives of Jocelyn and her mother-in-law, but it is the 1500s relationship that caused problems for Jocelyn in this lifetime. Her difficulties with the husband were magnified by the aggravations of the mother-in-law. What an interesting way chosen to meet the karma of wife-abuse! Another marriage "made in heaven" in the sense of having spiritual purpose and good in it, though definitely not of bliss and happiness!

ARLENE AND BEAU

Arlene felt that her husband Beau had invented the word infidelity. She couldn't understand why she had stayed with a man who for twenty years had repeatedly betrayed her. Although there had been good times, Arlene also wondered if her marriage had been made in hell.

Early in the life reading, Dr. John described a feminine lifetime for Arlene in France during the Napoleonic era. She observed the effects of the wars but was not too greatly caught up in them, and it was a rather normal incarnation for Arlene. Later she asked about Beau and Dr. John replied:

> Dr. John: This may surprise her, but he is a cosmic family member. He is a much younger soul. He is in the latter part of the second stage, the well-started stage, and verging towards entering the third stage. He also is an early masculine incarnation from a feminine soul.
>
> She may ask us later on, conductor, and you probably will know, whether or not this marriage should continue. Just from what I have said already, one who is acquainted with reincarnation and the flow of purpose in relationships and in individual patterns would know that such a question at least has crossed her mind upon occasion, and may be now or sometime in the past or future rather prominent in her mind.
>
> The answer is yes. It is hoped that the marriage will continue, for his sake more than for hers, but for her sake as well. He was born in 1937. He is coming to the time, within another ten years anyway and perhaps already, when he should be beginning to mellow a bit.
>
> The feminine soul in masculine incarnation sometimes has difficulty living up to its own ideas of what a man should be.

There are even more difficulties in that the feminine soul in early masculine incarnations—or the masculine soul in early feminine incarnations—may emphasize some one aspect of the nonnative gender expression and do fairly well in developing it, but at the cost of many weaknesses in the total picture.

Arlene's council is nodding. Every one of them is nodding his or her head. The one present from the supervisory council has sort of a knowing smile on his face. He, of course, is an Individuated-God-Being farther along. He says, 'Yes, this is the way it goes, and the earth councils learn this and can see it usually better than their earth incarnate proteges can.' Which is so true.

They were together in a way, let me say they were acquainted, in that lifetime in France. There was about a ten-year age difference. That, too, was an early masculine incarnation of the present husband's feminine soul. He was a boy in the village in which the then incarnation of the Arlene soul was a girl.

He was old enough to get caught up in the go-to-war fervor engendered by Napoleon, but he wasn't a very good soldier. In marching, you could almost say he would either start off with both feet together or not even start and then have to catch up. He was not too well coordinated physically, and that bothered him. He was not exactly a stumble-bum or a klutz, but he wasn't too far from that.

He survived the war and came home. Of course, for every man, no matter how situated, there is always a woman who will accept. So he did get married, but it was to somebody else. There was no romantic outreach of either of these toward the other. The age differential, for one thing, was too much. Then, the girl was more coordinated, more—there are some popular terms these days, 'she had her head together,' was 'with it' more, 'knew where she was coming from and where she was at,' and this sort of thing.

It was an introduction of the two, and that was good. The cosmic family relationship did not express much then, and it was purposefully held down so there would not be a closeness of the two.

When that life was over, both of these souls were brought together and evaluated the life of the present husband more, and the idea of their coming as husband and wife was broached and was accepted. The Arlene soul knew very well this would be sort of a teaching lifetime. She would be moved into the role of teacher to the other one. But it would have to be done in subtle ways in truly feminine fashion, because the soul of the present husband was really distressed by the awkwardness of the incarnation of the personality it had helped to form and through which it had functioned—or malfunctioned—in the 1700-1800s life in France.

This time it was going to come as a well-coordinated, strong, agile, physical man. That is all right, but when that is the emphasis, other things are left out. A young soul very often needs to emphasize one or two qualities in an incarnation, and it is growing in this way. The older soul volunteering to come in as wife knew there would be some difficulties to be experienced.

But the soul did not sigh. The soul said, 'Well, fine. This is a good service I can render to my younger cosmic sister soul. It may be a service beyond what he the person suspects is coming, but if I'm not there he could very well marry someone who would give him a much rougher time and fewer opportunities; less chance for growth into the larger understandings.'

The difficulties experienced by Arlene in this relationship are in themselves learning experiences, but only because her soul is old enough to take them in that way. A younger soul could have been completely devastated by the kind of life her husband brought to his wife.

Even though the person of the husband has been quite a prodigal, 'spending his substance in riotous living,' yet let Arlene, as did the father of the prodigal, look for his return. Which in his case may take a period of some years of gradual reversing of opinions and behavior. But something much better than they have now could develop in that marriage. It would surprise the husband, but it would gratify him too, although it might take him a while to say so.

Conductor: Arlene wanted to know why they were together in this lifetime. She thought it might be karmic, and you have answered this question. Another question she has—well, the major problem is that he has other women, in affair after affair after affair. It has been very disturbing to her, to the point now that, as she says, there are no more tears, there is no respect or love. She is wondering why she stuck with him all this time. Is this because of the service her soul is rendering his soul?

Jocelyn and Nicholas are not cosmically related, were only together this one past time and won't be together in the future—not even in the afterlife. But they are, we might say, karmically related because of the Italian father's example to the son.

What about the 1500s Italian wife? Interestingly enough, she was found when Jocelyn asked about her mother-in-law:

> Conductor: The mother-in-law is (name, birth given).
> Dr. John: Yes, she is the one. She was the wife in that Italian life. She somewhat got her revenge in this life. Not so much consciously and deliberately, but more from being the type of person she was and from forces set in motion in that other life which are venting or which did vent at least to quite some extent, I believe sufficiently, in this life when she was in a position where she could vent them, as she could not vent her emotions against her husband. He would not have understood and would not have tolerated such a thing in his wife. She would have been 'slapped silly' if she had told him certain things or rebelled against his demands, his treatment.
> That is one of the interesting things about life in the reincarnational pattern. The things that one person in a relationship feels and cannot express towards another in that relationship in one life, will usually get expressed in another relationship in a different incarnational pattern. The bully loses his position from which he could bully, and will experience some of the consequences when he is not in the favored position of strength and forcing his own way. It is just as simple as that.
> Several questions arise. Have they other pastlife acquaintance? Yes. Oddly enough, these two are cosmic cousins. On the soul level they do not bear one another animosity. But neither has yet gained the skill needed, and the experience, to guide its incarnations, its personhoods, through some of the temptations and situations and events of human living.
> They are sort of learning together. They may bump heads, accidentally or deliberately, but they will work things through into a good relationship before they are finished because they must, and because as souls they really want to. Although they don't know quite how to handle some of the more obstreperous kinds of personhoods. (A1292:7-13)

Dr. John: The service, and the cosmic family bond. The 'affair after affair after affair' does two things. It keeps up the ego of this very insecure male, and it represents a certain masculine accomplishment, let us say. The young soul has accomplished in that way, and possibly in another one or two ways. But with the total picture being quite unbalanced and incomplete and unsatisfactory.

She can help his soul to pass this life with a much better grade in the years ahead, over that which it has achieved to date. But it has achieved a passing grade. there is such a mixture of good and bad, positive and negative qualities, and strengths and weaknesses and so forth with him.

Conductor: Thank you, Dr. John. I think this will certainly bring her much more understanding of her husband. (A617:12,1-17,21)

In an early nonnative gender lifetime promiscuity is not unusual. Because the young soul is really trying to make a good man—or woman, as the case may be—it may latch onto the idea of proving through sex its masculine or feminine prowess. There are other reasons for infidelity, too many for this chapter: In some instances it is condoned; in others it is not.

Arlene's service to her younger cosmic sister has been no picnic, but it has been a favor lovingly given. On the soul level she better understands Beau's weaknesses. Through the reading, the Arlene person now sees the kindness she is extending to a younger cosmic friend. Despite the purgatory it brings her, this marriage was made in heaven.

HUBERT AND BELLE

Our prior illustration showed Dr. John counseling Arlene to stick with Beau. He is trying to be a good man, and time should mellow him. In an early nonnative gender life the soul must work hard to receive a passing grade, and even then the resulting person won't be the finest. But God is patient, and souls must become so.

However, a soul volunteer is not expected to stay with a mate who is not striving to do well. It behooves the young soul to try, for help will be removed if it does not.

Hubert—the second child in a family of seven siblings—is a hand-some, successful, young man in his thirties. He loves his wife Belle very much but is appalled at her lacks. The youngest of three children, she is beautiful, has social graces, but refuses to clean house and expects to be waited on. Yet she is quick to fault Hubert any chance she can. Hubert wants to keep this marriage together, but the problems are tearing him apart.

In the life reading for Hubert we find that both husband and wife are in their nonnative gender; however, Hubert is an older soul. The marriage was planned as a growing experience for them both, but Belle is refusing to budge past the accomplishment of a beautiful body and social graces. Dr. John cautions Hubert against keeping the marriage alive if Belle does not shape up. Although the feminine soul wants to be a supportive husband to its younger cosmic friend, that support could encourage the laziness of the wife's masculine soul.

We start the reincarnational life reading story after the conductor has given Belle's name and birth date:

> Dr. John: Well, this is quite interesting. They are cosmic family members. She is slightly, not very much but appreciably, younger than he and despite appearances to the contrary, she is from the masculine half of her whole soul.
>
> It was planned before they came into this incarnation that they do come and become husband and wife, and it was known there would be much to work out; and with the fact that they are not old souls, that meant there would be much difficulty in their life together.
>
> Let us take a look at Belle. The soul honestly and earnestly wanted to make a good success of the present life but…well, the essence of what I'm saying is that the soul concentrated on making a very feminine body and has congratulated itself on being a very good woman in that respect and has not really seen much or gone much beyond that, and has used that achievement to defend itself from even considering that it should go further.
>
> In the world in which they actually live, Hubert is a young prince. He is of fine body, of fine mind attainment, of fine position. He is a young prince. And the Belle soul has created

what it feels to be a young princess to walk beside the young prince. Well, I should drop the terms young there. They are a prince and princess. But there is more that is required, and partly because of the sibling placement of each and the family upbringing of each, but the sibling placement perhaps more, and majorly because of the soul outlook, the Belle personality has dug in its heels against proceeding further.

They are cosmic family members. There is a deep love between them as souls. There is a very honest urge on the part of the older soul to be with the younger soul and to bring it along into true success in the present lifetime.

But it is not certain how far that success will go and the prince is not to consider that he must stay with the princess all through the experience if she will not grow. He would be nearly devastated if it did not take place, partly because of his own love nature, partly because of the nurturing nature of that feminine soul, partly because of his own idealization and expectation of what his marriage should be, growing out of the marriage and home of his parents.

There is a double background of forebearing in the Hubert person towards the Belle person because of the feminine nature and because of the soul relationship, the cosmic family relationship. Unfortunately, there is not such a degree of forebearing on the part of the Belle person, because it is of the masculine nature and it tends to be seeking to assert itself rather than to nurture others to success. I have pointed out that one characteristic of masculine success is how far a male person can rise above other male persons, and one component of feminine success is how she can nurture her husband, her children, her church, her clubs, her associations, to their success. But in this case, the feminine concept of success has not really been instilled in the person of Belle and is not too well grasped by the soul.

The soul is ahead of the person in the case of Belle because it does comprehend more but it doesn't quite know what to do with the Belle person, who has 'taken her head,' or 'taken the bit in her teeth' and is insisting on running her own way. So even though the soul—and the same can be said of her council—is doing what it and they can, they are not as definitive in shaping the conduct of Belle as they wish they could be.

So, Hubert has a problem on his hands. The background, however, which must be remembered at all times, is that they are cosmic family members, that they have a deep love for each other on that level, that the Belle soul is depending upon the Hubert soul to do all he can, for he is in a closer position and can do more in some ways than her own soul can do with her.

Likewise, the Hubert person should know that his purpose, his relationship with life in the most basic way, is not defined by his wife. He must not, and I really need not say that because he will not, sever this relationship lightly, and it may be the relationship need not be severed. This is something that is not yet known.

It is also possible that if Belle does not measure up, that one of the most telling educational factors would be if she lost her prince. She may feel that that would not really matter too much; that she is herself and she is the princess and always will be. But a woman, even an attractive woman, who loses her husband in the present life, in the present culture, and in almost any culture, and has not been able to 'hold on' to him, and especially a woman who loses a man as attractive as Hubert is, particularly in the eyes of others but in very real actuality as well, that woman has failed and society, whereas it may outwardly sympathize with her and cluck, cluck, cluck with her, knows she has failed. She has failed to hold her husband, and when the nature of the husband is known as it is to some and would be known to others to be as really fine, as really outgoing, as really wanting a loving relationship and home, a partner in life, as Hubert does, then the condemnation of failure upon the wife is even stronger.

Dr. John has delineated five ways of learning: insight, education, personal experience, suffering, and failure. Failure is of course the hardest way to learn, but is very effective.

Dr. John: The soul is saying, 'Look, I have made a beautiful woman. I am very gracious in society. I am capable of being the socially acceptable and envied wife of a successful man. What more in heaven's name is required of me?'

Well, in heaven's name a great deal more is required of her, because she is to grow spiritually as well. She is to utilize the good things in her life for growth, not simply for pleasure. And God is never content with a soul nor an incarnation, a personhood of a soul, that is content itself to just stay where it is and count its achievements rather than pushing on.

So Hubert is faced with really a magnificent opportunity of bringing her further along. But if she will not, he is not to demote himself and hold himself from growth and from fulfillment, to fit into the smaller framework into which she would try to force him. It's a very interesting challenge and lifetime for Hubert.

Hubert and Belle were together as sisters in the 600s in Africa, but that lifetime does not affect this one. Dr. John continues:

Dr. John: Well, I am told I should go on. Perhaps at the end if we have additional time we can come back and trace in several more. They have not had extensive pastlife acquaintance. They have had more togetherness in certain schools of learning on the other side as souls, and this is part of the weakness of the relationship now, that there is not really a strong pastlife relationship built up. It is more the carryover of relationship from other realms of beingness and planes of expression, and these have their strengths. Each has a very basic strength and in some ways is stronger but in some ways leave the relationship with certain lacks of strength on the personal level.

Conductor: Thank you very much, Dr. John. Of course, they will be together in the future since they are cosmic family members?

Dr. John: Yes, but if this marriage does not turn out right, it may be quite a way in the future. The Belle soul may have to earn the right to come back, especially if it hurts the Hubert person. If the Belle person hurts the Hubert person, then it may have to go through a thousand years or more of incarnations aside from him before coming back. This would not be unusual; it's not a great penalty, but a very logical thing. If a younger family member makes a mess of a life with an older family member, then the younger one is removed from the older one's picture for a while. That is logical. And the force of it is used to motivate the younger one to do better. (A1388)

If Belle continues dragging her feet, it is only fair that she be separated from Hubert. Separation from a beloved cosmic friend can be a very effective teaching experience.

A postscript to the story of Hubert and Belle was received. Hubert is putting his foot down, refusing to accept Belle's lacks. In sessions with a marriage counselor, Hubert shocked Belle by asking for a divorce. It appears that this action awakened Belle from her lethargy, and Hubert now has hope that the marriage will survive and become truly good. Made in heaven, it has its purposes.

REUBEN AND AMY

Reuben and Any have been married for more than forty years. They were high school sweethearts and, for the most part, have had a good marriage. A successful and steady man in all ways, Reuben requested a life reading for deeper understandings. Among other things, he was told that his marriage had been made in heaven, "long before his father smiled upon his mother."

More than two hundred years ago the Amy soul had a tragic incarnation from which she is still recovering. In the 1800s Reuben was a supportive older brother, and he volunteered to be Amy's loving husband in this present lifetime, helping her to complete her healing. Dr. John relates the details:

> Dr. John: Amy, yes. This is a cosmic family member, a younger cosmic family member, from the feminine half of her soul.
> They were together in the 1800s. He was in the masculine and she in the feminine, she as a younger sister. This was back in the British Isles. It may have been in England or it may have been in Wales. The sister was frail. She did not marry. This brother was seven years and several months older, and when the parents died the brother took over the care of the sister, even though he was married. She died in her twentieth year but before her twentieth birthday.
> Her frailty goes back to a previous experience which was in her life and not in his. He was not present in the lifetime, but I shall endeavor to diverge now from his records to hers, as I seldom do in a life reading, as you know. But this is important.

She, in the 1700s or 1600s, had been caught up in an unexpected persecution. It was in France, and she was a very happy young girl. Her parents loved each other and loved their children. They had their own rather happy community within the city where they lived, a rather major city. The father was in business. They were members of a religious group which, although honest and honored and with its own dignity and constructive character, was set upon rather unexpectedly by the group that had the blessing of the king.

This girl saw all the life she had known destroyed by evil, because it was evil. She couldn't see why this should happen, and it should not have happened. She saw her father executed and her mother dishonored and left to die, and an older brother killed. She went quite distraught. She was only seven or eight years old at the time. Her happiness and gentleness and the love she had known had not prepared her for anything like this, and she quite lost her mind.

I can see her running, disheveled, crying, screaming, hiding, and in a panic. Then her mind broke. I do not like to look much further at the details. After her mind broke, she lived, I believe, about a week, but there were no provisions for her. There was a great upheaval at that time and she did not know friend from foe. She reverted somewhat to an animal status of simply seeking shelter, and she died. I think she was killed, but death really was rather merciful in her state there.

This was a horrible experience, and it has taken several incarnations to really recover from it and for the soul to regain strength and assurance. The soul pretty soon will come into some masculine lives in which certain additional strengths will be gained. It has had some masculine lives, and more feminine lives.

So the life in the immediately prior time as sister was definitely a healing life. They were together not simply for her sake. It was another life for him as well, a rather quiet farming life, really. Not caught up in the Industrial Revolution, not caught up in any revolution. Some would call it a rather dull life, but it had its reasons and its satisfactions and its quiet strengths. It was a life that took faithfulness to tend the animals, to love the ground, to produce the crops.

In the present life—and remember they are cosmic family

members, and the older cosmic brother has a real compassion for the younger cosmic sister—they have come into the husband-wife relationship. They will be together in the future, but not necessarily in this relationship.

He has provided her a life in which she has been protected, she has been loved, she has a framework which has carried her throughout life. When were they married?

Conductor: 1940.

Dr. John: There's forty-two years of a marriage, and that is good. He has been faithful to her. She has benefited on the soul level as much as on the personal level, possibly more. The quietness of this life, although it's not been all quiet, has been healing. He has been a shield and protector and a healing for her on the soul level in this life and its experiences.

Is there further question?

Conductor: His question, I believe, has to do with his misunderstanding of some of the teachings: 'Do I have unresolved karma to work out with her?'

Dr. John: Yes, but let us point out that karma is essentially learning. Yes, it means reaction, so there is karma. There is a continuing regard for her on the soul level from the cosmic relationship, although his soul and her guides see that her soul is largely healed from the trauma that came.

Her soul made a mistake in that traumatic child life by coming closer when, really, it should have withdrawn. The girl was hopelessly lost, and had her soul been wiser and taken a more impersonal attitude it could have withdrawn itself more. But instead, in compassion and love and fright and hurt, it came close to try to protect its little incarnation, and hence its own consciousness was more deeply affected by the trauma of the things that happened to her, you see. But the soul is getting righted, and that is good.

They will have future, and this will be karmic. Not in any aspect of debt or negativism, but her soul has a gratitude for his soul and for him as a person in its own way. The soul knows more, of course, than the person of the wife knows. They will have some future times as different persons, in different settings, different relationships, with perhaps more fun involved.

So the karma is not all resolved, but this is not a negative thing. It has been a positive achievement in the present life.

His responsibility for her healing in this particular trauma is over. When they meet again as different persons, with quite different personalities, it will be good, it will be very good. There is a reward which he has won. (A2399:7-9)

Evil **is** in this world and tragedies do occur. It may seem strange that the proper thing for the Amy soul would have been to draw back rather than help the little girl. But the soul—the larger beingness—should have protected itself. Dr. John has said it is as though during war a squadron of bombers sees one injured plane fall behind. The rest must go on or the whole group can be lost. Actually, there will be less hurt for the person if the soul consciousness is withdrawn a bit, somewhat numbing the person.

People who see only one life do not realize the magnificent give-and-take of souls with each other. Reuben is helping the Amy soul now and when they meet again on earth he will be rewarded in some appropriate way, as her soul expresses its gratitude to him.

DULCIE AND PRICE

Souls can also learn and grow in happy marriages, for happiness is a good medium for growth. Dulcie and Price had a very good marriage and she, of course, inquired about him in her life reading. As background for their close union Dr. John brought out several happy, shared pastlives. Then the conductor asked Dulcie's only question, "What is the purpose of our marriage?" Dr. John's reply:

> Dr. John: Well, they love each other, don't they?
> Conductor: Yes.
> Dr. John: They enjoy sharing life together, don't they?
> Conductor: Yes.
> Dr. John: They—you say he's had a previous marriage?
> Conductor: Yes, Dr. John.
> Dr. John: And with children?
> Conductor: Yes.
> Dr. John: Well then they certainly have a certain interest in children together. In vocations or hobbies or anything, do they have shared interest?
> Conductor: In music, yes.
> Dr. John: Well, it looks as though there are several answers

to that question, aren't there.

Conductor: Yes.

Dr. John: Marriages are not formed only to carry on some deep dark karmic bond or to aspire to high golden heights. Marriage is a provision for daily living upon earth. It's a wise provision, although sometimes that which can provide the greatest good can provide the greatest hurt as well and even the greatest manifestation of evil.

But having admitted that as being one of the natural hazards of that which can be so good, it is to be pointed out and seen that marriage has a value, has many values in and of itself, regardless of past lives and almost regardless of spiritual growth excepting that as the marriage is good, spiritual growth just naturally takes place. Happiness is a very infectious ground for spiritual growth. Yes.

Conductor: Very good, Dr. John. Thank you. I like that.

Dr. John: Marriage can be valued in and of itself, not simply as a means for achieving something extra. (A4660:12,13)

DOROTHY AND LAZARUS

Most married couples have been together in one relation or another in a previous life. Often happy marriages stem from good past forces. If a close association is cut short by death, it will usually be resumed at a future time. In God's world nothing good is lost.

Dorothy and Lazarus have been a very happily married couple for more than thirty years. Dorothy says of her husband, "My life began when I married him." When she asked about Lazarus in her reading Dr. John answered:

> Dr. John: He is a cosmic first cousin. They were together in the immediately prior lifetime, in the 1800s. They came from England to the new country. This was in the early 1800s. They were settlers. They were married in England; they were husband and wife as in the present life.
>
> The families of each had some members who had come to the new country and established themselves. They had been here quite a while. They were in the mid-Atlantic area, the Virginia-North Carolina area rather than the Maryland or Delaware. They had a large farm, small plantation.

This young couple came over to work with them and get a start, and then go on in whatever way proved best. But the husband died after they had been here not quite two years. This was a real blow. He was healthy. The wife and the husband both had been looking forward to a full life. She had already borne their first child. The child was about three months old when the father died.

The father died of some disease that he got, some infection or some parasite. The young wife and her baby went back to England about three months after his death. The family members were very fine. They did not press her. They let it be her decision. She thought things over very carefully. She liked the new world but she recognized her roots were back in England and she instinctively wanted to get back to her roots, which she did.

Actually, that was the right thing to do, because within a year she was married again to a man who had known her husband and had respected him very much. This was a somewhat younger man, several years younger, and he was happy to adopt the child, a boy, and the couple then made a good life. She did not come again to America but stayed in England.

In the present life, as it were, they picked up the marriage to complete it. (A1337:10)

The loss that the young wife felt in the 1800s when her husband died is being satisfied in their present long, happy marriage. The pattern is being happily completed. The "made in heaven" tag on this marriage is a happy one.

COLLEEN AND JOEL

If strong desires are denied in one life, the forces will be used at another time. By helping Colleen, Joel had sacrificed a truly fulfilling marriage in the 1200s. Six hundred years later Colleen hungered for Joel's love but it was withheld. This lifetime finds the forces from both pastlives merging in a long and happy union—more than forty years of wedded bliss between Colleen and Joel.

In her life reading Colleen was told of a lifetime in the 1800s in the American South. As a young girl she had set her cap for a man who turned her down. The 1800s girl was devastated, but finally recovered

and married someone else. With this background, let's go now to
Dr. John's response when Colleen asks about pastlives with Joel:

> Dr. John: Yes. He was the love interest in the immediately
> prior life of which I have spoken as the one who 'got away.'
> He was a fine young man then and went on into a good life
> of his own.
>
> But this really goes back to a very interesting and rather in-
> volved relationship of the two of them in Italy in the 13...in
> the 1200s A.D. I see there was another life then for this soul,
> the Colleen soul, in the 1300s in Italy, but in the 1200s she was
> in the feminine gender expression and really was born into an
> environment that was very disadvantageous.
>
> The soul somewhat jumped in over its head in that life. It
> knew it should have an incarnation with bad heredity, bad up-
> bringing. It jumped into a ghetto in one of the cities of Rome—
> excuse me, one of the cities of Italy. It was not Rome. It was
> a seaport city with—well, this one was born into an area that
> had some of the riff-raff found sometimes in seaport areas
> where visiting rough and tumble sailors will be looking for the
> quick pleasures of a short shore-leave and such.
>
> Her parents were poor excuses as parents but they func-
> tioned somewhat in the general pattern of some others in that
> ghetto. They spawned children, more or less provided a place
> for them to sleep and eat, but survival was dependent actually
> upon the child's ingenuity and energy. There was a lot of
> thievery. There was a lot of mistreatment of others, such as
> drugging them, robbing them; 'rolling' and 'mugging' I think
> are modern names for some of this. And, of course, as the girl
> came to womanhood there was prostitution with solicitation.
>
> And then something quite wondrous and redeeming took
> place. When she was about fifteen—she was in her midteens,
> oh, fifteen or sixteen or so—she solicited an older man, he was
> thirty, who was obviously of a better social class. He was well-
> dressed. He was clean. He had good clothes, indicating if not
> affluence at least a certain solid prosperity. And led him into
> a trap where he was robbed, but he was strong and able and
> wise and she was apprehended. Some of the actual thieves were
> quicker and got away but she was apprehended and it would
> have gone extremely hard for her in the court.
>
> She could well have been sentenced to a quick death, but

he had both compassion and a certain sense of social justice. He realized that the ghettos were an open sore upon the city, and this weighed upon his conscience to where he intervened with the court and after suitable investigation and with suitable safeguards the court allowed him to, as it were, take custody of the girl. She was somewhat paroled to him.

He was not married. He lived with his mother. He took the girl to his mother's home, and the girl responded, and so for several years there she was reeducated to life and she had real possibilities. So she became a quite decent young woman within that Italian framework. She lived in a completely different part of the city, and the break with her family and her former way of life was enforced. It was a complete break enforced by the court and by her patron. In about four years or so he married her and by this time she was truly in love with him, very appreciative of what he had done for her, for truly he was her savior, and this grew also into quite an affection for him, a rather fiery affection which, in a sense, did not have as deep roots as it might have had. But this also could be expected because she was only four or five years old in her new life when they were married.

They had a child, a very close child to her, and now the picture began to change. Because she did not have the greater roots, her affection became centered upon the child and the husband-wife relationship began to recede in importance. The husband gave her two more children to broaden her life so it would not be focused upon this one child only, and that was good. But the husband-wife relationship did deteriorate simply because the young woman did not have enough to her to encompass all of her new life.

And the life lived on and was acceptable, although it missed some of the richness that it should have had in the marriage relationship.

Out of this then she loved and lost him in the 1800s. And in the present life, the 1900s, he was her husband once again and she was a very good wife and companion and they had a good rich full marriage. Yes.

They are cosmic family members as well. Is there a question?

Conductor: Very interesting, Dr. John, thank you. Of course, they will be together in future lifetimes?

Dr. John: Definitely, yes.

In the 1200s the Joel soul bailed Colleen out of a tough situation. This act of kindness led to his eventually unhappy marriage. So it was fair that Colleen be denied in the 1800s, and this denial of desire fed into the present life to make their marriage rich and full. One more example of how God can cover all bases, with justice and reward for each person concerned.

That the Colleen soul needed to come into a disadvantageous environment needs clarification. The conductor asked Dr. John if every soul had to come into a ghetto-type life. His answer:

> Dr. John: Well, it doesn't have to be quite as disadvantageous as that one chose. The soul was too confident of itself, too ignorant of some of the degradations in earthliving, and that could have been a rather disastrous experience for the soul had it not been rescued by its cosmic family member, the older man who became the husband. Yes. (A1279:9-11)

In its youth, the Colleen soul came into a more deprived situation than she could handle. Thankfully, she was rescued, but it could have been disastrous. Every soul must recognize its limitations and act accordingly.

JACK AND CHLOE

A marriage may be made in heaven but still not materialize on earth. The person's decisions can change an intended pattern, for God's structure gives us free will.

Jack and Chloe dated for four years, lived together for two, and then went their separate ways. In his life reading Jack inquired about Chloe:

> Conductor: We will next go to Jack's old girlfriend, Chloe...
> Dr. John: You say an old girlfriend?
> Conductor: Yes.
> Dr. John: They did not marry?
> Conductor: No, they lived together for two years. They went together for four years, then they lived together for two years. But they did not marry. They separated, very friendly, but their ideals seemed to be different so they did not marry.

Dr. John: Well, from (chuckling) the akashic records I can see converging forces that could have produced a marriage.

I turn to the council. They just rather smile and indicate nothing. They want to see what I will do with this. Not just what I will do with it, but what the akashic records indicate.

There was a lifetime in the 1700s when these two almost did marry. I need to sort this out. It was in a rather matriarchal society in South America, the southern part, probably the area now known as Brazil. Yes. It was not on the Amazon River but it was in an economy affected by the river, the river as an avenue of trade and some civilization although this was a village some miles back from the river. The then incarnation of the Jack soul was in masculine expression. The then incarnation of this other one, the Chloe soul, was in feminine. As young people they did not meet until they were—well he was nine and she was seven, but they were then somewhat thrown together—I do not see just why, maybe something as simple as the parents of one putting up a house or taking a house very close to the other.

The two children were congenial and as the bodies ripened, as they were on the verge of doing when they met, there was the bodily outreach each to the other. There was no exploration of the body of the other by either, but there was the expectation of marriage on the part of their parents and on the part of each of them. And then it did not take place. I think the parents of the girl moved. I think they were associated with some family members who had a large boat and whose major livelihood came from the big river, so they moved for unknown reason or maybe almost no reason to some other spot, another little encampment. Had the boy kept the girl and married her, why, she would have stayed, but he did not.

Now this leads to an interesting situation and really an interesting learning condition. In almost any generation prior to now, not all but most, these two would have married and that would have meant then that any differences would have been worked out between them rather than differences almost being encouraged and allowed to put them asunder, apart.

Now it is not that in this life it was intended that they marry to the extent that since they haven't the pattern is brought to shipwreck. Patterns are more available and are more flexible now and what would have been shipwreck at some former time is now just a change of course, a seeking of new currents.

However, I do not see any other new currents bringing someone else to Jack or Jack to someone else at the present. The current had brought these two together, and now since they have diverged instead of melding their lives in working out any difficulties between them, now, oh, there will be other currents, but they are not yet flowing in Jack's life.

And these two will not be together in the future, at least not in the near future. (A4295:8:10)

There is no condemnation on Jack or Chloe for breaking the intended pattern. Since they may not be together in future lives, the forces between them which might have been expended through the time they lived together will now be expended with other persons. Some marriages are mapped out with stronger purpose, or greater negative karmic roots. A soul sidestepping that type of union would be reprimanded, but that is not the case with Jack and Chloe.

CHARLOTTE AND KERMIT

Just as an intended marriage may be evaded by a personality's decision, some weddings occur which are not made in heaven, and are not intended. Psychological forces of loneliness, need, attraction, compatibility can produce a union which has no cosmic or pastlife rootage. These may be happy or may be quite miserable marriages.

Charlotte rued the day she married Kermit. At the time she had been quite lonely. Her beloved husband of thirty years had died some years earlier, and she wrongly assumed that Kermit would make a good companion.

In her life reading Dr. John revealed that Charlotte and her deceased husband were cyclemates. They had a long past in common, with future lives to come. But when the present husband, Kermit, was asked about, Dr. John replied:

> Dr. John: Well, why is he her husband?
> Conductor: I think she's wondering the same thing, Dr. John. She feels that he lied to her quite a bit before the wedding. She thought that he would be a companion in the things she liked to do. She believed that he had more money. He

pushed her for marriage and she found after the wedding that he had lied about almost everything. She found from other sources that he had lied to everyone. He's even had two marriages that failed. He's also not a companion for her.

Dr. John: Well, she has lied to herself as well. She cannot blame him entirely for this. She was willing to be deceived. She was willing to believe that she would get these things that she wanted but really she was not convinced of it, she had not taken the proper steps to ascertain the truth of his nature.

Now he's quite honest in himself, with himself, in terms of what he is; and what he wanted in this marriage is what he has gotten.

She has not gotten what she wanted and what she had led herself to expect in it. True, he represented this and such; and she took his representations much too eagerly and too easily.

There is no cosmic acquaintance between them. There is no pastlife experience and it is not intended that there be future. Her council is saying to me this marriage was a mistake; it was not an accident like the 1800s life-ending accident, it was simply a mistake. And now it is up to her to bring the realism and the good judgment that she has, and which her father tried to teach her and certainly showed, to whether or not she wants to continue with this marriage with Kermit.

Now quite possibly she will, and quite possibly things can develop between them which will have more good than negativity in their experience. Even then it is doubtful if they will ever be together in any future earthlife because there is just not the likeness of nature between them that would cause them to establish a resonance each with the other to produce bonds to draw them together again.

Now let her use her good mind. Let her possibly develop a bit of impersonality as she stands back and quietly judges the situation. It has its advantages. She is a married woman. They do share living expenses or at least living accommodations. There are some further possibilities. She could make certain demands which she has not made. They could share more equally in expenses and thus make possible a better life for them both together than each could afford alone. She could demand certain legal safeguards should he die, a certain assignment to her of some of his assets or possibly insurance if he has such.

Then there are various disadvantages. They are not basically congenial. They are not cosmically associated. Their purposes are different.

Now this decision should, of course, consider his welfare but not paramountly. His welfare should be no more than one-third and possibly not more than ten percent of the factors in her considerations. Of course, he would like her to continue to take care of him and on the present basis. She's a very cheap nurse and cook and housekeeper. But her own welfare and her own wishes should be paramount, should be ninety percent of the decision. She has much living she can yet do. Even if the physical activity is a bit limited by finances or advancing age or whatever, the mental activity and the spiritual activity can increase.

But if the continued marriage with Kermit is limiting her accomplishments in this incarnation, then unless there are some significant compensation factors, it is hardly worth it, is it. (A4186)

Throughout the life readings Dr. John stresses the importance of using discrimination. No one is excused from the results of his own decisions. Whether or not a marriage is made in heaven, it must be evaluated on its own merits.

EDNA AND HANLEY

In our previous illustration, there were no cosmic reasons for Charlotte and Kermit's marriage. Sometimes there is pastlife momentum strong enough for wedlock, but without the substance to sustain it. Such a union may be almost destined to end in divorce.

Edna was not too sure she wanted to marry Hanley, but somehow she felt she must. Their marriage lasted a few years, then terminated, but they remained friends.

When Edna inquired about Hanley, her life reading brought the background for this strange, short relationship:

Conductor: We go now to Edna's ex-husband and friend, Hanley...

Dr. John: They were acquainted in Scotland, in the mid 1500s. Again she was in the feminine, and was betrothed to him, or at least the initial steps of betrothment. She had a fey quality about her which he completely lacked. He had his porridge every morning, thick and without milk. This characterized him.

He had sheep and he smelled like a sheep. He was sturdy and he met the practical demands of life in a very practical way. This girl, as he more and more extended his claim upon her, felt stifled and smothered, and she ran away from him. Or perhaps I should say she escaped him.

She found another young man much more to her liking. With her mother's connivance, the two of them became betrothed and very quickly married. The other man, who was older than she—I was going to say he said nothing, but he said a great deal, he said plenty, which was unusual for him, to begin with when she escaped him, and then he said nothing.

He found a woman who would submit to his pattern and be molded by him. He married her and they had quite a number of children. But the name of this first girl never crossed his lips again. Even though they lived in the same village, if he perchance saw her or one of her children, he acted as though he had not seen that one; or the husband.

There was one exception. There was one time when his own righteous wrath and his sense of being cheated and rejected by someone inferior to himself did get the better of him. He came up rather menacingly to the husband, who was of a slighter build, but the husband prudently put some space between them, and a few other men who were present kept the stronger man, the older man—well, he wasn't too much older, half a dozen years or maybe ten—from threatening the younger man or doing him bodily harm.

It was that sort of a situation. Actually, of course, the girl had made the correct choice. But she always felt a little guilty about it, because the other one, the jilted man, always felt so self-righteous and so sure about himself and the course of action he had laid out for her.

So she was not completely sure in her own mind that she had done the right thing, which left room for a little guilt complex. She was seventy to eighty percent sure, but there was twenty to thirty percent doubt, and the twenty to thirty percent doubt carried perhaps a fifteen percent guilt element with it. This is quite interesting.

> I do not see other past acquaintance with them. I do see a purpose in this, though. That the Edna soul, which is feminine, learn to stand up for itself in its own integrity of beingness, and not let an overlay of beingness be put upon it which is foreign to it, and not accept a consciousness which is not its own. (A1169)

Edna's guilt should not have pushed her into an unwise marriage with Hanley, but if she can learn the lesson of respecting her own integrity then the union was profitable. Yes, the God-child is to be considerate, but even a good thing can be taken too far. When consideration causes one to feel so guilty that he denies his own worth, his priorities need to be adjusted.

EDNA AND EDWARD

In the same reading Edna asked about an ex-boyfriend, Edward. Dr. John brought in several pastlives they had together and then went into the major life which birthed their current love:

> Dr. John: We find him with her in the late 1700s, but mainly the early 1800s, in this country. She again in the feminine, he in the masculine and her husband. This was in the southern part of the country. Not the far south—Kentucky, Tennessee.
>
> He traveled. He was not exactly a 'horse merchant,' but he had a pretty good business in the buying and selling of horses. The landed gentry in the southern part, the Louisiana and Alabama areas and such, knew him and came to trust him. If they wanted a horse, they could tell him what kind. If they wanted a horse perhaps for the wife, or a pony for the children, or a hunting horse for themselves, or a show horse, they would expect him to find it for them. They would entrust him to find it. They would place an order, as it were.
>
> He had contacts with the people who raised horses, which was more in the Kentucky-Tennessee area, his contacts anyway. So he could provide them. He was a shrewd trader, but an honest one. He knew the value of a horse, he knew what he could buy it for, and he got a good markup on its price as he sold it. He knew what he was doing, and his buyers and his sellers knew. It was a good relationship and a good life, and provided him a livelihood.

He did some other things as well. I do not see just what. He was not all the time moving around. He was at home quite a bit. These two had a very fine homelife together. There was a genuine love, there was a courtesy, there was the 'southern gentleman chivalry' about him. To which she responded with, you might say, opening all the doors of her feminine beingness.

She was gracious, she was pretty, she was light and limber. She kept her body in good shape. She bore several children and was a good mother to them. She was a good hostess. She was a good wife, a good partner. She was a southern gentlewoman. Not of the established society top rank, but in the good sense of it, meeting the honest gentlemanliness of her husband.

It was a good life. It was a pleasant streamlet of human experience in which to take an incarnation. There was no particular trauma in it, and nothing that you might call very deep. But their love was deep, and their joy was a flowing stream.

There was music in that life, too. She played. She had one of these long, rectangular pianos. She sang, she taught the children to sing. There was a little girl and a little boy, and they had some other instruments. The girl, I believe, had a violin. The boy had something he blew. It may have been a flute.

The husband did not play an instrument. He was not musical. He did not even sing. He did not have a tone sense or a good voice for singing. But he thoroughly enjoyed his family as they did. He really enjoyed it, he did not simply tolerate it. He enjoyed not only them but the music they produced, and this contributed to the enrichment of his life. The beingness of all involved melded together into a larger family beingness, which was quite good.

They are cosmic cousins. They will be together in the future, I believe in the second and third incarnations after this one, and quite possibly in more as well. Is there a question?

Conductor: Not exactly a question, Dr. John. This is a relationship that she has not been able to really release. She still feels in love with him, although next month he is planning to marry someone else. It seems rather hopeless. She refused to marry him at one time, and she's sorry now that she did. Do you have any comments?

Dr. John: They had a very fine marriage, so why repeat it?

The lesson to be learned from reincarnation is not that one should seek the past for what one has attained to make the present more enjoyable or easier, but that the soul progresses from the past to the present, to the future. This involves different experiences, different relationships, different partners.

Again, let there be a flow of growth in her beingness. I can bring this to her consciousness and say they are not intended to marry this time. There are fine forces of love between them, and that is fine. But there is a force and a flow of purpose which is bigger than they are, and carrying them to heights of beingness greater than their present beingness, each of them.

Find this perspective, and let her beingness respond to this which I have brought to her in her consciousness now.

Conductor: I think this will be very helpful to her, because she had felt that she stopped something which should have been and would have made her happier.

Dr. John: She would not have been happy, because there are purposes involved and with quite some power, some force of flow, which would have made that other relationship unhappy. Because the happiness in it was really a reversion to what had been rather than a going forward to what is to be with her and with him, separately. (A1169:7-12)

The major purpose in earthliving is growth. If the good has been received from a past pattern, there is no purpose in repeating it. This does not mean that Edna and Edward will never again come together in matrimony. Probably they will marry at a future time—with personalities and goals that are different from the 1800s couple. But their destinies this life lie in divergent directions.

DORA AND KENNETH

Even when the plans of God call for a marriage, the timing must be right. Dora loved Kenneth very much. Although they seriously dated for several years, the relationship never ended in wedlock. But Dora did not completely forget Kenneth. When she inquired about him in her life reading, Dr. John replied:

Dr. John: Well, there is not too much of a relationship here, but what there was was pretty strong.

This was in the immediately prior life, the 1800s Italian life, and these two as young people had been close, and it was rather expected by their families that they marry. And it would have been quite all right had they done so.

But then the girl decided to become a nun instead. It was rather a hasty decision on her part, to become a nun, and part of that decision was a little flare-up of feeling unsure. Well, that was still an early feminine expression for this masculine soul. It had had feminine expressions with motherhood and grandmotherhood, and yet that fear flared up again a bit, and particularly since she had this very good friend who was a nun, she chose to become a nun.

Actually, that was all right. It was a different pattern, but either pattern was quite all right for that phase of experience. She couldn't have both, but she could have one or the other. And so when there was this little flare-up, it was honored. And the nun life was a success, and she was very honestly a nun.

But the love force carried over. Nothing good is ever lost. Nothing bad is ever just laid away and forgotten, either. It has to be dealt with. It can be discharged and eradicated, and needs to be. But of course this was a good thing, their love, and came into an expression in this life beyond what it had before.

These two probably will be together as man and wife somewhere up ahead, but possibly at that time the Dora soul will be the husband. It doesn't really matter—and this is not a sure thing—but it is a distinct possibility and I believe a probability. There are forces which would make it a very good thing, at which time the Dora soul could very likely bring some of the growth she is acquiring to the other one, even as he would bring the growth he is acquiring to the two of them. Yes.

Conductor: All right, Dr. John. There still is a very strong attraction-obsession to him. She was wondering perhaps if this one was the one she should have married, or if you see anything like that in the future in this life?

Dr. John: Probably not.

For one thing the nun did think of her boyfriend a number of times, but would rather quickly push the thought back, which of course meant that she was pushing it into the subconscious mind where it still lived and still maintained its force. It is that force which is expressing in the present life.

Conductor: Very interesting. Very interesting.

Dr. John: Actually these two personalities, it seems to me,

in their present makeup would not make a very good
twosome—not a very good oneness out of their twoness, as
I see it. Yes. (A4406:15,16)

The timing is wrong for Dora and Kenneth, and a marriage between
them now would be unfortunate. But God does not waste love, and
these two should marry in a future life, when the personalities, with
their flows of purpose, will be more compatible.

"A marriage made in heaven" has become a slang phrase for a relationship filled with happiness and idyllic bliss. And there are marriages like that. But it is important for us to realize that *all* life
patterns—not just marriage but birth, parentage, native culture, sibling placement, gender, characteristics of personality, abilities and
life happenings—all are "made in heaven," all have spiritual basis
and purpose. Human life flows with meaning from the great design
and purposefulness of the Creator.

And the second thing to realize as one takes a deeper look at marriages made in heaven is that even a divinely-intended union may
bring with it difficulties, unpleasantnesses, problems to be worked
through. Growth, not happiness, is God's overriding primary purpose for souls, and marriage is that relationship within which so much
of growth can take place. Patience, respect for others, broader and
deeper understandings, discovery of good in other modes, the
development of strengths of body and mind and emotions and spirit,
character-building, service to others and to one's own deep needs,
new and expanding experiences—there is an endless stream of good
things which the close and long-continued relationship of marriage
can nurture.

So we can see that most marriages are made in heaven, for the growth
of the souls involved. The husband and wife relationship can prop-
agate so many different kinds of learning, and a happy, smooth marriage may provide the right medium to develop both souls.

However, a "marriage made in hell"—or at least in purgatory—
also has its place, and in a strange way may be actually "made in
heaven" because unhappy marriages are often intended to teach
needed lessons. There could be negative karma to erase, or a younger
soul in a difficult lifetime could need support. When one soul is help-

ing another, both learn and grow—though the lessons may be different. At times the real learning in an unpleasant union is how to develop the discernment and decision-power to break a marriage, for not all marriages made in heaven should continue an entire lifetime.

The bases of many romantic relationships lie in pastlives or in cosmic relationships. Some should culminate in marriage; others should not. There is so much more in the picture of matrimony than one can see at first glimpse. With an understanding of reincarnation, karma, and the forces which make or break a marriage, a more complete picture emerges.

CHAPTER SIXTEEN

WHAT WE LEARN FROM KARMA, THE GREAT TEACHER

What do we learn from karma, the great teacher?

First, that no one gets away with anything. The things we did wrong, the character-building we sidestepped, the times we chose expediency over principle—these come back to haunt us, if not in this lifetime, then in another. We find those same principles and problems waiting on our doorstep, to be faced again and yet again until we get it right.

Likewise, nothing good is ever lost. Reaction follows action, results follow causes, as surely as night follows day. Carried-over problems are incompleted masteries, unfinished learnings. But all that we do right, all that we learn, accumulates within the soul just as a bank account builds up, to be used at a later time for need or pleasure. Even war, with its experiences of good and bad, does not negate this framework of all experiences.

Second, we learn from karma, the great teacher, that the justice of God is tempered by, and really is a part of, His loving purpose for us. We have a God-nature and possess latent God-powers, and the purpose of our beneficent, parental Creator—the great demandment laid upon us by God—is that we grow in compatibility with Him. Each of us is to discover and develop our God-nature and our God-powers in the godlike, rather than the demonic, way. Karma, the pre-eminent teacher for that growth in the cosmic school of earth, is the way of a loving God.

For God's great purposes we as souls take our experience of earth in a number of different incarnations, each one a different person, each person tailor-made for that particular lifetime. This planned purpose may be for one life or a cycle of lives, may include a crippled body or mind, may hold a specific marriage or none at all—from the full gamut of races, creeds and philosophies, economic, social and religious statuses. All of these bring something to the soul, for earth is good and not to be despised, and a soul which stays away from earth too long may find itself in trouble.

Even though lives are planned ahead, God allows free will and not all souls carry through each incarnation productively. Occasionally a soul may even start off in the wrong lifetime!

God's plan for the soul provides companionship as we journey through earth. Cosmic families encompassing about three dozen to fifty souls mean that each one incarnates many times with souls that have a loving care and a personal regard one for the other. Cyclemates make it possible for individuals to incarnate with one other soul many times, in many different relationships. Cosmic cousins enlarge our spirit-family circle by another 200 or so, and other souls and persons of temperament congenial with ours extend our circle of friends.

Along with this emerging picture of the soul taking its earth learnings in a succession of incarnations, we find a new dimension to the person. For the person is not ended when the soul has a new incarnation. The person, at the death of the physical body, goes into its excarnate (out-of-body) phase, which can be a larger, longer, more achieving and glorious life period than the incarnate (in-the-body) phase was. This is dependent upon the spiritual potentials of that person, the start it has made on things such as character, aspiration and consciousness, while here on earth. The person who dies in a very low consciousness may not ever realize he has entered a new plane, and may rather quickly waste away without ever looking upward to find what is beyond death.

Reincarnation research is beginning to bring some of the answers to just who we are, why we are here, what we are attempting to do, what is our major purpose. This research is providing new tools for understanding our individual roles in this rich and complex system God has created.

Dr. John refers to the third stage (around-the-midpoint) as the major karma stage since this is when the soul does its most serious growing and has its most difficult incarnations. Approximately fifty to sixty percent of the soul's incarnations are in this stage. This book, *Karma, The Great Teacher*, and the next (third) book in this series, *Growth Is the First Spiritual Law*, cover this "middle soul" stage.

In this third stage one finds life after life rich in karmic inter-relatedness, and people asking, "What did I do to deserve this? Why is that person in my life? What karma brought this situation?" More often than not one sees the cause not in some villainy but in souls correcting their past weaknesses, learning new lessons, building new qualities, testing their new strengths. This stage provides the incarnations necessary to make the soul resilient, wise and strong, helping it on its pathway of growth in God-Beingness.

Our next book, *Growth Is the First Spiritual Law*, continues the engaging saga of the soul's travels through incarnate life as we go into the long-cycle lives which cover major learnings. These cycles usually hold about seven lifetimes with a central purpose such as developing ability in the nonnative gender, or the proper merging of physical and spiritual qualities while on earth, or cultural develop-ment with the soul taking a series of lives in one or related cultures, etc. Also explored is the changing role of woman in this new age, and what it means for both sexes and to the world.

Outside of our personal connection to God, the most precious rela-tionship that exists is that of soulmates, and our next book examines this phenomenon. Other subjects include the early building of spiritual beingness, conscious awareness, various qualities of character; quantity lives, "bulk" incarnational experiences; homosexuality and reincarnation; material success (including several millionaires) or limitation; births and adoptions; etc.

The double-barreled research of reincarnation, through pastlife recalls and the Loehr-Daniels Life Readings, reveals how we learn a great deal from karma, the great teacher. To know that there is purpose, cosmic purpose, in life makes whatever we are going through more understandable, more meaningful, more bearable. And we reach out anew for the hand and heart of God reaching out to us.

BOOKS AVAILABLE

LOEHR-DANIELS LIFE READINGS

Dr. John: He Can Read Your Past Lives, Hussey & Sherrod 1983

*Cross-Correspondence Among the Loehr-Daniels
Life Readings,* Amidon,1985

Incarnation and Reincarnation, Roy Smith, 1975

Destiny of the Soul, Roberts, 1981, 1986

Reincarnation Quickbooks:
   Karmic Roots
   Karmic Justice for Women

RELIGIOUS RESEARCH

The Power of Prayer on Plants, Loehr, 1959

Diary After Death, Loehr, 1975, 1986

*Science & Religion, and the Development of Religion
as a Science,* Loehr, 1983

*My Father With the Sweet Name,
Conversations with the Deity,* Goulding 1983

These Came Back, Webb, 1975

IN PROCESS

Growth is the First Spiritual Law, Roberts

Death With Understanding, Religious Research Staff

FREE: Life Reading information

GNOSTICOEURS PUBLISHERS
Box 208 Grand Island
Florida 32735 U.S.A.